Writing as Discovery

ELIZABETH MORGAN
Eastern College

DAVID HERRSTROM
Queens College

RONALD MORGAN
Eastern College

WINTHROP PUBLISHERS, INC.
Cambridge, Massachusetts

Library of Congress Cataloging in Publication Data
Morgan, Elizabeth
    Writing as discovery.

    Includes bibliographical references.
      1. English language—Rhetoric.   2. College readers.
I. Herrstrom, David, joint author.   II. Morgan, Ronald,
joint author.   III. Title.
PE1417.M619   808'.04275   75-35652
ISBN 0-87626-972-2

Cover: Paul Klee, "Once Emerged from the Gray of Night." Paul Klee Foundation, Museum of Fine Arts, Berne. © COSMOPRESS, Genève and SPADEM, Paris.

© *1976 by Winthrop Publishers, Inc.*
    17 Dunster Street, Cambridge, Massachusetts 02138

Contents

Chapter Three

Writing About Other People   79

Chapter Four

Writing About Your Culture   127

Preface

Our main premise in this book is that analytical thinking and writing are the tools human beings use to discover who they are and what they experience. Our goal is to make students aware of the various kinds of thinking that are used when they remember their childhood, describe their best friends or worst enemies, argue points that are important to them, or respond to short stories and films. We are convinced that writers must think clearly to write effectively, and our book is planned to guide students through these kindred processes. Through experience we have learned that as our students discover how they think about the kinds of subjects grouped in each chapter (and they do this by playing games, by reading, by sharing what's going on in their heads with each other in class), they also discover ways to get these thoughts into writing. It is for these reasons that we have called this book *Writing as Discovery*. We are not trying to make students do things they have never done before. We are trying to help them to see how they think about things important to them, and to help them to use written language to articulate those thoughts and discover new ones.

In short, we are asking students to participate in the analytical process. Whenever a writer looks at a subject (whether it is his childhood or a political opinion), when he asks questions that help him discern its make-up, and when he draws conclusions about its significance, he is practicing analysis. And whenever a writer articulates these conclusions and the evidence that supports them, he is both defining his own thoughts and revealing them to his audience.

The text of Chapter One and the introductions to Chapters Two through Five are our attempts to make the kindred processes of thinking and writing clear. The readings in each chapter provide the students with a chance to see written analysis in operation. And the suggestions for writing ask them to prepare an analysis of their own.

Only key rhetorical terms are used in this book. We have isolated and named writing techniques minimally in order to perpetuate the students' awareness that writing is a *total process*, not a series of "steps," and to avoid the confusion of technical jargon. This becomes particularly obvious in Chapter Five, where most of the writing assignments ask students to analyze short stories. Rather than introducing the specialized vocabulary of literary analysis here, we have attempted to apply the rhetorical concerns of the preceding four chapters to the examination of a "symbolic world." Our goal is to illustrate that all analysis, regardless of subject, follows a basic pattern. For this reason, and because "symbolic worlds" encompass dreams and fantasies, as well as fictions, we have deliberately avoided taking up a special set of terms and continued to refer to the concerns involved in analyzing oneself, another person, and one's culture.

This book developed as a series of "discoveries." As members of the composition staff at Queens College, we gradually accumulated a syllabus of workable games, readings, discussion topics, and writing assignments that was used in several Freshman English classes. As the insights mentioned above were being shaped by our successes and failures in the classroom, our list of games, readings, and discussion and writing topics was supplemented by the suggestions of other instructors using the syllabus. Our book is a course we have "discovered" with our colleagues and our students over the past five years. And its complementary Instructor's Companion elaborates our resulting classroom practice.

We'd like to extend our special thanks to Bob Lyons, the head of Queens' composition staff for these five years, who taught us to take composition seriously in the first place, to our colleagues who shared and argued with us, and to the reviewers of the text who gave us invaluable help in seeing and correcting its faults.

Acknowledgments

Maya Angelou, "Stamps, Arkansas," from *I Know Why the Caged Bird Sings,* by Maya Angelou. Copyright © 1969 by Maya Angelou. Reprinted by permission of Random House, Inc.

Joan Baez, "My Father," excerpted from *Daybreak* by Joan Baez. Copyright © 1966, 1968. by Joan Baez. Used with permission of The Dial Press.

Russell Baker, "Interpretations on a Tuffet." © 1969 by the New York Times Company. Reprinted by permission.

James Baldwin, "Autobiographical Notes," from *Notes of a Native Son* by James Baldwin. Copyright © 1955 by James Baldwin. Reprinted by permission of Beacon Press.

John Berryman, "Winter Landscape." Reprinted with the permission of Farrar, Straus & Giroux, Inc., from *Short Poems* by John Berryman. Copyright 1948 by John Berryman.

Henry Beston, "Waves" from *The Outermost House* by Henry Beston. Copyright 1928. 1949, © 1956 by Henry Beston Reprinted by permission of Holt, Rinehart and Winston, Publishers.

Bruno Bettelheim, "Joey: A Mechanical Boy." Reprinted with permission. Copyright © 1959 by Scientific American, Inc. All rights reserved.

Rachel L. Carson, "The Sea Surface," from *The Sea Around Us* by Rachel L Carson. Copyright © 1950, 1951, 1961 by Rachel L. Carson. Reprinted by permission of Oxford University Press, Inc.

Anton Chekhov, "Gooseberries." Reprinted by permission of Macmillan Publishing Co.. Inc. from *The Wife and Other Stories* by Anton Chekhov. Translated from the Russian by Constance Garnett. Copyright 1918 by Macmillan Publishing Co., Inc., renewed 1946 by Constance Garnett.

Joseph Conrad, "A Gale," from *The Mirror of the Sea and A Personal Record,* by Joseph Conrad, edited by Morton Dauwen Zabel. Copyright © 1960. Reprinted by permission of Doubleday and Company, Inc.

Cox, Harvey, "Sex and Secularization." Reprinted by permission of Macmillan Publishing Co., Inc. from *The Secular City,* revised edition, by Harvey Cox. Copyright Harvey Cox 1965, 1966.

Ralph Ellison, "Battle Royal." Copyright 1947 by Ralph Ellison. Reprinted from *Invisible Man* by Ralph Ellison, by permission of Random House, Inc.

Jerry Farber, "The Student as Nigger." Copyright © 1970 by Jerry Farber. Reprinted from *The Sudent as Nigger* by permission of the author.

Joseph Fletcher, "Ethics and Unmarried Sex." Reprinted from *The 99th Hour: Population Crisis in the United States.* Copyright © 1967, by permission of the University of North Carolina Press.

Robert Frost, quoted in Roger Kahn, "Encountering Frost," from *The Poetry of Robert Frost,* edited by Edward Connery Lathem. Copyright 1928, © 1969 by Holt, Rinehart and Winston, Inc. Copyright 1936, © 1956 by Robert Frost. Copyright © 1964 by Lesley Frost Ballantine. Reprinted by permission of Holt, Rinehart and Winston, Publishers.

George F. Gilder, "Suicide of the Sexes." Copyright © 1973 by George F. Gilder. Reprinted by permission of Quadrangle/The New York Times Book Co. from "The Suicide of the Sexes" from *Harper's Magazine,* July 1973. Adapted from *Sexual Suicide* by George F. Gilder.

Nathaniel Hawthorne, "The Birthmark." Reprinted from *The Complete Works of Nathaniel Hawthorne,* copyright 1882, by permission of Houghton Mifflin Company.

Roger Kahn, "Encountering Frost," excerpts from *How the Weather Was* by Roger Kahn. Copyright © 1973 by Roger Kahn. By permission of Harper & Row, Publishers.

Alfred Kazin, "The Subway to the Synagogue," from *A Walker in the City,* copyright 1951 by Alfred Kazin. Reprinted by permission of Harcourt Brace Jovanovich, Inc.

Hugh Kenner, "Don't Send Johnny to College," copyright © 1964 by Hugh Kenner. Reprinted from *Saturday Evening Post* by permission of the Sterling Lord Agency.

Martin Luther King, Jr., "To Fellow Clergymen," from pp. 84–90 "Letter from Birmingham Jail"—April 16, 1963—in *Why We Can't Wait,* by Martin Luther King, Jr. Copyright © 1963 by Martin Luther King, Jr. By permission of Harper & Row, Publishers.

Norbert Krapf, "Returning from the Hunt." Copyright © 1974 by The Modern Poetry Association. Reprinted by permission of the Editor of *Poetry.* The poem first appeared in *Poetry,* September 1974.

Mary McCarthy, "Names," from *Memories of a Catholic Girlhood,* copyright © 1957 by Mary McCarthy. Reprinted by permission of Harcourt Brace Jovanovich, Inc.

H. L. Mencken, "The Politician," copyright 1924 by Alfred A. Knopf, Inc., and renewed 1952 by H. L. Mencken. Reprinted from *A Mencken Chrestomathy,* by H. L. Mencken, by permission of the publisher.

Pablo Neruda, "A Lemon." Reprinted by permission of Grove Press, Inc. Copyright © 1965 by Grove Press, Inc.

Joyce Carol Oates, "Four Summers." © 1967 by Joyce Carol Oates. Reprinted from *The Wheel of Fire and Other Stories* by permission of Vanguard Press. "The Visionary Art of Flannery O'Connor" from *New Heaven, New Earth: The Visionary Experience in Literature.* © 1974 by Joyce Carol Oates. Reprinted by permission of Vanguard Press.

Flannery O'Connor, "Revelation," from *Everything That Rises Must Converge* by Flannery O'Connor. Copyright © 1964, 1965 by the Estate of Mary Flannery O'Connor.

George Orwell, "Ecclesiastes," from *Shooting an Elephant and Other Essays,* Harcourt Brace Jovanovich, Publishers. Reprinted by permission.

Donn Pearce, "Those Truck Drivin' Men." Reprinted by permission of *Esquire Magazine* © 1972 by Esquire, Inc.

Francis Ponge, "Rain" and "Orange" from *The Voice of Things* by Francis Ponge, edited and translated by Beth Archer. Copyright © 1972 by Herder and Herder, Inc. Reprinted by permission of McGraw-Hill Book Company.

Marcel Proust, "The Glass Sea." Copyright 1924 and renewed 1952 by Random House, Inc. Reprinted from *Remembrance of Things Past, Volume I,* by Marcel Proust, by permission of the publisher.

Alain Robbe-Grillet, "The Balustrade" and "The Brush Descends." Reprinted by permission of Grove Press, Inc. Copyright © 1961 by Grove Press, Inc.

Lillian Smith, "When I Was a Child," reprinted from *Killers of the Dream* by Lillian Smith. By permission of W. W. Norton & Company, Inc. Copyright 1949, © 1961 by Lillian Smith.

Wallace Stevens, "Study of Two Pears." Copyright 1942 by Wallace Stevens and renewed 1970 by Holly Stevens. Reprinted from *The Collected Poems of Wallace Stevens,* by permission of Alfred A. Knopf, Inc.

Jonathan Swift, "A Modest Proposal," from *Irish Tracts 1728–1733* by Jonathan Swift. Reprinted by permission of Basil Blackwell, Publisher.

Leo Tolstoy, "Advice to a Draftee." Translated by Rodney Dennis. Copyright © 1968 by *Atlantic.* Reprinted by permission of the Houghton Library, Harvard University.

John Updike, "The Staircase," from *The Centaur,* copyright © 1963. Reprinted by permission of Alfred A. Knopf, Inc.

Naomi Weisstein, " 'Kinder, Kuche, Kirche' as Scientific Law: Psychology Constructs the Female." Copyright © 1971 by Naomi Weisstein. Reprinted from *Journal of Social Education,* April, 1971, by permission of Naomi Weisstein.

William Carlos Williams, "The Hunters in the Snow," from William Carlos Williams, *Pictures from Brueghel and Other Poems.* Copyright © 1962 by William Carlos Williams. Reprinted by permission of New Directions Publishing Corporation. "The Red Wheelbarrow," from William Carlos Williams, *Collected Earlier Poems.* Copyright 1938 by New Directions Publishing Corporation. Reprinted by permission of New Directions Publishing Corporation.

 *Chapter One*

Discovering the Nature of Writing

INTRODUCTION

We have all participated in some game or other—field hockey, tennis, poker, or even Monopoly. Our enjoyment of, and success in, these games requires the mastery of two kinds of specific skills: proficiency in knowing and obeying the rules of the game and prowess in taking advantage of these rules. A game such as tennis assumes a set of arbitrary rules which must be followed if the "game" is to have any point. This is the first and most basic way in which writing, or composing with words, is similar to playing a game.

Playing tennis without the net would be just as meaningless and unsatisfying for both players and spectators as writing a letter to a friend in which you continually make up your own words and arrange the words in your sentences according to the throw of dice. In the movie *Bang the Drum Slowly*, for example, the main character is wickedly sharp at TEGWAR, a card game guaranteed to relieve the sucker of his money every time. The Exciting Game Without Any Rules, however, is only fun for the players who set up the patsy, because they make up their rules as they go. With their hilariously brilliant double-talk, they convince the sucker that it's a real game and they succeed in stinging him.

Yet, as you know, even in a legitimate game merely obeying the rules does not necessarily make a good tennis player; neither does it necessarily produce a good writer. Correct punctuation and grammar alone no more constitute good writing than rules by themselves constitute the game. Sports, then, are popular not because we enjoy observing someone follow rules, but because we delight in seeing a skilled athlete take advantage of the rules. And participating in games is enjoyable for the same reason. We know that there are an infinite number of possible plays within the boundaries set by the rules. Our success is wholly dependent on our skill at discovering the right play to solve the immediate problem. We delight in these discoveries, and the more skillful we are, the more adept we are at discovering solutions.

But this skill cannot be exercised outside the actual playing of the game itself. Only through participation in the sport can we discover what is beautifully successful, the perfect forced play or volley. Only in the *process* of playing can we discover more efficient solutions to problems such as betting on a "full house" or returning a difficult spin. Similarly, only in the *activity* of writing can we find a solution to the problem of clarifying a particular subject. The great modern poet W. H. Auden refers to this activity when he exclaims: "How can I know what I think until I see what I say."

Discovering *how* to play comes only in the actual playing of the game. Discovering *how* to express yourself comes only in the actual fiddling with words. Merely being told how to pole vault before banging your shin on the bar or to write before setting pen to paper is insufficient. Yet, if you are going to try to catapult yourself into the air and over the bar, you must observe the smallest details of the motion that you wish to express with your own body. You have to observe the *minute particulars* of the way that the pole is balanced in the hands as speed increases, the exact position of the arms as the long awkward pole is planted with a bone-breaking jolt in the box, and the precise movement of the legs as their potent bend echoes the pole's, exploding the body into the air. There can be no great vault without precise and subtle observation. Similarly, there can be no good writing without detailed observation of the object, emotion, or idea that you want to express.

However, watching and noting in detail the distinct, minute steps of the vault are not sufficient to make the jump yourself. For, to clear the distant bar, you must get a sense of the complete motion that you want to express. It is necessary to see the *shape* of all the discrete movements together—the precise way in which they are related to each other and make a unity. That is, you have to imagine the completed action flowing from your first step down the run-way, through the loft and the final torque as you whisper across the bar and relax heavily into the sawdust.

Likewise, in writing, close observation of the subject is not enough. You must have a compelling purpose that gives "shape" to the details you have observed. Specifically, this shape is determined by: 1. the relationship of minute particulars to general ideas; 2. the correspondence of various minute particulars to one another; and 3. the relationship of writers to their material. Together, this set of relationships makes writing a whole experience no less than muscle coordination makes pole vaulting a complete motion. Chapter One shows how to test and define these associations, beginning with the relationship of writers to their subject matter.

FACING YOURSELF

AN EXPERIMENT

Let's perform an experiment. Its purpose is to show that each person interacts with concrete details in a unique way. You may be surprised at what else it reveals.

> *Step 1:* Choose some inanimate object in the room (for example, the blackboard, a piece of chalk, a table, a "creation" of building blocks made by several students, or an old shoe or piece of fruit provided by your teacher).
> *Step 2:* Look at the object or construction closely and write a "neutral" description of it. There should be no discussion of the word *neutral;* just be guided by what you assume it would mean to most people.

What conclusions can we draw? Let's say you chose to describe a clock in your classroom. Though the "facts" each of you noted are "objective," you will find that your descriptions differ greatly. How can this be true? The answer to this is simple once you realize that all observers, because they are individuals, see everything, even a clock, from a unique perspective which inevitably manifests itself in their writing.

This perspective results from the interaction of the writer with the particulars, and so determines the *kind* of clock the reader will see. It determines whether the clock will be a solid or a flat disk, whether it will be made of "glaring chrome" or "smooth metal," or whether the hands will be "rods," "indicators," or "long needle-shaped objects." There is a great difference between "rods" and "needle-shaped objects." (And notice that only "indicators" reveal function.) We can call the writers' perspective their *point of view,* and we can define point of view in physical, emotional, or cultural terms. A writer standing across the room from the clock will see the object differently than one standing underneath it. The writer late for a desired rendezvous will see it differently than one due at the dentist's office in half an hour. Similarly, we take it for granted that the physicist will see a "different" clock than the electrician or the interior decorator. Therefore, our experiment has shown the following:

> *Observation:* Writing is never neutral. All your writing, whether you intend it to or not, has a unique point of view—yours.
> *Proposition:* Since you cannot possibly keep yourself out of your writing, since there is no such thing as writing without a unique perspective, you might as well choose your point of view (and you'll have to if you want to communicate clearly and forcefully), or it will choose you. (That is, your language will inevitably embody an unexamined or unintentional point of view.)

A GAME

The following interpretations of "Little Miss Muffet" depend mainly on caricature and occupational jargon rather than on detailed description. But the interpretations dramatically reveal the great difference between points of view on the same subject. After reading the passages carefully, decide on the basis of the facts included in each and the way in which they are presented what each author is interested in. On the basis of your inferences form generalizations about each person's way of seeing. Then match the list of people following the article with their view of the nursery rhyme. Give reasons for your choices, pointing to individual words and phrases that influenced you.

"Interpretations on a Tuffet"/*Russell Baker*

Little Miss Muffet, as everyone knows, sat on a tuffet eating her curds and whey when along came a spider who sat down beside her and frightened Miss Muffet away. While everyone knows it, the significance of the event had never been analyzed until a conference of thinkers recently brought their special insights to bear upon it. Following are excerpts from the transcript of their discussion:

1. We are clearly dealing with a prototypical illustration of a highly tensile social structure's tendency to dis- or perhaps even de-structure itself under the pressures created when optimum minimums do not obtain among the disadvantaged. Miss Muffet is nutritionally underprivileged, as evidenced by the subminimal diet of curds and whey upon which she is forced to subsist, while the spider's cultural disadvantage is evidenced by such phenomena as legs exceeding standard norms, odd mating habits and so forth.

In this instance, spider expectations lead the culturally disadvantaged to assert demands to share the tuffet with the nutritionally under-privileged. Due to a communications failure, Miss Muffet assumes with-out evidence that the spider will not be satisfied to share her tuffet, but will also insist on eating her curds and whey. Thus, the failure to pre-establish selectively optimum norm structures leads to. . . .

2. Second-strike capability, sir! That's what was lacking. If Miss Muffet had developed a second-strike capability instead of squandering her resources on curds and whey, no spider on earth would have dared launch a first strike capable of carrying him right to the heart of her tuffet. I am confident that Miss Muffet had adequate notice from experts

that she could not afford both curds and whey and at the same time support an early-spider-warning system. Yet curds alone were not good enough for Miss Muffet. She had to have whey, too. Tuffet security must be the first responsibility of every diner. . . .

3. Written on several levels, this searing, sensitive exploration of the arachnid heart illuminates the agony and splendor of Jewish family life with a candor that is at once breath-taking in its simplicity and soul-shattering in its implied ambiguity. Some will doubtless be shocked to see such subjects as tuffets and whey discussed without flinching, but hereafter writers too timid to call a tuffet a tuffet will no longer. . . .

4. Why has the Government not seen fit to tell the public all it knows about the so-called curds-and-whey affair? It is not enough to suggest that this was merely a random incident involving a lonely spider and a young diner. In today's world, poised as it is on the knife edge of. . . .

5. Little Miss Muffet is, of course, neither little, nor a miss. These are obviously the self she has created in her own fantasies to escape the reality that she is a gross divorcee whose superego makes it impossible for her to sustain a normal relationship with any man, symbolized by the spider, who, of course, has no existence outside her fantasies. She may, in fact, be a man with deeply repressed Oedipal impulses who sees in the spider the father he would like to kill, and very well may some day unless he admits that what he believes to be a tuffet is, in fact, probably the dining room chandelier and that the whey he thinks he is eating is, in fact, probably. . . .

6. This beautiful kid is on a bad trip. Like. . . .

7. Little Miss Muffet, tuffets, curds, whey and spiders are what's wrong with education today. They're all irrelevant. Tuffets are irrelevant. Curds are irrelevant. Whey is irrelevant. Meaningful experience! How can you have relevance without meaningful experience? And how can there ever be meaningful experience without understanding? With understanding and meaningfulness and relevance, there can be love and good and deep seriousness and education today will be freed of slavery and Little Miss Muffet, and life will become meaningful. . . .

8. This is about a little girl who gets scared by a spider.

(The child was sent home when the conference broke for lunch. It was agreed that the child was too immature to add anything to the sum of human understanding and should not come back until he had grown up.)

a. a militarist
b. a child
c. a sociologist
d. an editorial writer
e. a psychiatrist
f. a flower child

g. a book reviewer

h. a student demonstrator

A WRITING EXERCISE

Write a description of a lemon from a blind person's point of view. Write one from the point of view of a doctor, a French chef, an Eskimo (who has probably never seen or heard of a lemon), or a biologist. (You can add your own.) Exchange these in class and guess which point of view is represented. Discuss what facts are and are not appropriate given the chosen point of view.

A READING EXERCISE

After carefully reading the two descriptions below, consider them in the same way that you have considered your own descriptions, and answer the questions that follow.

"The Balustrade"/*Alain Robbe-Grillet*

The wood of the balustrade is smooth to the touch, when the fingers follow the direction of the grain and the tiny longitudinal cracks. A scaly zone comes next; then there is another smooth surface, but this time without lines of orientation and stippled here and there with slight roughnesses in the paint.

In broad daylight, the contrast of the two shades of gray—that of the naked wood and that, somewhat lighter, of the remaining paint—creates complicated figures with angular, almost serrated outlines. On the top of the handrail, there are only scattered, protruding islands formed by the last vestiges of paint. On the balusters, though, it is the unpainted areas, much smaller and generally located toward the middle of the uprights, which constitute the spots, here incised, where the fingers recognize the vertical grain of the wood. At the edge of the patches, new scales of the paint are easy to chip off; it is enough to slip a fingernail beneath the projecting edge and pry it up by bending the first joint of the finger; the resistance is scarcely perceptible.

"The Staircase"/*John Updike*

The country staircase, descending between a plaster wall and a wood partition, was narrow and steep. At the bottom, the steps curved in narrow worn wedges; there should have been a railing. My father was sure that my grandfather with his clouded downward vision was going to fall some day; he kept vowing to put up a bannister. He had even bought the bannister, for a dollar in an Alton junk shop. But it leaned forgotten in the barn. Most of my father's projects around this place were like that. Tripping in grace notes like Fred Astaire, I went downstairs, in my descent stroking the bare plaster on my right. So smoothskinned, this wall shallowly undulated like the flank of a great calm creature alive with the chill communicated through stone from the outdoors. The walls of this house were thick sandstone uplifted by mythically strong masons a century ago.

1. The sense of touch is important in both descriptions, but what are the differences in the way this sense is used? In which passage is the sense of sight most important? What is the significance of this?
2. Both descriptions made us feel as if we were looking through a camera. Which one is a moving picture, and which a snapshot? What are the specific observations and details that make us feel this difference?
3. What difference between the two points of view is indicated by noting that it is a *wooden* balustrade and a *country* staircase?
4. Why is the "balustrade" significant? Why is the "staircase" significant?
5. What difference in the angle of vision is revealed by the fact that the second passage has a context (a physical setting and a "history")? How would you describe this context?
6. Which description and which author do you feel closest to? Why? What does this indicate about the difference between the two writers' points of view?
7. Which description seeks to create an impression, and which attempts to provide information? Do they both create an impression? Do they both give information? Do these seem like valid or false distinctions?

The relationship between you as writer and your subject is obviously an intimate one. Furthermore, since what you *are* inevitably appears in your writing, it is best consciously to *choose* and *control* your point of view. "But how?" you ask. The answer is not simple. It involves a continual awareness of how you are "seeing" your subject. And it involves a close consideration of two other relationships that help to determine the shape a piece of writing takes: the connections between the details the writers have observed about their subject, and the relationship of these details to their central ideas.

The next section examines the network of concrete details or minute particulars that comprise writers' basic material. We will discuss how writers can improve their *powers* of observation, and we will explore the means by which writers narrow the *scope* of their observation in the course of any given writing exercise—the means by which they present a web of *related* details rather than a mixed bag of haphazard facts.

EXPANDING YOUR SENSES AND FOCUSING

The poet William Carlos Williams rightfully insists that

so much depends
upon

a red wheel
barrow

glazed with rain
water

beside the white
chickens

Everything depends, in fact, on the minute particulars of experience. As you have seen in your own descriptions and in those of the balustrade and the staircase, significance and interest are determined by how clearly the concrete details are observed and by how carefully the most representative ones are chosen. Without the observing, however, there can be no choosing. If we want to write well, we must be willing to say with the poet Rimbaud that our taste is for "earth and stones," the particulars of experience. We must learn to revel in things, observing them sharply and celebrating their dense presence.

In order to see the minute particulars, we must employ all of our senses, forcing them to become more alert. Like the five-year-old meandering home from school, we must become transfixed with the prickly texture and strange odor of a leaf, or astonished at the weird geometric shapes and striations in the ice on a mud puddle. With practice this is possible. William Blake, a late eighteenth century English poet-painter-prophet, believed that the sense of touch was the most glorious and perfect of the senses because it alone covers the whole body.

And analogously he assumed that our other senses used to be this way, eyes covering us, and the ability to hear and smell pervading the body. Through lack of use, these senses have become shrunken to mere remnants, two ears, two eyes, and only one nose. Blake felt that we could restore our contracted senses to their full power by increased use. Perhaps you will never have eyes all over your body, but you can expand your powers of observation by continually exercising your senses as you do your muscles.

The following game may help to expand your senses.

A GAME

Sit in a circle in the classroom. Then pass a lemon (or an apple, shoe, or the like) around the circle. Each of you must make a concrete observation about the object. Use all your senses and try to be as detailed as you can, using the most precise words possible. Keep passing it until someone can't think of anything more to add. That person loses. After you have done this, pass it around again, only this time everyone must compare it to something else which reveals more about that object. (Notice how one observation seems to conjure or suggest another.) Your instructor may record your observations on the blackboard as you proceed so that afterwards you can consider which are the most illuminating or which should be grouped together to support a particular point of view. Some kind of pattern may be present in the list itself due to the "power of suggestion."

A WRITING EXERCISE

Select two lemons (or trees, shoes, and so on) that look alike. Write a description of one in such a way that your reader could choose the same one you have. Read these to each other and try to guess which object is being described.

A READING EXERCISE

The following readings are examples of close observation and expansion of the senses. In each passage we are invited to examine what seems to be a familiar object. But we find ourselves forced into an experience of so many more details than we have ever encountered before that the object becomes unfamiliar and delightfully surprising. Yet, none of these readings are merely exercises in observation for its own sake. In each, all the minute particulars are unified by a consistent point of view, giving us a unique experience of a lemon, a pear, and an orange. After you read each of the following carefully, discuss which senses are appealed to in each description, the differences of appeal from writer to writer, as well as the directions in which these senses are expanded. Questions follow the readings.

"A Lemon"/*Pablo Neruda*

Out of lemon flowers
loosed
on the moonlight, love's
lashed and insatiable
essences,
sodden with fragrance,
the lemon tree's yellow
emerges,
the lemons
move down
from the tree's planetarium.

Delicate merchandise!
The harbors are big with it—
bazaars
for the light and the
barbarous gold.
We open
the halves
of a miracle,
and a clotting of acids
brims
into the starry
divisions:
creation's
original juices,
irreducible, changeless,
alive:
so the freshness lives on
in a lemon,
in the sweet-smelling house of the rind,
the proportions, arcane and acerb.

Cutting the lemon
the knife
leaves a little
cathedral:
alcoves unguessed by the eye
that open acidulous glass
to the light; topazes
riding the droplets,
altars,
aromatic façades.

So, while the hand
holds the cut of the lemon,
half a world
on a trencher,
the gold of the universe
wells
to your touch:
a cup yellow
with miracles,
a breast and a nipple
perfuming the earth;
a flashing made fruitage,
the diminutive fire of a planet.

"Study of Two Pears"/*Wallace Stevens*

I
Opusculum paedagogum.
The pears are not viols,
Nudes or bottles.
They resemble nothing else.

II
They are yellow forms
Composed of curves
Bulging toward the base.
They are touched red.

III
They are not flat surfaces
Having curved outlines.
They are round
Tapering toward the top.

IV
In the way they are modelled
They are bits of blue.
A hard dry leaf hangs
From the stem.

V
The yellow glistens.
It glistens with various yellows,
Citrons, oranges and greens
Flowering over the skin.

VI

The shadows of the pears
Are blobs on the green cloth.
The pears are not seen
As the observer wills.

"The Orange"/Francis Ponge

Like the sponge, the orange aspires to regain face after enduring the ordeal of expression. But where the sponge always succeeds, the orange never does; for its cells have burst, its tissues are torn. While the rind alone is flabbily recovering its form, thanks to its resilience, an amber liquid has oozed out, accompanied, as we know, by sweet refreshment, sweet perfume—but also by the bitter awareness of a premature expulsion of pips as well.

Must one take sides between these two poor ways of enduring oppression? The sponge is only a muscle and fills up with air, clean or dirty water, whatever: a vile exercise. The orange has better taste, but is too passive—and this fragrant sacrifice . . . is really too great a kindness to the oppressor.

However, merely recalling its singular manner of perfuming the air and delighting its tormentor is not saying enough about the orange. One has to stress the glorious color of the resulting liquid which, more than lemon juice, makes the larynx open widely both to pronounce the word and ingest the juice without any apprehensive grimace of the mouth, or raising of papillae.

And one remains speechless to declare the well-deserved admiration of the covering of the tender, fragile, russet oval ball inside that thick moist blotter, whose extremely thin but highly pigmented skin, bitterly flavorful, is just uneven enough to catch the light worthily on its perfect fruit form.

At the end of too brief a study, conducted as roundly as possible, one has to get down to the pip. This seed, shaped like a miniature lemon, is the color of the lemon tree's whitewood outside, and inside is the green of a pea or tender sprout. It is within this seed that one finds—after the sensational explosion of the Chinese lantern of flavors, colors and perfumes which is the fruited ball itself—the relative hardness and greenness (not entirely tasteless, by the way) of the wood, the branch, the leaf; in short, the puny albeit prime purpose of the fruit.

1. What are the differences among the three writers in the qualities of the fruit that they are especially interested in?
2. What is the difference between saying that a halved lemon is "a breast and a nipple," and that "The pears are not viols." Are pears in any way like viols? Why does Stevens insist that they are *not?*
3. Both Stevens' and Ponge's descriptions are called "studies." How are these different from Neruda's description? Could his be called a "study"? Why or why not?
4. Which writer in your opinion gives the fullest description and why? What do you mean by "fullest"?
5. Stevens says that "The pears are not seen/As the observer wills." What do you think this means? Is it also true of the lemon and the orange? What hints does this statement give you about Stevens' purpose in writing the poem?
6. What is the purpose of each description? What are the main differences in purpose between the writers? How are these differences reflected in the details chosen for each of the descriptions and in the sequence or order in which the details are arranged?

In the preceding exercises, you have gradually shifted your attention from observation itself to the necessity of grouping and editing observations in writing. This is what is meant by *focusing*—keeping your eyes on a particular aspect of an object, experience, or concept because of what you want to say about it or where you "stand" in relation to it.

You may want to describe a car in such a way that the reader feels its objective presence, its "car-ness," very strongly. You will, therefore, *focus* on its physical properties—size, color, weight, texture, number of parts—and leave such observations as speed, maneuverability, efficiency, history of repairs, cost of operation, likeness to other vehicles for another day. If, on the other hand, you want to prove that your car has been a financial liability, or that you are a victim of Detroit's carelessness, you will probably focus on some of the latter qualities and only mention physical properties in passing. You will select details that best suit your purpose and your point of view.

The following game and reading exercise help to make clearer the necessity and process of focusing.

A GAME

A movie consists of a series of "shots." Each shot is simply what the camera is focused on from the time it starts to the time it stops (usually not more than fifteen seconds). A two-hour film, for example, will have about 600 shots.

In the first selection for the following reading exercise, study carefully the description of rain and, as a class, pretend you have to film it. Divide the *first* paragraph into shots, and record these by numbering them separately on the blackboard. Discuss why each shot was selected and the reasons for the particular order of these shots in light of the observations in the last three short paragraphs of the passage. What specific quality or aspect of the rain is focused on primarily? What possible shots are left out? Arrange alternate orders of the shots, and discuss what alternate last paragraphs would then be appropriate.

A READING EXERCISE

Consider the relationship of focus and selection in the following paragraphs of Francis Ponge and Alain Robbe-Grillet. Read both passages carefully. Discuss as a class whether the focus in these descriptions is primarily on rain and hair or on the rhythm of raining and brushing. Compare the writers' methods of achieving their focus. How do they use sight and sound? How are the various details related to one another? Considering the mechanical nature of the action involved, how do the writers manage to avoid monotony?

"Rain"/*Francis Ponge*

Rain, in the courtyard where I watch it fall, comes down at very different speeds. At the center it is a sheer uneven curtain (or net), an implacable but relatively slow descent of fairly light drops, an endless precipitation without vigor, a concentrated fraction of the total meteor. Not far from the walls to the right and left, heavier individuated drops fall more noisily. Here they seem the size of wheat kernels, there large as peas, elsewhere big as marbles. Along the window sills and mouldings the rain streaks horizontally, while on the underside of these obstacles it hangs suspended like lozenges. It ripples along, thinly coating the entire surface of a little zinc roof beneath my glance, moiréed with the various currents caused by the imperceptible rises and falls of the covering. From the nearby gutter, where it flows with the effort of a shallow brook poorly sloped, it plummets sharply to the ground in a perfectly vertical, thickly corded trickle where it shatters and rebounds like glistening icicles.

Each of its forms has a particular speed, accompanied by a particular sound. All of it runs with the intensity of a complex mechanism, as precise as it is unpredictable, like a clockwork whose mainspring is the weight of a given mass of precipitating vapor.

The pealing of the vertical jets on the ground, the gurgling of the gutters, the tiny gong strokes, multiply and resound together in a concert neither monotonous nor unsubtle.

When the mainspring has unwound, some wheels go on turning for a while, more and more slowly, until the whole machinery stops. Should the sun then reappear, everything is soon effaced; the glimmering mechanism evaporates: it has rained.

"The Brush Descends" / *Alain Robbe-Grillet*

The brush descends the length of the loose hair with a faint noise something between the sound of a breath and a crackle. No sooner has it reached the bottom than it quickly rises again toward the head, where the whole surface of its bristles sinks in before gliding down over the black mass again. The brush is a bone-colored oval whose short handle disappears almost entirely in the hand firmly gripping it.

Half of the hair hangs down the back, the other hand pulls the other half over one shoulder. The head leans to the right, offering the hair more readily to the brush. Each time the latter lands at the top of its cycle behind the nape of the neck, the head leans farther to the right and then rises again with an effort, while the right hand, holding the brush, moves away in the opposite direction. The left hand, which loosely confines the hair between the wrist, the palm and the fingers, releases it for a second and then closes on it again, gathering the strands together with a firm, mechanical gesture, while the brush continues its course to the extreme tips of the hair. The sound, which gradually varies from one end to the other, is at this point nothing more than a dry, faint crackling, whose last sputters occur once the brush, leaving the longest hair, is already moving up the ascending part of the cycle, describing a swift curve in the air which brings it above the neck, where the hair lies flat on the back of the head and reveals the white streak of a part.

To the left of this part, the other half of the black hair hangs loosely to the waist in supple waves. Still further to the left the face shows only a faint profile. But beyond is the surface of the mirror, which reflects the image of the whole face from the front, the eyes—doubtless unnecessary for brushing—directed straight ahead, as is natural.

Let's review before we go on. Some of the basic realizations beginning writers have to make are that:

1. They have a unique relationship with everything they write about be-

cause *they* are the ones who perceive it and because *they* are the ones who choose the words that present it.

2. One of the most essential qualities of good writers is that they look closely at the world; they see in *detail* the material they want to present in their writing.

3. Effective writers do not just grab handfuls of observations to fill up their pages, but they *select* details carefully according to how the details relate to one another, according to their chosen point of view, and according to their reasons for writing. This is their *focus*.

This last point leads us into the relationship of concrete details to general ideas. In the process of *focusing* writers allow one or two concerns or ideas to control their selection of materials—to train their eyes, or to narrow their observations to a particular *kind* of detail. But as they write, as they turn their material into a unified statement, how do they keep general ideas and specific details in a *continuing* relationship? How do they demonstrate that these ideas and details *constantly* reinforce one another? A consideration of concrete and abstract language provides us with a number of insights into this on-going relationship.

HANDLING ABSTRACT AND CONCRETE LANGUAGE

A famous movie director once complained that he couldn't picture "work" on the screen, only individual acts of working: hammering, sewing, lifting, painting, scrubbing. We, too, can often have this problem. It reveals an important characteristic of language, that it constantly moves between the abstract (general principles) and the concrete (sensory details), from "work" to "scrubbing" and back again.

The reason for this movement is simple. Because all that we call reality is a process (even a seemingly solid chair consists of the rapid movement of atoms), the word "work" is simply a name for the shared element that we select or "abstract" from the processes of "sewing," "lifting," "painting," and "scrubbing." However, we don't have to stop here. We can divest these processes of even more of their unique characteristics, their minute particulars, and call the resulting common factor "activity." "Work," then, is a more abstract word than "scrubbing," but "activity" is more abstract than "work." "Abstract" and "concrete," therefore, are relative terms.

What we have been calling the "minute particulars" are the "concrete," and can be opposed to the general impression we abstract from them. The following passages, a verse from *Ecclesiastes* and George Orwell's satiric translation of it, vividly reveal the difference between the two:

I returned, and saw under the sun, that the race is
not to the swift, nor the battle to the strong,
neither yet bread to the wise, nor yet riches to men
of understanding, nor yet favor to men of skill; but
time and chance happeneth to them all.

Objective consideration of contemporary phenomena
compels the conclusion that success or failure in
competitive activities exhibits no tendency to be
commensurate with innate capacity, but that a
considerable element of the unpredictable must
invariably be taken into account.

The "sun," "battle," and "bread" are concrete things we can see, feel, and taste. In the context of this comparison, "contemporary phenomena" is an abstraction on such a high level that it becomes humorous. The only thing that would make it "make sense" would be a clearly defined connection with the "raw material" it supposedly represents. In the absence of this connection, the abstract phrase is vague and meaningless.

Orwell is being deliberately obscure in order to make his point. But, like the movie director, we are often genuinely frustrated because a generalization won't do. We must connect it to our specific observations—that is, the concrete details that gave rise to our generalization. You looked out the window this morning and you were depressed, but what specifically did you see that produced this emotion? Rain? A wino lying in the gutter? Though being specific is time consuming, and frustrating on occasion, this is exactly where the excitement of writing lies. By forcing ourselves to connect our general impressions to concrete perceptions, we discover what we really think or feel, what lies underneath our tendency to dismiss vaguely our experience, and say: "I'm just depressed, that's all. You know." We don't know. What you mean by "depressing," and what someone else means, of course, can be worlds apart. Good writing connects the abstract and the concrete; it reminds us that ideas and perceptions constantly reinforce one another.

The following game and exercises are designed to increase your awareness of how interdependent concrete and abstract statements are. They will also give you practice in moving from one to the other.

A GAME

The Chinese language consists of conventionalized and abbreviated pictures (called ideograms) of concrete *things*, such as 人 for "man." Consequently, for example, they have no word for poetry in *general*, but only individual ideograms for different kinds of poetry. Likewise, they express the abstraction "red" by combining the pictures:

ROSE	CHERRY
IRON RUST	FLAMINGO

Similarly, we could express "fear" by combining the pictures:

SWORD	SYRINGE
WOLF'S TOOTH	BAYONET

On the model of the Chinese ideogram, give at least four concrete word pictures which could be combined to convey the meaning of each of the following more abstract words:

1. yellow	6. cruelty
2. loud	7. hate
3. stench	8. kindness
4. sour	9. happiness
5. hot	10. love

When you have done this, read them to each other and discuss the variations of each word. You could also choose your own abstractions, write the word-pictures for them separately, and have the class guess what the abstraction is in each case.

A READING EXERCISE

The following poems all deal with winter and are based on the sixteenth century painting by Pieter Brueghel the Elder, entitled "The Return of the Hunters." First, look at the picture carefully, then read the poems and discuss the questions.

"Returning from the Hunt"/*Norbert Krapf*

The last specks of sunlight
sparkle in the wisps of snow
balanced on the branches
of the stark, unyielding trees.
Perched way above the action,
crows gaze down coldly upon
a pack of hounds poking their
noses in the crusty snow.

Pieter Brueghel the Elder, "The Return of the Hunters." 1565, Kunsthistorisches Museum, Vienna.

The smell of blood has curdled
in their nostrils; tails curl
with enthusiasm but bottoms
sag. Although already within
the village, they force
a few last hopeful yaps
into the heavy evening air.

Just in front of the hounds
the masters lean their brawny
shoulders into the January
evening. Their boots trudge
homeward in the deep snow.
One man feels the body warmth
of the slain animal slumped
against the small of his back.
From here on it is downhill.
They will coast down to their
cottages and prop their feet
up against a blazing hearth.
After darkness has swooped
down upon the valley like
a vulture, they will consume
rustic food that has simmered
on the fire for hours. Later
they will go to bed with their
women and know a pleasure which,
like their appetite for food
and the hunt, never diminishes
with fulfillment. Soon they
will be in the field again.

"The Hunters in the Snow"/*William Carlos Williams*

The over-all picture is winter
icy mountains
in the background the return

from the hunt it is toward evening
from the left
sturdy hunters lead in

their pack the inn-sign
hanging from a
broken hinge is a stag a crucifix

between his antlers the cold
inn yard is
deserted but for a huge bonfire

that flares wind-driven tended by
women who cluster
about it to the right beyond

the hill is a pattern of skaters
Brueghel the painter
concerned with it all has chosen

a winter-struck bush for his
foreground to
complete the picture.

"Winter Landscape"/*John Berryman*

The three men coming down the winter hill
In brown, with tall poles and a pack of hounds
At heel, through the arrangement of the trees,
Past the five figures at the burning straw,
Returning cold and silent to their town,

Returning to the drifted snow, the rink
Lively with children, to the older men,
The long companions they can never reach,
The blue light, men with ladders, by the church
The sledge and shadow in the twilit street,

Are not aware that in the sandy time
To come, the evil waste of history
Outstretched, they will be seen upon the brow
Of that same hill: when all their company
Will have been irrecoverably lost,

These men, this particular three in brown
Witnessed by birds will keep the scene and say
By their configuration with the trees,
The small bridge, the red houses and the fire,
What place, what time, what morning occasion

Sent them into the wood, a pack of hounds
At heel and the tall poles upon their shoulders,
Thence to return as now we see them and
Ankle-deep in snow down the winter hill
Descend, while three birds watch and the fourth flies.

1. What are the differences in the details noticed by each of the writers?
2. Different minor details are important to each writer. Why are the "cottages" so significant to Krapf, the "broken hinge" to Williams, and the "birds" to Berryman?
3. Krapf and Berryman both add details that are not actually visible in the painting. What are they and why are they added?
4. Why does Williams call attention to "Brueghel the painter," not allowing us to forget that he is describing a painting?
5. What is the difference in the point of view among the three writers? (Where does each poet "stand"—physically and emotionally—in relation to the winter scene?) You might begin by considering differences between the titles.
6. What is the difference in the focus of each poem? (What segment of the painting has each writer chosen to pay attention to? And why?) In this light, what is the significance of the different titles?
7. If you consider each of these poems as a large ideogram, what abstraction would you assign to each? How does each detail support this central abstraction (which we could call the "theme")? Does each writer make clear what his theme is? How?

A WRITING EXERCISE

Choose a theme (an abstraction) of your own about Brueghel's painting, or about an experience you have had of winter. Express this in your first sentence, and write a paragraph clarifying your idea, by choosing only those concrete details that support your theme. Try to keep your point of view and focus consistent; that is, try to select only those details that relate specifically to your abstraction.

DISCOVERING STYLE

You should be realizing in this chapter that point of view (knowing where you are in relation to your subject), focus (your deliberate limitation of your subject), and the constant interaction of concrete details with abstract ideas, are all part of the same process.

Beginning writers must expand their senses; they must get a "respect for the sensory aspect of things." But, more than this, they must learn to *react* to what they see according to where and who they are. They must practice *abstracting* general impressions from the "sensory aspect of things." Their reactions and general impressions will determine where their chief interest lies and, therefore, provide a focus for their attention. This focus, in turn, should bring them back into contact with their store of concrete details and aid them in seeing the importance of these details.

In short, the relationships we have been discussing—that of writer to subject, of minute particulars to general ideas, and of minute particulars to each other— are all merely contributing concerns to the major concern of expressing yourself clearly and originally. They create a total verbal effect that is called *style*. They give the shape to a piece of writing that renders it a whole experience.

Note: You may want to ask here if we've left something important out of our definition of *style*. What has happened to the relationship of subject to audience? That relationship, while one of special importance, is also implicit in the others. Writers' points of view and focus are both chosen with an eye toward what the writers want their audience to "see." The impressions that all writers abstract from their observations and the concrete details they choose to illustrate them are all recorded in an effort to bring the reader into a particular understanding of the subject. We will be discussing this relationship further in future chapters, but its place in the writing process should be clear to you from the very beginning.

The reading exercise that follows is designed to help you put all of the considerations of Chapter One together, to see how *style* is a dynamic product of the interactions of point of view, focus, abstract ideas and concrete details.

A READING EXERCISE

In the following excerpts the ocean is the subject. The questions that follow each selection ask you to examine various aspects of the authors' styles, considering how each writer interacts with and represents the sea. Carson and Proust both focus on the surface of the sea in their descriptions. But while Carson is the more objective scientist, delighting in pointing out to a lay audience the myriad details that a specially trained person sees, Proust is overwhelmingly concerned with himself. (Notice however how he uses meticulously observed and arranged details to generate his interests.) Similarly, though Beston and Conrad both focus on the tremendous force of the gale, their points of view differ. Whereas Beston is primarily concerned with experiencing the winds and waves, Conrad is more consciously haunted by the need to "interpret" his experience.

"The Sea Surface"/*Rachel L. Carson*

Nowhere in all the sea does life exist in such bewildering abundance as in the surface waters. From the deck of a vessel you may look down, hour after hour, on the shimmering discs of jellyfish, their gently pulsating bells dotting the surface as far as you can see. Or one day you may notice early in the morning that you are passing through a sea that has taken on a brick-red color from billions upon billions of microscopic creatures, each of which contains an orange pigment grannule. At noon you are still moving through red seas, and when darkness falls the waters shine with an eerie glow from the phosphorescent fires of yet more billions and trillions of these same creatures.

And again you may glimpse not only the abundance but something of the fierce uncompromisingness of sea life when, as you look over the rail and down, down into water of a clear, deep green, suddenly there passes a silver shower of finger-long fishlets. The sun strikes a metallic gleam from their flanks as they streak by, driving deeper into the green depths with the desperate speed of the hunted. Perhaps you never see the hunters, but you sense their presence as you see the gulls hovering, with eager, mewing cries, waiting for the little fish to be driven to the surface.

Or again, perhaps, you may sail for days on end without seeing anything you could recognize as life or the indications of life, day after day of empty water and empty sky, and so you may reasonably conclude that there is no spot on earth so barren of life as the open ocean. But if you had the opportunity to tow a fine-meshed net through the seemingly lifeless water and then to examine the washings of the net, you would find that life is scattered almost everywhere through the surface waters like a fine dust. A cupful of water may contain millions upon millions of tiny plant cells, each of them far too small to be seen by the human eye; or it may swarm with an infinitude of animal creatures, none larger than a dust mote, which live on plant cells still smaller than themselves.

1. Using some of her own phrases, summarize Carson's attitude toward the sea. What abstractions give her sketch unity?
2. Is Carson's feeling about the sea consistent throughout the passage?
3. How does her physical point of view change from the beginning to the end of her description? How is this change related to her theme?
4. What sense does she use primarily? How does she achieve variety in her description despite the predominant reliance on a single sense?
5. How is her point of view confining? How does she make it seem revealing instead?

"The Glass Sea"/*Marcel Proust*

I went into my room. Regularly, as the season advanced, the picture that I found there in my window changed. At first it was broad daylight, and dark only if the weather was bad: and then, in the greenish glass which it distended with the curve of its round waves, the sea, set among the iron uprights of my window like a piece of stained glass in its leads, ravelled out over all the deep rocky border of the bay little plumed triangles of an unmoving spray delineated with the delicacy of a feather or a downy breast from Pisanello's pencil, and fixed in that white, unalterable, creamy enamel which is used to depict fallen snow in Gallé's glass.

Presently the days grew shorter and at the moment when I entered my room the violet sky seemed branded with the stiff, geometrical, travelling, effulgent figure of the sun (like the representation of some miraculous sign, of some mystical apparition) leaning over the sea from the hinge of the horizon as a sacred picture leans over a high altar, while the different parts of the western sky exposed in the glass fronts of the low mahogany bookcases that ran along the walls, which I carried back in my mind to the marvellous painting from which they had been detached, seemed like those different scenes which some old master executed long ago for a confraternity upon a shrine, whose separate panels are now exhibited side by side upon the wall of a museum gallery, so that the visitor's imagination alone can restore them to their place on the predella of the reredos. A few weeks later, when I went upstairs, the sun had already set. Like the one that I used to see at Combray, behind the Calvary, when I was coming home from a walk and looking forward to going down to the kitchen before dinner, a band of red sky over the sea, compact and clear-cut as a layer of aspic over meat, then, a little later, over a sea already cold and blue like a grey mullet, a sky of the same pink as the salmon that we should presently be ordering at Rive-belle reawakened the pleasure which I was to derive from the act of dressing to go out to dinner. Over the sea, quite near the shore, were try-ing to rise, one beyond another, at wider and wider intervals, vapours of a pitchy blackness but also of the polish and consistency of agate, of a visible weight, so much so that the highest among them, poised at the end of their contorted stem and overreaching the centre of gravity of the pile that had hitherto supported them, seemed on the point of bringing down in ruin this lofty structure already half the height of the sky, and of precipitating it into the sea. The sight of a ship that was moving away like a nocturnal traveller gave me the same impression that I had had in the train of being set free from the necessity of sleep and from confine-ment in a bedroom. Not that I felt myself a prisoner in the room in which I now was, since in another hour I should have left it and be getting into the carriage. I threw myself down on the bed; and, just as if I had been lying in a berth on board one of those steamers which I could see quite near to me and which, when night came, it would be strange to see stealing slowly out into the darkness, like shadowy and silent but un-sleeping swans, I was on all sides surrounded by pictures of the sea.

1. Is the focus of the passage on Proust or on the sea? Does the focus shift throughout? If so, where? And what is the relationship between the sea and the "I"?
2. What is Proust's physical point of view? What is his psychological point of view? How are these related? What do the differences between Carson's and Proust's physical points of view have to do with other differences between the descriptions?
3. Pick out all the words and phrases in the passage that have to do with pic-tures or painting, and all those that are concerned with religion. How are these two patterns of images related? How do these patterns unify the de-scription? How are they related to Proust's main idea or theme?
4. What does Proust's comparison of the "red sky over the sea" to a "layer of aspic over meat" indicate about his point of view and theme? Why does Proust use a number of comparisons and Carson none?
5. What is gained by focusing on the "sight of a ship" toward the end of the description?
6. Both Carson and Proust rely primarily on the sense of sight in their descrip-

tions, yet the two passages are extremely different. What are the differences in the way that each expands the sense of sight?

"Waves"/*Henry Beston*

They say here that great waves reach this coast in threes. Three great waves, then an indeterminate run of lesser rhythms, then three great waves again. On Celtic coasts it is the seventh wave that is seen coming like a king out of the grey, cold sea. The Cape tradition, however, is no half-real, half-mystical fancy, but the truth itself. Great waves do indeed approach this beach by threes. Again and again have I watched three giants roll in one after the other out of the Atlantic, cross the outer bar, break, form again, and follow each other in to fulfilment and destruction on this solitary beach. Coast guard crews are all well aware of this triple rhythm and take advantage of the lull that follows the last wave to launch their boats.

It is true that there are single giants as well. I have been roused by them in the night. Waked by their tremendous and unexpected crash, I have sometimes heard the last of the heavy overspill, sometimes only the loud, withdrawing roar. After the roar came a briefest pause, and after the pause the return of ocean to the night's long cadences. Such solitary titans, flinging their green tons down upon a quiet world, shake beach and dune. Late one September night, as I sat reading, the very father of all waves must have flung himself down before the house, for the quiet of the night was suddenly overturned by a gigantic, tumbling crash and an earthquake rumbling; the beach trembled beneath the avalanche, the dune shook, and my house so shook in its dune that the flame of a lamp quivered and pictures jarred on the wall.

The three great elemental sounds in nature are the sound of rain, the sound of wind in a primeval wood, and the sound of outer ocean on a beach. I have heard them all, and of the three elemental voices, that of ocean is the most awesome, beautiful, and varied. For it is a mistake to talk of the monotone of ocean or of the monotonous nature of its sound. The sea has many voices. Listen to the surf, really lend it your ears, and you will hear in it a world of sounds: hollow boomings and heavy roarings, great watery tumblings and tramplings, long hissing seethes, sharp, rifle-shot reports, and sometimes vocal sounds that might be the half-heard talk of people in the sea. And not only is the great sound varied in the manner of its making, it is also constantly changing its tempo, its pitch, its accent, and its rhythm, being now loud and thundering, now almost placid, now furious, now grave and solemn-slow, now a simple measure, now a rhythm monstrous with a sense of purpose and elemental will.

Every mood of the wind, every change in the day's weather, every phase of the tide—all these have subtle sea musics all their own. Surf of the ebb, for instance, is one music, surf of the flood another, the change in the two musics being most clearly marked during the first hour of a rising tide. With the renewal of the tidal energy, the sound of the surf grows louder, the fury of battle returns to it as it turns again on the land, and beat and sound change with the renewal of the war.

Sound of surf in these autumnal dunes—the continuousness of it, sound of endless charging, endless incoming and gathering, endless fulfilment and dissolution, endless fecundity, and endless death. I have been trying to study out the mechanics of that mighty resonance. The dominant note is the great spilling crash made by each arriving wave. It may be hollow and booming, it may be heavy and churning, it may be a tumbling roar. The second fundamental sound is the wild seething cataract roar of the wave's dissolution and the rush of its foaming waters up the beach—this second sound *diminuendo*. The third fundamental sound is the endless dissolving hiss of the inmost slides of foam. The first two sounds reach the ear as a unisonance—the booming impact of the tons of water and the wild roar of the up-rush blending—and this mingled sound dissolves into the foam-bubble hissing of the third. Above the tumult, like birds, fly wisps of watery noise, splashes and counter splashes, whispers, seethings, slaps, and chucklings. An overtone sound of other breakers, mingled with a general rumbling, fells earth and sea and air.

1. What is the central focus of this description?
2. With what sense primarily does Beston experience the sea? With what three things is the sea compared?
3. What is the dominant idea or theme throughout the passage?
4. What kinds of progression are there in the description from beginning to end?
5. How are the references to the "king out of the grey, cold sea" (para. 1), "giants" (para. 1), "rhythm monstrous with a sense of purpose and elemental will" (para. 3), and "endless fecundity, and endless death" (para. 5) related to Beston's point of view?
6. Beston announces a classification, "The three great . . ." (para. 3), but is he primarily interested in classification? Why does he make these kind of announcements? How are they related to his theme? What does this tendency reveal about his interaction with the sea, which is so different from Proust's?

"A Gale"/*Joseph Conrad*

It seems to me that no man born and truthful to himself could declare that he ever saw the sea looking young as the earth looks young in spring. But some of us, regarding the ocean with understanding and affection, have seen it looking old, as if the immemorial ages had been stirred up from the undisturbed bottom of ooze. For it is a gale of wind that makes the sea look old.

From a distance of years, looking at the remembered aspects of the storms lived through, it is that impression which disengages itself clearly from the great body of impressions left by many years of intimate contact.

If you would know the age of the earth, look upon the sea in a storm. The greyness of the whole immense surface, the wind furrows upon the faces of the waves, the great masses of foam, tossed about and waving, like matted white locks, give to the sea in a gale an appearance of hoary age, lustreless, dull, without gleams, as though it had been created before light itself. . . .

For after all, a gale of wind, the thing of mighty sound, is inarticulate. It is a man who, in chance phrase, interprets the elemental passion of his enemy. Thus there is another gale in my memory, a thing of endless, deep, humming roar, moonlight, and a spoken sentence.

It was off that other cape which is always deprived of its title as the Cape of Good Hope is robbed of its name. It was off the Horn. For a true expression of dishevelled wildness there is nothing like a gale in the bright moonlight of a high latitude.

The ship, brought to and bowing to enormous flashing seas, glistened wet from deck to trucks; her one set sail stood out a coal-black shape upon the gloomy blueness of the air. I was a youngster then, and suffering from weariness, cold, and imperfect oilskins which let water in at every seam. I craved human companionship, and, coming off the poop, took my place by the side of the boatswain (a man whom I did not like) in a comparatively dry spot where at worst we had water only up to our knees. Above our heads the explosive booming gusts of wind passed continuously, justifying the sailor's saying "It blows great guns." And just from that need of human companionship, being very close to the man, I said, or rather shouted:

"Blows very hard, boatswain."

His answer was:

"Ay, and if it blows only a little harder things will begin to go. I don't mind as long as everything holds, but when things begin to go it's bad."

The note of dread in the shouting voice, the practical truth of these words, heard years ago from a man I did not like, have stamped its peculiar character on that gale.

A look in the eyes of a shipmate, a low murmur in the most sheltered spot where the watch on duty are huddled together, a meaning moan from one to the other with a glance at the windward sky, a sigh of weariness, a gesture of disgust passing into the keeping of the great wind, become part and parcel of the gale. The olive hue of hurricane clouds presents an aspect peculiarly appalling. The inky ragged wrack, flying before a nor'-west wind, makes you dizzy with its headlong speed that depicts the rush of the invisible air. A hard sou'-wester startles you with its close horizon and its low grey sky, as if the world were a dungeon wherein there is no rest for body or soul. And there are black squalls, white squalls, thunder squalls, and unexpected gusts that come without a single sign in the sky; and of each kind no one of them resembles another.

There is infinite variety in the gales of wind at sea, and except for the peculiar, terrible, and mysterious moaning that may be heard sometimes passing through the roar of a hurricane—except for that unforgettable sound, as if the soul of the universe had been goaded into a mournful groan—it is, after all, the human voice that stamps the mark of human consciousness upon the character of a gale.

1. Both Beston and Conrad use the word "elemental" in their descriptions. But do they share the same point of view? If not, how do they differ? What is Conrad's theme or controlling idea?
2. What is the "character" (para. 8, 10) of the gale? How does the description of its "character" further Conrad's theme?
3. Conrad attempts to classify the winds, much as Beston does the waves, but how does it serve to develop his description differently?
4. How are the senses of hearing and seeing related in the passage? What sense is dominant? Why?
5. Conrad concludes by saying that it is, "after all, the human voice that stamps the mark of human consciousness upon the character of a gale." Show how this assumption determines the focus of the whole description. What is Conrad's main purpose for writing this passage?
6. Compare what Conrad and Proust find of the "human" in the sea.

 *Chapter Two*

Writing About Yourself

INTRODUCTION

By now, you should have some idea of what elements make up the writing process. You have exercised your powers of observation, explored the need for clear point of view and focus in writing, and have become sensitive to the intricate relationships between the concrete particulars or details of experience and the general ideas they inspire. We will continue to be concerned with these things, but in future chapters you will be asked to apply them to particular kinds of subject matter (yourself, other people, your culture, and a symbolic world), all of which require some form of *analysis*.

What, then, do we mean by analysis? And how do concerns such as point of view and focus relate to analysis? In its simplest form analysis is the process of taking some object, experience, or idea apart to *discover* and *understand* its structure. If you want to know how your favorite wind-up mouse works (or why it doesn't work), you'll have to look inside the mechanism, see how the various gears and parts relate to one another, and comprehend the sequence of movements. Similarly, if you want to know how Politician X won the mayoral contest, you'll have to look inside the campaign platform, see how the various programs relate to social problems and the "party line," and comprehend how these various programs moved the voters' sympathies. Thus, analysis is the process by which all thinking people question, discover, and understand the world around them.

Written analysis is the setting forth of these understandings, the discovery in language of how a particular subject can be clarified. *Point of view* enters in as the writers' feelings about, and relationship to, their subject. (Does the writer describe the wind-up mouse from the perspective of an adept mechanic, a curious child, a detached observer, or a sentimental owner?) *Focus* is the area of concentration that writers-analyzers define for themselves. (Does the writer concentrate on Politician X's social programs as being more revolutionary—and therefore more significant in assessing his success—than his financial programs?) *Concrete details* are the evidence that writers consider to arrive at an understanding or clarification of their subject; and *abstract ideas* are the understandings they strive for.

The first subject we are going to ask you to analyze is yourself.

I. HOW DOES ANALYSIS RELATE TO PERSONALITY?

As you are becoming aware, analysis is a constant mental process, not a specialized tool to be embraced and discarded at will. Every subject that thinking people look at—their reflection in the mirror as well as a statistical chart on population distribution—inspires questions, reactions, and ideas. ("I bet I look so robust today because of my red turtleneck;" or "Perhaps most wage earners in North Carolina live in the Piedmont area because of the growth of universities there.") Analysis is a function of *how* you look at the world, not of a special kind of subject matter.

This basic understanding should make it easier for us to talk about *self-analysis*—what it entails and how it is best articulated. You have probably written numerous autobiographical essays in previous English classes. "What did you do this summer"? and "What is the most exciting experience you've ever had"? are standard assignments. We're asking you to do something more complex than merely describing an event, however. We're asking you to take some of the pertinent "facts" of your existence and hold them up to the light, turning them slowly so that the full meaning is disclosed. We're asking you to select certain moments from your life and turn a clear questioning eye on them. James Baldwin, a contemporary writer of essays and fiction, goes so far as to claim that this kind of examination is, in fact, the source of *all* writing. He says, "One writes out of one thing only—one's own experience. Everything depends on how relentlessly one forces from this experience the last drop, sweet or bitter, it can possibly give."

No one can pretend that this kind of self-assessment is easy. The facts of our lives often become like comfortable old sticks of furniture; we know their shape but could hardly describe the pattern of the upholstery or the origin of their presence in the family room. We're asking you to look carefully at the "sticks of furniture" in your life to discover how they came into your possession, but more important, to discern why you still keep them around. If you can apply the analytical process to yourself, you will begin to discover who you are, and you will become comfortable with evaluative, critical thinking.

Now, exactly what do we mean by the important "facts" of your life? That can be answered several ways. It can mean memories of childhood experience, remembrances of family and friends, religious and ethical inheritances, ethnic associations, or any factor, past or present, that you feel has a vital connection with what you are right now.

To be worth analyzing, a "fact" of your life must present to you some aspect of your origins, your social milieu, your likes, your dislikes, your talents, or your blind spots. But it should also intrigue you so that unraveling its accompanying sights, sounds, feelings, and gestures is interesting and self-motivating. Analysis is only dull when you (the analyst) don't care at all about the object of your attention. Your life, of all the things around you, probably intrigues you the most and, therefore, is a good place to begin "examining" the world.

2. HOW DO YOU BEGIN ANALYZING YOURSELF?

How do you begin? You become reflective, and you practice discrimination. You pretend that you have been given one small photograph album to hold the thousands of color snapshots that memorialize your life. Then you select the most representative, the most sharply etched, and the most enigmatic shots. You pull out moments, friends, and favorite places that most clearly build a portrait of your "roots," your habits, and your goals. Be aware, meanwhile, that the decisions that you are making are themselves "facts" of your existence. Ask yourself occasionally, "Why did I select the third day of kindergarten rather than the first"? or "Why did I select Aunt Sarah over Uncle Harry"?

Now you need to carry your album to a bright light and study the "frozen moments" at length. See how many details you can remember for each "fact"— how many raised eyebrows and chipped teeth you can associate with each person, how many stifled laughs and nearly imperceptible gestures you can associate with each event. You will find that some moments or persons engender more strong feelings and more concrete memories than others. These are the most likely subjects for meaningful self-analysis. Spend extra time examining them. Make sure the raw material is clearly written on your mind.

Third, ask yourself questions about these chief events—"Why did Aunt Sarah's eyes narrow with pleasure when I came into the room?" or "Why did I cry so easily when Sister Rosalie came near?" Consider what might have been the source of your anxiety in fearful moments, what might have been the reasons for your brashness in others. Let your mind play with what you see, with what you already know of yourself. Decide how you feel about these events. (This will eventually become your point of view.) And decide what aspects of the events most clearly reinforce these feelings. (This will become your focus.)

Finally, draw some thoughtful conclusions, and see if the evidence supports them. Entertain explanations for your behavior, and see if they hold true. Keep going back to the evidence or details for verification and new clues. Allow the observed details to generate ideas about your personality, and allow these ideas to lead you to new observations. At this point you are discovering who you are; if you have thought carefully about the "facts," you will be analyzing yourself with conviction. The results should be enlightening to both yourself and others.

A WRITING EXERCISE

Your class might want to try an exercise in remembering. Take ten minutes to write a description of your very first memory. Read the results to the rest of the class and explain *why* you think this is your first memory. What makes it remarkable? It will be interesting to see if any of your events and explanations are similar.

Likewise, take ten minutes to describe your first "love object" (mother, teddy bear, pet cat). Again, read the accounts aloud and offer explanations for your choices.

Or you might want to take ten minutes to describe a decision you have made sometime in the past that has had unforeseen consequences. Describe the situation that prompted the decision and the actual process of deciding. Read your description to the class, and tell them where this choice has led you.

To summarize, analyzing yourself means selecting moments from the "rag and bone shop" of your life, looking at them with a lucid eye, asking them questions (and letting them ask you questions), and finally attempting to put the pieces together.

3. WHAT PROBLEMS WILL YOU FACE IN FOCUSING AND ORGANIZING YOUR SELF-ANALYSIS?

These problems could range from "Who in the world would want to know about me, anyhow?" to "Where should the commas go in a noun of direct address?" There are many questions you're *likely* to meet; but we're going to concentrate on two problems you're *sure* to face. How much material constitutes an analyzable memory? And, how do anecdote (the narration of a self-contained event) and analysis (the process by which events are understood) fit together in a single paper?

The first question involves the "size" of your subject. Is an analyzable "memory" made up of the events of an hour, an afternoon, or of incidents that spread out over a period of years? The answer lies in the nature of the memory and the writer's approach to it. In her essay, "When I was a Child," Lillian

Smith uses a single incident to suggest a whole set of value conflicts that surrounded her childhood in the South. She tells of a "white" child who was discovered living in the black section of town. According to her parents' cardinal rule—"white and colored people do not live together"—the child had to be removed to a white home, in this case, their own. But the incident becomes most remarkable at the point where the white-looking child is discovered to be "black," and Lillian Smith's parents must either amend their rule or play a cruel trick on the child.

As the writer points out, this is not the only time that the racist values of her parents and their friends were called into question, but it is vivid enough to suggest the nature of these conflicts and, therefore, can stand alone. She has focused on one event and made it speak of many things.

Other subjects require the use of several closely related incidents. In her short story, "Four Summers," Joyce Carol Oates chooses four separate incidents in a young girl's life to demonstrate her changing relationship to her parents. (Sections I and IV are reproduced here.) All four take place in the same picnic grove, involve the same basic characters, and are narrated by the young girl herself. Oates' focus is on the complex relationship between "Sissie" and her parents, and her four related events demonstrate this relationship. (Here the *controlling idea* or *theme* of the story is closely related to the *focus* and the *point of view*. One might well say that the *theme* of any given work is equal to the *correspondence* of its focus, point of view, concrete details and general impressions. The theme both determines and is determined by how these various elements come together.)

Another kind of self-analysis requires that incidents be loosely arranged to create a kaleidoscopic effect. This occurs when writers want to present the total *impression* that some period in their life leaves behind. They therefore move quickly from one incident to another just as your eyes might sweep the pages of a photograph album.

Maya Angelou creates this effect in "Stamps, Arkansas" where she moves abruptly from one memory of her childhood to another, from a crisis with the redneck sheriff to a trip across town with her brother Bailey. But a close look at the incidents reveals several binding threads—her love for Bailey, Uncle Willie's afflictions, her mother's store which functions as "home base." And all the incidents contribute to the impression of what life was like for a small black child in rural Arkansas.

Thus, there is no such thing as a given circumference for your subject matter. You may use one, three, or five incidents as long as some aspect of your life is "set off" by the selection, and as long as your focus is clear.

The second question you are bound to face is how anecdotes relate to analysis (the process of evaluation). Once you are aware that the events of your life have consequences worth analyzing, how do you write about both events and your understanding of them in one essay? (This is, of course, a variation of a problem we have already faced—how does the writer keep concrete details and abstract ideas in a continuing relationship?) Just as with the previous question, there is no single answer.

The most straightforward method is to recreate the incident and then discuss its consequences. Lillian Smith does this to some extent in "When I was a Child." She gives the reader a general portrait of the South, as seen by a white child. Then she tells the story of how Janie, a child of indeterminate race, entered this environment and brought all of its inconsistencies to light. She ends by explaining how this event affected her at the time it happened and how she responded to it some thirty years later. In essence, she prepares the reader for her anecdote, tells it, then considers its ramifications. But the reader should also notice that all of Smith's speculations about why this event occurred are not reserved for the last section. The telling of the event itself exhibits a correspondence of detail and general comment, of concrete and abstract statements. As we saw in Chapter One, the two can rarely be kept completely separate, although certain "groupings" of concrete evidence and abstract evaluation can be utilized effectively.

In "Names," Mary McCarthy *surrounds* her anecdotes with evaluative comments, introducing the self-contained events as *examples* of abstract ideas. She begins by discussing the symbolic content of names, and then uses the school-girl practice of assigning comic, often cruel, nicknames to fellow students as an illustration of how this content "works." The use of nicknames to intimidate one's classmates, however, was only one form of oppression that operated in the convent school Mary McCarthy attended, as she points out to us in the mid-section of the selection. She illustrates this observation with an incident in which the nuns absolutely refused to believe her account of how blood appeared on her bedsheet. The essay then returns to the mysterious power of nicknames and a series of comments on how pretense is the logical outcome of emotional bullying. The writer's focus is on the relationship of oppression to falsehood, within the confines of a parochial school. McCarthy establishes her focus and supports her main idea or theme by presenting specific examples of this association.

But there are other personal essays in which the conclusions are so closely woven with the anecdotes that there is no obvious break, but rather, a perpetual use of physical events to clarify one another and to lead to a general understanding. In this strategy, as compared with the others, the events *contain* the evaluation.

For example, the first paragraph of Alfred Kazin's "From the Subway to the Synagogue" includes a vivid physical description of the exterior of the Brooklyn school which he attended with dread. Later he gives an even more vivid account of how his painful shyness about his speech made him physically ill on the days when he was forced by the school authorities to take special speech therapy lessons. Both descriptions are clear, vivid, and physical. However, they finally transcend the physical when Kazin associates all that he has been describing with a fly-specked druggist's display of digestion portrayed by a series of illustrations called "The Human Factory." In the end we learn that the starkness of his school building, the unapproachable sternness of his teachers, and the well-meant compulsion of his immigrant parents to have him speak flawless English repulsed the boy because they suggested to him a mindless, mechanical process of education which rubbed raw his every exposed nerve. He realizes, in fact, that his school is "A Human Factory."

Thus, there are several ways that individual events or anecdotes can be incorporated into a unified self-analysis. Similarly, there are various numbers of events that constitute an analyzable memory. Each of the examples we have used to alert you to this makes the same point, one that is central to our theme of discovery. The process of articulate self-analysis leads to the discovery of a writing strategy that will best express the experiences writers must look at to see who they are. For each of the writers represented below, discovery of self is bound up in discovery of a strategy that will aid them in looking at and learning from their experiences. Be aware of the alternatives these authors' works offer you in planning your own theme. Be sure to structure your essay so that your readers can see through your eyes the things you have seen.

READINGS

"Autobiographical Notes"/*James Baldwin*

Writing simultaneously about himself and the *process* of writing about himself, James Baldwin focuses on the basic dilemma of all writers: bringing out of the disorder of their own experience an ordered account that has the power to communicate. But in this prologue to *Notes of A Native Son,* a collection of autobiographical–critical essays, Baldwin probes this dilemma further. He discovers its *personal* aspect, that as a black writer he is prohibited from examining his own experience too closely "by the tremendous demands and the very real dangers" of his social situation. Thus, in bringing order out of his experience, he is constantly thrust back to the central fact that, as a Negro, he must confront his blackness before he can describe it. We all have some "reality," perhaps a different one from Baldwin's, with which we must make a truce. As a result of confronting this problem, Baldwin realizes that before he can examine the present and look to the future, he must take a "long look back." And in doing so he both finds himself and grapples with the problems of writing about himself.

The very structure of "Notes" reveals this process. Baldwin begins with a "long look back," which leads to a confrontation with his personal dilemma, inseparable from the problem of writing, and ends with a series of present autobiographical facts. The middle section shifts focus as his dilemma looms large and he realizes that his life (or anyone's) is not inherently interesting. Only by its shape—its "order"—does it have power to smash the "indifference" of the world. His discovery of the solution to his dilemma is the essay itself, a piece of writing that will communicate. This desire for order unifies Baldwin's whole essay, but as you read, consider why it strikes us as "Notes" and how he has prepared us to be concerned about his many "interests."

I was born in Harlem thirty-one years ago. I began plotting novels at about the time I learned to read. The story of my childhood is the usual bleak fantasy, and we can dismiss it with the restrained observation that I certainly would not consider living it again. In those days my mother was given to the exasperating and mysterious habit of having babies. As they were born, I took them over with one hand and held a book with the other. The children probably suffered, though they have since been kind enough to deny it, and in this way I read *Uncle Tom's Cabin* and *A Tale of Two Cities* over and over and over again; in this way, in fact, I read just about everything I could get my hands on—except the Bible, probably because it was the only book I was encouraged to read. I must also confess that I wrote—a great deal—and my first professional triumph, in any case, the first effort of mine to be seen in print, occurred at the age of twelve or thereabouts, when a short story I had written about the Spanish revolution won some sort of prize in an extremely short-lived church newspaper. I remember the story was censored by the lady editor, though I don't remember why, and I was outraged.

Also wrote plays, and songs, for one of which I received a letter of congratulations from Mayor La Guardia, and poetry, about which the less said, the better. My mother was delighted by all these goings-on, but my father wasn't; he wanted me to be a preacher. When I was fourteen I became a preacher, and when I was seventeen I stopped. Very shortly thereafter I left home. For God knows how long I struggled with the world of commerce and industry—I guess they would say they struggled with *me*—and when I was about twenty-one I had enough done of a novel to get a Saxton Fellowship. When I was twenty-two the fellowship was over, the novel turned out to be unsalable, and I started waiting on tables in a Village restaurant and writing book reviews—mostly, as it turned out, about the Negro problem, concerning which the color of my skin made me automatically an expert. Did another book, in company with photographer Theodore Pelatowski, about the storefront churches in Harlem. This book met exactly the same fate as my first—fellowship, but no sale. (It was a Rosenwald Fellowship.) By the time I was twenty-four I had decided to stop reviewing books about the Negro problem—which, by this time, was only slightly less horrible in print than it was in life—

and I packed my bags and went to France, where I finished, God knows how, *Go Tell It on the Mountain.*

Any writer, I suppose, feels that the world into which he was born is nothing less than a conspiracy against the cultivation of his talent—which attitude certainly has a great deal to support it. On the other hand, it is only because the world looks on his talent with such a frightening indifference that the artist is compelled to make his talent important. So that any writer, looking back over even so short a span of time as I am here forced to assess, finds that the things which hurt him and the things which helped him cannot be divorced from each other; he could be helped in a certain way only because he was hurt in a certain way; and his help is simply to be enabled to move from one conundrum to the next—one is tempted to say that he moves from one disaster to the next. When one begins looking for influences one finds them by the score. I haven't thought much about my own, not enough anyway; I hazard that the King James Bible, the rhetoric of the store-front church, something ironic and violent and perpetually understated in Negro speech—and something of Dickens' love for bravura—have something to do with me today; but I wouldn't stake my life on it. Likewise, innumerable people have helped me in many ways; but finally, I suppose, the most difficult (and most rewarding) thing in my life has been the fact that I was born a Negro and was forced, therefore, to effect some kind of truce with this reality. (Truce, by the way, is the best one can hope for.)

One of the difficulties about being a Negro writer (and this is not special pleading, since I don't mean to suggest that he has it worse than anybody else) is that the Negro problem is written about so widely. The bookshelves groan under the weight of information, and everyone therefore considers himself informed. And this information, furthermore, operates usually (generally, popularly) to reinforce traditional attitudes. Of traditional attitudes there are only two—For or Against—and I, personally, find it difficult to say which attitude has caused me the most pain. I am speaking as a writer; from a social point of view I am perfectly aware that the change from ill-will to good-will, however motivated, however imperfect, however expressed, is better than no change at all.

But it is part of the business of the writer—as I see it—to examine attitudes, to go beneath the surface, to tap the source. From this point of view the Negro problem is nearly inaccessible. It is not only written about so widely; it is written about so badly. It is quite possible to say that the price a Negro pays for becoming articulate is to find himself, at length, with nothing to be articulate about. ("You taught me language," says Caliban to Prospero, "and my profit on't is I know how to curse.") Consider: the tremendous social activity that this problem generates imposes on whites and Negroes alike the necessity of looking forward, of working to bring about a better day. This is fine, it keeps the waters troubled; it is all, indeed, that has made possible the Negro's progress. Nevertheless, social affairs are not generally speaking the writer's prime concern, whether they ought to be or not; it is absolutely necessary that he establish between himself and these affairs a distance which will allow, at least, for clarity, so that before he can look forward in any meaningful sense, he must first be allowed to take a long look back. In the context of the Negro problem neither whites nor blacks, for excellent reasons of their own, have the faintest desire to look back; but I think that the past is all that makes the present coherent, and further, that the past will remain horrible for exactly as long as we refuse to assess it honestly.

I know, in any case, that the most crucial time in my own development came when I was forced to recognize that I was a kind of bastard of the West; when I followed the line of my past I did not find myself in Europe but in Africa. And this meant that in some subtle way, in a really profound way, I brought to Shakespeare, Bach, Rembrandt, to the stones of Paris, to the cathedral at Chartres, and to the Empire State Building, a special attitude. These were not really my creations, they did not contain my history; I might search in them in vain forever for any reflection of myself. I was an interloper; this was not my heritage. At the same time I had no other heritage which I could possibly hope to use—I had certainly been unfitted for the jungle or the tribe. I would have to appropriate these white centuries, I would have to make them mine— I would have to accept my special attitude, my special place in this scheme—otherwise I would have no place in *any* scheme. What was the most difficult was the fact that I was forced to admit something I had always hidden from myself, which the American Negro has had to hide from himself as the price of his public progress; that I hated and feared white people. This did not mean that I loved black people; on the contrary, I despised them, possibly because they failed to produce Rembrandt. In effect, I hated and feared the world. And this meant, not only that I thus gave the world an altogether murderous power over me, but also that in such a self-destroying limbo I could never hope to write.

One writes out of one thing only—one's own experience. Everything depends on how relentlessly one forces from this experience the last drop, sweet or bitter, it can possibly give. This is the only real concern of the artist, to recreate out of the disorder of life that order which is art. The difficulty then, for me, of being á Negro writer was the fact that I was, in effect, prohibited from examining my own experience too closely by the tremendous demands and the very real dangers of my social situation.

I don't think the dilemma outlined above is uncommon. I do think, since writers work in the disastrously explicit medium of language, that it goes a little way towards explaining why, out of the enormous resources of Negro speech and life, and despite the example of Negro music, prose written by Negroes has been generally speaking so pallid and so harsh.

I have not written about being a Negro at such length because I expect that to be my only subject, but only because it was the gate I had to unlock before I could hope to write about anything else. I don't think that the Negro problem in America can be even discussed coherently without bearing in mind its context; its context being the history, traditions, customs, the moral assumptions and preoccupations of the country; in short, the general social fabric. Appearances to the contrary, no one in America escapes its effects and everyone in America bears some responsibility for it. I believe this the more firmly because it is the overwhelming tendency to speak of this problem as though it were a thing apart. But in the work of Faulkner, in the general attitude and certain specific passages in Robert Penn Warren, and, most significantly, in the advent of Ralph Ellison, one sees the beginnings—at least—of a more genuinely penetrating search. Mr. Ellison, by the way, is the first Negro novelist I have ever read to utilize in language, and brilliantly, some of the ambiguity and irony of Negro life.

About my interests: I don't know if I have any, unless the morbid desire to own a sixteen-millimeter camera and make experimental movies can be so classified. Otherwise, I love to eat and drink—it's my melancholy conviction that I've scarcely ever had enough to eat (this is because it's *impossible* to eat enough if you're worried about the next meal)—and I love to argue with people who do not disagree with me too profoundly, and I love to laugh. I do *not* like bohemia, or bohemians, I do not like people whose principal aim is pleasure, and I do not like people who are *earnest* about anything. I don't like people who like me because I'm a Negro; neither do I like people who find in the same accident grounds for contempt. I love America more than any other country in the world, and, exactly for this reason, I insist on the right to criticize her perpetually. I think all theories are suspect, that the finest principles may have to be modified, or may even be pulverized by the demands of life, and that one must find, therefore, one's own moral center and move through the world hoping that this center will guide one aright. I consider that I have many responsibilities, but none greater than this: to last, as Hemingway says, and get my work done.

I want to be an honest man and a good writer.

1. How is Baldwin's last sentence a summary of his thematic concerns and the structure of his "Notes"? How are "honest man" and "good writer" related? Why does he make this one sentence a single paragraph?
2. What is the purpose of the several short, simple sentences in the beginning and end of the essay? In what ways are the sentences of the last section repetitious? Why?

3. What is Baldwin's point of view? Why does he mention Shakespeare, Bach, Rembrandt, and Faulkner? How does this support his point of view?
4. What is the shift in focus from the first two paragraphs to the third? Why is this shift effective?
5. How is "Notes" an example of Baldwin's assertion that "one writes out of one thing only—one's own experience"? How is his discussion of the "dilemma" of the writer related to the opening sketch of the essay?
6. What unifies the series of "interests" in the next to the last paragraph?
7. How does Baldwin make us take notice of the first sentence of the second paragraph?

"When I was a Child"/*Lillian Smith*

In the following excerpt from her book-length reminiscence of life in the South, Lillian Smith recounts a childhood incident that "festers" in her memory. It involves a child of seemingly indeterminate race who lived in Smith's home for a short time, only to be whisked away for "social reasons." What "festers," however, is not the set of actions that made up this incident, but rather the net of hypocrisies that surrounded it, the labyrinth of equivocations that made her realize for the first time that her parent's strong Christianity was incompatible with their cultural conditioning, and that, in fact, they were "out of control."

We gradually become fully aware of this lack of control as we proceed through the clearly defined three-part structure of the excerpt. Lillian Smith first paints the scene or "backdrop," then presents the "drama" itself, and finally gives her mature evaluation of the experience. This final assessment of the incident, however, is implicit from the beginning. For in each part of the passage she analyzes her experience through the process of selecting and setting off aspects of her life, describing her impressions, and presenting her milieu. As you read, observe the way in which physical events (impressions or anecdotes) are related to abstract ideas (analysis), and in which the past is related to the present. How does the progression from a specific scene to its drama to explicit reflection on the drama, and from the past to the present, serve to clarify Smith's analysis of her experience?

I was born and reared in a small Deep South town whose population was about equally Negro and white. There were nine of us who grew up freely in a rambling house of many rooms, surrounded by big lawn, back yard, gardens, fields, and barn. It was the kind of home that gathers memories like dust, a place filled with laughter and play and pain and hurt and ghosts and games. We were given such advantages of schooling, music, and art as were available in the South, and our world was not limited to the South, for travel to far places seemed a simple, natural thing to us, and usually there was one of the family in a remote part of the earth.

We knew we were a respected and important family of this small town but beyond this knowledge we gave little thought to status. Our father made money in lumber and naval stores for the excitement of making and losing it—not for what money can buy nor the security which it sometimes gives. I do not remember at any time wanting "to be rich" nor do I remember that thrift and saving were ideals which our parents considered important enough to urge upon us. Always in the family there was an acceptance of risk, a mild delight even in burning bridges, an expectant "what will happen now!" We were not irresponsible; living according to the pleasure principle was by no means our way of life. On the contrary we were trained to think that each of us should do something that would be of genuine usefulness to the world, and the family thought it right to make sacrifices if necessary, to give each child adequate preparation for this life's work. We were also trained to think learning important, and books, but "bad" books our mother burned. We valued music and art and craftsmanship but it was people and their welfare and religion that were the foci around which our lives seemed naturally to move. Above all else, the important thing was what we "planned to do with our lives." That each of us must do something was as inevitable as breathing for we owed a "debt to society which must be paid." This was a family commandment.

While many of our neighbors spent their energies in counting limbs on the family tree and grafting some on now and then to give symmetry to it, or in reliving the old bitter days of Reconstruction licking scars to cure their vague malaise, or in fighting each battle and turn of battle of that Civil War which has haunted the southern conscience so long, my father was pushing his nine children straight into the future. "You have your heritage," he used to say, "some of it good, some not so good; and as far as I know you had the usual number of grandmothers and grandfathers. Yes, there were slaves, far too many of them in the family, but that was your grandfather's mistake, not yours. The past has been lived. It is gone. The future is yours. What are you going to do with it?" Always he asked this question of his children and sometimes one knew it was but an echo of the old question he had spent his life trying to answer for himself. For always the future held my father's dreams; always there, not in the past, did he expect to find what he had spent his life searching for.

We lived the same segregated life as did other southerners but our parents talked in excessively Christian and democratic terms. We were told ten thousand times that status and money are unimportant (though we were well supplied with both); we were told that "all men are brothers," that we are a part of a democracy and must act like democrats. We were told that the teachings of Jesus are real and important and could be practiced if we tried. We were told also that to be "radical" is bad, silly too; and that one must always conform to the "best behavior" of one's community and make it better if one can. We were taught that we were superior not to people but to hate and resentment, and that no member of the Smith family could stoop so low as to have an enemy. No matter what injury was done us, we must not injure ourselves further by retaliating. That was a family commandment too.

We had family prayers once each day. All of us as children read the Bible in its entirety each year. We memorized hundreds of Bible verses and repeated them at breakfast, and said "sentence prayers" around the family table. God was not someone we met on Sunday but a permanent member of our household. It never occurred to me until I was fourteen or fifteen years old that He did not see every act and thought and chalk up the daily score on eternity's tablets.

Despite the strain of living so intimately with God, the nine of us were strong, healthy, energetic youngsters who filled our days with play and sports and music and books and managed to live much of our lives on the careless level at which young lives should be lived. We had our times of profound anxiety of course, for there were hard lessons to be learned about the body and "bad things" to be learned about sex. Sometimes I have wondered how we ever learned them with a mother so shy with words.

She was a wistful creature who loved beautiful things like lace and sunsets and flowers in a vague inarticulate way, and took good care of her children. We always knew this was not her world but one she accepted under duress. Her private world we rarely entered, though the shadow of it lay at times heavily on our hearts.

Our father owned large business interests, employed hundreds of colored and white laborers, paid them the prevailing low wages, worked them the prevailing long hours, built for them mill towns (Negro and white), built for each group a church, saw to it that religion was supplied free, saw to it that a commissary supplied commodities at a high price, and in general managed his affairs much as ten thousand other southern businessmen managed theirs.

Even now, I can hear him chuckling as he told my mother how he won his fight for Prohibition. The high point of the campaign was election afternoon, when he lined up the entire mill force of several hundred (white and black), passed out a shining silver dollar to each one of them, marched them in and voted liquor out of our county. It was a great day in his life. He had won the Big Game, a game he was always playing with himself against all kinds of evil. It did not occur to him to scrutinize the methods he used. Evil was a word written in capitals; the devil was smart; if you wanted to win you outsmarted him. It was as simple as that.

He was a practical, hardheaded, warmhearted, high-spirited man born during the Civil War, earning his living at twelve, struggling through bitter decades of Reconstruction and post-Reconstruction, through populist movement, through the panic of 1893, the panic of 1907, on into the twentieth century accepting his region as he found it, accepting its morals and its mores as he accepted its climate, with only scorn for those who held grudges against the North or pitied themselves or the South; scheming, dreaming, expanding his business, making and losing money, making friends whom he did not lose, with never a doubt that God was always by his side whispering hunches as to how to pull off successful deals. When he lost, it was his own fault. When he won, God had helped him.

Once while we were kneeling at family prayers the fire siren at the mill sounded the alarm that the mill was on fire. My father did not falter from his prayer. The alarm sounded again and again—which signified that the fire was big. With quiet dignity he continued his talk with God while his children sweated and wriggled and hearts beat out of their chests in excitement. He was talking to God—how could he hurry out of the presence of the Most High to save his mills! When he finished his prayer, he quietly stood up, laid the Bible carefully on the table. Then, and only then, did he show an interest in what was happening in Mill Town. . . . When the telegram was placed in his hands telling of the death of his beloved favorite son, he gathered his children together, knelt down, and in a steady voice which contained no hint of his shattered heart, loyally repeated, "God is our refuge and strength, a very present help in trouble. Therefore will we not fear, though the earth be removed, and though the mountains be carried into the midst of the sea." On his deathbed, he whispered to his old Business Partner in Heaven: "I have fought the fight; I have kept the faith."

Against this backdrop the drama of the South was played out one day in my life:

A little white girl was found in the colored section of our town, living with a Negro family in a broken-down shack. This family had moved in only a few weeks before and little was known of them. One of the ladies in my mother's club, while driving over to her washerwoman's, saw the child swinging on a gate. The shack, as she said, was hardly more than a pigsty and this white child was living with ignorant and dirty and sick-looking colored folks. "They must have kidnapped her," she told her friends. Genuinely shocked, the clubwomen busied themselves in an attempt to do something, for the child was very white indeed. The

strange Negroes were subjected to a grueling questioning and finally
grew frightened and evasive and refused to talk at all. This only increased
the suspicion of the white group, and the next day the clubwomen,
escorted by the town marshal, took the child from her adopted family
despite their tears.

She was brought to our home. I do not know why my mother con-
sented to this plan. Perhaps because she loved children and always
showed tenderness and concern for them. It was easy for one more to fit
into our ample household and Janie was soon at home there. She roomed
with me, sat next to me at the table; I found Bible verses for her to say
at breakfast; she wore my clothes, played with my dolls and followed me
around from morning to night. She was dazed by her new comforts and
by the interesting activities of this big lively family; and I was as happily
dazed, for her adoration was a new thing to me; and as time passed a
quick, childish, and deeply felt bond grew up between us.

But a day came when a telephone message was received from a colored
orphanage. There was a meeting at our home, whispers, shocked exclamations. All afternoon the ladies went in and out of our house talking
to Mother in tones too low for children to hear. And as they passed us at
play, most of them looked quickly at Janie and quickly looked away
again, though a few stopped and stared at her as if they could not tear
their eyes from her face. When my father came home in the evening
Mother closed her door against our young ears and talked a long time
with him. I heard him laugh, heard Mother say, "But Papa, this is no
laughing matter!" And then they were back in the living room with us
and my mother was pale and my father was saying, "Well, work it out,
honey, as best you can. After all, now that you know, it is pretty simple."

In a little while my mother called my sister and me into her bedroom
and told us that in the morning Janie would return to Colored Town.
She said Janie was to have the dresses the ladies had given her and a few
of my own, and the toys we had shared with her. She asked me if I would
like to give Janie one of my dolls. She seemed hurried, though Janie was
not to leave until next day. She said, "Why not select it now?" And in
dreamlike stiffness I brought in my dolls and chose one for Janie. And
then I found it possible to say, "Why? Why is she leaving? She likes us,
she hardly knows them. She told me she had been with them only a
month."

"Because," Mother said gently, "Janie is a little colored girl."

"But she can't be. She's white!"

"We were mistaken. She is colored."

"But she looks——"

"She is colored. Please don't argue!"

"What does it mean?" I whispered.

"It means," Mother said slowly, "that she has to live in Colored Town
with colored people."

"But why? She lived here three weeks and she doesn't belong to them, she told me she didn't."

"She is a little colored girl."

"But you said yourself that she has nice manners. You said that," I persisted.

"Yes, she is a nice child. But a colored child cannot live in our home."

"Why?"

"You know, dear! You have always known that white and colored people do not live together."

"Can she come over to play?"

"No."

"I don't understand."

"I don't either," my young sister quavered.

"You're too young to understand. And don't ask me again, ever again, about this!" Mother's voice was sharp but her face was sad and there was no certainty left there. She hurried out and busied herself in the kitchen and I wandered through that room where I had been born, touching the old familiar things in it, looking at them, trying to find the answer to a question that moaned in my mind like a hurt thing. . . .

And then I went out to Janie, who was waiting, knowing things were happening that concerned her but waiting until they were spoken aloud.

I do not know quite how the words were said but I told her that she was to return in the morning to the little place where she had lived because she was colored and colored children could not live with white children.

"Are you white?" she said.

"I'm white," I replied, "and my sister is white. And you're colored. And white and colored can't live together because my mother says so."

"Why?" Janie whispered.

"Because they can't," I said. But I knew, though I said it firmly, that something was wrong. I knew my father and mother whom I passionately admired had done that which did not fit in with their teachings. I knew they had betrayed something which they held dear. And I was ashamed by their failure and frightened, for I felt that they were no longer as powerful as I had thought. There was something Out There that was stronger than they and I could not bear to believe it. I could not confess that my father, who had always solved the family dilemmas easily and with laughter, could not solve this. I knew that my mother who was so good to children did not believe in her heart that she was being good to this child. There was not a word in my mind that said it but my body knew and my glands, and I was filled with anxiety.

But I felt compelled to believe they were right. It was the only way my world could be held together. And, like a slow poison, it began to seep through me: *I was white. She was colored. We must not be together. It was bad to be together. Though you ate with your nurse when you were little, it was bad to eat with any colored person after that. It was bad just as other things were bad that your mother had told you. It was bad that she was to sleep in the room with me that night. It was bad. . . .*

I was suddenly full of guilt. For three weeks I had done things that white children are not supposed to do. And now I knew these things had been wrong.

I went to the piano and began to play, as I had always done when I was in trouble. I tried to play Paderewski's *Minuet* and as I stumbled through it, the little girl came over and sat on the bench with me. Feeling lonely, lost in these deep currents that were sweeping through our house that night, she crept closer and put her arms around me and I shrank away as if my body had been uncovered. I had not said a word, I did not say one, but she knew, and tears slowly rolled down her little white face. . . .

And then I forgot it. For more than thirty years the experience was wiped out of my memory. But that night, and the weeks it was tied to, worked its way like a splinter, bit by bit down to the hurt places in my memory and festered there. And as I grew older, as more experiences collected around that faithless time, as memories of earlier, more pro-found hurts crept closer and closer drawn to that night as if to a magnet, I began to know that people who talked of love and Christianity and democracy did not mean it. That is a hard thing for a child to learn. I still admired my parents, there was so much that was strong and vital and sane and good about them and I never forgot this; I stubbornly believed in their sincerity, as I do to this day, and I loved them. Yet in my heart they were under suspicion. Something was wrong.

Something was wrong with a world that tells you that love is good and people are important and then forces you to deny love and to humili-ate people. I knew, though I would not for years confess it aloud, that in trying to shut the Negro race away from us, we have shut ourselves away from so many good, creative, honest, deeply human things in life. I began to understand so slowly at first but more and more clearly as the years passed, that the warped, distorted frame we have put around every Negro child from birth is around every white child also. Each is on a different side of the frame but each is pinioned there. And I knew that what cruelly shapes and cripples the personality of one is as cruelly shaping and crippling the personality of the other. I began to see that though we may, as we acquire new knowledge, live through new experi-ences, examine old memories, gain the strength to tear the frame from us, yet we are stunted and warped and in our lifetime cannot grow straight again any more than can a tree, put in a steel-like twisting frame when young, grow tall and straight when the frame is torn away at maturity.

1. What is the purpose of the carefully drawn backdrop against which the "Janie" incident is played out? Does it simply provide "regional insights," or is it thematically related to the incident?
2. At what point did Lillian Smith know that she was inescapably "white"? How did she arrive at this realization? What did it mean to her as a child? What does it mean to her now?
3. What does this essay reveal about guilt and a child's experience of it? Does the author experience a different kind of guilt now?
4. How is Smith's conflict with her parents, and with Janie, expressed by their conversation? Are these "spoken words" unnecessary "facts" or are they essential to her analysis of the conflicts?
5. Pick out your three favorite analogies (for example, Smith's house is the "kind of home that gathers memories like dust"). How do they work to make the conflicts in the essay come alive for you? What do they reveal about Smith's attitudes toward this childhood incident?
6. How do analysis and anecdote weave together in this essay? How are the anecdotes which are primarily examples of abstract ideas related to paragraphs which are mainly analytical?

"Stamps, Arkansas"/*Maya Angelou*

Maya Angelou's book, *I Know Why the Caged Bird Sings,* traces her experiences as a black girl growing up in a small southern town. In the following excerpts, as in the whole book, we hear the author "singing" as well as feel her confinements; we learn of her loves and joys as well as her frustrations and fears. She transports us back into the innocence of childhood but never lets us forget that the adult author knows very well what that innocence has cost.

But more than simply describing several memorable incidents from her childhood, Angelou helps us to see them within the framework of her growing consciousness. She "places" these incidents by presenting them simultaneously from two points of view, innocence and experience, that of the child and the adult. By focusing on her uncle, on the sheriff, and on "whitefolks" from this double perspective, she is able to use humor as well as explicit psychological analysis in developing her theme. As you read the passages, notice specifically how Angelou uses this interplay between points of view, and between humor and gravity to evaluate her experience.

When Bailey was six and I a year younger, we used to rattle off the times tables with the speed I was later to see Chinese children in San Francisco employ on their abacuses. Our summer-gray pot-bellied stove bloomed rosy red during winter, and became a severe disciplinarian threat if we were so foolish as to indulge in making mistakes.

Uncle Willie used to sit, like a giant black Z (he had been crippled as a child), and hear us testify to the Lafayette County Training Schools' abilities. His face pulled down on the left side, as if a pulley had been attached to his lower teeth, and his left hand was only a mite bigger than Bailey's, but on the second mistake or on the third hesitation his big overgrown right hand would catch one of us behind the collar, and in the same moment would thrust the culprit toward the dull red heater, which throbbed like a devil's toothache. We were never burned, although once I might have been when I was so terrified I tried to jump onto the stove to remove the possibility of its remaining a threat. Like most children, I thought if I could face the worst danger voluntarily, and *triumph,* I would forever have power over it. But in my case of sacrificial effort I was thwarted. Uncle Willie held tight to my dress and I only got close enough to smell the clean dry scent of hot iron. We learned the times tables without understanding their grand principle, simply because we had the capacity and no alternative.

The tragedy of lameness seems so unfair to children that they are embarrassed in its presence. And they, most recently off nature's mold, sense that they have only narrowly missed being another of her jokes. In relief at the narrow escape, they vent their emotions in impatience and criticism of the unlucky cripple.

Momma related times without end, and without any show of emotion, how Uncle Willie had been dropped when he was three years old by a woman who was minding him. She seemed to hold no rancor against the baby-sitter, nor for her just God who allowed the accident. She felt it necessary to explain over and over again to those who knew the story by heart that he wasn't "born that way."

In our society, where two-legged, two-armed strong Black men were able at best to eke out only the necessities of life, Uncle Willie, with his starched shirts, shined shoes and shelves full of food, was the whipping boy and butt of jokes of the underemployed and underpaid. Fate not only disabled him but laid a double-tiered barrier in his path. He was also proud and sensitive. Therefore he couldn't pretend that he wasn't cripple, nor could he deceive himself that people were not repelled by his defect.

Only once in all the years of trying not to watch him, I saw him pretend to himself and others that he wasn't lame.

Coming home from school one day, I saw a dark car in our front yard. I rushed in to find a strange man and woman (Uncle Willie said later they were schoolteachers from Little Rock) drinking Dr. Pepper in the cool of the Store. I sensed a wrongness around me, like an alarm clock that had gone off without being set.

I knew it couldn't be the strangers. Not frequently, but often enough, travelers pulled off the main road to buy tobacco or soft drinks in the only Negro store in Stamps. When I looked at Uncle Willie, I knew what was pulling my minds' coattails. He was standing erect behind the counter, not leaning forward or resting on the small shelf that had been built for him. Erect. His eyes seemed to hold me with a mixture of threats and appeal.

I dutifully greeted the strangers and roamed my eyes around for his walking stick. It was nowhere to be seen. He said, "Uh . . . this this . . . this . . . uh, my niece. She's . . . uh . . . just come from school." Then to the couple—"You know . . . how, uh, children are . . . th–th–these days . . . they play all d–d–day at school and c–c–can't wait to get home and pl–play some more."

The people smiled, very friendly.

He added, "Go on out and pl–play, Sister."

The lady laughed in a soft Arkansas voice and said, "Well, you know, Mr. Johnson, they say, you're only a child once. Have you children of your own?"

Uncle Willie looked at me with an impatience I hadn't seen in his face even when he took thirty minutes to loop the laces over his high-topped shoes. "I . . . I thought I told you to go . . . go outside and play."

Before I left I saw him lean back on the shelves of Garret Snuff, Prince Albert and Spark Plug chewing tobacco.

"No, ma'am . . . no ch–children and no wife." He tried a laugh. "I have an old m–m–mother and my brother's t-two children to l-look after."

I didn't mind his using us to make himself look good. In fact, I would have pretended to be his daughter if he wanted me to. Not only did I not feel any loyalty to my own father, I figured that if I had been Uncle Willie's child I would have received much better treatment.

The couple left after a few minutes, and from the back of the house I watched the red car scare chickens, raise dust and disappear toward Magnolia.

Uncle Willie was making his way down the long shadowed aisle be-tween the shelves and the counter—hand over hand, like a man climbing out of a dream. I stayed quiet and watched him lurch from one side, bumping to the other, until he reached the coal-oil tank. He put his hand behind that dark recess and took his cane in the strong fist and shifted his weight on the wooden support. He thought he had pulled it off.

I'll never know why it was important to him that the couple (he said later that he'd never seen them before) would take a picture of a whole Mr. Johnson back to Little Rock.

He must have tired of being crippled, as prisoners tire of penitentiary bars and the guilty tire of blame. The hightopped shoes and the cane, his uncontrollable muscles and thick tongue, and the looks he suffered of either contempt or pity had simply worn him out, and for one afternoon, one part of an afternoon, he wanted no part of them.

I understood and felt closer to him at that moment than ever before or since. . . .

Throwing scoops of corn to the chickens and mixing sour dry mash with leftover food and oily dish water for the hogs were among our evening chores. Bailey and I sloshed down twilight trails to the pig pens, and standing on the first fence rungs we poured down the unappealing concoctions to our grateful hogs. They mashed their tender pink snouts down into the slop, and rooted and grunted their satisfaction. We always grunted a reply only half in jest. We were also grateful that we had concluded the dirtiest of chores and had only gotten the evil-smelling swill on our shoes, stockings, feet and hands.

Late one day, as we were attending to the pigs, I heard a horse in the front yard (it really should have been called a driveway, except that there was nothing to drive into it), and ran to find out who had come riding up on a Thursday evening when even Mr. Steward, the quiet, bitter man who owned a riding horse, would be resting by his warm fire until the morning called him out to turn over his field.

The used-to-be sheriff sat rakishly astraddle his horse. His nonchalance was meant to convey his authority and power over even dumb animals. How much more capable he would be with Negroes. It went without saying.

His twang jogged in the brittle air. From the side of the Store, Bailey and I heard him say to Momma, "Annie, tell Willie he better lay low tonight. A crazy nigger messed with a white lady today. Some of the boys'll be coming over here later." Even after the slow drag of years, I remember the sense of fear which filled my mouth with hot, dry air, and made my body light.

The "boys"? Those cement faces and eyes of hate that burned the clothes off you if they happened to see you lounging on the main street downtown on Saturday. Boys? It seemed that youth had never happened to them. Boys? No, rather men who were covered with graves' dust and age without beauty or learning. The ugliness and rottenness of old abominations.

If on Judgment Day I were summoned by St. Peter to give testimony to the used-to-be Sheriff's act of kindness, I would be unable to say anything in his behalf. His confidence that my uncle and every other Black man who heard of the Klan's coming ride would scurry under their houses to hide in chicken droppings was too humiliating to hear. Without waiting for Momma's thanks, he rode out of the yard, sure that things were as they should be and that he was a gentle squire, saving those deserving serfs from the laws of the land, which he condoned.

Immediately, while his horse's hoofs were still loudly thudding the ground, Momma blew out the coal-oil lamps. She had a quiet, hard talk with Uncle Willie and called Bailey and me into the Store.

We were told to take the potatoes and onions out of their bins and knock out the dividing walls that kept them apart. Then with a tedious and fearful slowness Uncle Willie gave me his rubber-tipped cane and bent down to get into the now-enlarged empty bin. It took forever before he lay down flat, and then we covered him with potatoes and onions, layer upon layer, like a casserole. Grandmother knelt praying in the darkened Store.

It was fortunate that the "boys" didn't ride into our yard that evening and insist that Momma open the Store. They would have surely found Uncle Willie and just as surely lynched him. He moaned the whole night through as if he had, in fact, been guilty of some heinous crime. The heavy sounds pushed their way up out of the blanket of vegetables and I pictured his mouth pulling down on the right side and his saliva flowing into the eyes of new potatoes and waiting there like dew drops for the warmth of morning. . . .

Throughout the year, until the next frost, we took our meals from the smokehouse, the little garden that lay cousin-close to the Store and from the shelves of canned foods. There were choices on the shelves that could set a hungry child's mouth to watering. Green beans, snapped always the right length, collards, cabbage, juicy red tomato preserves that came into their own on steaming buttered biscuits, and sausage, beets, berries and every fruit grown in Arkansas.

But at least twice yearly Momma would feel that as children we should have fresh meat included in our diets. We were then given money —pennies, nickles, and dimes entrusted to Bailey—and sent to town to buy liver. Since the whites had refrigerators, their butchers bought the meat from commercial slaughterhouses in Texarkana and sold it to the wealthy even in the peak of summer.

Crossing the Black area of Stamps which in childhood's narrow measure seemed a whole world, we were obliged by custom to stop and speak to every person we met, and Bailey felt constrained to spend a few minutes playing with each friend. There was a joy in going to town with money in our pockets (Bailey's pockets were as good as my own) and time on our hands. But the pleasure fled when we reached the white part of town. After we left Mr. Willie Williams' Do Drop Inn, the last stop before whitefolksville, we had to cross the pond and adventure the railroad tracks. We were explorers walking without weapons into man-eating animals' territory.

In Stamps the segregation was so complete that most Black children didn't really, absolutely know what whites looked like. Other than that they were different, to be dreaded, and in that dread was included the hostility of the powerless against the powerful, the poor against the rich, the worker against the worked for and the ragged against the well dressed.

I remember never believing that whites were really real.

Many women who worked in their kitchens traded at our Store, and when they carried their finished laundry back to town they often set the big baskets down on our front porch to pull a singular piece from the starched collection and show either how graceful was their ironing hand or how rich and opulent was the property of their employers.

I looked at the items that weren't on display. I knew, for instance, that white men wore shorts, as Uncle Willie did, and that they had an opening for taking out their "things" and peeing, and that white women's breasts weren't built into their dresses, as some people said, because I saw their brassieres in the baskets. But I couldn't force myself to think of them as people. People were Mrs. LaGrone, Mrs. Hendricks, Momma, Reverend Sneed, Lillie B, and Louise and Rex. Whitefolks couldn't be people because their feet were too small, their skin too white and see-throughy, and they didn't walk on the balls of their feet the way people did—they walked on their heels like horses.

People were those who lived on my side of town. I didn't like them all, or, in fact, any of them very much, but they were people. These others, the strange pale creatures that lived in their alien unlife, weren't considered folks. They were whitefolks.

1. In what passages is Maya Angelou seeing her life from the point of view of a child? In what passages does she write from the adult perspective? How does the contrast support her conclusions about her "roots" (geographical, social, familial)?

2. What is the child's view of white people? How is this view revealed by the "facts" (impressions, incidents) the author chooses to report? Does this view still hold for her?

3. How does Maya Angelou use humorous anecdotes and observations to develop her theme?

4. How does Angelou's choice of words and use of conversation and analogy make her incidents come alive for the reader? How does she use these

techniques to draw her conclusions about racial consciousness and to make them convincing?

5. What specific themes unify Angelou's childhood memories? How does she make the "threads" obvious, and how does she use these themes to structure the passages?

6. Both Maya Angelou and Lillian Smith are concerned with being "closed in" by race, but their experiences differ. In expressing these experiences, how do their respective ways of handling the relationship between anecdote and analysis also differ?

"Four Summers"/*Joyce Carol Oates*

In the two sections of the short story that follow, Joyce Carol Oates takes her main character back to the same picnic grove in two different summers of her life. This device is used to "bridge time." It also allows us to examine the changes Sissie undergoes in relation to herself and to her environment. Through the sharp juxtaposition of Sissie's past and present existence, Oates reveals these changes to us. We are also made aware of them by the way in which Oates forces us to focus on people and objects from Sissie's point of view. We hear and see only what Sissie hears and sees. And the continuities and discontinuities between what her two selves hear and see lead us to conclusions about the nature of her coming into maturity—into freedom and love as well as confinement and hate. As she discovers herself, Sissie, as narrator, finds language to express this discovery. Thus, you will find that section IV presents a more complete analysis than section I.

I

It is some kind of special day. "Where's Sissie?" Ma says. Her face gets sharp, she is frightened. When I run around her chair she laughs and hugs me. She is pretty when she laughs. Her hair is long and pretty.

We are sitting at the best table of all, out near the water. The sun is warm and the air smells nice. Daddy is coming back from the building with some glasses of beer, held in his arms. He makes a grunting noise when he sits down.

"Is the lake deep?" I ask them.

They don't hear me, they're talking. A woman and a man are sitting with us. The man marched in the parade we saw just awhile ago; he is a volunteer fireman and is wearing a uniform. Now his shirt is pulled open because it is hot. I can see the dark curly hair way up by his throat; it looks hot and prickly.

A man in a soldier's uniform comes over to us. They are all friends, but I can't remember him. We used to live around here, Ma told me, and then we moved away. The men are laughing. The man in the uniform leans back against the railing, laughing, and I am afraid it will break and he will fall into the water.

"Can we go out in a boat, Dad?" says Jerry.

He and Frank keep running back and forth. I don't want to go with them. I want to stay by Ma. She smells nice. Frank's face is dirty with sweat. "Dad," he says, whining, "can't we go out in a boat? Them kids are going out."

A big lake is behind the building and the open part where we are sitting. Some people are rowing on it. This tavern is noisy and everyone is laughing; it is too noisy for Dad to think about what Frank said.

"Harry," says Ma, "the kids want a boat ride. Why don't you leave off drinking and take them?"

"What?" says Dad.

He looks up from laughing with the men. His face is damp with sweat and he is happy. "Yeah, sure, in a few minutes. Go over there and play and I'll take you out in a few minutes."

The boys run out back by the rowboats, and I run after them. I have a bag of potato chips.

An old man with a white hat pushed down over his forehead is sitting by the boats, smoking. "You kids be careful," he says.

Frank is leaning over and looking at one of the boats. "This here is the best one," he says.

"Why's this one got water in it?" says Jerry.

"You kids watch out. Where's your father?" the man says.

"He's gonna take us for a ride," says Frank.

"Where is he?"

The boys run along, looking at the boats that are tied up. They don't bother with me. The boats are all painted dark green, but the paint is peeling off some of them in little pieces. There is water inside some of them. We watch two people come in, a man and a woman. The woman is giggling. She has on a pink dress and she leans over to trail one finger in the water. "What's all this filthy stuff by the shore?" she says. There is some scum in the water. It is colored a light brown, and there are little seeds and twigs and leaves in it.

The man helps the woman out of the boat. They laugh together. Around their rowboat little waves are still moving; they make a churning noise that I like.

"Where's Dad?" Frank says.

"He ain't coming," says Jerry.

They are tossing pebbles out in to the water. Frank throws his sideways, twisting his body. He is ten and very big. "I bet he ain't coming," Jerry says, wiping his nose with the back of his hand.

After awhile we go back to the table. Behind the table is the white railing, and then the water, and then the bank curves out so that the weeping willow trees droop over the water. More men in uniforms, from the parade, are walking by.

"Dad," says Frank, "can't we go out? Can't we? There's a real nice boat there—"

"For Christ's sake, get them off me," Dad says. He is angry with Ma. "Why don't you take them out?"

"Honey, I can't row."

"Should we take out a boat, us two?" the other woman says. She has very short, wet-looking hair. It is curled in tiny little curls close to her head and is very bright. "We'll show them, Lenore. Come on, let's give your kids a ride. Show these guys how strong we are."

"That's all you need, to sink a boat," her husband says.

They all laugh.

The table is filled with brown beer bottles and wrappers of things. I can feel how happy they all are together, drawn together by the round table. I lean against Ma's warm leg and she pats me without looking down. She lunges forward and I can tell even before she says something that she is going to be loud.

"You guys're just jealous! Afraid we'll meet some soldiers!" she says.

"Can't we go out, Dad? Please?" Frank says. "We won't fight. . . ."

"Go and play over there. What're those kids doing—over there?" Dad says, frowning. His face is damp and loose, the way it is sometimes when he drinks. "In a little while, okay? Ask your mother."

"She can't do it," Frank says.

"They're just jealous," Ma says to the other woman, giggling. "They're afraid we might meet somebody somewhere."

"Just who's gonna meet this one here?" the other man says, nodding with his head at his wife.

Frank and Jerry walk away. I stay by Ma. My eyes burn and I want to sleep, but they won't be leaving for a long time. It is still daylight. When we go home from places like this it is always dark and getting chilly and the grass by our house is wet.

"Duane Dorsey's in jail," Dad says. "You guys heard about that?"

"Duane? Yeah, really?"

"It was in the newspaper. His mother-in-law or somebody called the police, he was breaking windows in her house."

"That Duane was always a nut!"

"Is he out now, or what?"

"I don't know, I don't see him these days. We had a fight," Dad says.

The woman with the short hair looks at me. "She's a real cute little thing," she says, stretching her mouth. "She drink beer, Lenore?"

"I don't know."

"Want some of mine?"

She leans toward me and holds the glass by my mouth. I can smell the beer and the warm stale smell of perfume. There are pink lipstick smudges on the glass.

"Hey, what the hell are you doing?" her husband says.

When he talks rough like that I remember him: we were with him once before.

"Are you swearing at me?" the woman says.

"Leave off the kid, you want to make her a drunk like yourself?"

"It don't hurt, one little sip. . . ."

"It's okay," Ma says. She puts her arm around my shoulders and pulls me closer to the table.

"Let's play cards. Who wants to?" Dad says.

"Sissie wants a little sip, don't you?" the woman says. She is smiling at me and I can see that her teeth are darkish, not nice like Ma's.

"Sure, go ahead," says Ma.

"I said leave off that, Sue, for Christ's sake," the man says. He jerks the table. He is a big man with a thick neck; he is bigger than Dad. His eyebrows are blond, lighter than his hair, and are thick and tufted. Dad is staring at something out on the lake without seeing it. "Harry, look, my goddam wife is trying to make your kid drink beer."

"Who's getting hurt?" Ma says angrily.

Pa looks at me all at once and smiles. "Do you want it, baby?"

I have to say yes. The woman grins and holds the glass down to me, and it clicks against my teeth. They laugh. I stop swallowing right away because it is ugly, and some of the beer drips down on me. "Honey, you're so clumsy," Ma says, wiping me with a napkin.

"She's a real cute girl," the woman says, sitting back in her chair. "I wish I had a nice little girl like that."

"Lay off of that," says her husband.

"Hey, did you bring any cards?" Dad says to the soldier.

"They got some inside."

"Look, I'm sick of cards." Ma says.

"Yeah, why don't we all go for a boat ride?" says the woman. "Be real nice, something new. Every time we get together we play cards. How's about a boat ride?"

"It better be a big boat, with you in it," her husband says. He is pleased when everyone laughs, even the woman. The soldier lights a cigarette and laughs. "How come your cousin here's so skinny and you're so fat?"

"She isn't fat," says Ma. "What the hell do you want? Look at yourself."

"Yes, the best days of my life are behind me," the man says. He wipes his face and then presses a beer bottle against it. "Harry, you're lucky you moved out. It's all going downhill, back in the neighborhood."

"You should talk, you let our house look like hell," the woman says. Her face is blotched now, some parts pale and some red. "Harry don't sit out in his back yard all weekend drinking. He gets something done."

"Harry's younger than me."

Ma reaches over and touches Dad's arm. "Harry, why don't you take the kids out? Before it gets dark."

Dad lifts his glass and finishes his beer. "Who else wants more?" he says.

"I'll get them, you went last time," the soldier says.

"Get a chair for yourself," says Dad. "We can play poker."

"I don't want to play poker, I want to play rummy," the woman says.

"At church this morning Father Reilly was real mad," says Ma. "He said some kids or somebody was out in the cemetery and left some beer bottles. Isn't that awful?"

"Duane Dorsey used to do worse than that," the man says, winking.

"Hey, who's that over there?"

"You mean that fat guy?"

"Isn't that the guy at the lumberyard that owes all that money?"

Dad turns around. His chair wobbles and he almost falls; he is angry.

"This goddamn place is too crowded," he says.

"This is a real nice place," the woman says. She is taking something out of her purse. "I always liked it, didn't you, Lenore?"

"Sue and me used to come here a lot," says Ma. "And not just with you two, either."

"Yeah, we're real jealous," the man says.

"You should be," says the woman.

The soldier comes back. Now I can see that he is really a boy. He runs to the table with the beer before he drops anything. He laughs.

"Jimmy, your ma wouldn't like to see you drinking!" the woman says happily.

"Well, she ain't here."

"Are they still living out in the country?" Ma says to the woman.

"Sure. No electricity, no running water, no bathroom—same old thing. What can you do with people like that?"

"She always talks about going back to the Old Country," the soldier says. "Thinks she can save up money and go back."

"Poor old bastards don't know there was a war," Dad says. He looks as if something tasted bad in his mouth. "My old man died thinking he could go back in a year or two. Stupid old bastards!"

"Your father was real nice. . . ." Ma says.

"Yeah, real nice," says Dad. "Better off dead."

Everybody is quiet.

"June Dieter's mother's got the same thing," the woman says in a low voice to Ma. "She's had it a year now and don't weigh a hundred pounds —you remember how big she used to be."

"She was big, all right," Ma says.

"Remember how she ran after June and slapped her? We were there— some guys were driving us home."

"Yeah. So she's got it too."

"Hey," says Dad, "why don't you get a chair, Jimmy? Sit down here."

The soldier looks around. His face is raw in spots, broken out. But his eyes are nice. He never looks at me.

"Get a chair from that table," Dad says.

"Those people might want it."

"Hell, just take it. Nobody's sitting on it."

"They might—"

Dad reaches around and yanks the chair over. The people look at him but don't say anything. Dad is breathing hard. "Here, sit here," he says. The soldier sits down.

Frank and Jerry come back. They stand by Dad, watching him. "Can we go out now?" Frank says.

"What?"

"Out for a boat ride."

"What? No, next week. Do it next week. We're going to play cards."

"You said—"

"Shut up, we'll do it next week." Dad looks up and shades his eyes. "The lake don't look right anyway."

"Lot's of people are out there—"

"I said shut up."

"Honey," Ma whispers, "let him alone. Go and play by yourselves."

"Can we sit in the car?"

"Okay, but don't honk the horn."

"Ma, can't we go for a ride?"

"Go and play by yourselves, stop bothering us," she says. "Hey, will you take Sissie?"

They look at me. They don't like me, I can see it, but they take me with them. We run through the crowd and somebody spills a drink—he yells at us. "Oops, got to watch it!" Frank giggles.

We run along the walk by the boat. A woman in a yellow dress is carrying a baby. She looks at us like she doesn't like us.

Down at the far end some kids are standing together.

"Hey, lookit that," Frank says.

A blackbird is caught in the scum, by one of the boats. It can't fly up.

One of the kids, a long-legged girl in a dirty dress, is poking at it with a stick.

The bird's wings keep fluttering but it can't get out. If it could get free it would fly and be safe, but the scum holds it down.

One of the kids throws a stone at it. "Stupid old goddamn bird," somebody says. Frank throws a stone. They are all throwing stones. The bird doesn't know enough to turn away. Its feathers are all wet and dirty. One of the stones hits the bird's head.

"Take that!" Frank says, throwing a rock. The water splashes up and some of the girls scream.

I watch them throwing stones. I am standing at the side. If the bird dies, then everything can die, I think. Inside the tavern there is music from the jukebox. . . .

IV

Jesse says, "Let's stop at this place. I been here a few times before."

It's the Lakeside Bar. That big old building with the grubby siding, and a big pink neon sign in front, and the cinder driveway that's so bumpy. Yes, everything the same. But different too—smaller, dirtier. There is a custard stand nearby with a glaring orange roof, and people are crowded around it. That's new. I haven't been here for years.

"I feel like a beer," he says.

He smiles at me and caresses my arm. He treats me as if I were something that might break; in my cheap linen maternity dress I feel ugly and heavy. My flesh is so soft and thick that nothing could hurt it.

"Sure, honey. Pa used to stop in here too."

We cross through the parking lot to the tavern. Wild grass grows along the sidewalk and in the cracks of the sidewalk. Why is this place so ugly to me? I feel as if a hand were pressing against my chest, shutting off my breath. Is there some secret here? Why am I afraid?

I catch sight of myself in a dusty window as we pass. My hair is long, down to my shoulders. I am pretty, but my secret is that I am pretty like everyone is. My husband loves me for this but doesn't know it. I have a pink mouth and plucked darkened eyebrows and soft bangs over my forehead; I know everything, I have no need to learn from anyone else now. I am one of those girls younger girls study closely, to learn from. On buses, in five-and-tens, thirteen-year-old girls must look at me solemnly, learning, memorizing.

"Pretty Sissie!" my mother likes to say when we visit, though I told her how I hate that name. She is proud of me for being pretty, but thinks I'm too thin. "You'll fill out nice, after the baby," she says. Herself, she is fat and veins have begun to darken on her legs; she scuffs around the house in bedroom slippers. Who is my mother? When I think of her I can't think of anything—do I love her or hate her, or is there nothing there?

Jesse forgets and walks ahead of me, I have to walk fast to catch up. I'm wearing pastel-blue high heels—that must be because I am proud of my legs. I have little else. Then he remembers and turns to put out his hand for me, smiling to show he is sorry. Jesse is the kind of man thirteen-year-old girls stare at secretly; he is not a man, not old enough, but not a boy either. He is a year older than I am, twenty. When I met him he was wearing a navy uniform and he was with a girl friend of mine.

Just a few people sitting outside at the tables. They're afraid of rain—the sky doesn't look good. And how bumpy the ground is here, bare spots and little holes and patches of crab grass, and everywhere napkins and junk. Too many flies outside. Has this place changed hands? The screens at the windows don't fit right; you can see why flies get inside. Jesse opens the door for me and I go in. All bars smell alike. There is a damp, dark odor of beer and something indefinable—spilled soft drinks, pretzels getting stale? This bar is just like any other. Before we were married we went to places like this, Jesse and me and other couples. We had to spend a certain amount of time doing things like that—and going to movies, playing miniature golf, bowling, dancing, swimming—then we got married, now we're going to have a baby. I think of the baby all the time, because my life will be changed then; everything will be different. Four months from now. I should be frightened, but a calm laziness has come over me. It was so easy for my mother. . . . But it will be different with me because my life will be changed by it, and nothing ever changed my mother. You couldn't change her! Why should I think? Why should I be afraid? My body is filled with love for this baby, and I will never be the same again.

We sit down at a table near the bar. Jesse is in a good mood. My father would have liked him, I think; when he laughs Jesse reminds me of him. Why is a certain kind of simple, healthy, honest man always destined to lose everything? Their souls are as clean and smooth as the muscular line of their arms. At night I hold Jesse, thinking of my father and what happened to him—all that drinking, then the accident at the factory—and I pray that Jesse will be different. I hope that his quick, open, loud way of talking is just a disguise, that really he is someone else —slower and calculating. That kind of man grows old without jerks and spasms. Why did I marry Jesse?

Someone at the bar turns around, and it's a man I think I know—I have known. Yes. That man outside, the man I met outside. I stare at him, my heart pounding, and he doesn't see me. He is dark, his hair is neatly combed but is thinner than before; he is wearing a cheap gray suit. But is it the same man? He is standing with a friend and looking around, as if he doesn't like what he sees. He is tired too. He has grown years older.

Our eyes meet. He glances away. He doesn't remember—that frightened girl he held in his arms.

I am tempted to put my hand on Jesse's arm and tell him about that man, but how can I? Jesse is talking about trading in our car for a new one. . . . I can't move, my mind seems to be coming to a stop. Is that the man I kissed, or someone else? A feeling of angry loss comes over me. Why should I lose everything? Everything? Is it the same man, and would he remember? My heart bothers me, it's stupid to be like this: here I sit, powdered and sweet, a girl safely married, pregnant and secured to the earth, with my husband beside me. He still loves me. Our love keeps on. Like my parents' love, it will subside someday, but nothing surprises me because I have learned everything.

The man turns away, talking to his friend. They are weary, tired of something. He isn't married yet, I think, and that pleases me. Good. But why are these men always tired? Is it the jobs they hold, the kind of men who stop in at this tavern? Why do they flash their teeth when they smile, but stop smiling so quickly? Why do their children cringe from them sometimes—an innocent upraised arm a frightening thing? Why do they grow old so quickly, sitting at kitchen tables with bottles of beer? They are everywhere, in every house. All the houses in this neighborhood and all neighborhoods around here. Jesse is young, but the outline of what he will be is already in his face; do you think I can't see it? Their lives are like hands dealt out to them in their innumerable card games. You pick up the sticky cards, and there it is: there it is. Can't change anything, all you can do is switch some cards around, stick one in here, one over here . . . pretend there is some sense, a secret scheme.

The man at the bar tosses some coins down and turns to go. I want to cry out to him, "Wait, wait!" But I cannot. I sit helplessly and watch him leave. Is it the same man? If he leaves I will be caught here, what can I do? I can almost hear my mother's shrill laughter coming in from outside, and some drawling remark of my father's—lifting for a moment above the music. Those little explosions of laughter, the slap of someone's hand on the damp table in anger, the clink of bottles accidentally touching—and there, there, my drunken aunt's voice, what is she saying? I am terrified at being left with them. I watch the man at the door and think that I could have loved him. I know it.

He has left, he and his friend. He is nothing to me, but suddenly I feel tears in my eyes. What's wrong with me? I hate everything that springs upon me and seems to draw itself down and oppress me in a way I could never explain to anyone. . . . I am crying because I am pregnant, but not with that man's child. It could have been his child, I could have gone with him to his car; but I did nothing, I ran away, I was afraid, and now I'm sitting here with Jesse, who is picking the label off his beer bottle with his thick squarish fingernails. I did nothing. I was afraid. Now he has left me here and what can I do?

I let my hand fall onto my stomach to remind myself that I am in love: with this baby, with Jesse, with everything. I am in love with our house and our life and the future and even this moment—right now— that I am struggling to live through.

1. What images and/or objects appear repeatedly in Sissie's two visions? Does the repetition express similarities between these two views or does it create a sense of radical difference between them? If you see a difference, define Sissie's change in perspective.
2. How do the physical descriptions of Sissie's parents change from the first to the last section? What parts of the descriptions indicate physical changes in her parents? What parts signal changes in her attitude toward her parents?
3. Why does Oates structure her story by formal division into sections? How are I and IV related?
4. By the end of the story we see Sissie become self-conscious about her identity. How does Oates use point of view and focus to express this self-consciousness? What is the value of Sissie's knowledge of herself? Is she trapped or freed by what she has discovered in the process of maturing?
5. At no point in this story does Joyce Carol Oates formally analyze Sissie's development. How, then, does analysis take place in the story?
6. How does the relationship between abstract and concrete language shift from the first to the last section of the story?

"Names"/*Mary McCarthy*

As a young girl, Mary McCarthy attended a convent school. As she describes it, the choice to send her there was all wrong, but not for the obvious reasons. The nuns were kind, the education decent, and the students normal adolescent girls. The "wrongness" came from inside herself. In the following excerpt from *Memories of a Catholic Girlhood* Mary McCarthy examines this wrongness within the context of several convent incidents. She weaves the incidents together in an anecdotal fashion. But McCarthy's strategy for revealing the nature of her failure to "fit in," and the puzzle that that failure has presented to her ever since, is to begin and end her essay with a consideration of names as symbols of behavior.

She announces at the outset that her own name can mean either "bitter" or "star of the sea," but in reading the piece we realize with the writer that "bitter" is the most appropriate meaning. This framework becomes a means by which McCarthy probes the paradox of her relationship to the convent: she liked it but did not fit in because of an inner sense of wrongness. And all of the anecdotes she uses to reveal these divided feelings focus on a conflict between her and the "system." Thus, the clash between Mary's assigned name and her sense of its wrongness affords her a way both of revealing the hypocrisy of the convent school and of expressing her inner conflict.

Names have more significance for Catholics than they do for other people; Christian names are chosen for the spiritual qualities of the saints they are taken from; Protestants used to name their children out of the Old Testament and now they name them out of novels and plays, whose heroes and heroines are perhaps the new patron saints of a secular age. But with Catholics it is different. The saint a child is named for is supposed to serve, literally, as a model or pattern to imitate; your name is your fortune and it tells you what you are or must be. Catholic children ponder their names for a mystic meaning, like birthstones; my own, I learned, besides belonging to the Virgin and Saint Mary of Egypt, originally meant "bitter" or "star of the sea." My second name, Therese, could dedicate me either to Saint Theresa or to the saint called the Little Flower, Soeur Thérèse of Lisieux, on whom God was supposed to have descended in the form of a shower of roses. At Confirmation, I had added a third name (for Catholics then rename themselves, as most nuns do, yet another time, when they take orders); on the advice of a nun, I had taken "Clementina," after Saint Clement, an early pope—a step I soon regretted on account of "My Darling Clementine" and her number nine shoes. By the time I was in the convent, I would no longer tell anyone what my Confirmation name was. The name I had nearly picked was "Agnes," after a little Roman virgin martyr, always shown with a lamb, because of her purity. But Agnes would have been just as bad, I recognized in Forest Ridge Convent—not only because of the possibility of "Aggie," but because it was subtly, indefinably *wrong*, in itself. Agnes would have made me look like an ass.

The fear of appearing ridiculous first entered my life, as a governing motive, during my second year in the convent. Up to then, a desire for prominence had decided many of my actions and, in fact, still persisted. But in the eighth grade, I became aware of mockery and perceived that I could not seek prominence without attracting laughter. Other people could, but I couldn't. This laughter was proceeding, not from my classmates, but from the girls of the class just above me, in particular from two boon companions, Elinor Heffernan and Mary Harty, a clownish pair—oddly assorted in size and shape, as teams of clowns generally are, one short, plump, and baby-faced, the other tall, lean, and owlish—who entertained the high-school department by calling attention to the oddities of the younger girls. Nearly every school has such a pair of satirists, whose marks are generally low and who are tolerated just because of their laziness and non-conformity; one of them (in this case, Mary Harty, the plump one) usually appears to be half asleep. Because of their low standing, their indifference to appearances, the sad state of their uniforms, their clowning is taken to be harmless, which, on the whole, it is, their object being not to wound but to divert; such girls are bored in school. We in the eighth grade sat directly in front of the two wits in study hall, so that they had us under close observation; yet at first I was not afraid of them, wanting, if anything, to identify myself with their laughter, to be initiated into the joke. One of their specialties was giving people nicknames, and it was considered an honor to be the first in the eighth grade to be let in by Elinor and Mary on their latest invention. This often happened to me; they would tell me, on the playground, and I would tell the others. As their intermediary, I felt myself almost their friend and it did not occur to me that I might be next on their list.

I had achieved prominence not long before by publicly losing my faith and regaining it at the end of a retreat. I believe Elinor and Mary questioned me about this on the playground, during recess, and listened with serious, respectful faces while I told them about my conversations with the Jesuits. Those serious faces ought to have been an omen, but if the two girls used what I had revealed to make fun of me, it must have been behind my back. I never heard any more of it, and yet just at this time I began to feel something, like a cold breath on the nape of my neck, that made me wonder whether the new position I had won for myself in the convent was as secure as I imagined. I would turn around in study hall and find the two girls looking at me with speculation in their eyes.

It was just at this time, too, that I found myself in a perfectly absurd situation, a very private one, which made me live, from month to month, in horror of discovery. I had waked up one morning, in my convent room, to find a few small spots of blood on my sheet; I had somehow scratched a trifling cut on one of my legs and opened it during the night. I wondered what to do about this, for the nuns were fussy about bed-making, as they were about our white collars and cuffs, and if we had an inspection those spots might count against me. It was best, I decided, to ask the nun on dormitory duty, tall, stout Mother Slattery, for a clean bottom sheet, even though she might scold me for having scratched my leg in my sleep and order me to cut my toenails. You never know what you might be blamed for. But Mother Slattery, when she bustled in to look at the sheet, did not scold me at all; indeed, she hardly seemed to be listening as I explained to her about the cut. She told me to sit down: she would be back in a minute. "You can be excused from athletics today," she added, closing the door. As I waited, I considered this remark, which seemed to me strangely munificent, in view of the unimportance of the cut. In a moment, she returned, but without the sheet. Instead, she produced out of her big pocket a sort of cloth girdle and a peculiar flannel object which I first took to be a bandage, and I began to protest that I did not need or want a bandage; all I needed was a bottom sheet. "The sheet can wait," said Mother Slattery, succinctly, handing me two large safety pins. It was the pins that abruptly enlightened me; I saw Mother Slattery's mistake, even as she was instructing me as to how this flannel article, which I now understood to be a sanitary napkin, was to be put on.

"Oh, no, Mother," I said, feeling somewhat embarrassed. "You don't understand. It's just a little cut, on my leg." But Mother, again, was not listening; she appeared to have grown deaf, as the nuns had a habit of doing when what you were saying did not fit in with their ideas. And now that I knew what was in her mind, I was conscious of a funny con- straint; I did not feel it proper to name a natural process, in so many words, to a nun. It was like trying not to think of their going to the bath- room or trying not to see the straggling iron-grey hair coming out of their coifs (the common notion that they shaved their heads was false). On the whole, it seemed better just to show her my cut. But when I offered to do so and unfastened my black stocking, she only glanced at my leg, cursorily. "That's only a scratch, dear," she said. "Now hurry up and put this on or you'll be late for chapel. Have you any pain?" "No, no, Mother!" I cried. "You don't understand!" "Yes, yes, I understand," she replied soothingly, "and you will too, a little later. Mother Superior will tell you about it some time during the morning. There's nothing to be afraid of. You have become a woman."

"I know all about that," I persisted. "Mother, please listen. I just cut my leg. On the athletic field. Yesterday afternoon." But the more excited I grew, the more soothing, and yet firm, Mother Slattery became. There seemed to be nothing for it but to give up and do as I was bid. I was in the grip of a higher authority, which almost had the power to persuade me that it was right and I was wrong. But of course I was not wrong; that would have been too good to be true. While Mother Slattery waited, just outside my door, I miserably donned the equipment she had given me, for there was no place to hide it, on account of drawer inspection. She led me down the hall to where there was a chute and explained how I was to dispose of the flannel thing, by dropping it down the chute into the laundry. (The convent arrangements were very old-fashioned, dating back, no doubt, to the days of Louis Philippe.)

The Mother Superior, Madame MacIllvra, was a sensible woman, and all through my early morning classes, I was on pins and needles, chafing for the promised interview with her which I trusted would clear things up. *"Ma Mère,"* I would begin, "Mother Slattery thinks . . ." Then I would tell her about the cut and the athletic field. But precisely the same impasse confronted me when I was summoned to her office at recess-time. I talked about my cut, and she talked about becoming a woman. It was rather like a round, in which she was singing "Scotland's burning, Scotland's burning," and I was singing "Pour on water, pour on water." Neither of us could hear the other, or, rather, I could hear her, but she could not hear me. Owing to our different positions in the convent, she was free to interrupt me, whereas I was expected to remain silent until she had finished speaking. When I kept breaking in, she hushed me, gently, and took me on her lap. Exactly like Mother Slattery, she attributed all my references to the cut to a blind fear of this new, un-expected reality that had supposedly entered my life. Many young girls, she reassured me, were frightened if they had not been prepared. "And you, Mary, have lost your dear mother, who could have made this easier for you." Rocked on Madame MacIllvra's lap, I felt paralysis overtake me and I lay, mutely listening, against her bosom, my face being tickled by her white, starched, fluted wimple, while she explained to me how babies were born, all of which I had heard before.

There was no use fighting the convent. I had to pretend to have be-come a woman, just as, not long before, I had had to pretend to get my faith back—for the sake of peace. This pretense was decidedly awkward. For fear of being found out by the lay sisters downstairs in the laundry (no doubt an imaginary contingency, but the convent was so very thorough), I reopened the cut on my leg, so as to draw a little blood to stain the napkins, which were issued me regularly, not only on this occasion, but every twenty-eight days thereafter. Eventually, I abandoned this bloodletting, for fear of lockjaw, and trusted to fate. Yet I was in awful dread of detection; my only hope, as I saw it, was either to be re-leased from the convent or to become a woman in reality, which might take a year, at least, since I was only twelve. Getting out of athletics once a month was not sufficient compensation for the farce I was going through. It was not my fault; they had forced me into it; nevertheless, it was I who would look silly—worse than silly; half mad—if the truth ever came to light.

I was burdened with this guilt and shame when the nickname finally found me out. "Found me out," in a general sense, for no one ever did learn the particular secret I bore about with me, pinned to the linen band. "We've got a name for you," Elinor and Mary called out to me, one day on the playground. "What is it?" I asked, half hoping, half fearing, since not all their sobriquets were unfavorable. "Cye," they answered, looking at each other and laughing. " 'Si'?" I repeated, supposing that it was based on Simple Simon. Did they regard me as a hick? "C.Y.E.," they elucidated, spelling it out in chorus. "The letters stand for something. Can you guess?" I could not and I cannot now. The closest I could come to it in the convent was "Clean Your Ears." Perhaps that was it, though in later life I have wondered whether it did not stand, simply, for "Clever Young Egg" or "Champion Young Eccentric." But in the convent I was certain that it stood for something horrible, something even worse than dirty ears (as far as I knew, my ears were clean), something I could never guess because it represented some aspect of myself that the world could see and I couldn't, like a sign pinned on my back. Everyone in the convent must have known what the letters stood for, but no one would tell me. Elinor and Mary had made them promise. It was like halitosis; not even my best friend, my deskmate, Louise, would tell me, no matter how much I pleaded. Yet everyone assured me that it was "very good," that is, very apt. And it made everyone laugh.

This name reduced all my pretensions and solidified my sense of *wrongness*. Just as I felt I was beginning to belong to the convent, it turned me into an outsider, since I was the only pupil who was not in the know. I liked the convent, but it did not like me, as people say of certain foods that disagree with them. By this, I do not mean that I was actively unpopular, either with the pupils or with the nuns. The Mother Superior cried when I left and predicted that I would be a novelist, which surprised me. And I had finally made friends; even Emilie von Phul smiled upon me softly out of her bright blue eyes from the far end of the study hall. It was just that I did not fit into the convent pattern; the simplest thing I did, like asking for a clean sheet, entrapped me in consequences that I never could have predicted. I was not bad; I did not consciously break the rules; and yet I could never, not even for a week, get a pink ribbon, and this was something I could not understand, because I was trying as hard as I could. It was the same case as with the hated name; the nuns, evidently, saw something about me that was invisible to me.

The oddest part was all that pretending. There I was, a walking mass of lies, pretending to be a Catholic and going to confession while really I had lost my faith, and pretending to have monthly periods by cutting myself with nail scissors; yet all this had come about without my volition and even contrary to it. But the basest pretense I was driven to was the acceptance of the nickname. Yet what else could I do? In the convent, I could not live it down. To all those girls, I had become "Cye McCarthy." That was who I was. That was how I had to identify myself when telephoning my friends during vacations to ask them to the movies: "Hello, this is Cye." I loathed myself when I said it, and yet I succumbed to the name totally, making myself over into a sort of hearty to go with it—the kind of girl I hated. "Cye" was my new patron saint. This false personality stuck to me, like the name, when I entered public high school, the next fall, as a freshman, having finally persuaded my grandparents to take me out of the convent, although they could never get to the bottom of my reasons, since, as I admitted, the nuns were kind, and I had made many nice new friends. What I wanted was a fresh start, a chance to begin life over again, but the first thing I heard in the corridors of the public high school was that name called out to me, like the warmest of welcomes: "Hi, there, Si!" That was the way they thought it was spelled. But this time I was resolute. After the first weeks, I dropped the hearties who called me "Si" and I never heard it again. I got my own name back and sloughed off Clementina and even Therese—the names that did not seem to me any more to be mine but to have been imposed on me by others. And I preferred to think that Mary meant "bitter" rather than "star of the sea."

1. "There was no use fighting the convent" just about sums up Mary McCarthy's comments in this essay. But why did she feel this overwhelming sense of futility? What kind of authority did the place and its guardians extend? Was it an authority of love, guilt, or power?

2. What is the connection between the "nickname" incident and Mary McCarthy's misunderstanding with the nuns about her "womanhood"? Do any words, analogies, or observations carry over from one account to the other? Are the conclusions the same?

3. How does McCarthy's point of view aid in expressing her strong sense of her "wrongness"? How do the facts that Elinor and Mary sought her out as a confidant and that the Mother Superior cried when she left also reinforce her feeling of not fitting in?

4. Are the conclusions that McCarthy draws in *writing* about these "facts" of her life similar to those she drew at the point when she decided to leave the convent school? What does this suggest to you about the relationship of writing to analysis?

5. Mary McCarthy "surrounds" her convent incidents with a discussion of names and their symbolic significance. How does this unify the selection and emphasize the significance of the anecdotes? In her opening discussion of names, how does McCarthy prepare us for her thematic concerns?

6. Why does McCarthy's nickname solidify her "sense of wrongness," and why is acceptance of it her "basest pretense"? How do the anecdotes serve to define this "wrongness"? What is revealed about McCarthy's situation by the fact that the abstraction "Cye" has such a concrete impact?

"From the Subway to the Synagogue"/*Alfred Kazin*

In the following essay Alfred Kazin recalls his school days with excruciating accuracy. This accuracy stems from the kind of all-encompassing pain that makes the sufferer acutely aware of the slightest change in his position. The agony of Kazin's adolescent fears has etched into his memory the most minute details of the "machinery" that inspired these terrors. We know from the first paragraph that the educational system that paralyzed him at fourteen still has the power to make him shudder at middle-age. And the essay is written as part exorcism, part explanation of the atrocities that such bureaucracies, and their accompanying expectations, can inflict.

To clarify and release his pain, Kazin plunges us into an overwhelming amount of detail, immersing us until we gasp for air and feel the oppression that was his within those "five city blocks" of his childhood experience. The massed minute particulars are there in order that we may clearly examine Kazin's pain, but they also provide a pattern that points us to the reasons for this pain. His detailed description of the school, its activity, his teacher, and his handicap always have a larger significance. The teacher is like a god but the school superintendent is "God Himself." Kazin drops his sandwich down a grate in the street, but this brings a vision of the "Human Factory," as well as a profound resolve never to succumb to despair. As you read Kazin's memories and his evaluation of them, observe how he moves from remembered particulars to their larger significance and back again.

All my early life lies open to my eye within five city blocks. When I passed the school, I went sick with all my old fear of it. With its standard New York public-school brown brick courtyard shut in on three sides of the square and the pretentious battlements overlooking that cockpit in which I can still smell the fiery sheen of the rubber ball, it looks like a factory over which has been imposed the façade of a castle. It gave me the shivers to stand up in that courtyard again; I felt as if I had been mustered back into the service of those Friday morning "tests" that were the terror of my childhood.

It was never learning I associated with that school: only the necessity to succeed, to get ahead of the others in the daily struggle to "make a good impression" on our teachers, who grimly, wearily, and often with ill-concealed distaste watched against our relapsing into the natural savagery they expected of Brownsville boys. The white, cool, thinly ruled record book sat over us from their desks all day long, and had remorselessly entered into it each day—in blue ink if we had passed, in red ink if we had not—our attendance, our conduct, our "effort," our merits and demerits; and to the last possible decimal point in calculation, our standing in an unending series of "tests"—surprise tests, daily tests, weekly tests, formal midterm tests, final tests. They never stopped trying to dig out of us whatever small morsel of fact we had managed to get down the night before. We had to prove that we were really alert, ready for anything, always in the race. That white thinly ruled record book figured in my mind as the judgment seat; the very thinness and remote blue lightness of its lines instantly showed its cold authority over me; so much space had been left on each page, columns and columns in which to note down everything about us, implacably and forever. As it lay there on a teacher's desk, I stared at it all day long with such fear and anxious propriety that I had no trouble believing that God, too, did nothing but keep such record books, and that on the final day He would face me with an account in Hebrew letters whose phonetic dots and dashes looked strangely like decimal points counting up my every sinful thought on earth.

All teachers were to be respected like gods, and God Himself was the greatest of all school superintendents. Long after I had ceased to believe that our teachers could see with the back of their heads, it was still understood, by me, that they knew everything. They were the delegates of all visible and invisible power on earth—of the mothers who waited on the stoops every day after three for us to bring home tales of our daily triumphs; of the glacially remote Anglo-Saxon principal, whose very name was King; of the incalculably important Superintendent of Schools who would someday rubberstamp his name to the bottom of our diplomas in grim acknowledgment that we had, at last, given satisfaction to him, to the Board of Superintendents, and to our benefactor the City of New York—and so up and up, to the government of the United States and to the great Lord Jehovah Himself. My belief in teachers' unlimited wisdom and power rested not so much on what I saw in them—how impatient most of them looked, how wary—but on our abysmal humility, at least in those of us who were "good" boys, who proved by our ready compliance and "manners" that we wanted to get on. The road to a professional future would be shown us only as we pleased *them. Make a good impression the first day of the term, and they'll help you out. Make a bad impression, and you might as well cut your throat.* This was the first article of school folklore, whispered around the classroom the opening day of each term. You made the "good impression" by sitting firmly at your wooden desk, hands clasped; by silence for the greatest part of the live-long day; by standing up obsequiously when it was so expected of you; by sitting down noiselessly when you had answered a question; by "speaking nicely," which meant reproducing their painfully exact enunciation; by "showing manners," or an ecstatic submissiveness in all things; by outrageous flattery; by bringing little gifts at Christmas, on their birthdays, and at the end of the term—the well-known significance of these gifts being that they came not from us, but from our parents, whose eagerness in this matter showed a high level of social consideration, and thus raised our standing in turn.

It was not just our quickness and memory that were always being tested. Above all, in that word I could never hear without automatically seeing it raised before me in gold-plated letters, it was our *character*. I always felt anxious when I heard the word pronounced. Satisfactory as my "character" was, on the whole, except when I stayed too long in the playground reading; outrageously satisfactory, as I can see now, the very sound of the word as our teachers coldly gave it out from the end of their teeth, with a solemn weight on each dark syllable, immediately struck my heart cold with fear—they could not believe I really had it. Character was never something you had; it had to be trained in you, like a technique. I was never very clear about it. On our side *character* meant demonstrative obedience; but teachers already had it—how else could they have become teachers? They had it; the aloof Anglo-Saxon principal whom we remotely saw only on ceremonial occasions in the assembly was positively encased in it; it glittered off his bald head in spokes of triumphant light; the President of the United States had the greatest conceivable amount of it. Character belonged to great adults. Yet we were constantly being driven onto it; it was the great threshold we had to cross. *Alfred Kazin, having shown proficiency in his course of studies and having displayed satisfactory marks of character* . . . Thus someday the hallowed diploma, passport to my further advancement in high school. But there —I could already feel it in my bones—they would put me through even more doubting tests of character; and after that, if I should be good enough and bright enough, there would be still more. *Character* was a bitter thing, racked with my endless striving to please. The school—from every last stone in the courtyard to the battlements frowning down at me from the walls—was only the stage for a trial. I felt that the very atmosphere of learning that surrounded us was fake—that every lesson, every book, every approving smile was only a pretext for the constant probing and watching of me, that there was not a secret in me that would not be decimally measured into that white record book. All week long I lived for the blessed sound of the dismissal gong at three o'clock on Friday afternoon.

I was awed by this system, I believed in it, I respected its force. The alternative was "going bad." The school was notoriously the toughest in our neighborhood, and the dangers of "going bad" were constantly impressed upon me at home and in school in dark whispers of the "reform school" and in examples of boys who had been picked up for petty thievery, rape, or flinging a heavy inkwell straight into a teacher's face. Behind any failure in school yawned the great abyss of a criminal career. Every refractory attitude doomed you with the sound "Sing Sing." Anything less than absolute perfection in school always suggested to my mind that I might fall out of the daily race, be kept back in the working class forever, or—dared I think of it?—fall into the criminal class itself.

I worked on a hairline between triumph and catastrophe. Why the odds should always have felt so narrow I understood only when I realized how little my parents thought of their own lives. It was not for myself alone that I was expected to shine, but for them—to redeem the constant anxiety of their existence. I was the first American child, their offering to the strange new God; I was to be the monument of their liberation from the shame of being—what they were. And that there was shame in this was a fact that everyone seemed to believe as a matter of course. It was in the gleeful discounting of themselves—what do we know?—with which our parents greeted every fresh victory in our savage competition for "high averages," for prizes, for a few condescending words of official praise from the principal at assembly. It was in the sickening invocation of "Americanism"—the word itself accusing us of everything we apparently were not. Our families and teachers seemed tacitly agreed that we were somehow to be a little ashamed of what we were. Yet it was always hard to say why this should be so. It was certainly not—in Brownsville!—because we were Jews, or simply because we spoke another language at home, or were absent on our holy days. It was rather that a "refined," "correct," "nice" English was required of us at school that we did not naturally speak, and that our teachers could never be quite sure we would keep. This English was peculiarly the ladder of advancement. Every future young lawyer was known by it. Even the Communists and Socialists on Pitkin Avenue spoke it. It was bright and clean and polished. We were expected to show it off like a new pair of shoes. When the teacher sharply called a question out, then your name, you were expected to leap up, face the class, and eject those new words fluently off the tongue.

There was my secret ordeal: I could never say anything except in the most roundabout way; I was a stammerer. Although I knew all those new words from my private reading—I read walking in the street, to and from the Children's Library on Stone Avenue; on the fire escape and the roof; at every meal when they would let me; read even when I dressed in the morning, propping my book up against the drawers of the bureau as I pulled on my long black stockings—I could never seem to get the easiest words out with the right dispatch, and would often miserably signal

from my desk that I did not know the answer rather than get up to
stumble and fall and crash on every word. If, angry at always being put
down as lazy or stupid, I did get up to speak, the black wooden floor
would roll away under my feet, the teacher would frown at me in amazement, and in unbearable loneliness I would hear behind me the groans
and laughter: *tuh-tuh-tuh-tuh.*

The word was my agony. The word that for others was so effortless
and neutral, so unburdened, so simple, so exact, I had first to meditate in
advance, to see if I could make it, like a plumber fitting together odd
lengths and shapes of pipe. I was always preparing words I could speak,
storing them away, choosing between them. And often, when the word
did come from my mouth in its great and terrible birth, quailing and
bleeding as if forced through a thornbush, I would not be able to look the
others in the face, and would walk out in the silence, the infinitely echoing silence behind my back, to say it all cleanly back to myself as I
walked in the streets. Only when I was alone in the open air, pacing the
roof with pebbles in my mouth, as I had read Demosthenes had done to
cure himself of stammering; or in the street, where all words seemed to
flow from the length of my stride and the color of the houses as I remembered the perfect tranquility of a phrase in *Beethoven's Romance
in F* I could sing back to myself as I walked—only then was it possible
for me to speak without the infinite premeditations and strangled silences
I toiled through whenever I got up at school to respond with the expected, the exact answer.

It troubled me that I could speak in the fullness of my own voice only
when I was alone on the streets, walking about. There was something
unnatural about it; unbearably isolated. I was not like the others! I was
not like the others! At midday, every freshly shocking Monday noon, they
sent me away to a speech clinic in a school in East New York, where I
sat in a circle of lispers and cleft palates and foreign accents holding a
mirror before my lips and rolling difficult sounds over and over. To be
sent there in the full light of the opening week, when everyone else was
at school or going about his business, made me feel as if I had been ex-
pelled from the great normal body of humanity. I would gobble down my
lunch on my way to the speech clinic and rush back to the school in time
to make up for the classes I had lost. One day, one unforgettable dread
day, I stopped to catch my breath on a corner of Sutter Avenue, near the
wholesale fruit markets, where an old drugstore rose up over a great
flight of steps. In the window were dusty urns of colored water floating
off iron chains; cardboard placards advertising hairnets, Ex-Lax; a great
illustrated medical chart headed THE HUMAN FACTORY, which showed
the exact course a mouthful of food follows as it falls from chamber to
chamber of the body. I hadn't meant to stop there at all, only to catch

my breath; but I so hated the speech clinic that I thought I would delay my arrival for a few minutes by eating my lunch on the steps. When I took the sandwich out of my bag, two bitterly hard pieces of hard salami slipped out of my hand and fell through a grate onto a hill of dust below the steps. I remember how sickeningly vivid an odd thread of hair looked on the salami, as if my lunch were turning stiff with death. The factory whistles called their short, sharp blasts stark through the middle of noon, beating at me where I sat outside the city's magnetic circle. I had never known, I knew instantly I would never in my heart again submit to, such wild passive despair as I felt at that moment, sitting on the steps before THE HUMAN FACTORY, where little robots gathered and shoveled the food from chamber to chamber of the body. They had put me out into the streets, I thought to myself; with their mirrors and their everlasting pulling at me to imitate their effortless bright speech and their stupefaction that a boy could stammer and stumble on every other English word he carried in his head, they had put me out into the streets, had left me high and dry on the steps of that drugstore staring at the remains of my lunch turning black and grimy in the dust.

1. In Kazin's memory, doing what was correct, what was necessary to become a well-educated American, is often presented through images of coldness, sterility and sternness. What images contradict these and suggest that Kazin's own warm, passionate nature was being repressed by such attitudes? Where does this conflict lead him?

2. What details in Kazin's account help to establish the impression that he sees his youth as somehow sordid, untidy, even disgusting? Is he recording his childhood disgust or are these images the result of his looking back?

3. Why is Kazin's inability to speak English properly of such central importance to this selection?

4. How does the idea of being tested link Kazin's presentation of his childhood views of education, citizenship and religion?

5. Both Alfred Kazin and Mary McCarthy clarify their inner sense of "wrongness." But McCarthy begins and ends with a consideration of abstractions—names; Kazin opens and closes his essay with a focus on concrete particulars. What is the relation of these different strategies to the respective differences in the authors' self-revelations?

6. How is the opening description, its focus and the details Kazin selects, related to his theme? What is the relationship between the abstract "Human Factory" and the concrete details of the scene below the grate at the close?

SUGGESTIONS FOR WRITING

1. Have you ever had a hero or heroine? What was your relationship to this person? Why did you choose him or her as a model or object of imitation and admiration? What does this reveal about the kind of person you were at the time, or perhaps still are?

2. Try to recapture your first awareness of yourself as a sexual person, or your first realization of the inevitability of death. What physical details are associated with this memory? What was the meaning of this awareness to you at the time? How has it made you what you are today?

3. Visit a place associated with your childhood. Remember how you used to see it. How has it changed? What has really changed, you or the spot? You may want to write two separate descriptions of this place, taking first the voice of a child, and second, your present voice. Or you may want to write entirely in your present voice but reflect on your childhood views. In either case, the reader should get a real sense of "then" and "now."

4. Explore your earliest feelings of being a particular *kind* of person within the context of your cultural, national, or religious background (that is, a political or religious conversion experience; the sense of being "Jewish" or "Catholic"; the sense of being black or white). Consider carefully whether this exploration requires one symbolic event, several similar events, or a wide-ranging collection of incidents. And remember that your purpose is self-definition not simple description.

5. When have you felt ostracized or arbitrarily disliked (laughed at by your family, ignored at dances, defeated in an election, barred from joining an organization)? Define the relationship between you and the group from which you felt excluded. Does this exclusion still rankle with you? (Focus on the nature and significance of your feelings, not just on the events that motivated them.)

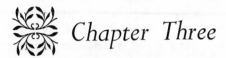 Chapter Three

Writing About Other People

INTRODUCTION

I. HOW DO YOU LOOK AT ANOTHER PERSON ANALYTICALLY?

So far we have asked you to analyze yourself—to discover how your personality is "put together," to practice revealing yourself through the selection and presentation of events from your past. Now we want you to turn your attention to other people. The movement is an obvious one. You have probably already discovered that many of your most private emotions and attitudes—from delight to disgust—depend upon other people whose lives have become entangled with your own.

But how do writers begin to sort out the tangle, to separate themselves from the persons they want to reveal? What methods of observation can help them distinguish themselves from the persons they choose to describe?

Sometimes a complete separation is impossible, even undesirable. Let's say you want to write about how you chose to go to college X to escape the gangly, pimply-faced boy next door who had been plaguing you for a date since seventh grade, and who later became the star center of the basketball team at Y college, where you really wanted to go in the first place. You can't get yourself out of your character sketch, can you? The very heart of your project involves the remarkable change in your perception of this transformed ugly duckling. There are times when your description of a person must include you; when, in fact, it will reveal almost as much about you as it does about your subject. For example, the selection by Joan Baez describes her father. She wants her readers to see the man, but her own life is so bound up in the life of her subject that the anecdotes she uses to present her character all have a double significance. We always see the subject sketched in relation to the author. Her point of view, then, is one of intimate connection to, and concern for, her subject. And she focuses on the effects that her subject's life has had on her own thinking and experience.

In direct contrast to the *autobiographical* way of looking at a person there is the *case study* where the author maintains a clinical detachment from the subject. The idea is to describe and analyze the behavior of the subject without becoming personally involved in that behavior. When authors are observing their subjects for this kind of essay, they are likely to note factual details rather than personal anecdotes. And as much as possible, they are likely to leave out of their accounts how they feel about the behavior of the characters they are describing. Of course, such objectivity is never entirely possible.

In his case study, "Joey: The Mechanical Boy," Bruno Bettelheim produces an objective description of this child who classified himself as a machine. Bettelheim gives an analyis of the conditions of Joey's upbringing that drove him to this self-classification. For us to see clearly what Joey was, and how he got to be what he was, the author has had to suppress his own horror at what he observed of the boy's mechanical behavior, and his outrage that Joey's parents could be so blind to the effects of their rejection of the child. Nevertheless, the reader cannot help but feel the writer's dismay at Joey's inhuman condition and his relief when human emotions begin to become part of Joey's world. While these feelings are never stated overtly, they are clearly suggested by the *kind* of details Bettelheim has chosen in order to recreate Joey's condition and treatment.

In the case study, the author's intention is to describe and analyze the subject's behavior as it is observed, without deliberately coloring the portrayal with personal feelings or judgments. The author's point of view is one of professional detachment, and the focus is on the subject. In the "autobiographical" character study, as we have seen, such detachment is neither necessary nor desirable. But there is a similarity in both of these strategies. In each the author chooses a method of observation that will lay bare some essential insight about a character who is probably unfamiliar to the reader.

But if the subject is a public figure, another method of observation may be called for. To be sure, a close relative or associate of Senator X or President Y could write an intimate sketch of him, and to his psychoanalyst he may appear as simply another case study. But, in addition, interested writers may choose to observe this kind of person by noting the *contrast* between the public official and the private man or woman. Writers may choose to show what personal strengths and weaknesses contribute to their subjects' public status. Or they may analyze the effect public life has had on the private lives of their characters. In either case, the author is focusing on the contrast between the public mask and the private face and increasing the reader's understanding of how these two spheres correspond.

In spite of their obvious differences, all of the approaches to characterization that we have suggested have one thing in common. They attempt to present to the audience some essential characteristics and understandings of a single individual. But there is an additional approach. A writer may elect to explore and present the distinctive traits of a whole *class* of people—"hippies," "radicals," "feminists," for example. In the selection, "A Politician," H. L. Mencken uses this approach to suggest that the chief characteristic of all politicians, as well as clergymen, policemen, and even journalists, is their attempt to hoodwink the public for their own personal gain. His point of view is that of a cynical citizen, and his focus is on the hypocrisy of "public servants."

Before we go on, let's review the possibilities we have been discussing. A character study can be: 1. an *intimate portrait* of someone with whom the writer is closely connected; 2. a *case study* of an intriguing individual that the writer has observed in a detached fashion; 3. a *comparative study* of the public and private faces of a key personality; and 4. a *group portrait* of persons who share a particular function (garbagemen, politicians), an ideal (poetry lovers, feminists), or a life style (hippies, aristocrats).

These approaches to character study are not meant to be exhaustive. Add your own, or combine approaches, but make sure your strategy is the product of a clearly defined point of view, a distinct focus, and, as previous examples illustrate, an *intention* toward the readers. Do you want to introduce them to a new character, educate them in the complexities of human nature, deepen their awareness of a popular personality, or persuade them that a certain group of people is dangerous or admirable? Know what you want your readers to think and feel when they finish reading your essay. Let this *intention* help to determine your *point of view,* your *focus,* and your *theme* or controlling idea which is, in turn, a function of all of these things.

2. HOW DO YOU PREPARE TO WRITE ABOUT A PERSON?

Getting started is the most difficult part of any writing assignment. We'd like to suggest some activities and exercises that can help you collect and edit data for an essay that analyzes a person who interests you.

You have all composed a character sketch at some time or other, even if just in passing. ("You remember him, Ruth, the tall bony one with frizzy red hair, size fourteen feet, and the weirdest sense of humor imaginable.") Very often character sketches are put together for the primary purpose of identifying the subject, of making the person immediately recognizable. But we'd like to have you go beyond merely "pointing out" your subject to explore some of the less obvious, more subtly revealing aspects of the subject: nervous gestures, tone of voice, sleeping habits, walking speed, favorite breakfast, and so on. This, of course, requires close observation.

TWO WRITING EXERCISES

1. As a way of practicing this kind of observation, you may want to try the following exercise. With your class sitting in a circle so that all members are within your range of vision, pick someone to describe. You are not allowed to use that person's name, hair color, or present clothing. Concentrate on details such as body language, *usual* style of dress, gregariousness, sense of humor, type of features, and write a short profile of your choice. Then read your profile to the class. If you have done a good job, the class should not only know who you are describing when you are finished, but they should see something new about this person.

2. Changing point of view can also help you to look for the unobvious. Another activity your class might try is to construct a situation that involves two or three persons (a confrontation at home between Mother, Father, and twenty-year-old daughter; a confrontation at work between boss, svelt secretary, and naive errand boy). When the situation is clearly defined, try to adopt the perspective of each participant in turn and describe the actions and motives of the other two. You should wind up with three *different* accounts. Read them aloud and see what kind of details appear in each description. You will probably find that each "role" brought new "facts" to light.

Once you have sharpened your "people-watching" eye, you should begin to consider a subject for your essay. One fertile "hunting ground" is your family and circle of close friends. Pick someone very close to you whom you *almost* know inside out but whom you could still rediscover in the process of writing. In short, if you are going to write about someone close to you, make sure there is something you still want to learn about the person. A motiveless essay is the very dullest kind.

A WRITING EXERCISE

If a number of students in the class choose to describe someone close to them, you may want to try the following exercise. Imagine that at the very moment your class is meeting, your mother or father is walking into your room. Adopt his or her voice and take ten minutes to describe what you, as mother or father, see and say. Read your efforts to the class. Although what is being described is technically the room with its people and activity, you will, in fact, have brought some close observations of your parent to bear in taking his or her point of view. Try this same kind of exercise with other subjects; to describe someone intimately, it helps to walk around in that person's skin for a while.

Another place to search for a subject is the public arena. Look for individual characters or character types that intrigue you in subways and restaurants. Take a notebook along and see how much you can say about a person you've never met simply through observing the person's nods, smiles, wrinkles, and shirt color. Keep a collection of portraits from which you can eventually choose a subject to develop. Someone you know you can return to—a waitress, florist, traffic cop—is a safe bet.

You may not be interested in either extreme—the complete stranger or the intimate friend—but rather, you may be intrigued by someone you know superficially or "know of": the college dean, a campus celebrity, the student government president. Consider interviewing that person with questions carefully suited to his or her interests and to what you want to know about that person. Then, using his or her answers, as well as personal observations you have made during the course of the interview, compose a unified character analysis.

AN ACTIVITY

You might want to try doing this as a class. Pick a well known figure on campus and, in class, write a set of leading questions to use in an interview. Have several students conduct the interview and either tape or transcribe the encounter for the whole group. Then, as a class, edit the material, deciding on a central idea or theme and choosing what information will and will not contribute to it.

One other source you can go to for subjects and data on these subjects is the media. Pick a public personality and collect articles on your subject, trying to vary the sources and nature of the articles. See if the various roles (for example, Rockefeller as millionaire, politician, husband, and father) complement or contradict one another. Or you might want to select a group of persons (a social, economic, or political group) and scan the media for accounts of their activities and values. See if the general characteristics of this group hold up under an examination (your own or that of the media) of its individual members.

Whether you are observing, interviewing, or scanning the media for data, you should be aware of the danger of *stereotyping*. Rather than helping you to discover others, stereotyping prevents discovery. Stereotyping is the act of automatically making your observations of other people conform to a preconceived idea about the group to which they belong. Your idea, then, is a fixed and rigid point of view which dictates an almost reflex response to individuals. As a result, you automatically assume that each individual of a group, solely because they are members of that group, has certain traits. (For example, "Welfare recipients are lazy," "Most women are emotional and naturally intuitive," or "Long-haired students are radicals.") This kind of assumption is dangerous because it prevents you from really seeing other people. As an analysis of experience it is always false because it ignores the minute particulars, individual people with their variety of unique traits.

Stereotyping, however, shouldn't be confused with generalizing. For generalizations begin with minute particulars, while stereotypes begin with preconceived, fixed notions. A good generalization always comes after observation and experience, but a stereotype invariably precedes observation. And, of course, generalizing about character "types" is necessary. It allows us to talk about people we don't know personally and to classify our impressions of people. But when the classifications become sweeping and rigid ("Of course he's irresponsible, he's a student," or "She must be absent-minded, she's a professor."), they become stereotypes and destroy the whole process of analysis. They stop being a means toward the understanding of personality and become mere prejudices. In your own writing, make sure the conclusions you draw are justified by the minute particulars you observe. Make sure they depend on a continuing relationship of concrete details and abstract ideas.

In summary, this section presents ways of getting to know your subjects, of becoming aware of what and who they are. As we have seen before, careful observation or examination of the subject matter is the very backbone of analysis. As you observe your subjects, you discover how you relate to them (point of view), what areas of their life are most characteristic and interesting (focus), what you would like your readers to think or feel about them (intention), and the general impression or idea that you want to present (theme). Once these things are clear in your mind, you are ready to begin organizing your essay; in fact, you have begun.

3. HOW DO YOU ORGANIZE A CHARACTER SKETCH?

There are several ways of putting a character analysis together. Very often the methods overlap or appear simultaneously in a single portrait, but in every readable analysis, you will find some principle of organization at work.

A series of revealing anecdotes is one way of presenting a character. This is particularly effective if you are writing about a person you've known for a while or whose career you've been watching for some time. Joan Baez uses this method in describing her father, as does Bruno Bettelheim in analyzing "Joey." In one case, the anecdotes are personal; in the other, they are factual. But the principle works the same way in both essays. Each anecdote reveals a new insight that adds to a collective impression of what the subject is like.

The chronological arrangement of events and insights is a pattern related to the one we have been discussing. This pattern is useful if your character has undergone a significant change in personality or situation that you wish to focus on. It helps you explain the causes and effects of the alteration. Both Baez and Bettelheim order their anecdotes chronologically, which illustrates the compatability of these two methods. But the chronology does not have to be anecdotal; it can present emotional or intellectual history as well as the history of relevant events.

Another pattern for character analysis involves an initial clear statement of the author's central idea, followed by a systematic arrangement of observations proving its verity. In "A Politician," H. L. Mencken begins by discussing the duplicity that accompanies public life. He shows that neither clergymen nor policemen deserve our respect and then goes on to assert that the same holds true for politicians. Having established his major idea, Mencken devotes the rest of his essay to presenting and evaluating the false assumptions politicians would have us believe.

One other method of developing subjects is to describe them within their given world, concentrating not only on who they are but on how they color and reflect the world they inhabit. For example, if you have chosen to describe a waitress in the local coffee shop, you will probably want to place her in her context, to describe the piled cups, stained formica, and stale doughnuts as part of the "reality" she represents. Donn Pearce does this with the "truck drivin' men," using their attitudes to trucks, coffee-house waitresses, and lack of sleep as a means of revealing their gruffness and isolation. In this case, his central idea or theme depends on the *correspondence* between truck drivers and their world.

What we have discussed so far in this chapter is: 1. approaches to character analysis; 2. ways of collecting information about a character; and 3. methods of organizing the material you collect about your subject. When you begin to write your essay, be aware of the many combinations of techniques that are open to you.

For example, suppose you decide to write about your best friend, Beth Ann, whose occasional desire for absolute solitude puzzles you. You may choose: to write an intimate portrait in which the reader feels the strong flow of affections that binds you to her, or to "back off" and do an objective "case study." Let's say you choose the "case study." You can then decide: 1. to present a series of incidents in which Beth Ann has illustrated her desire to retreat from the world, perhaps arranging them chronologically to reveal the constancy of this trait, or 2. to describe Beth Ann within her solitary world, moving over the furniture and memorabilia in her room, then focusing on Beth Ann lying in the middle of the bed and staring at the ceiling, and ending with an assessment of what she gains from these retreats.

What you choose to do will depend on what point of view seems most comfortable to you, what material you think is most valuable to focus on, what impression you want to leave with your readers, and what, in the final analysis, you really want to say about Beth Ann. You have a large number of options available to you. Don't limit yourself arbitrarily, but let your attitudes toward your subject and toward your audience determine the best strategy for you.

READINGS

"My Father"/*Joan Baez*

This description of her father is from Joan Baez's autobiography *Daybreak*.
Despite its place in the larger picture of *her* life, the sketch also gives us insights
into the man the author chooses to present. There is little question, for example,
that her father is a deeply committed idealist, and that his personal ethics have
influenced his daughter. What is perhaps more intriguing, however, are the
cloudy antitheses of love and hate, approval and disapproval, which seem to
shadow their relationship. Baez says her father can rarely compliment her, or
agree that she is right, yet she gives several cases when he does both. She says
she has never been able to show an interest in his commitment to academia, yet
she clearly admires his success as an author and teacher.

It's only in the context of this special relationship that her father is revealed.
We don't see him as a teacher in the classroom, or as the subject of a detached
description, but rather in relation to the author. Baez's choice of the series of
anecdotes by which she reveals her father is guided by this concern with their
relationship. And as we read the sketch we notice how this relationship also
determines her choice of details.

My father is short, honest, dark, and very handsome. He's good, he's a
good man. He was born in Mexico, and brought up in Brooklyn. His
father was a Mexican who left the Catholic church to become a Methodist
minister. My father worked hard in school. He loved God and the church
and his parents. At one time in his life he was going to be a minister, but
the hypocrisy of the church bothered him and he became a scientist instead. He has a vision of how science can play the major role in saving
the world. This vision puts a light into his eyes. He is a compulsive
worker, and I know that he will never stop his work long enough to have
a look at some of the things in his life which are blind and tragic. But it's
not my business to print. About me and my father I don't know. I keep
thinking of how hard it was for him to say anything nice about me to my
face. Maybe he favored me and felt guilty about it, but he couldn't say
anything nice. A lot of times I thought he would break my heart. Once
he complimented me for something I was wearing. "You ought to wear
that kind of thing more often," he said, and I looked into the mirror and
I was wearing a black dress which I hated. I was fourteen then and I
remember thinking, "Hah. I remind him of his mother in this thing."

My father is the saint of the family. You work at something until you exhaust yourself, so that you can be good at it, and with it you try to improve the lot of the sad ones, the hungry ones, the sick ones. You raise your children trying to teach them decency and respect for human life. Once when I was about thirteen he asked me if I would accept a large sum of money for the death of a man who was going to die anyway. I didn't quite understand. If I was off the hook, and just standing by, and then the man was killed by someone else, why shouldn't I take a couple of million? I told him sure, I'd take the money, and he laughed his head off. "That's immoral," he said. I didn't know what immoral meant, but I knew something was definitely wrong taking money for a man's life.

Once in my life I spent a month alone with my father. In 1950, when he was assigned to a project in Baghdad, Iraq, for UNESCO, my sisters got jaundice, and couldn't leave the States. My father left on schedule, for a month of briefing in Paris before going to Baghdad. I had jaundice too, but I didn't tell anyone. I wanted very badly to go to Paris. So despite bad pains in my stomach and black urine which I flushed in a hurry so he wouldn't see, and a general yellow hue which was creeping over my skin, and sometimes seemed to be tinting everything I looked at, I took full advantage of that time with my old man in Gay Paree. We bicycled everywhere, and bought long fresh bread and cheese and milk. We sat in outdoor cafés and had tea, and while he was busy at UNESCO house, I would run the elevators and visit secretaries and draw pictures of everyone and go off to feed pigeons in the park. Neither of us spoke French, but we faked it. One night in a restaurant, we couldn't understand anything on the dessert menu, so my father took a gamble and said, *"Ça, s'il vous plaît,"* pointing to the word *"Confiture,"* and they brought him a dish of strawberry jam, which he ate.

Once the family was together in Baghdad, I developed a terrible fear that my father was going to die. The fact is he almost killed himself tampering with the stupid brick oven which had to be lit in order to get hot bath water. He was "experimenting" with it—trying to determine how fast he could get the fire going by increasing the flow of kerosene into the oven. It exploded in his face, setting his clothes on fire and giving him third degree burns on his hands and face. He covered his eyes instinctively, or he would probably have been blinded, but his eyelashes and eyebrows were burned off anyway. Pauline passed out after telling Mother that "Popsy is on fire," and Mother wrapped him up in a sheet and called the English hospital for an ambulance. While we waited for the ambulance, my father tapped his feet in rhythm on the kitchen tiles, and cleared his throat every four or five seconds. He smelled terrible, and except for Mother, we just stood there. I was probably praying. Mother took me to the hospital to see him once, and I felt bad because I got dizzy when I saw his hands. They had big pussy blisters on them, and his face looked like a Rice Krispie, and I wanted to make him feel better, but I also wanted to go stick my head out the window and get some fresh air. When he came home from the hospital he was bandaged so that all you could see were his eyes and his ears. He held classes for his students at home. He is a brilliant teacher, and they loved him. I know they loved him, because the room smelled so awful from burnt flesh and Middle East medication that I felt sick every time I passed his door. And they came every day to learn and to see him.

My father teaches physics. He is a Ph.D. in physics, and we all wish he'd had just one boy who wasn't so opposed to school, to degrees, to formal education of any kind. One child to show some interest when he does physics experiments at the dinner table. But then it must be partly because we felt obligated to be student-types that we have all rebelled so completely. I can barely read. That is to say, I would rather do a thousand things before sitting down to read.

He used to tell us we should read the dictionary. He said it was fun and very educational. I've never gotten into it.

When we lived in Clarence Center, New York (it was a town of eight hundred people, and as far as they knew, we were niggers; Mother says that someone yelled out the window to me, "Hey, nigger!" and I said, "You ought to see me in the summertime!"), my father had a job working in Buffalo. It was some kind of armaments work. I just knew that it was secret, or part of it was secret, and that we began to get new things like a vacuum cleaner, a refrigerator, a fancy coffee pot, and one day my father came home with a little Crosley car. We were so excited about it that we drove it all over the front lawn, around the trees and through the piles of leaves. He was driving, Mother was in the front seat, and we three kids were in the back. The neighbors knew we were odd to begin with, but this confirmed it. Mother was embarrassed and she kept clutching my father's arm and saying, "Oh, Abe!" but he would take a quick corner around a tree and we'd all scream with laughter and Mother gave up and had hysterics.

Then something started my father going to Quaker meetings. We all had to go. It meant we had to sit and squelch giggles for about twenty minutes, and then go off with some kind old lady who planted each of us a bean in a tin can, and told us it was a miracle that it would push its little head up above the damp earth and grow into a plant. We knew it was a miracle, and we knew she was kind, but we made terrible fun of her the entire time and felt guilty about it afterwards.

While we were in the side room with the kind old lady, watching our beans perform miracles, my father was in the grown-up room, the room where they observe silence for a whole hour, and he was having a fight with his conscience. It took him less than a year of those confrontations with himself in that once a week silence to realize that he would have to give up either the silences or his job. Next thing I knew we were packing up and moving across the country. My father had taken a job as a professor of physics at the University of Redlands for about one-half the pay, and one-tenth the prestige—against the advice of everyone he knew except my mother. Since leaving Buffalo in 1947, he's never accepted a job that had anything to do with armaments, offense, defense, or whatever they prefer to call it. Last night I had a dream about him. I dreamed he was sitting next to himself in a theater. One of him was as he is now, and the other was the man of thirty years ago. I kept trying to get him to look at himself and say hello. Both faces smiled very understandingly, but neither would turn to greet the other.

I don't think he's ever understood me very well. He's never understood my compulsiveness, my brashness, my neuroses, my fears, my anti-nationalism (though he's changing on that), my sex habits, my loose way of handling money. I think often I startle him, and many times I please him. Sometimes I have put him through hell, like when I decided to live with Michael when I was twenty. "You mean you're going to . . . *live* with him?" "Yes," I said, and my father took a sleeping bag and went to the beach for two days, because Michael was staying in the house. Years later he sent me an article by Bertrand Russell, whom he respects very much, underlining the part which said that if young people could have a chance at "experimental marriages" while they were in college, they might know more about what it's all about before they actually got married. My father wrote that it always amazed him how I came to conclusions intuitively which took him years to realize.

1. What part does direct statement play in Baez's establishment of her father's integrity? How do anecdotes contribute to these same goals? What is the relation of statement to anecdote?

2. What kind of language does the author use to handle her disagreements with her father? Is she sympathetic, angry, amused? Why do you think she chooses to "sound" the way she does?

3. What is Baez's focus? Does she concentrate on her father's eccentricities, her own insecurities, or the nature of their relationship?

4. What is the central theme of this sketch? What strategies hold the essay together?

5. Baez's sketch opens with a number of short, declarative sentences that produce a somewhat halting rhythm. How is this way of writing related to her attitude toward her father? Does this rhythm continue throughout the sketch? Why?

6. Why does Baez relate her anecdotes in the order she does? Are they chronological? How does she get from one anecdote to another? What aspects of her father does this particular order emphasize?

"Joey: A Mechanical Boy"/*Bruno Bettelheim*

In this case study, Bettelheim, a psychologist, presents the portrait of a child whose abnormal behavior he treated over a period of several years. Adopting a clinical perspective, he focuses on Joey's strange withdrawal from humanity. His examination of Joey's illness as a case study, however, doesn't mean that he lacks concern for Joey, only that his concern is subordinated to a desire for explanation. Joey becomes a phenomenon to be analyzed so that he can be helped and so that we can prevent his illness in other children. Understanding the boy's behavior and its causes, then, is Bettelheim's primary intention. His selection of a detached, somewhat objective point of view allows him to explain the sequence of causes and effects which constitute this particular "mechanical boy."

Bettelheim's purpose, to explain Joey, determines his selection of details and anecdotes that describe the boy's autistic personality, and gives a thematic unity to the essay's basically chronological structure. Yet Bettelheim's intention also raises the problem of how to present Joey dispassionately but kindly, how to regard him as both an object of study and a child. For it's possible to become objective to the point where Joey is dehumanized by the psychologist's very act of scientific observation. In reading Bettelheim's case study you'll find that he recognizes this problem, but more important, observe the strategies he employs to prevent himself from giving us a portrait of Joey done by a coldly inhuman, mechanical scientist.

Joey, when we began our work with him, was a mechanical boy. He functioned as if by remote control, run by machines of his own powerfully creative fantasy. Not only did he himself believe that he was a machine but, more remarkably, he created this impression in others. Even while he performed actions that are intrinsically human, they never appeared to be other than machine-started and executed. On the other hand, when the machine was not working we had to concentrate on recollecting his presence, for he seemed not to exist. A human body that functions as if it were a machine and a machine that duplicates human functions are equally fascinating and frightening. Perhaps they are so uncanny because they remind us that the human body can operate without a human spirit, that body can exist without soul. And Joey was a child who had been robbed of his humanity.

Not every child who possesses a fantasy world is possessed by it. Normal children may retreat into realms of imaginary glory or magic powers, but they are easily recalled from these excursions. Disturbed children are not always able to make the return trip; they remain withdrawn, prisoners of the inner world of delusion and fantasy. In many ways Joey presented a classic example of this state of infantile autism.

At the Sonia Shankman Orthogenic School of the University of Chicago it is our function to provide a therapeutic environment in which such children may start life over again. I have previously described in this magazine the rehabilitation of another of our patients ["Schizophrenic Art: A Case Study"; SCIENTIFIC AMERICAN, April, 1952]. This time I shall concentrate upon the illness, rather than the treatment. In any age, when the individual has escaped into a delusional world, he has usually fashioned it from bits and pieces of the world at hand. Joey, in his time and world, chose the machine and froze himself in its image. His story has a general relevance to the understanding of emotional development in a machine age.

Joey's delusion is not uncommon among schizophrenic children today. He wanted to be rid of his unbearable humanity, to become completely automatic. He so nearly succeeded in attaining this goal that he could almost convince others, as well as himself, of his mechanical character. The descriptions of autistic children in the literature take for their point of departure and comparison the normal or abnormal human being. To do justice to Joey I would have to compare him simultaneously to a most inept infant and a highly complex piece of machinery. Often we had to force ourselves by a conscious act of will to realize that Joey was a child. Again and again his acting-out of his delusions froze our own ability to respond as human beings.

During Joey's first weeks with us we would watch absorbedly as this at once fragile-looking and imperious nine-year-old went about his mechanical existence. Entering the dining room, for example, he would string an imaginary wire from his "energy source"—an imaginary electric outlet—to the table. There he "insulated" himself with paper napkins and finally plugged himself in. Only then could Joey eat, for he firmly believed that the "current" ran his ingestive apparatus. So skillful was the pantomime that one had to look twice to be sure there was neither wire nor outlet nor plug. Children and members of our staff spontaneously avoided stepping on the "wires" for fear of interrupting what seemed the source of his very life.

For long periods of time, when his "machinery" was idle, he would sit so quietly that he would disappear from the focus of the most conscientious observation. Yet in the next moment he might be "working" and the center of our captivated attention. Many times a day he would turn himself on and shift noisily through a sequence of higher and higher gears until he "exploded," screaming "Crash, crash!" and hurling items from his ever present apparatus—radio tubes, light bulbs, even motors or, lacking these, any handy breakable object. (Joey had an astonishing knack for snatching bulbs and tubes unobserved.) As soon as the object thrown had shattered, he would cease his screaming and wild jumping and retire to mute, motionless nonexistence.

Our maids, inured to difficult children, were exceptionally attentive to Joey; they were apparently moved by his extreme infantile fragility, so strangely coupled with megalomaniacal superiority. Occasionally some of the apparatus he fixed to his bed to "live him" during his sleep would fall down in disarray. This machinery he contrived from masking tape, cardboard, wire and other paraphernalia. Usually the maids would pick up such things and leave them on a table for the children to find, or disregard them entirely. But Joey's machine they carefully restored: "Joey must have the carburetor so he can breathe." Similarly they were on the alert to pick up and preserve the motors that ran him during the day and the exhaust pipes through which he exhaled.

How had Joey become a human machine? From intensive interviews with his parents we learned that the process had begun even before birth. Schizophrenia often results from parental rejection, sometimes combined ambivalently with love. Joey, on the other hand, had been completely ignored.

"I never knew I was pregnant," his mother said, meaning that she had already excluded Joey from her consciousness. His birth, she said, "did not make any difference." Joey's father, a rootless draftee in the wartime civilian army, was equally unready for parenthood. So, of course, are many young couples. Fortunately most such parents lose their indifference upon the baby's birth. But not Joey's parents. "I did not want to see or nurse him," his mother declared. "I had no feeling of actual dislike—I simply didn't want to take care of him." For the first three months of his life Joey "cried most of the time." A colicky baby, he was kept on a rigid four-hour feeding schedule, was not touched unless necessary and was never cuddled or played with. The mother, preoccupied with herself, usually left Joey alone in the crib or playpen during the day. The father discharged his frustrations by punishing Joey when the child cried at night.

Soon the father left for overseas duty, and the mother took Joey, now a year and a half old, to live with her at her parents' home. On his arrival the grandparents noticed that ominous changes had occurred in the child. Strong and healthy at birth, he had become frail and irritable; a responsive baby, he had become remote and inaccessible. When he began to master speech, he talked only to himself. At an early date he became preoccupied with machinery, including an old electric fan which he could take apart and put together again with surprising deftness.

Joey's mother impressed us with a fey quality that expressed her insecurity, her detachment from the world and her low physical vitality. We were struck especially by her total indifference as she talked about

Joey. This seemed much more remarkable than the actual mistakes she made in handling him. Certainly he was left to cry for hours when hungry, because she fed him on a rigid schedule; he was toilet-trained with great rigidity so that he would give no trouble. These things happen to many children. But Joey's existence never registered with his mother. In her recollections he was fused at one moment with one event or person; at another, with something or somebody else. When she told us about his birth and infancy, it was as if she were talking about some vague acquaintance, and soon her thoughts would wander off to another person or to herself.

When Joey was not yet four, his nursery school suggested that he enter a special school for disturbed children. At the new school his autism was immediately recognized. During his three years there he experienced a slow improvement. Unfortunately a subsequent two years in a parochial school destroyed this progress. He began to develop compulsive defenses, which he called his "preventions." He could not drink, for example, except through elaborate piping systems built of straws. Liquids had to be "pumped" into him, in his fantasy, or he could not suck. Eventually his behavior became so upsetting that he could not be kept in the parochial school. At home things did not improve. Three months before entering the Orthogenic School he made a serious attempt at suicide.

To us Joey's pathological behavior seemed the external expression of an overwhelming effort to remain almost nonexistent as a person. For weeks Joey's only reply when addressed was "Bam." Unless he thus neutralized whatever we said, there would be an explosion, for Joey plainly wished to close off every form of contact not mediated by machinery. Even when he was bathed he rocked back and forth with mute, engine-like regularity, flooding the bathroom. If he stopped rocking, he did this like a machine too; suddenly he went completely rigid. Only once, after months of being lifted from his bath and carried to bed, did a small expression of puzzled pleasure appear on his face as he said very softly: "They even carry you to your bed here."

For a long time after he began to talk he would never refer to anyone by name, but only as "that person" or "the little person" or "the big person." He was unable to designate by its true name anything to which he attached feelings. Nor could he name his anxieties except through neologisms or word contaminations. For a long time he spoke about "master paintings" and "a master painting room" (*i.e.,* masturbating and masturbating room). One of his machines, the "criticizer," prevented him from "saying words which have unpleasant feelings." Yet he gave personal names to the tubes and motors in his collection of machinery. Moreover, these dead things had feelings; the tubes bled when hurt and sometimes got sick. He consistently maintained this reversal between animate and inanimate objects.

In Joey's machine world everything, on pain of instant destruction, obeyed inhibitory laws much more stringent than those of physics. When we came to know him better, it was plain that in his moments of silent withdrawal, with his machine switched off, Joey was absorbed in pondering the compulsive laws of his private universe. His preoccupation with machinery made it difficult to establish even practical contacts with him. If he wanted to do something with a counselor, such as play with a toy that had caught his vague attention, he could not do so: "I'd like this very much, but first I have to turn off the machine." But by the time he had fulfilled all the requirements of his preventions, he had lost interest. When a toy was offered to him, he could not touch it because his motors and his tubes did not leave him a hand free. Even certain colors were dangerous and had to be strictly avoided in toys and clothing, because "some colors turn off the current, and I can't touch them because I can't live without the current."

Joey was convinced that machines were better than people. Once when he bumped into one of the pipes on our jungle gym he kicked it so violently that his teacher had to restrain him to keep him from injuring himself. When she explained that the pipe was much harder than his foot, Joey replied: "That proves it. Machines are better than the body. They don't break; they're much harder and stronger." If he lost or forgot something, it merely proved that his brain ought to be thrown away and replaced by machinery. If he spilled something, his arm should be broken and twisted off because it did not work properly. When his head or arm failed to work as it should, he tried to punish it by hitting it. Even Joey's feelings were mechanical. Much later in his therapy, when he had formed a timid attachment to another child and had been rebuffed, Joey cried: "He broke my feelings."

Gradually we began to understand what had seemed to be contradictory in Joey's behavior—why he held on to the motors and tubes, then suddenly destroyed them in a fury, then set out immediately and urgently to equip himself with new and larger tubes. Joey had created these machines to run his body and mind because it was too painful to be human. But again and again he became dissatisfied with their failure to meet his need and rebellious at the way they frustrated his will. In a recurrent frenzy he "exploded" his light bulbs and tubes, and for a moment became a human being—for one crowning instant he came alive. But as soon as he had asserted his dominance through the self-created explosion, he felt his life ebbing away. To keep on existing he had immediately to restore his machines and replenish the electricity that supplied his life energy.

What deep-seated fears and needs underlay Joey's delusional system? We were long in finding out, for Joey's preventions effectively concealed the secret of his autistic behavior. In the meantime we dealt with his peripheral problems one by one.

During his first year with us Joey's most trying problem was toilet behavior. This surprised us, for Joey's personality was not "anal" in the Freudian sense; his original personality damage had antedated the period of his toilet-training. Rigid and early toilet-training, however, had certainly contributed to his anxieties. It was our effort to help Joey with this problem that led to his first recognition of us as human beings.

Going to the toilet, like everything else in Joey's life, was surrounded by elaborate preventions. We had to accompany him; he had to take off all his clothes; he could only squat, not sit, on the toilet seat; he had to touch the wall with one hand, in which he also clutched frantically the vacuum tubes that powered his elimination. He was terrified lest his whole body be sucked down.

To counteract this fear we gave him a metal wastebasket in lieu of a toilet. Eventually, when eliminating into the wastebasket, he no longer needed to take off all his clothes, nor to hold onto the wall. He still needed the tubes and motors which, he believed, moved his bowels for him. But here again the all-important machinery was itself a source of new terrors. In Joey's world the gadgets had to move their bowels, too. He was terribly concerned that they should, but since they were so much more powerful than men, he was also terrified that if his tubes moved their bowels, their feces would fill all of space and leave him no room to live. He was thus always caught in some fearful contradiction.

Our readiness to accept his toilet habits, which obviously entailed some hardship for his counselors, gave Joey the confidence to express his obsessions in drawings. Drawing these fantasies was a first step toward letting us in, however distantly, to what concerned him most deeply. It was the first step in a year-long process of externalizing his anal preoccupations. As a result he began seeing feces everywhere; the whole world became to him a mire of excrement. At the same time he began to eliminate freely wherever he happened to be. But with this release from his infantile imprisonment in compulsive rules, the toilet and the whole process of elimination became less dangerous. Thus far it had been beyond Joey's comprehension that anybody could possibly move his bowels without mechanical aid. Now Joey took a further step forward; defecation became the first physiological process he could perform without the help of vacuum tubes. It must not be thought that he was proud of this ability. Taking pride in an achievement presupposes that one accomplishes it of one's own free will. He still did not feel himself an autonomous person who could do things on his own. To Joey defecation still seemed enslaved to some incomprehensible but utterly binding cosmic law, perhaps the law his parents had imposed on him when he was being toilet-trained.

It was not simply that his parents had subjected him to rigid, early training. Many children are so trained. But in most cases the parents have a deep emotional investment in the child's performance. The child's response in turn makes training an occasion for interaction between them and for the building of genuine relationships. Joey's parents had no emotional investment in him. His obedience gave them no satisfaction and won him no affection or approval. As a toilet-trained child he saved his mother labor, just as household machines saved her labor. As a machine he was not loved for his performance, nor could he love himself.

So it had been with all other aspects of Joeys' existence with his parents. Their reactions to his eating or noneating, sleeping or wakening, urinating or defecating, being dressed or undressed, washed or bathed did not flow from any unitary interest in him, deeply embedded in their personalities. By treating him mechanically his parents made him a machine. The various functions of life—even the parts of his body—bore no integrating relationship to one another or to any sense of self that was acknowledged and confirmed by others. Though he had acquired mastery over some functions, such as toilet-training and speech, he had acquired them separately and kept them isolated from each other. Toilet-training had thus not gained him a pleasant feeling of body mastery; speech had not led to communication of thought or feeling. On the contrary, each achievement only steered him away from self-mastery and integration. Toilet-training had enslaved him. Speech left him talking in neologisms that obstructed his and our ability to relate to each other. In Joey's development the normal process of growth had been made to run backward. Whatever he had learned put him not at the end of his infantile development toward integration but, on the contrary, farther behind than he was at its very beginning. Had we understood this sooner, his first years with us would have been less baffling.

It is unlikely that Joey's calamity could befall a child in any time and culture but our own. He suffered no physical deprivation; he starved for human contact. Just to be taken care of is not enough for relating. It is a necessary but not a sufficient condition. At the extreme where utter scarcity reigns, the forming of relationships is certainly hampered. But our society of mechanized plenty often makes for equal difficulties in a child's learning to relate. Where parents can provide the simple creature-comforts for their children only at the cost of significant effort, it is likely that they will feel pleasure in being able to provide for them; it is this, the parents' pleasure, that gives children a sense of personal worth and sets the process of relating in motion. But if comfort is so readily available that the parents feel no particular pleasure in winning it for their children, then the children cannot develop the feeling of being worthwhile around the satisfaction of their basic needs. Of course parents and children can and do develop relationships around other situations. But matters are then no longer so simple and direct. The child must be on the receiving end of care and concern given with pleasure and without the exaction of return if he is to feel loved and worthy of respect and consideration. This feeling gives him the ability to trust; he can entrust his well-being to persons to whom he is so important. Out of such trust the child learns to form close and stable relationships.

For Joey relationship with his parents was empty of pleasure in comfort-giving as in all other situations. His was an extreme instance of a plight that sends many schizophrenic children to our clinics and hospitals. Many months passed before he could relate to us; his despair that anybody could like him made contact impossible.

When Joey could finally trust us enough to let himself become more infantile, he began to play at being a papoose. There was a corresponding change in his fantasies. He drew endless pictures of himself as an electrical papoose. Totally enclosed, suspended in empty space, he is run by unknown, unseen powers through wireless electricity.

As we eventually came to understand, the heart of Joey's delusional system was the artificial, mechanical womb he had created and into which he had locked himself. In his papoose fantasies lay the wish to be entirely reborn in a womb. His new experiences in the school suggested that life, after all, might be worth living. Now he was searching for a way to be reborn in a better way. Since machines were better than men, what was more natural than to try rebirth through them? This was the deeper meaning of his electrical papoose.

As Joey made progress, his pictures of himself became more dominant in his drawings. Though still machine-operated, he has grown in self-importance.

Another great step forward is represented in another picture. Now he has acquired hands that do something, and he has had the courage to make a picture of the machine that runs him. Later still the papoose became a person, rather than a robot encased in glass.

Eventually Joey began to create an imaginary family at the school: the "Carr" family. Why the Carr family? In the car he was enclosed as he had been in his papoose, but at least the car was not stationary; it could move. More important, in a car one was not only driven but also could drive. The Carr family was Joey's way of exploring the possibility of leaving the school, of living with a good family in a safe, protecting car.

Joey at last broke through his prison. In this brief account it has not been possible to trace the painfully slow process of his first true relations with other human beings. Suffice it to say that he ceased to be a mechanical boy and became a human child. This newborn child was, however, nearly 12 years old. To recover the lost time is a tremendous task. That work has occupied Joey and us ever since. Sometimes he sets to it with a will; at other times the difficulty of real life makes him regret that he ever came out of his shell. But he has never wanted to return to his mechanical life.

One last detail and this fragment of Joey's story has been told. When Joey was 12, he made a float for our Memorial Day parade. It carried the slogan: "Feelings are more important than anything under the sun." Feelings, Joey had learned, are what make for humanity; their absence, for a mechanical existence. With this knowledge Joey entered the human condition.

1. Why does Bettelheim organize his essay chronologically? In what places does he violate the general chronology by tracing the chronology of special traits? Why is this necessary?
2. What proportion of Bettelheim's case study is description of Joey's behavior? What proportion is analysis? How does Bettelheim move from one to the other?
3. Where does Bettelheim interject his, and his staff's, personal feelings about Joey's behavior? For what reasons does he include those responses? Are these interjections consistent with his point of view?
4. How does Bettelheim relate Joey's malady to the culture into which he was born? How central is this insight to the essay as a whole? What can we infer from this concern about Bettelheim's intentions?
5. When Bettelheim shifts attention to Joey's mother and father, how does he still keep his focus on Joey? Does he subordinate Joey to his illness?
6. Bettelheim calls his essay a "fragment of Joey's story." How does he convince us that it's not *merely* a fragment? In what ways does Bettelheim lay bare Joey's essential characteristics and give them significance?

"Those Truck Drivin' Men"/*Donn Pearce*

This essay describes the thousands of truck drivers that cruise American roads every day. It doesn't ignore their private lives or their idiosyncracies, but it does suggest through a meticulous description of roadside truck-stops, wrecks, and pressing schedules that their lives are bound by their work. "Roger," "Jim," and "Harry" exist in a world where mistakes are fatal, sleep is rare, and coffee is watered down. And they exist in this world for such a large proportion of their time that its effects are pervasive. They are victimized, yet ruthless; uneducated, yet worldly wise.

The brutal frankness of the truck drivers' world and the toughness of the truckers themselves are inseparable. Pearce's equally frank language and his strategy in making a class of people come alive by constructing their world rests on this assumption. By piling up the minute particulars of the truckers, their trucks, their loads, and their stops, by describing truckers and trucks as if they were the same kind of objects, Pearce builds up, piece by piece, a world which becomes believable largely because of the sheer amount of concrete detail we are forced to experience. But this extraordinary attention to detail could backfire and undermine his intent to reveal "Those Truck Drivin' Men." Ask yourselves, as you read this essay then, why the details don't get in our way, diverting Pearce's focus and completely obscuring the character of the drivers instead of revealing it.

Here he comes; roaring east out of Portland, Oregon, on Interstate 80-N, doing the limit and just a little bit more, shifting up and shifting down through sixteen gears, pushing a rig that is eight feet wide and fifty-five feet long and weighs seventy-two thousand pounds, a dozen different tags fastened to the bumper and fuel permits plastered all over the door, waving to a girl in a golden Mustang as he pulls down on the overhead lanyard and lets go with a long blast of the air horn.

Here he comes; his bloodshot eyes blinking nine feet above the concrete, staring through the windshield at forty-eight of the fifty states, two long black smudges of soot along the top edges of the mud-spattered aluminum trailer, twin chrome-plated exhaust pipes belching smoke high up in the air. This is the guy delivering your orange juice and frozen pizzas, a TV set, a new window screen, cigarettes, a typewriter, your cat food and your fertilizer. He's got one hand on the steering wheel and one on the stick, double-clutching as he goes, mashing the accelerator down on the floor, all pilled-up with a Black Molly or a West Coaster or a Turnaround, bouncing, jiggling, jerking his way on his long-haul, over-the-road run. He's got kidney trouble, back trouble and piles. He hasn't been home in three weeks and hasn't slept in two days. Behind him, stretched like a curtain across the length of the sleeper berth, is a big Confederate flag. And as he whizzes by with a dropped octave and a diminishing roar, you can look at the mudguards fluttering behind each set of wheels and read the big white

ALABAMA   ALABAMA

There are two kinds of truck drivers, the slicks and the hicks; those who like Dick Tracy's bad guys and those who look like Li'l Abner's.

They have skinny legs and bulging bellies, square heads, short hair and wrinkles and every one of them looks ten years older than he really is. There was a time when caps were very much in vogue, those with chromed elastic bands stretched over the visors and with all sorts of buttons and badges. Everyone had to have a king-size wallet hanging out of his hip pocket, fastened to a belt loop by a long chain, an Eisenhower jacket and a wide belt with a gold replica of a truck embossed on an enormous silver buckle. This tradition is still being carried on by a few blacks and, here and there, a Texan, but generally the style has gone. All that is left are the boots; either cowboy boots or the motorcycle kind.

You can see them at the truck stops, their bearded jowls, the flab and the hard lines all green and blue under the fluorescence. They sit there hunched over the counters; the Flattops, the Prunefaces and the Plentys, the Floogles, the Yokums and the Scraggs. They drink watery coffee and eat quarter-inch hamburgers made of some shiny substance slapped between two white cushions of dry fluff. They smoke continuously. Some will try to joke with the waitresses, the one with the funny-looking ass and the super-boobs or the one with the acne and no boobs at all. Miniature toy trucks decorate the walls, identified by company colors and names. Etchings of classic vehicles are framed under glass.

Outside, on a five-acre parking lot, you can see their rigs; cattle trucks and low-boys, reefers, open-tops and tankers, five-axle jobs, screw-tractors, cab-over-engines, Whites, Macks, Kenworths; all side by side, diesels idling, Thermo Kings refrigerating, air brakes gasping out of the greasy neon shadows.

And there goes Roger, zipping past Harrisburg along the Turnpike, cautious but anxious to get out of what he calls Pennslowmania. Roger is the kind of guy who just naturally doesn't give a shit. He is twenty-five and single. He earns $300 a week and more. Womanizing is his hobby. But he doesn't dare let himself get caught driving in his own home state. When he visits his family at Christmas, he comes in at night and parks his truck at the county line. He calls up his father, who comes out and picks him up. Roger jumped a $1,000 bond after he was caught driving while intoxicated while his license was revoked. His license had been revoked because he had been caught driving while his license was under suspension. It had been suspended because he had been given three tickets for speeding within one thirty-day period.

Roger is the kind of guy who will go out for a sandwich and promise to return in ten minutes but may not come back for three or four hours. Or he will promise faithfully to call the next morning and then smile at you with disarming blue-eyed innocence if you should be lucky enough to catch him two days later. Like many over-the-road truck drivers, he is moody and itchy, anxious to start out on another long haul, preferring to drive by himself without a helper. At other times he feels lazy, overcome with a sudden yearning for deep-sea fishing.

After a three-day binge, Roger stumbled home to his efficiency apartment one night, collapsing blind-drunk in his bed. Burglars broke in while he was sleeping it off and completely cleaned him out. They took everything. They emptied his closet and his bureau drawers. They took his watch and his ring. They removed all the beer from the refrigerator and a bottle of whiskey from the kitchen cabinet. They took his shoes. Shifting his head to get under his pillow, they took a check and $150 in cash from his wallet, but very carefully put a single dollar bill back inside. Roger slept through it all. When he woke up, he called the police. A squad car arrived and two cops promptly put Roger in handcuffs and took him to jail. Some time before, he had been given a traffic ticket for failure to yield the right-of-way. He had ignored the ticket and there was a warrant out for his arrest. He waited three hours in a cell before his boss arrived to bail him out.

Roger spent a year and a half in Vietnam where the Army taught him how to drive a tank transporter, a rig consisting of a twenty-ton tractor and a twenty-ton trailer that carried a single tank out of combat. The tank weighed fifty-two tons. Roger just finished reading *Black Like Me*. One of his girl friends is a schoolteacher and a liberal and she is trying to convert him. He himself is a segregationist. While over in Nam, he had two black buddies with whom he was very close. They fought their war together, they talked and drank their beer together. But then they went their separate ways. Roger resents the integration of schools and all those other pressure programs to persist in pushing blacks into jobs regardless of their qualifications. He claims few blacks drive over-the-road. At certain truck stops in South Carolina and Alabama there are signs that say: "All money spent here by colored drivers will be donated to the K.K.K."

Roger drives an automobile carrier, a privately owned rig which is not for hire. The company has about twenty outlets all over the country and acts as a broker, buying whatever is available and selling it whenever there is a demand. The truck is therefore a rolling used-car lot. It services an involved network of contacts and connections and associates who haunt the auctions, the factories and the dealers, everything done on a fast, cash, spot-transaction basis. The company's phone bill is about $500 a month. Speed and the dependability of delivery is an essential part of the business, which is why Roger is paid twenty-five percent of the gross earnings of the truck. His trips average seven days but sometimes stretch to thirty. He is guaranteed a minimum of $150 per week and has made as much as $700. On one typical trip he carried four Cadillacs, a Triumph Spitfire and a Lincoln Continental to Louisville, Kentucky. He took a load from Akron to Atlanta and then deadheaded up to Flint to pick up six new Buicks.

Roger has to load and unload the truck by himself which takes him about an hour and forty-five minutes. Clearance is the deciding factor because sometimes the bridges and tunnels are very low. Once, on Jerome

Avenue in the Bronx, Roger peeled the tops off two Volvos. He kept right on going. . . .

Just as trucks can be separated vertically by the kinds of loads they carry, they can also be classified horizontally by the length of the trips they make. Dump trucks, cement mixers, milk, gasoline and delivery trucks are all local. The drivers work regular hours and sleep in their own beds every night. The routemen usually drive back and forth, hauling freight several hundred miles between the same two or three terminals and sleeping in their own beds two or three times each week. The over-the-road men make the long hauls. They get home once a week or perhaps once a month, depending on what they carry, their luck, or the season of the year. And then there are the gypsies who will carry anything anywhere at any time and never come home at all unless someone pays them to.

On U. S. 301, in South Carolina, a Chrysler Imperial is parked on the edge of the truck-stop apron. The door clicks open and closes. A woman walks over to a parked truck, the gasoline motor on its refrigeration apparatus raucous and tireless in the night. She knocks on the door of the cab. In a moment the door opens. Nervously looking around her, she speaks in a low voice. A light goes on, revealing her pudgy figure, her smile cracking the thick makeup, the lipstick seeming black in the darkness. The woman laboriously clambers up into the cab. The door closes. The light goes out.

The rest area on Interstate 78 in New Jersey is crowded with parked cars, a house trailer, a boat trailer, a U-Haul-It trailer. In the other parking lane are the trucks. A shadowy male figure approaches a dark-green Diamond Reo, raps lightly on the door and steps back into full view of the window, calling out softly in a lilting, effeminate voice, "Hi. You looking for company?" The figure moves off toward another truck. Ten minutes later, another man approaches, tall, thin, moving gracefully. He knocks. Suddenly the truck motor starts, compressed air gasping as the parking brakes are released, the exhaust roaring as the semi pulls away, hesitates at the edge of the road and drives on.

Just outside Stockton, California, on U. S. 99, a driver knocks on the cab door of a truck, calling out in a loud, gruff voice, "Hey, buddy. You mind pullin' up a couple feet? You got me blocked." The motor starts. The truck moves ahead. "Yeah. Fine. That's plenty. Thanks, buddy." Later, the driver wakes up and gets out of the sleeper bunk, climbing down out of the cab to go to the john. Then he discovers that he has driven his rig up on two-inch planks placed in front of the inside tires of each double wheel. All the outside wheels have been stolen.

Jim doesn't push a rig anymore. He used to drive a tanker, hauling fifty-six hundred gallons of gasoline down to Key West, squeezing through the narrow spots of the antiquated Overseas Highway, over Bahia Honda and the Seven Mile Bridge. Occasionally, he used to scrape his tires along the curbs and once he passed a Greyhound bus so close the two vehicles banged their side mirrors together.

Just before dawn, two days after Christmas, still glowing with the contentment of the holidays, the security of a comfortable, three-year job, good health, a recent safe-driver award, a lovely wife and two small children, Jim had a wreck. He was driving a substitute rig. While reaching out the window to adjust the mirror, the tractor bounced over the dips and potholes of Krome Avenue outside Miami and momentarily he ran off the road, the right front wheel hitting a soft, sandy spot on the shoulder. He whipped the tractor back but miscalculated the steering characteristics of the shorter wheelbase. The semitrailer began to fishtail. In ten seconds, a trail 448 feet long was cut through the countryside. Four royal palms were broken off, a frame house was narrowly averted and six tires were blown out. Jim tried frantically to regain control of the thirty-five-ton runaway as it rolled down the embankment, turned, started back, turned over two and a half times and landed against a tree in a flood of gasoline, ten feet short of an electric utility pole. The roof of the cab was smashed flat, the steering column bent back, Jimmy pinned in the wreckage so tight he could move only one arm, hanging there upside down, his back arched, drenched by fifty gallons of fuel leaking out of a saddle tank.

It was dark and it was quiet. At first he actually thought he was dead. Then he made one great, desperate try at pulling himself out of the wreckage. When the back of his leather jacket split open he felt the pain in his spine and he knew it was broken. He also knew he had lost his left leg. His left ear was full of blood and he realized he was deaf. Waiting for the imminent explosion and the flames, Jim began to scream. As dawn broke and the sun came up, he hung there, hysterical, for one hour and forty-five minutes.

But he had been heard by a woman in the nearby house who didn't have the stomach to go down personally to such an impossible wreck. But she did call the Highway Patrol. A trooper arrived with a wrecker. In disbelief, Jim watched them rig a chain around the cab. He tried to stop them but by then he couldn't talk. Because of his fear and the strain of his screaming, he was literally speechless. And it happened. He watched the winch take up the slack on the chain and he felt the tractor move. Then the hook slipped, the chain jerked away. He saw the sparks flying.

They decided to use hydraulic jacks. Eventually they righted the cab and pried him loose, laying him on an ambulance stretcher. Jim very nearly fainted when he saw the crowd of a hundred bystanders, silent and awed, most of them actually standing in the spilled gasoline, any of them capable of lighting up a cigarette.

But it all ended well. Jim's back was not broken and his leg was fine.

He suffered a few bruises and a dozen small cuts on his scalp from fragments of the smashed windshield. The largest was on the back of his ear. His most serious injury was a stiff arm which he couldn't raise over his head. The company safety inspectors gave the actuarial odds for survival in such a wreck as about a thousand-to-one.

Jim drove again for about ninety days. Then he quit. In his office he still has a framed color photograph of the truck and trailer which had been washed and waxed the day before the accident. He has another picture taken the day after the accident. One of the things that saved him was the breaking of the kingpin that connects the trailer to the fifth wheel of the tractor. This permitted the mangled, squashed remains of the truck to roll away from the fifty-six-hundred-gallon cargo. The pin is about three inches in diameter and made of a tough alloy steel. They say it is impossible to break a kingpin. Jim salvaged his from the wreck. He had it chrome-plated and now uses it as a paperweight on his desk.

In Phoenix, Arizona, there is a businessman who was once a policeman in a large Midwestern city. He was on traffic duty the night a personal friend had a similar accident in a similar truck. He too was hopelessly pinned in the wreckage. But this time the gasoline caught fire. The driver was screaming. He begged to be put out of his agony. The policeman drew his pistol and shot his friend in the head. . . .

Mr. and Mrs. Dell are from Price, Utah. They are a husband-and-wife driving team and they own their tractor which they lease to Franklin Transport, a company specializing in extra-heavy, long-distance hauling. Mrs. Dell has a block of wood rigged to the accelerator when she is driving so she can reach it with her foot. The Dells operate as a typical team, keeping their rig moving twenty-four hours a day. Before women drivers became so common, they had trouble with the police who used to stop them frequently to check Mrs. Dell's credentials.

For some time now they have been hauling guided missiles and loads of high explosives. They have a television set in the cab and also a coffee maker. It is all air-conditioned and they have a stereo cartridge tape player. One of their favorite pieces is by the Sharecroppers, the singer accompanied by fiddles, base and guitars:

> Pour me another cup of coffee
> For it is the best in the land
> I'll put a quarter in the jukebox
> And play The Truck Driving Man

Their pet dog, a Boston terrier, goes along with them on their trips. Mrs. Dell doesn't like Los Angeles or New York because of the heavy traffic. Her hobby is collecting souvenirs from her travels. She has two hundred salt and pepper shakers in her collection. . . .

Harry hasn't missed a Christmas at home in the twenty-four years he's been driving. Sometimes he has had to come in on the fly and sometimes he has had to park his rig and take the Greyhound. But he always made it.

Winter is the dead season for moving vans and getting home for Christmas is usually no problem. Some years Harry is home for thirty days at a time. But in the summer he is constantly on the go, at times running out to California from the East Coast, sometimes to Oregon and Washington. It is a crazy business, alternating between winter's lethargy and summer's frenzy. It is a sick business in which no one can ever be satisfied.

Originally it was very wildcat. Anyone with a truck and a telephone could set himself up. But then the I.C.C. stepped in as well as public commissions in every state, sometimes controlling the business right down to the local level. Rules were set up, certificates issued and prices regulated. But by then it was too late. The competition is still very ferocious.

Each outfit operates as a network of agencies scattered all over the country with one big headquarters acting as the brain center, dispatching trucks from here to there to pick up a load, a half load or part of a load and to deliver it somewhere else. This outfit must have all the necessary permits which the I.C.C. rarely issues.

The process of moving a family's possessions to a new location usually begins with an informer. Often it is your friendly neighborhood real-estate agent who sometimes gets a five-percent commission for a good tip-off. Do not bother to ask him about this practice because he will deny it. This is a violation of the rules of confidence for realtors. Other informers could be almost anyone you know who has a connection with the salesman who gets a commission of eight to ten percent from the agency. And he is the guy who causes most of the problems. Because he is the one who estimates the weight of your furniture, calculates how much it will cost you to move and insinuates it is a flat price while underestimating the final cost every time. Then he makes all those glorious promises as to when the stuff will be picked up and when delivered. He will promise you absolutely anything you want to hear. Then he takes his commission and runs. Everyone in the business knows that you never get a repeat customer.

And guess who is in the middle? Right. The truck driver.

Again, the standard arrangement is for the trucker to lease his own tractor to the company who provides the trailer bearing the company emblem. The freight is calculated on distance and weight, so much per hundred pounds per mile. The driver will get fifty percent of the charges and must pay all costs and expenses. He must also load the van, using local helpers for extra muscle. He must prepare a manifest, itemizing everything and noting its condition. And right here is another area of endless hassling. That kitchen chair is just a plain old kitchen chair to anyone else, but to its owner it has a fantastic emotional significance. And how many people realize the extent of the dents and the cat scratches and the spider webs and the baby puke and the crud that has collected over the years in the secret half-light under the table?

Finally comes the easy part—driving a couple thousand miles over mountains and through rainstorms, pushing day and night to fulfill some jerk salesman's fantastic promises. He has to pop a few pills and falsify a few log entries. But what the hell? All this is almost relaxing compared to what comes at delivery time, because all the while the Great Conspiracy has been at work. Mr. X has decided that his stuff cannot arrive on the thirteenth after all because his boss fouled him up and made him work overtime two nights in a row. But Mr. X's junk just happens to be on the top of the heap. Mrs. Y has contacted the central dispatcher, in tears because her daughter has eloped, her husband is drunk, the dog ran away. And couldn't they possibly be reasonable and deliver her very own personal lifetime belongings two days early? But Mrs. Y's crap is all loaded on the bottom.

And then Mr. Z refuses to pay up in cash before his stuff is unloaded. This is the standard agreement. You must sign a contract at the beginning and this particular clause is always emphasized, pointed out, bordered, starred and heavily underlined. Before the driver even arrives on the scene he will call up long-distance to warn everyone of his expected arrival time and to gently remind them about the money. And to give them the exciting news about the final bill. So what happens? The house is empty when he gets there. Three hours later the consignee arrives. But no money. Instead he has a shotgun, a committee of incensed male relatives, a cop, a lawyer and two old ladies in black, crying hysterically. The driver stands there in the sweat of a July Kansas afternoon. He hasn't slept in three days. He was supposed to be in Montana yesterday with a load he was supposed to pick up in Nevada. The truck isn't running right. On the phone his wife said she was tired of his fooling around with all those waitresses and if he isn't back home in Connecticut by tomorrow, forget it. Meanwhile, this ten-year-old brat keeps screaming, "Where's my roller skates?"

So he gets it all unloaded. He is in a high-labor area and has to pay double for his helpers. One moves with the grace of a constipated turtle and the other feels his individual integrity is threatened if he picks up anything weighing more than twenty-two pounds. Finally, all ten tons are unloaded. There is an old, beat-up stool in the back corner of the truck. But the leg was broken off in transit, perhaps that time that tourist was coming down the highway backward with no taillights while gawking at a motel sign and the truck driver had to slam on the brakes. But what the hell? It's only a stool. Oh, yeah? That stool was whittled out of a solid-hickory stump by hand in the year 1734 by a first cousin of Paul Revere. And where in the hell is the birdbath? Didn't anybody load the birdbath?

The small, old-fashioned, greasy-spoon truck stop is now giving way to the super-huge, full-service, motel-and-department-store, chain-operated establishment constructed just off the wide, fast, nonstop interstate highways at engineer-calculated intervals. They are like busy miniature harbors beside concrete rivers offering all-weather shelter to the merchant wanderers who drift in and drop anchor. Veering high above the reefs and the rocks are the lighthouses—signs, if you prefer—rotating and blinking, neon and fluorescent towers with translucent panels, beacons giving the code names of their locations. There may be ten acres of paved parking area. Hundreds of trucks are scattered in clumps and rows and lines. Diesel fuel pumps are ready. The grease monkeys are standing by. You can have a fast lubrication job. You can have your oil changed. You can order a new air filter, an oil filter and a fuel filter. The complete servicing will cost about $80, including the labor, the parts and about thirty-six quarts of oil. For another $30 you can have the entire rig steam-cleaned and washed.

Inside, all is Muzak and indirect lighting. There is a modernistic picture window in the front with a rubber tree growing up the shaft beside a spiral staircase. There are toilets and free showers for the men, free showers and powder rooms for the ladies. Rooms are available, both single and double, for mixed couples or homogeneous.

There is a mail room and a game room and a recreation room. There is a coffee shop and a dining room. There is an exchange counter where you can swap tape cartridges. Upstairs there is a truck broker's office. The cashier will accept your credit card and the trucker's discount will be paid over immediately in cash. Trip sheets are rubber-stamped to prove the amount of fuel taxes paid while in transit in that particular state. Ordinary tourists driving simple little cars are allowed on the premises but they have segregated facilities. Somewhere in the jungle of service lanes, hoses, pumps, and racks, he might even be able to get some gas.

You can buy anything you need—funny greeting cards, knives, wrenches, flashlights, stereo tapes, plaid shirts, cigarettes, sunglasses, belts, logbooks, socks, briar pipes, paperback books, pillows, suitcases, underarm deodorant spray, gloves, rotating signal lights, distress flares, stay-awake tablets, padlocks, magnetic dashboard paper clips, watchbands, underwear, key chains, toothpaste, work pants, dress pants, cans of salted peanuts—and somewhere on the premises, if you know the right guy, you can buy those black capsules, the RX-7's or you can even get some RJS's.

Again, there are the red eyes and the wrinkles. Sample truck tires are on display everywhere. The waitress tries her best to be sassy. The truck driver tries his best to look horny and tough. The tradition is studiously maintained of keeping your coffee cup full. As the waitress flits by, she splashes in a little more, without hesitation, without asking. If you like your coffee at a certain temperature and at a certain sweetness, it can drive you right out of your mind.

And this is where you hear the stories, the rumors, the reports, the gossip and the lies. Like sailors of old in the waterfront grogshops, they speak of their adventures, their favorite ports, the girls, the storms, the monsters they have encountered outside in the night.

"Man, it's cold. I was in Savannah Thursday and it was down to seventeen. And I didn't bring any coat with me this trip."

"Yeah. It was twelve Tuesday down in San Antonio."

"Anybody know where I can buy some charcoal? I'm supposed to deliver this load of oranges at Minneapolis at thirty-eight degrees. But it was colder than that when they loaded me up in Orlando. And the goddamn company took the Thermo King off the rig to save some weight during the winter season. So I gotta heat the damn trailer up somehow. If I can get some charcoal and some buckets I can build some fires and stick the embers inside. See?"

"I knew a guy once. Had a load of frozen pies. Trouble was thermostat was busted. Thermometer said zero. But when they opened up the doors. Wow. It was hot in there. Every one of 'em thawed out. They refused to accept delivery and it cost him four thousand bucks. Even after the insurance paid off. And so then what do you do? With twenty tons of gooey wet pies on your hands?"

It is right here that you get all those little bits of information which together can make up a portrait of this way of life. You can hear bitching, the pissing and the moaning, the laughter, the brag and the fact all mixed in with the sound of a cash register, the clinking of spoons, the deep salvos of the pistons as somewhere outside a truck casts off. A guy tells you how he once peeked through a hole cut in a partition wall at a company terminal and actually saw the dispatcher being pieced off by a ruthless, competitive driver. Because just having a lease agreement is not really enough. The company can play favorites. And you can get gypped. You may not get a load even if it is your turn. Or you will get a low-paying load. Or the statement you get will be deliberately vague or incomplete or just plain false.

Bribery is very much a part of this world. At the top level, certain officials are paid off to permit a "hot load" to go through. This will be an overweight load or a commodity for which the company doesn't have a proper permit. It may even be contraband; untaxed cigarettes or whiskey or a hijacked cargo. Normally, the scales at a weighing station are open twenty-four hours a day. But for various reasons they sometimes close down at odd, unannounced times. Unless some arrangement has been made in advance. This explains the dilemma of the driver who gets ahead of schedule and must kill two or three hours at a truck stop, waiting for the hour when the scales will be closed.

The I.C.C. and the state public commissions have roving patrols, their investigators stopping trucks on the road or at the scales, checking documents, cargos, safety devices and general equipment, looking for unauthorized riders or for amphetamines. But the pay is low and appropriations are inadequate for full patrols. Enforcement of the laws and the regulations is inept at best. At worst it is corrupt. Almost any trucker will describe how overweight problems can be smoothed over with a ten-dollar bill to the scaleman. Otherwise, he may drive some forty-odd miles along dirt roads and back routes to bypass the station altogether.

The situation varies, according to the locality and the state. It also varies according to the size and the nature of the problem. A favorite trick of drivers is to hide their pills in a small bottle buried in a can of cup grease. A company trick is to have all its vehicles inspected at one time, a so-called "fleet inspection." But very likely the Man will never leave the front office. The next day, inspection stickers are issued to the drivers by the handful.

There are many instances of cheap, inadequate repairs, retreaded tires, faulty brakes, loose steering connections, exhaust leakage into the cab, bad lights or a loose fifth wheel. And it isn't necessarily the gypsy who is the worst offender. He has to make his living with his rig and often takes care of it like a baby carriage, whereas a dollar here and a dollar there can add up to big money when you are operating a fleet of hundreds. The Teamsters are very much down on this kind of practice. They have the contractual right to "red-tag" a vehicle when they feel it needs repair work. The dispatcher is notified and the tag remains on the truck until the problem is rectified. And yet certain Teamster drivers will never red-tag a truck, afraid of being cut out of a load.

And you listen to the stories of the hijackers, how they will back up to a warehouse with a pirate rig flying the false colors of a counterfeit company and altered P.U.C. numbers and stolen license tags. They have all the I.D. cards you could ask for, all with phony names. They will load up with a cargo of cigarettes or whiskey worth more than a hundred thousand dollars and then drive off and disappear. Or a gang will pull into a truck stop where a loaded trailer has been parked. They will back up the tractor, hook up the fifth wheel, crank up the trailer's landing gear and take off.

A purple truck drives into the Wildwood Trucker Paradise. Behind it, three other tractors are hooked up in a line, the front of each one raised off the ground and connected to the fifth wheel of the tractor in front of it. It is like a line of circus elephants waiting for the applause and the peanuts. Or it is like a daisy chain of queer bulls standing on their hind legs and humping each other.

The trucks are all brand-new, being transported from Pontiac, Michigan, down to some G.M.C. agency. There is an immediate crowd. The driver is wearing a business suit and tie. As his wife takes his three little kids inside for a pee-stop and for some lunch, he talks to the guys about the purple monster he is driving, all chrome and all aglitter. It is an Astro 95. The bunk is three feet wide and more than seven feet long. The cab is completely padded with shining black vinyl. The instrument panel bends around the driver's seat in a semicircle of dials and guages, all indicating expertise and authority. The truck has a three-speed axle and an adjustable steering wheel. It is air-conditioned and has a transistorized radio. The governor is set at ninety-four miles an hour and, with all of the available options, it costs $35,000.

The men mutter and joke. They stand and gawk at the purple truck. Every possible style of cool is being displayed right here in this one group; the pursed lips and squinched eyes, the knotted jaws, the chewing gum, a dozen ways of holding a cigarette and taking a drag, hips cocked to the left or to the right, arms crossed, arms akimbo, boots resting on their heels, boots crossed while the weight is on one leg, hands in pockets, hands cupping chins. But they all see and hear one thing; the booming of an engine echoing among the cliffs, the flashing of a silver trailer through the moonlight, the Purple Ghost whistling out of the wind, its twin chrome-plated bugles singing of balls and glory.

1. In what way are "Roger," "Jim," and "Harry" symbolic characters? How does Donn Pearce let you know this?
2. The essay is chiefly anecdotal. What structural similarities hold the anecdotes together? What themes unify the piece?
3. Why is Pearce almost obsessed with detail in this essay? How is this related to the obsession of his drivers? How does this use of detail work to unify the sketch?
4. Try to distinguish characterization from background in this essay. Is it possible? If not, why not?
5. In what way does analysis enter this essay? Is it subtle or obvious? Use specific passages to prove your point.
6. In the first paragraph we are immediately plunged into a trucker's world of power and speed. What specific words and phrases make us feel this power and speed? How does the structure of the opening paragraph itself also convey a sense of speed? What strategies in this paragraph for revealing a person are used throughout the essay?

"The Politician"/H. L. Mencken

The subject of Mencken's character sketch is the "nature" of the politician. Although he makes topical references to some politicians of the 1920's, Mencken does not attack them personally. Instead he denounces the public's belief that there are "good" and "bad" politicians. Mencken contrives his sketch to convince the reader that such a belief is not "realistic," and that the political scene would be clarified by the honest acceptance of *duplicity* as the central personal quality of *all* politicians.

Mencken clearly is more intent on convincing us of the reality of this duplicity than on merely characterizing politicians; the real basis of his argument is the relation of this group of people to the public. As a result, he does not paint politicians in minute and careful detail, but with broad, bold strokes, using his characterization as example—evidence for an abstract idea. He is not interested in the color of an individual politician's eyes or in the way he dresses, but in the general outlook of politicians as a group. And he establishes this interest by focusing on a fundamental attitude they all share. Yet this strategy raises some questions. Does he deal only with stereotypes? If so, how does he make them convincing? Or does his sketch fall into caricature? If not, how does he avoid caricature?

Half the sorrows of the world, I suppose, are caused by making false assumptions. If the truth were only easier to ascertain the remedy for them would consist simply of ascertaining it and accepting it. This business, alas, is usually impossible, but fortunately not always: now and then, by some occult process, half rational and half instinctive, the truth gets itself found out and an ancient false assumption goes overboard. I point, in the field of the social relations, to one which afflicted the human race for millenniums: that one, to wit, which credited the rev. clergy with a mysterious wisdom and awful powers. Obviously, it has ceased to trouble all the superior varieties of men. It may survive in those remote marches where human beings go to bed with the cows, but certainly it has vanished from the cities. Asphalt and the apostolic succession, indeed, seem to be irreconcilable enemies. I can think of no clergyman in any great American city today whose public dignity and influence are much above those of an ordinary Class I Babbitt. It is hard for even the most diligent and passionate of the ancient order to get upon the first pages of the newspapers; he must make a clown-show, discreditable to his fraying cloth, or he must blush unseen. When bishops begin launching thunderbolts against heretics, the towns do not tremble; they laugh. When elders denounce sin, sin only grows more popular. Imagine a city man getting a notice from the ordinary of his diocese that he had been excommunicated. It would trouble him far less, I venture, than his morning *Katzenjammer.*

The reason for all this is not hard to find. All the superior varieties of men—and even the lowest varieties of city workmen are at least superior to peasants—have simply rid themselves of their old belief in devils. Hell no longer affrights and palsies them, and so the magic of those who profess to save them from it no longer impresses them. That profession, I believe, was bogus, and its acceptance was therefore a false assumption. Being so, it made men unhappy; getting rid of it has delivered them. They are no longer susceptible to ecclesiastical alarms and extortions; *ergo,* they sleep and eat better. Think of what life must have been under such princes of damnation as Cotton Mather and Jonathan Edwards, with even bartenders and metaphysicians believing in them! And then compare it to life under Bishop Manning and the Rev. Dr. John Roach Straton, with only a few half-wits believing in them! Or turn to the backwoods of the Republic, where the devil is still feared, and with him his professional exterminators. In the country towns the clergy are still almost as influential as they were in Mather's day, and there, as everyone knows, they remain public nuisances, and civilized life is almost impossible. In such Neolithic regions nothing can go on without their consent, on penalty of anathema and hell-fire; as a result, nothing goes on that is worth recording. It is this survival of sacerdotal authority, I begin to believe, and not hookworm, malaria or the event of April 9, 1865, that is chiefly responsible for the cultural paralysis of the late Confederate States. The South lacks big cities; it is run by its country towns—and in every country town there is some Baptist *mullah* who rules by scaring the peasantry. The false assumption that his pretensions are sound, that he can actually bind and loose, that contumacy to him is a variety of cursing God—this false assumption is what makes the yokels so uneasy, so nervous, and hence so unhappy. If they could throw it off they would burn fewer Aframericans and sing more songs. If they could be purged of it they would be purged of Ku Kluxry too.

The cities got rid of that false assumption half a century ago, and have been making cultural progress ever since. Somewhat later they got rid of its brother, to wit, respect for government, and, in particular, respect for its visible agents, the police. That respect—traditional, and hence irrational—had been, for years, in increasingly unpleasant collision with a great body of obvious facts. The police, by assumption austere and almost sacrosanct, were gradually discovered to be, in reality, a pack of rogues and but little removed, save by superior impudence and enterprise, from the cut-throats and purse-snatchers they were set to catch. When, a few decades ago, the American people, at least in the big cities, began to accept them frankly for what they were—when the old false assumption of their integrity and public usefulness was quietly abandoned and a new and more accurate assumption of their roguery was adopted in its place—when this change was effected there was a measurable increase, I believe, in the public happiness. It no longer astonished anyone when policemen were taken in evildoing; indignation therefore abated, and with it its pains. If, before that time, the corps of Prohibition enforcement officers—i.e., a corps of undisguised scoundrels with badges—had been launched upon the populace, there would have been a great roar of wrath, and much anguished gnashing of teeth. People would have felt themselves put upon, injured, insulted. But with the old false assumption about police-men removed from their minds, they met the new onslaught calmly and even smilingly. Today no one is indignant over the fact that the extortions of these new *Polizei* increase the cost of potable alcohol. The false as-sumption that the police are altruistic agents of a benevolent state has been replaced by the sound assumption that they are gentlemen engaged assiduously, like the rest of us, in finding meat and raiment for their families and in laying up funds to buy Liberty Bonds in the next war to end war. This is human progress, for it increases human happiness.

So much for the evidence. The deduction I propose to make from it is simply this: that a like increase would follow if the American people could only rid themselves of another and worse false assumption that still rides them—one that corrupts all their thinking about the great business of politics, and vastly augments their discontent and unhappiness—the assumption, that is, that politicians are divided into two classes, and that one of those classes is made up of good ones. I need not argue, I hope, that this assumption is almost universally held among us. Our whole politics, indeed, is based upon it, and has been based upon it since the earliest days. What is any political campaign save a concerted effort to turn out a set of politicians who are admittedly bad and put in a set who are thought to be better? The former assumption, I believe, is always sound; the latter is just as certainly false. For if experience teaches us anything at all it teaches us this: that a good politician, under democracy, is quite as unthinkable as an honest burglar. His very existence, indeed, is a standing subversion of the public good in every rational sense. He is not one who serves the common weal; he is simply one who preys upon the commonwealth. It is to the interest of all the rest of us to hold down his powers to an irreducible minimum, and to reduce his com-pensation to nothing; it is to his interest to augment his powers at all hazards, and to make his compensation all the traffic will bear. To argue that these aims are identical is to argue palpable nonsense. The politician, at his ideal best, never even remotely approximated in practise, is a necessary evil; at his worst he is an almost intolerable nuisance.

What I contend is simply that he would be measurably less a nuisance if we got rid of our old false assumption about him, and regarded him in the cold light of fact. At once, I believe, two-thirds of his obnoxiousness would vanish. He would remain a nuisance, but he would cease to be a swindler; the injury of having to pay freight on him would cease to be complicated by the insult of being rooked. It is the insult and not the injury that makes the deeper wounds, and causes the greater permanent damage to the national psyche. All of us have been trained, since infancy, in putting up with necessary evils, plainly recognized *as* evils. We know, for example, that the young of the human species commonly smell badly; that garbage men, bootblacks and messenger boys commonly smell worse. These facts are not agreeable, but they remain tolerable because they are universally assumed—because there is no sense of having been tricked and cozened in their perennial discovery. But try to imagine how distressing fatherhood would become if prospective fathers were all taught that the human infant radiates an aroma like the rose—if the truth came constantly as a surprise! Each fresh victim of the deception would feel that he had been basely swindled—that his own child was somehow bogus. Not infrequently, I suppose, he would be tempted to make away with it in some quiet manner, and have another—only to be shocked again. That procedure would be idiotic, admittedly, yet it is exactly the one we follow in politics. At each election we vote in a new set of politicians, insanely assuming that they are better than the set turned out. And at each election we are, as they say in the Motherland, done in.

Of late the fraud has become so gross that the plain people begin to show a great restlessness under it. Like animals in a cage, they trot from one corner to another, endlessly seeking a way out. If the Democrats win one year, it is a pretty sure sign that they will lose the next year. State after State becomes doubtful, pivotal, skittish; even the solid South begins to break. In the cities it is still worse. An evil circle is formed. First the poor taxpayers, robbed by the politicians of one great party and then by those of the other, turn to a group of free-lance rogues in the middle ground— non-partisan candidates, Liberals, reformers or what not: the name is unimportant. Then, flayed and pillaged by these gentry as they never were by the old-time professionals, they go back in despair to the latter, and are flayed and pillaged again. Back to Bach! Back to Tammany! Tammany reigns in New York because the Mitchel outfit was found to be intolerable —in other words, because the reformers were found to be even worse than the professionals. Is the fact surprising? Why should it be? Reformers and professionals are alike politicians in search of jobs; both are trying to bilk the taxpayers. Neither ever has any other motive. If any genuinely honest and altruistic politician had come to the surface in America in my time I'd have heard of him, for I have always frequented newspaper offices, and in a newspaper office the news of such a marvel would cause a dreadful tumult. I can recall no such tumult. The unanimous opinion of all the journalists that I know, excluding a few Liberals who are obviously somewhat balmy—they all believed, for example, that the late war would end war,—is that, since the days of the national Thors and Wotans, no politician who was not out for himself, and for himself alone, has ever drawn the breath of life in the United States.

The gradual disintegration of Liberalism among us, in fact, offers an excellent proof of the truth of my thesis. The Liberals have come to grief by fooling their customers, not merely once too often, but a hundred times too often. Over and over again they have trotted out some new hero, usually from the great open spaces, only to see him taken in the immemorial malpractises within ten days. Their graveyard, indeed, is filled with cracked and upset headstones, many covered with ribald pencilings. Every time there is a scandal in the grand manner the Liberals lose almost as many general officers as either the Democrats or Republicans. Of late, racked beyond endurance by such catastrophes at home, they have gone abroad for their principal heroes; losing humor as well as hope, they now ask us to venerate such astounding paladins as the Hon. Bela Kun, a gentleman who, in any American State, would not only be in the calaboose, but actually in the deathhouse. But this absurdity is only an offshoot of a deeper one. Their primary error lies in making the false assumption that some politicians are better than others. This error they share with the whole American people.

I propose that it be renounced, and contend that its renunciation would greatly rationalize and improve our politics. I do not argue that there would be any improvement in our politicians; on the contrary, I believe that they would remain substantially as they are today, and perhaps grow even worse. But what I do argue is that recognizing them frankly for what they are would instantly and automatically dissipate the indignation caused by their present abominations, and that the disappearance of this indignation would promote the public contentment and happiness. Under my scheme there would be no more false assumptions and no more false hopes, and hence no more painful surprises, no more bitter resentment of fraud, no more despair. Politicians, in so far as they remained necessary, would be kept at work—but not with any insane notion that they were archangels. Their rascality would be assumed and discounted, as the rascality of the police is now assumed and discounted. Machinery would be gradually developed to limit it and counteract it. In the end, it might be utilized in some publicly profitable manner, as the insensitiveness to filth of garbage men is now utilized, as the reverence of the clergy for capitalism is now utilized. The result, perhaps, would be a world no better than the present one, but it would at least be a world more intelligent.

In all this I sincerely hope that no one will mistake me for one who shares the indignation I have spoken of—that is, for one who believes that politicians can be made good, and cherishes a fond scheme for making them so. I believe nothing of the sort. On the contrary, I am convinced that the art and mystery they practise is essentially and incurably anti-social—that they must remain irreconcilable enemies of the common weal until the end of time. But I maintain that this fact, in itself, is not a bar to their employment. There are, under Christian civilization, many necessary offices that demand the possession of anti-social talents. A professional soldier, regarded realistically, is much worse than a professional politician, for he is a professional murderer and kidnaper, whereas the politician is only a professional sharper and sneakthief. A clergyman, too, begins to shrink and shrivel on analysis; the work he does in the world is basically almost indistinguishable from that of an astrologer, a witch-doctor or a fortune-teller. He pretends falsely that he can get sinners out of hell, and collects money from them on that promise, tacit or express. If he had to go before a jury with that pretension it would probably go hard with him. But we do not send him before a jury; we grant him his hocus-pocus on the ground that it is necessary to his office, and that his office is necessary to civilization, so-called. I pass over the journalist delicately; the time has not come to turn State's evidence. Suffice it to say that he, too, would probably wither under a stiff cross-examination. If he is no murderer, like the soldier, then he is at least a sharper and swindler, like the politician.

What I plead for, if I may borrow a term in disrepute, is simply *Realpolitik*, i. e., realism in politics. I can imagine a political campaign purged of all the current false assumptions and false pretenses—a campaign in which, on election day, the voters went to the polls clearly informed that the choice between them was not between an angel and a devil, a good man and a bad man, an altruist and a go-getter, but between two frank go-getters, the one, perhaps, excelling at beautiful and nonsensical words and the other at silent and prehensile deeds—the one a chautauqua orator and the other a porch-climber. There would be, in that choice, something candid, free and exhilarating. Buncombe would be adjourned. The voter would make his selection in the full knowledge of all the facts, as he makes his selection between two heads of cabbage, or two evening papers, or two brands of chewing tobacco. Today he chooses his rulers as he buys bootleg whiskey, never knowing precisely what he is getting, only certain that it is not what it pretends to be. The Scotch may turn out to be wood alcohol or it may turn out to be gasoline; in either case it is not Scotch. How much better if it were plainly labelled, for wood alcohol and gasoline both have their uses—higher uses, indeed, than Scotch. The danger is that the swindled and poisoned consumer, despairing of ever avoiding them when he doesn't want them, may prohibit them even when he does want them, and actually enforce his own prohibition. The danger is that the hopeless voter, forever victimized by his false assumption about politicians, may in the end gather such ferocious indignation that he will abolish them teetotally and at one insane swoop, and so cause government by the people, for the people and with the people to perish from this earth.

1. Construct a brief outline of Mencken's central points (three or four sentences). How are his character sketches of clergymen, policemen and politicians all related to these central logical points?
2. Why does Mencken begin with a discussion of clergymen and policemen? What are the ways in which Mencken makes a transition from clergymen to policemen to politicians?
3. What is the focus of Mencken's essay? Does he concentrate on the traits of public servants or on the nature of hypocrisy? How do you know this?
4. What is Mencken's point of view in this essay (concentrate on the first three paragraphs)? Is he approaching his subject as judge, as participant (remember that he includes journalists in his list of characters), or as observer?
5. What techniques does Mencken use to shock his reader into attending to, if not agreeing with, his characterization of politicians?
6. Instead of relying on descriptive details as Pearce does, Mencken continually employs overstatement in his portrait of a class of people. How are these strategies similar?

"Encountering Frost"/*Roger Kahn*

The following character study results from an interview Roger Kahn conducted with poet Robert Frost in his Vermont retreat. The encounter was an informal one, and the language of the essay is also informal. Rather than reproducing the questions and answers of the interview, Kahn has chosen to synthesize Frost's words, gestures, and surroundings into a three dimensional portrait. He summarizes material where it seems expedient, quotes Frost's words where appropriate, and pays particular attention to the facial expressions and tones of voice that accompany each response. The result is an intimate and full portrait, one in which the readers are invited to share the whole experience of the author's meeting with Frost, not just a distilled transcript of the verbal exchange.

Roger Kahn gives depth to this portrait not by revealing a series of expanded anecdotes, but by exhibiting Frost's own voice and manner in a precisely described setting. The correspondence of the writer's gently entreating voice—"come with me"—with the sound of Frost's playfully firm voice reinforces our feeling of intimacy and Kahn's informal but persistent focus on the man Frost. Throughout the essay we are made aware that he is a writer, and that our interest in the man derives initially from this fact. But by expanding the interview to reveal Frost's interest in everything from sports to politics and religion, Kahn gives his portrait fullness. This strategy for conveying a sense of fullness while keeping Frost the *poet* in the foreground is one of Kahn's strongest techniques, one well worth emulating in your own character sketch.

To find Robert Frost, the great poet who wrote so fondly of New Hampshire, one drove deep into the Green Mountains of Vermont. The paradox amused Mr. Frost. It made his green eyes twinkle and moved him to soft laughter. Beyond his eighty-fifth birthday, Frost wore the seasons lightly and humor ran strong and young within him.

If America anointed Poets Laureate, Robert Frost, of course, would have been chosen. His poems won him four Pulitzer prizes, a special Congressional medal and, more important, earned for him and the craft of poetry the admiration of millions who found Pound, Stevens, Eliot, obscure and puzzling.

"I never like to read anyone who seems to be saying, 'Let's see you understand this, you damn fool,' " Frost said. "I haven't any of that spirit and I don't like to be treated with that spirit." The spirit Frost did possess, scholarly, independent, questioning, sage, reached out, a golden beacon across an uncertain land.

What sort of talk did one hear on paying Frost a visit? Talk about poetry, to be sure; good talk that stirred the mind. But more than that, one heard about scores of other things: Fidel Castro's revolution and John Thomas' high jumping; the feel of farming and the sight of beatniks; loneliness and love and religion and Russia, and how important it is for a man to know how to live poor. Somewhat sadly, too, one heard about the Boston Red Sox. Frost rooted for the Red Sox, but cheerlessly. He felt that they played baseball in the manner of Boston gentlemen and, although Frost appreciated Boston gentlemen in their place, he did not feel that their place is on a ball field. "Spike 'em as you go around the bases," he suggested.

Frost was not a poet by accident, and much of what one heard came in phrases which, like his poems, were vivid and exciting. It was not surprising to find here such sure command of English, but what may surprise you is the freshness with which the patriarchal Frost looked at the world. He once wrote:

I never dared be radical when young
For fear it would make me conservative when old.

At eighty-six he was neither radical nor conservative. He was simply Robert Frost, one man unique in his time and in ours.

Come with me then backward in time to the year 1960 on a cool, pleasant afternoon when Vermont summer is changing into fall. The route, up from the south, leads past mountains and farmland almost into Middlebury, the college town. Then you turn off the main highway into a side road that runs through the village of Ripton and, for a time, follows the course of a swift-running stream. A few miles beyond Ripton, approaching a spine of the Green Mountains, you turn down a dirt road, and when the dirt road stops, you get out of the car and walk up to the brow of a hill. There, in an unpretentious house of weathered timber, Frost lives by himself.

Two old friends, Mr. and Mrs. Theodore Morrison, occupy a large farmhouse at the bottom of the hill. Morrison is a novelist and a member of the English faculty at Harvard. Mrs. Morrison is unofficial secretary to Frost, handling his correspondence, screening visitors, helping the poet with such mundane matters as income-tax returns. The Ripton farm is Frost's home from May until October. During the winter he lives by himself at Cambridge, Massachusetts, when he is not traveling to recite and talk about poetry.

"Are you going to use a tape recorder?" Mrs. Morrison asked in the farmhouse. She is a sprightly, cultured lady who has been close to, and perhaps suffered, writers for most of her life.

"No, I thought I'd set up my typewriter and just type as he talks."

"Good," Mrs. Morrison said. "He's had a lot to do with tape recorders, and he doesn't like them very much. He feels they make one watch every word, make every word permanent, whether it's really meant to be permanent or not. Come. Let's start up the hill."

Entering Frost's home, one walks into a small, screened porch. The porch leads to a rectangular living room, with a stone fireplace in one long wall and a window, opening onto the countryside, opposite. Above the hearth, two red roses sat in tiny vases. "We're here," Mrs. Morrison called.

Frost emerged from the bedroom, walking very straight, and shook hands firmly. He was wearing blue slacks, a gray sweater and a white shirt, open at the throat. He is not tall, perhaps five feet seven, but his body is strong and solid as one might expect in a man who has spent years behind a plow. His hair, once red, is white and luxuriant. His face, with its broad nose and resolute chin, is marked by time, but firm. It is a memorable face, mixing as it does strength and sensitivity.

"No tape recorder," Mrs. Morrison said.

"Good," Frost said. "Very good."

Mrs. Morrison helped set up my typewriter on a table she uses when taking dictation and excused herself. The poet walked to one of two large chairs in the room and motioned for me to sit in the other. "You're a journalist?" Frost asked.

"Yes, mostly. I write a few other things, too."

"Nearly everybody has two lives," Frost said, smiling. "Poets, sculptors. Nearly everybody has to lead two lives at the least."

"What life have you been leading recently?" I asked. "What have you been doing?"

"I never am doing anything, really," Frost said, "and I can't talk about my plans until I see how the plans work out. If I were writing a novel or an epic, I could tell you what I've been doing, but I don't write novels or epics.

"I don't have any routine," Frost said. "I don't have any hours. I don't have any desk. I don't have any letter business with people, except I dictate one once in a while. Lectures? Lecture is the wrong word. I'm going to about twenty or twenty-five places from here to California, but lecture is the wrong word. I talk, and then I read. I never wrote out a lecture in my life. I never wrote a review, never a word of criticism. I've possibly written a dozen essays, but no more. You couldn't call mine a literary life." Frost chuckled and gestured at the typewriter.

"You use that thing pretty well," he said.

"Thanks," I said.

"Never learned to type, myself," Frost said.

"The world," I said. "Khrushchev and Castro—what do you think about what the world's been doing lately?"

"I wonder," Frost said, "if God hasn't looked down and turned away and said, 'Boys, this isn't for me. You go ahead and fight it out with knives and bombs.' ". . .

There are two bookcases in Frost's living room, and on the window seat between our chairs books rested in three small stacks. His recent reading ranged from Latin poetry to a work about contemporary architecture. But the room was not overrun with books. The average publishing-house editor lives among more books than does Robert Frost.

"We came to southern New Hampshire after my father died," Frost said. "I escaped school until I was twelve. I'd try it for a week, and then the doctor would take me out. They never knew what the matter was, but I seemed to be ailing. I got so I never wanted to see school. The first time I liked it was in New Hampshire. I liked the noon hour and the recess. I didn't want to miss what went on then, and so I became interested in the rest of it, the studies.

"It was a little country school. There was no grading. I could go as fast as I wanted, and I made up the whole eight years in a year and a half without realizing I was doing it. Then they sent me down to Lawrence [Massachusetts] to live with my grandfather and go to the high school where my father had gone. It was just the luck of that year in the country, that country school. Otherwise, I might not have made it.

"In high school I had only Greek, Latin and mathematics. I began to write in my second year, but not for any teacher. There were no English teachers. We had an active school magazine that the teachers had nothing to do with. I must have been reading Prescott's *Conquest of Mexico,* because my first poem was a ballad about the night the Indians fought Cortez. People say, 'You were interested in Indians the way children are interested in cops and robbers.' But it wasn't that way at all. I was interested in Indians because of the wrongs done to them. I was wishing the Indians would win all the battles.

"The magazine would surprise you if you saw it. We did it for pleasure. When they do it nowadays, they have teachers, and that spoils the whole thing. They say, 'I can't finish this, teacher, help me.' That spoils it. We had poems, stories, editorials, and we did it all ourselves. I edited the magazine the last year, and I had eighteen assistant editors. One day I got mad at them. They weren't giving me enough material. I got sore and went down to the printing room, and in a day or two I wrote the whole damn thing. I wrote it all. I even made up a story about the debating union and wrote the whole debate. I wrote it all, the whole thing, then I resigned." Frost smiled at me as he remembered something he had done seventy years before of which he was still proud.

"Dartmouth is my chief college," he said, "the first one I ran away from. I ran from Harvard later, but Dartmouth first. In a little library at Dartmouth I saw a magazine, and on the front page there was a poem. There was an editorial inside about the poem, so evidently that magazine was in favor of poetry. I sent them a poem, "My Butterfly." It's in the big collection. They bought it so easily I thought I could make a living this way, but I didn't keep selling 'em as fast as that. The magazine was called the *New York Independent,* and after they bought the poem they asked that when I sent them more, would I please spell the name of the magazine correctly. I'd made a mistake, but they bought my poem.

"When I told Grandfather Frost I wanted to be a poet, he wasn't pleased. He was an old-line Democrat, the devil take the hindmost, and here I was, making good grades, and wanting, he thought, to waste my life. 'I give you one year to make it, Rob,' he said. I put on an auctioneer's voice. 'I'm offered one, give me twenty, give me twenty, give me twenty,' I said. My grandfather never brought up poetry again."

Frost married Elinor White, his co-valedictorian at Lawrence High, in 1895, and set about rearing a family and dividing his life among poetry, teaching and farming. "I had to find other means than poems," he said. "They didn't sell fast enough, and I didn't send my poems out much. Oh, I wanted them to want my poems. Some say, 'Do you write for yourself entirely?' 'You mean into the wastebasket?' I say. But I had pride there. I hated rejection slips. I had to be very careful of my pride. Love me little, love me long. Did you hear that? Were you brought up on that? Love me little, love me long." Frost smiled. "But not too little," he said.

He placed a hand before his eyes again. "One of the most sociable virtues or vices is that you don't want to feel queer. You don't want to be too much like the others, but you don't want to be clear out in nowhere. 'She mocked 'em and she shocked 'em and she said she didn't care.' You like to mock 'em and to shock 'em, but you really do care.

"You are always with your sorrows and your cares. What's a poem for if not to share them with others? But I don't like poems that are too crudely personal. The boy writes that the girl has jilted him, and I know who the boy is and who the girl is, and I don't want to know. Where can you be personal and not in bad taste? In poetry, but you have to be careful. If anybody tries to make you say more—they have to stop where you stop.

" 'What does this poem mean?' some ask.

" 'It means what it says.'

" 'I know what it means to me, but I don't know just what it means to you,' they say.

" 'Maybe I don't want you to.' "

Frost was sitting back comfortably, his mind at work. "We have all sorts of ways to hold people," he said. "Hold them and hold them off. Do you know what the sun does with the planets? It holds them and holds them off. The planets don't fall away from the sun, and they don't fall into it. That's one of the marvels. Attraction and repulsion. You have that with poetry, and you have that with friendships.". . .

In many of Frost's poems, loneliness is a strong theme. His wife died in 1938, and only two of his five children survive. I wondered how he had come to terms with solitude.

"In the big newspaper office," Frost said, "where everyone sits alongside the other and writes—I couldn't do that. Even reading. I've got to be totally absorbed when I read. Where there are other people reading, too, I don't feel very happy.

"Alone you take all your traits as if you were bringing 'em to market. You bring them from the quiet of the garden. But the garden is not the marketplace. That's a big trouble to some: how you mix living with people with not living with people; how you mix the garden with the marketplace.

"I like the quiet here, but I like to have a big audience for my talks, to have a few turned away. I like to feel all that warmth in the room. At Kansas City once they told me, 'You see that hazy look down the end of the hall. That's whiskers. Them's beatniks.' They came and I wish 'em well, but I do like some form in the things that I read."

Suddenly Frost sat up straight. "I'm sorry I can't entertain you," he said. "I'm not set up here for that sort of thing."

He meant drinks, and I asked if he took a drink himself.

"A daiquiri once in a while," he said, "but not much, and not serious. I don't care for those parties where everyone does. They take just a little too much, and they say just a little too much. I've always been shy. I get uncomfortable."

Outside in the late-afternoon sun, the grass looked bright and fresh. "Used to play softball out past there," Frost said. "I pitched. They don't let me do all the things I want to any more, but if we had a ball, I'd pitch to you a little, and I'd surprise you." He grinned.

"You like sports?"

"Oh, yes," he said. "You get a certain glory out of being translated, but no, no, it doesn't work. So much is lost. There are other arts that are international. Boxing, and high jumping seven feet two inches. Anyone can understand that. Just think of that boy from Boston [John Thomas] going right up in the air higher than anybody but a basketball player."

Then we were serious again, and I asked about another strong theme in Frost's work, the theme of God. "Don't make me out to be a religious man," Frost said. "Don't make me out to be a man who has all the answers. I don't go around preaching God. I'm not a minister. I'm always pleased when I see people comfortable with these things. There's a rabbi near here, a friend of mine, who preaches in Cincinnati in the winter. He talks at the Methodist church here sometimes and tells the people in Cincinnati that he's a summer Methodist.

"People have wondered about him at the Methodist church. One lady was troubled and said to me, 'How do they differ from us?'

" 'What you got there on that table?' I said.

" 'That's a Bible,' she said.

"I didn't say any more.

" 'Oh,' she said. 'Oh, the Old Testament. Why can't you have a Jew in church?' she said, and she understood."

Frost's voice was strong. "There's a good deal of God in everything you do," he said. "It's like climbing up a ladder, and the ladder rests on nothing, and you climb higher and higher and you feel there must be God at the top. It can't be unsupported up there. I'd be afraid, though, of any one religion being the whole thing in one country, because there would probably come a day when they would take me down to the cellar and torture me—just for my own good."

He smiled briefly. "There is more religion outside church than in,"

Frost said, "more love outside marriage than in, more poetry outside verse than in. Everyone knows there is more love outside the institutions than in, and yet I'm kind of an institutional man."

We turned back to poetry then. "They ask me if I have a favorite," Frost said, "but if a mother has a favorite child, she has to hide it from herself, so I can't tell you if I have a favorite, no."

"Is there one basic point to all fine poetry?" I asked.

"The phrase," Frost said slowly, clearly, "and what do I mean by a phrase? A clutch of words that gives you a clutch at the heart."

His own phrases, his own words, were all about me in the little house. Afternoon was fading, and I realized how much we had discussed; and how Frost had ranged from the profound to the simple, as his own life, which seems so simple, has in reality been so profound. I remembered his poems, too.

Some summing up seemed in order and, for want of a better term, I intended to say that this visit had brought me into the presence of greatness. "I feel as though—" I began.

"Now, none of that," Frost said, anticipating. "We've had a fine talk together, haven't we? And we've talked to some purpose. Come now, and I'll walk with you down the hill." He got up from his chair and started out the door and down the steep path, pausing to look at the sunset as he went.

1. What purpose do the incidental descriptions (Frost's dress, the countryside) serve in this essay? How does Kahn make them an integral part of this encounter with Frost?

2. Kahn varies his essay by summarizing some of Frost's comments and reproducing others. What is the proportion of summary to quotation? Is it an effective balance? Why?

3. How would you assess Kahn's performance as an interviewer? Does he ask important questions? Does he allow himself to be led by the subject's responses?

4. The interview was obviously a far-reaching one, touching on poetic theory, politics, sports, religion, and personal history. How does Kahn unify his diverse material in turning it into a character sketch? Is all of the material essential to the portrait he is attempting to construct?

5. What similarities exist between Frost's phrasing in answering the questions and Kahn's phrasing in setting up the essay? How do you account for these similarities?

6. What is Kahn's intention in writing this essay? Does he want his readers to go out and buy Frost's books of poems? Does he want them to observe the difference between Frost's role as *poet* and his role as genteel old man? Does he merely want to entertain them with a lively account of an admirable man?

SUGGESTIONS FOR WRITING

1. Examine a person very close to you. Starting with a brief description of that person, define some area of his or her personality that still intrigues or disturbs you. Choose details and anecdotes from your subject's life that shed light on this peculiarity and try to discover its source.

2. Reveal the character or "being" of an unassuming, uncharismatic person by showing that person *within* his or her world (for example, a night janitor in a lonely building, a typist in a typing pool, a truck driver on the open road). What is the significant relationship between the person and his or her work and/or environment?

3. Examine a person in public life (a politician, rock singer, professional athlete). Choose one of the following perspectives:

    a. His contribution to the profession practiced. (Is her music innovative? Has he made race car driving a safer sport?)

    b. The effect of personal idiosyncracies, political views and private life on his public career.

    c. His attempts to maintain a private world that exists apart from the public arena.

4. Examine a particular group of people (hippies, rednecks, homosexuals). What is and is not characteristic of this group? How do you account for these characteristics? One way of getting into this kind of essay is to focus on one or two members of the group, examining their views, and then to move to generalizations about the *kind* of people they represent.

5. Conduct an interview of a "campus character." Do not reproduce the interview verbatim, but construct a character analysis from it. As you conduct the interview, be aware of nonverbal communication and note it. Then listen to or read the interview several times, watching for a central theme. Using this theme, decide which material to delete from the essay and which to incorporate.

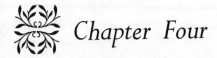 *Chapter Four*

Writing About
Your Culture

INTRODUCTION

1. HOW DO YOU ANALYZE CULTURE?

By now you've become accustomed to using language to elaborate your experience rather than to close it off. You have been using writing to discover and explore your feelings and perceptions rather than merely to reinforce prejudices about yourself: "I was just born lazy I guess," or about the people around you: "If he's religious, he must be easily led." In using language to analyze, to clarify your perceptions of yourself and the people you meet every day, you have also found that certain techniques are useful, such as the ability to isolate and identify distinct aspects of experience, or the ability to correlate specific observations with important ideas about personality. We are, of course, still concerned with seeing these things. But in this chapter we are going to ask you to broaden your concern with yourself and others and to explore a third, more inclusive category—culture.

This word may immediately conjure up visions for you of haughty, mink-coated matrons leaning on the arms of penguin-like men strutting into the opera. But culture is really more than this caricatured picture: it is something we all share; it doesn't confine itself to a special time, place, or class of people. In fact, culture is inescapable, for it is anything that people create and pass on to the next generation: artifacts, including everything from opera to knives and forks; ideas, such as freedom and justice; and institutions, such as religion and law. In its largest sense, culture is what distinguishes humans from the animals.

One of the most important aspects of culture is language itself. Language is so much the matrix of our experience that we rarely ever think of it as of human origin, as symbolic, or as depending on a set of rules. For example, because we generally don't think of language as a cultural artifact, we assume that all dogs go "woof-woof," "bow-wow," and "arf-arf" as they do in English. But German dogs go "wau-wau"; Chinese dogs, "wang-wang"; Japanese dogs, "wan-wan"; and Yiddish dogs, "how-how." And an American duck would certainly be surprised to hear the German frog, who croaks, "quak-quak." It is almost as hard for us to become conscious of our own language, and *all* such pervasive aspects of our culture, as it would be for a fish to become conscious of the water it swims in.

Yet, if we are to begin to analyze culture, a relatively detached point of view is necessary. We can never exist *totally* outside our culture, just as the fish cannot exist for long out of water. But because we have the power of imagination, we can imagine ourselves outside of a *particular* aspect of our culture. For example, you may enjoy participating in the frenzied sound of a rock festival, but you can also imagine yourself outside the event, viewing it *as if* you were not part of it. It may be more difficult, but similarly, with practice and persistence you can imagine yourself looking at your own religion as if it were something apart from you. Likewise, although sexuality is not a cultural object in itself, the various ways of handling one's sexuality are aspects of culture, and can be examined objectively as artificial constructs.

A point of view which places you outside of the aspect of culture you want to study allows you to ask probing (even disturbing) questions about your subject, about the rock music you couldn't live without, the institution of government, church or school which you can never remember not being part of, or the relationship between male and female that sometimes seems like a frustrating game. If, for example, you wish to analyze your own religion, you could begin by pretending you are an atheist. Then, imagine what aspects of religion, from this perspective, would stand out or look strange. This imaginative act will produce questions such as: "Why do priests and rabbis pray?" "Why do Catholics kneel before the cross?" "Why do Jews cover their heads in the temple?" "Why is (or isn't) Jesus special?" These questions lead to further, more generally applicable ones: "What is the cause of religion?" "When did religion first arise?" "What are the effects of religion?" The purpose of these questions is to reveal the basic assumptions that support religion. It is, most likely, one of these inclusive questions that will become the focus or limiting concern of your analysis. It will determine what aspects of religion you select for further study, and what details about religious practice you present in writing.

"So," you ask, "I've found and focused on my main question, but how do I develop it?" You do this by returning to and evaluating the concrete manifestations of your chosen aspect of culture. This doesn't mean that you have to analyze every facet of your subject (although a general awareness of the whole institution or practice is necessary), only that you must examine all the parts that are relevant to your focus and point of view. For example, we wouldn't normally think of the cafeteria or the restrooms as being parts of higher education, but notice how revealing these selected details become in Jerry Farber's essay, "The Student as Nigger":

> At Cal State L.A., . . . the students have separate and unequal dining facilities. If I take them into the faculty dining room, my colleagues get uncomfortable, as though there were a bad smell. If I eat in the student cafeteria, I become known as the educational equivalent of a niggerlover. In at least one building there are even rest rooms which students may not use.

Farber has examined specific practices that contribute to the general question of why students are second class citizens.

The process of moving from your central question to the material that inspired it in the first place, and that has the potential to answer it, involves a concern we have been discussing since Chapter One: the viable relationship between concrete details and abstract ideas. As you examine your material, answers to your question will begin to suggest themselves. For example, if you ponder the effects of religion, you will probably begin to observe the behavior of religious people very closely. You may conclude from this observation that, on the one hand, religious people tend to be kinder than atheists to persons in physical or emotional need, but, on the other hand, they are often intolerant of doctrines different from their own. As these discoveries occur, they will send you back to your material to look for additional answers and to collect reinforcements for the ones you have already defined.

Eventually, a general consensus should emerge from your solutions. To go back to our example of the effects of religion, you may eventually be led to conclude that the institutionalizing of religion restricts and "programs" the basic impulses of its believers, thus engendering intolerance and hypocrisy. Once you have arrived at this consensus, you have discovered your theme or controlling idea and can decide what you want your readers to think and feel about it. (This intention has, of course, been formulating all along.) Do you intend for them to be enraged by the hypocrisy of religious people, or do you want them to understand in a sympathetic fashion that no ideal can exist in its pure form?

Once you know where your analysis is going, what main ideas and specific observations are essential to an understanding of your chosen aspect of culture, you are ready to consider the best means of presenting this understanding to your audience.

2. HOW IS ANALYSIS OF CULTURE RELATED TO ARGUMENT?

As you have seen above, the process of analyzing culture is not substantially different from the process of analyzing yourself and others. But because culture is more inclusive than the other two categories, and because our reactions to it are more speculative (you are continually forced to comment on groups of people and their beliefs rather than on a single, closely observed person), your study of culture will need to be more systematic in procedure and in presentation than your study of yourself and of another person. We have been considering a procedure for analyzing culture which involves: 1. an initial detachment from your subject; 2. a careful questioning and examination of your material; and 3. a gradual extraction of general ideas from your observations.

But what about the presentation of these conclusions—what is important there? Many times in your college and professional life you are going to be asked to present an *argument* for or against a certain idea. Arguing well is a useful skill, one that incorporates all the writing elements we have been dealing with but that incorporates them within a tightly organized pattern of logic whose purpose is to persuade the readers. At the point where you are examining various aspects of your culture, it is appropriate to take up the nature of argument. The basic ideas and institutions that govern society are concerns that involve and affect your readers every bit as much as they do you. To be able to make them see and understand your observations about culture are to make them become more knowledgeable about the forces they must contend with everyday. Thus, your ability to sound reasonable to your audience, to convince them that you are correct, is particularly important here.

3. HOW DO YOU WRITE A CONVINCING ARGUMENT?

The proper Lady Bracknell, in a play by Oscar Wilde, openly condemns argument: "I dislike arguments of any kind. They are always vulgar, and often convincing." She is amusing, but not very accurate. A carefully considered and reasoned argument is one in which you, as writer, seek the common ground between you and your audience, and support your ideas by a logical presentation of evidence. True, some arguments seem to have a vulgar urgency about them, but these are usually lopsided presentations. Writing a balanced argument demands consideration of four basic elements: 1. your *proposition*, the answer to the question that is central to your analysis (we have been calling this main idea the theme; in argument, however, it is referred to as proposition); 2. the *reasons* why your proposition is true, including concrete evidence and the refutation of opposing points; 3. the *implications* of your case, a summary of the main effects of your proven proposition; and 4. the *voice* of your arguments, which involves the language you choose to fulfill your intention toward the audience. (If you want your readers to be morally outraged by a particular political practice, you will describe it in vivid, disparaging terms, but if you only want them to see that it is too expensive, you will use concise statistical language.)

DISCOVERING YOUR PROPOSITION

Your argument will be the development of a single idea, called the proposition or thesis, which answers a particular question about the nature of the aspect of culture you have analyzed. It may arise from a question concerning your relationship to that culture, such as: "How should I react to an unjust law?" "What should my attitude toward religion be?" "What should my relationship to the opposite sex be?" In any case, your essay is not a report, in which you merely describe the history or the facts surrounding a cultural phenomenon, but is instead a presentation of a conclusion that arises from your observation and analysis of relevant facts.

This conclusion or proposition will be the controlling idea for your whole essay. That is, everything in your essay will be subordinated to one aim, proving that your single proposition is true. Consequently, it is extremely important to narrow your subject at the outset. Instead of arguing that all unjust laws must be disobeyed, for example, focus on one law which you can make a case against, showing that your argument holds universally.

MUSTERING YOUR REASONS

Once you've discovered your proposition, you must present the reasons why you believe your proposition to be true. This demands that you produce evidence supporting your conclusion, fact or testimony. In some cases, statistics, examples, or reports may be the most relevant facts. Often, the opinion of the "man on the street" will hold weight, or the testimony of an expert, such as a scientist, but in most cases your argument will draw on both facts and testimonies in an effort to be convincing.

Yet you will also have to organize logically your evidence. Logical reasoning is compelling in argument because it underlies the three fundamental ways in which we reflect on issues and solve practical problems: deductively, inductively, and analogically. These are simply names for recurrent structures of thought, which you can use to shape your argument.

Deductive argument moves from the conclusions to the evidence. It usually begins with a statement that you believe in strongly and assume would get general assent from your audience. You then use this statement to get to other less abstract ones, which your audience is forced into accepting if they have already agreed to your first statement. For example, early in Martin Luther King, Jr.'s letter to his fellow clergymen in defense of his nonviolent actions, which they had called "unwise and untimely," he states: "I would agree with St. Augustine that 'an unjust law is no law at all,'" and thus doesn't require obedience. This is the major statement or premise which he assumes most fair thinking people would agree with. He lays this down and carefully defines his terms; a "just law" is "any law that uplifts human personality," and an "unjust law" is "any law that degrades human personality." Now, he moves to the particular laws, the "segregation ordinances," illustrating their effect and maintaining that since these laws don't uplift the human personality, they are "unjust" and don't need to be obeyed. Deductively, this display of evidence and application of principles follows logically from King's first statement.

The structure of an *inductive argument* moves in the reverse direction, from the evidence to the proposition. In a deductive argument our attention is drawn to the definition of terms, and the validity of the premises, but inductive argument focuses our attention primarily on the facts of our experience. We are reasoning inductively whenever we begin with specific facts, pile them up, and imply that if something has been observed to be true in a hundred cases then it will be true in the one hundred and first case. Because we have a number of examples, such as our friend's kneeling in prayer on the sidewalk in the middle of town, his shouting obscenities from the top of the English building, his dancing in the aisle of the bus on the way to school, his continual disruption of class with shouts of "the horror," "the horror," "the horror," and his insistence on wearing only a purple T-shirt and sneakers, we are justified in concluding that our friend is "acting strangely." That is, on the basis of our experience of particular facts, we form a generalization or proposition.

An *argument by analogy* doesn't move from the concrete to the abstract or vice versa, but in parallel motion; it always compares, asserting that *this* is like *that*. "Your going into the dean's office is like entering the lion's den." In our everyday arguments we use this method constantly because of its tendency to concrete imagery and succinctness. This is why it's commonly the basis for many folk expressions. Having trouble understanding how fast that football player is going? He's as "quick as a hiccup." Trying to convince your friend that it's dark? "It's darker in here than in a bull's belly with his tail shut down." You don't understand how quiet your friend is? He's "as quiet as a mosquito doing push-ups on a lemon meringue pie." You may be thinking that this is far removed from formal argument, but it follows the same logical structure. If you can convince your reader that United States involvement in Vietnam was parallel to Russian involvement in Hungary, then you've made a substantial point about American political motives.

But the evidence of fact and testimony, as well as the force of logic are never sufficient by themselves. You must also anticipate and refute opposing arguments. An attempt to prove that capital punishment should be abolished in all forms will fail unless you anticipate the counterargument that a decrease in crime occurs where capital punishment prevails, and refute the statistics that allegedly support this point. You could do this in many ways, including a flat denial in which you hope your reader will take your word over that of your opponent's. A direct retort, a presentation of your own statistics proving your proposition, however, would probably be more effective. Equally compelling would be to show that your opponent is intentionally or unintentionally deceitful in taking statistics out of context, or that the statistics are ambiguous and open to diverse interpretations, or that the authority of the social scientist who gathered the data is unreliable, or that the figures are simply ridiculous because they are irrelevant to the actual proposition in question. But the most forceful refutation is to find a weakness in your opponent's logic or to make a distinction, for example, between two basic definitions of capital punishment, and show that your opponent is arguing against the one which you are making no effort to defend.

DRAWING YOUR IMPLICATIONS

The conclusion of your attempt to convince should point your readers back to the original proposition and forward to the implications of your proven case. You can reinforce your main points here, and review the original question with its answer. But this is also the place to remind your readers of the consequences of their acceptance or rejection of your proposition. These consequences may be emotional, such as the feeling that they are doing the *right* thing by agreeing with you, that by giving assent to your argument against capital punishment, they are doing their part to ensure that no innocent man goes to his death by "legal" means. But remember that your delineation of implications is your last appeal to the readers. It is usually wise to make a final attempt to show them that they have a personal stake in the truth of your argument—for example, that they themselves might someday be in the need of pardon or reprieve.

CHOOSING YOUR VOICE

An important and continuous concern in writing an argument is how you, as writer, want to "sound" to your readers. In the argumentative situation, no less than in any writing, you must choose your intention as well as your proposition. Of course, your primary purpose here is to convince your audience to accept a particular answer to a question you have raised. But you must decide, further, whether you want to checkmate your readers, ruthlessly cutting off all escape, or to gain their admiration and generous approval. A decision one way or the other will determine how you phrase and qualify your proposition; it will determine the kind of language you employ to make this appeal to your audience. The way you phrase yourself, the way you sound to your audience, is what we call tone of voice.

To get a clearer idea of the relationship between the voice you project and your audience, let's examine for a moment perhaps the simplest kind of argument, an advertisement, such as the one shown on the next page. The purpose of this ad, of course, is to convince us to accept the proposition that Excedrin is more effective than regular aspirin. And its argument depends almost totally on skillful adaptation of voice to assumed audience.

"There's no room in my schedule for a headache."

"So when a headache comes along, I take two Excedrin and keep on going.
Sure, I've tried regular aspirin. But for me, Excedrin does a better job.
I've heard about two medical studies on pain, at a major hospital and a university medical center, where the doctors also found Excedrin was superior to the regular aspirin tablet.
I can see why Excedrin is known as the extra-strength pain reliever."

Significantly more effective than the regular aspirin tablet in two medical studies.

Excedrin

Excedrin

Excedrin

"For me, Excedrin works better than regular aspirin."

EXCEDRIN is a registered trademark of Bristol-Myers Company.

Our attention is immediately caught by the stylishly dressed woman staring intensely at us from the center of the page, a woman who clearly takes herself very seriously. She clasps her hands in well-meaning sincerity, as if she were just about to announce to us that in her professional opinion we should see a psychiatrist. And it's not only her demeanor that demands we take her seriously, it's her surroundings as well. From the art objects in the background, we infer that she has cultivated tastes, and from the photographs in the foreground, we are meant to infer that she has a job that requires creativity and responsible judgment.

We may not know for sure whether she is a film or magazine editor, or museum curator, but we do know that she is a "professional." Reinforcing this impression is the sound of her voice stating prominently: "There's no room in my schedule for a headache." It's a forceful voice because she's a busy, active woman determined to "keep on going." Despite her schedule, she's also well-informed, having heard about two medical studies, and yet she's not dogmatic. For she would never say flatly that "Excedrin works better than regular aspirin"; she's an open-minded woman and so must qualify, saying, "For me . . . ." (Clearly, point of view is closely connected with the voice of an argument.)

Her voice, given added credibility by her picture, inspires us with confidence. The strategy of the argument depends on our imaginatively accepting her voice as our own, replacing the image we have of our own voice with that of hers. Given this acceptance and assuming the writer's skill, we can infer the audience for which this ad is intended. Like this woman, the people in her audience want to view themselves as stylish, cultivated, creative, responsible, and certainly professional; in short, the kind of people who are taken seriously. This could perhaps describe the desires of an audience who read a magazine such as *Esquire,* but is this woman, in her dress and voice, trying to appeal primarily to the readers of such a magazine? The readers of *Playboy* then? Maybe *Vogue*? No, as you may have guessed, this rather insistent voice, with its relatively new image, is intended for readers of *Ms.* magazine.

Your arguments will, of course, be more complex than the one here, and choosing your voice will depend on more than assessing the life style of the audience. But you can see that taking into account the sound of your voice is crucial to your success, for it also leads to a determined effort to find common ground between you and your audience.

You will not be convincing if your audience feels threatened by your tone of voice, or cut off from the world of experience that you appear to be part of. Some men, for example, may feel sexually threatened by the business-like seriousness of the woman in the ad, and similarly some women may feel insecure in being forced to face someone who is so sure of herself that she is obviously not trying to ingratiate herself with a primarily male audience. As a result, like the writer of this ad, you should search for the common ground of shared knowledge, values, or social relationships between you and your audience. Clearly, people who value art, hard work, and independence are going to respond to this ad more readily than those who don't.

A GAME

Make up an ad to appear in a specific current magazine, including picture (described, cut out, or roughly sketched) and text, which sells a preposterous product, such as a left-handed monkey wrench. Lay it out exactly as you would want it to appear in the magazine. Bring these to class and discuss the impact of the whole and each of its elements—size, placement, and content of the picture and text. After examining the composition of the ad, discuss in detail the voice that the ad projects, and its appropriateness to the audience selected.

In summary, an argument is a tightly organized presentation of a central proposition in which all the other elements of writing are involved: focus, point of view, the relationship of concrete evidence to general ideas, the writers' intention toward an audience, and the voice used to carry it. Such an effort entails: 1. a clear knowledge of your main idea or proposition; 2. a careful and logical presentation of supportive evidence; 3. a clear determination of the consequences the readers will face as a result of accepting or rejecting your proposition, and 4. the adoption of a tone of voice that can best bring your point home to the audience. Look for these elements in the readings that follow, and then try to incorporate them into your own persuasive analysis of culture.

READINGS

"Advice to a Draftee"/*Leo Tolstoy*

"To Fellow Clergymen"/*Martin Luther King, Jr.*

The following letters are addressed to very specific audiences: a young man who has solicited Tolstoy's advice, and a group of colleagues who have opposed King's methods. Both writers are passionately concerned with the moral issues involved, and both hope to persuade their audience; but King is defending himself, while Tolstoy is expounding his beliefs. This difference in intention partially accounts for the different voices we hear in each letter. The relatively personal nature of the relationship between author and audience, on the other hand, accounts for some of the similarities in their attitudes and strategies.

A "letter" assumes certain conventional relationships between writer and audience, so it is revealing to see how Tolstoy and King differ in their handling of this form. You might begin your examination of these two arguments by considering what differences are attributable to the facts that King knew that his letter (which is here incomplete) would be published, while Tolstoy didn't, and that King is risking his life, while Tolstoy isn't.

"Advice to a Draftee"

In my last letter I answered your question as well as I could. It is not only Christians but all just people who must refuse to become soldiers— that is, to be ready on another's command (for this is what a soldier's duty actually consists of) to kill all those one is ordered to kill. The question as you state it—which is more useful, to become a good teacher or to suffer for rejecting conscription?—is falsely stated. The question is falsely stated because it is wrong for us to determine our actions according to their results, to view actions merely as useful or destructive. In the choice of our actions we can be led by their advantages or disadvantages only when the actions themselves are not opposed to the demands of morality.

We can stay home, go abroad, or concern ourselves with farming or science according to what we find useful for ourselves or others; for neither in domestic life, foreign travel, farming, nor science is there anything immoral. But under no circumstance can we inflict violence on people, torture or kill them because we think such acts could be of use to us or to others. We cannot and may not do such things, especially because we can never be sure of the results of our actions. Often actions which seem the most advantageous of all turn out in fact to be destructive; and the reverse is also true.

The question should not be stated: which is more useful to be a good teacher or to go to jail for refusing conscription? but rather: what should a man do who has been called upon for military service—that is, called upon to kill or to prepare himself to kill?

And to this question, for a person who understands the true meaning of military service and who wants to be moral, there is only one clear and incontrovertible answer: such a person must refuse to take part in military service no matter what consequences this refusal may have. It may seem to us that this refusal could be futile or even harmful, and that it would be a far more useful thing, after servicing one's time, to become a good village teacher. But in the same way, Christ could have judged it more useful for himself to be a good carpenter and submit to all the principles of the Pharisees than to die in obscurity as he did, repudiated and forgotten by everyone.

Moral acts are distinguished from all other acts by the fact that they operate independently of any predictable advantage to ourselves or to others. No matter how dangerous the situation may be of a man who finds himself in the power of robbers who demand that he take part in plundering, murder, and rape, a moral person cannot take part. Is not military service the same thing? Is one not required to agree to the deaths of all those one is commanded to kill?

But how can one refuse to do what everyone does, what everyone finds unavoidable and necessary? Or, must one do what no one does and what everyone considers unnecessary or even stupid and bad? No matter how strange it sounds, this strange argument is the main one offered against those moral acts which in our times face you and every other person called up for military service. But this argument is even more incorrect than the one which would make a moral action dependent upon considerations of advantage.

If I, finding myself in a crowd of running people, run with the crowd without knowing where, it is obvious that I have given myself up to mass hysteria; but if by chance I should push my way to the front, or be gifted with sharper sight than the others, or receive information that this crowd was racing to attack human beings and toward its own corruption, would I really not stop and tell the people what might rescue them? Would I go on running and do these things which I knew to be bad and corrupt? This is the situation of every individual called up for military service, if he knows what military service means.

I can well understand that you, a young man full of life, loving and loved by your mother, friends, perhaps a young woman, think with a natural terror about what awaits you if you refuse conscription; and perhaps you will not feel strong enough to bear the consequences of refusal, and knowing your weakness, will submit and become a soldier. I understand completely, and I do not for a moment allow myself to blame you, knowing very well that in your place I might perhaps do the same thing. Only do not say that you did it because it was useful or because everyone does it. If you did it, know that you did wrong.

In every person's life there are moments in which he can know

himself, tell himself who he is, whether he is a man who values his
human dignity above his life or a weak creature who does not know his
dignity and is concerned merely with being useful (chiefly to himself).
This is the situation of a man who goes out to defend his honor in a
duel or a soldier who goes into battle (although here the concepts of life
are wrong). It is the situation of a doctor or a priest called to someone
sick with plague, of a man in a burning house or a sinking ship who must
decide whether to let the weaker go first or shove them aside and save
himself. It is the situation of a man in poverty who accepts or rejects a
bribe. And in our times, it is the situation of a man called to military
service. For a man who knows its significance, the call to the army
is perhaps the only opportunity for him to behave as a morally free
creature and fulfill the highest requirement of his life—or else merely
to keep his advantage in sight like an animal and thus remain slavishly
submissive and servile until humanity becomes degraded and stupid.

For these reasons I answered your question whether one has to refuse
to do military service with a categorical "yes"—if you understand the
meaning of military service (and if you did not understand it then, you
do now) and if you want to behave as a moral person living in our
times must.

Please excuse me if these words are harsh. The subject is so important
that one cannot be careful enough in expressing oneself so as to avoid
false interpretation.

April 7, 1899

1. What voice is established by the word "Advice" in the title?
2. Tolstoy calls his words "harsh" (par. 11); what words is he referring to?
   He is also very conscious of the relationship between his subject and his
   projected voice, saying in the last paragraph: "The subject is so important
   that one cannot be careful enough in expressing oneself." How does this
   attitude affect the structure of the letter? Point to individual sentences or
   paragraphs that show evidence of this concern.
3. What is the primary question Tolstoy seeks to answer? What is his answer?
   What is the purpose of repeating this answer (his proposition) three times?
4. Why does Tolstoy so carefully define "Moral acts" in paragraph five? How
   does he use this definition in the remainder of his argument?
5. What is Tolstoy's principal assumption about the nature of rightness? Why
   is he so concerned to oppose the "useful" as a criterion for morality?
6. How effective are the analogical arguments in paragraphs four, seven, and
   nine? How are they related to each other?

"To Fellow Clergymen"

You express a great deal of anxiety over our willingness to break laws. This is certainly a legitimate concern. Since we so diligently urge people to obey the Supreme Court's decision of 1954 outlawing segregation in the public schools, at first glance it may seem rather paradoxical for us consciously to break laws. One may well ask: "How can you advocate breaking some laws and obeying others?" The answer lies in the fact that there are two types of laws: just and unjust. I would be the first to advocate obeying just laws. One has not only a legal but a moral responsibility to obey just laws. Conversely, one has a moral responsibility to disobey unjust laws. I would agree with St. Augustine that "an unjust law is no law at all."

Now, what is the difference between the two? How does one deter- mine whether a law is just or unjust? A just law is a man-made code that squares with the moral law or the law of God. An unjust law is a code that is out of harmony with the moral law. To put it in the terms of St. Thomas Aquinas: An unjust law is a human law that is not rooted in eternal law and natural law. Any law that uplifts human personality is just. Any law that degrades human personality is unjust. All segregation statutes are unjust because segregation distorts the soul and damages the personality. It gives the segregator a false sense of superiority and the segregated a false sense of inferiority. Segregation, to use the terminology of the Jewish philosopher Martin Buber, substi- tutes an "I–it" relationship for an "I–thou" relationship and ends up relegating persons to the status of things. Hence segregation is not only politically, economically and sociologically unsound, it is morally wrong and sinful. Paul Tillich has said that sin is separation. Is not segregation an existential expression of man's tragic separation, his lawful estrange- ment, his terrible sinfulness? Thus it is that I can urge men to obey the 1954 decision of the Supreme Court, for it is morally right; and I can urge them to disobey segregation ordinances, for they are morally wrong.

Let us consider a more concrete example of just and unjust laws. An unjust law is a code that a numerical or power majority group compels a minority group to obey but does not make binding on itself. This is *difference* made legal. By the same token, a just law is a code that a majority compels a minority to follow and that it is willing to follow itself. This is *sameness* made legal.

Let me give another explanation. A law is unjust if it is inflicted on a minority that, as a result of being denied the right to vote, had no part in enacting or devising the law. Who can say that the legislature of Alabama which set up that state's segregation laws was democratically elected? Throughout Alabama all sorts of devious methods are used to prevent Negroes from becoming registered voters, and there are some counties in which, even though Negroes constitute a majority of the population, not a single Negro is registered. Can any law enacted under such circumstances be considered democratically structured?

Sometimes a law is just on its face and unjust in its application. For instance, I have been arrested on a charge of parading without a permit. Now, there is nothing wrong in having an ordinance which requires a permit for a parade. But such an ordinance becomes unjust when it is used to maintain segregation and to deny citizens the First-Amendment privilege of peaceful assembly and protest.

I hope you are able to see the distinction I am trying to point out. In no sense do I advocate evading or defying the law, as would the rabid segregationist. That would lead to anarchy. One who breaks an unjust law must do so openly, lovingly, and with a willingness to accept the penalty. I submit that an individual who breaks a law that conscience tells him is unjust, and who willingly accepts the penalty of imprisonment in order to arouse the conscience of the community over its injustice, is in reality expressing the highest respect for law.

Of course, there is nothing new about this kind of civil disobedience. It was evidenced sublimely in the refusal of Shadrach, Meshach and Abednego to obey the laws of Nebuchadnezzar, on the ground that a higher moral law was at stake. It was practiced superbly by the early Christians, who were willing to face hungry lions and the excruciating pain of chopping blocks rather than submit to certain unjust laws of the Roman Empire. To a degree, academic freedom is a reality today because Socrates practiced civil disobedience. In our own nation, the the Boston Tea Party represented a massive act of civil disobedience.

We should never forget that everything Adolf Hitler did in Germany was "legal" and everything the Hungarian freedom fighters did in Hungary was "illegal." It was "illegal" to aid and comfort a Jew in Hitler's Germany. Even so, I am sure that, had I lived in Germany at the time, I would have aided and comforted my Jewish brothers. If today I lived in a Communist country where certain principles dear to the Christian faith are suppressed, I would openly advocate disobeying that country's antireligious laws.

I must make two honest confessions to you, my Christian and Jewish brothers. First, I must confess that over the past few years I have been gravely disappointed with the white moderate. I have almost reached the regrettable conclusion that the Negro's great stumbling block in his stride toward freedom is not the White Citizen's Counciler or the Ku Klux Klanner, but the white moderate, who is more devoted to "order" than to justice; who prefers a negative peace which is the absence of tension to a positive peace which is the presence of justice; who constantly says: "I agree with you in the goal you seek, but I cannot agree with your methods of direct action"; who paternalistically believes he can set the timetable for another man's freedom; who lives by a mythical concept of time and who constantly advises the Negro to wait for a "more convenient season." Shallow understanding from people of good will is more frustrating than absolute misunderstanding from people of ill will. Lukewarm acceptance is much more bewildering than outright rejection.

I had hoped that the white moderate would understand that law and order exist for the purpose of establishing justice and that when they fail in this purpose they become the dangerously structured dams that block the flow of social progress. I had hoped that the white moderate would understand that the present tension in the South is a necessary phase of the transition from an obnoxious negative peace, in which the Negro passively accepted his unjust plight, to a substantive and positive peace, in which all men will respect the dignity and worth of human personality. Actually, we who engage in nonviolent direct action are not the creators of tension. We merely bring to the surface the hidden tension that is already alive. We bring it out in the open, where it can be seen and dealt with. Like a boil that can never be cured so long as it is covered up but must be opened with all its ugliness to the natural medicines of air and light, injustice must be exposed, with all the tension its exposure creates, to the light of human conscience and the air of national opinion before it can be cured.

In your statement you assert that our actions, even though peaceful, must be condemned because they precipitate violence. But is this a logical assertion? Isn't this like condemning a robbed man because his possession of money precipitated the evil act of robbery? Isn't this like condemning Socrates because his unswerving commitment to truth and his philosophical inquiries precipitated the act by the misguided populace in which they made him drink hemlock? Isn't this like condemning Jesus because his unique God-consciousness and never-ceasing devotion to God's will precipitated the evil act of crucifixion? We must come to see that, as the federal courts have consistently affirmed, it is wrong to urge an individual to cease his efforts to gain his basic constitutional rights because the quest may precipitate violence. Society must protect the robbed and punish the robber.

I had also hoped that the white moderate would reject the myth concerning time in relation to the struggle for freedom. I have just received a letter from a white brother in Texas. He writes: "All Christians know that the colored people will receive equal rights eventually, but it is possible that you are in too great a religious hurry. It has taken Christianity almost two thousand years to accomplish what it has. The teachings of Christ take time to come to earth." Such an attitude stems from a tragic misconception of time, from the strangely irrational notion that there is something in the very flow of time that will inevitably cure all ills. Actually, time itself is neutral; it can be used either destructively or constructively. More and more I feel that the people of ill will have used time much more effectively than have the people of good will. We will have to repent in this generation not merely for the hateful words and actions of the bad people but for the appalling silence of the good people. Human progress never rolls in on wheels of inevitability; it comes through the tireless efforts of men willing to be co-workers with God, and without this hard work, time itself becomes an ally of the forces of social stagnation. We must use time creatively, in the knowledge that the time is always ripe to do right. Now is the time to make real the promise of democracy and transform our pending national elegy into a creative psalm of brotherhood. Now is the time to lift our national policy from the quicksand of racial injustice to the solid rock of human dignity.

1. King addresses his audience as "my Christian and Jewish brothers," but then associates them with the "white moderate," who he believes is a greater problem than the Ku Klux Klan (par. 9). Why wouldn't his audience necessarily be offended by this, and King's argument rendered a failure? What characteristics of the voice of his plea would convince his audience that he is sincere in calling them "brothers" despite his accusation? Tolstoy is quick to assert that he is not accusing (par. 8); do we believe him? Why or why not?

2. What specific analogies, authorities cited, and allusions should be particularly meaningful to King's audience? Does he use God as an authority in the same way as Tolstoy? Is King's comparison of himself to Jesus a shock? Why or why not? How does this comparison function within the total argument?

3. King's primary focus is on "justice." The entire letter is devoted to making a distinction between "justice" and "injustice," and "justice" and "order." Why is he so concerned to make these distinctions? How do they relate to each other? How do they relate to his argument?

4. As we have discussed in the introduction, King's main argument is deductive: major premise—"an unjust law is no law at all" (par. 1); minor premise and conclusion—"All segregation statutes are not laws, and need not be obeyed" (par. 3,6). But this argument has been completed by the sixth paragraph; what is the purpose of the remainder of his letter?

5. Like Tolstoy, King also uses much analogical argument. Where, and how effective is this strategy?

6. Examine the antitheses in paragraph nine, and show how they are indicative of the structure of the letter as a whole. What are some of the qualities of King's voice as projected here? Would Tolstoy describe King's words as "harsh"? What are the differences between a letter of "Advice" and a plea? How are the corresponding arguments different?

"The Student as Nigger"/*Jerry Farber*

"Don't Send Johnny to College"/*Hugh Kenner*

Both Farber and Kenner are critical of the institution of higher education, but they analyze this aspect of culture from vastly different points of view. Indicative of their radical difference is that *Esquire* magazine called Farber's angry indictment the first "underground classic," while Kenner's impassioned speech appeared in the "Speak Out" section of *The Saturday Evening Post,* whose wide circulation almost made it an institution in itself. Farber shows what it is to be an oppressed student; Kenner reveals what it is to be an oppressed professor.

Jerry Farber's strategy for gaining distance from the subject of his analysis is to imagine what the institution would look like from the perspective of a slave. He claims this perspective will explode the false assumption that higher education consists of dedicated teachers passing on their knowledge. After he focuses on a primary question—why students are niggers—he sustains his analysis by viewing all the parts of the educational institution from the slave's point of view. Similarly, Hugh Kenner imagines what the present situation of rampant "Johnnyism" would look like to a "real student." This strategy, like Farber's, reveals the falseness of one of the most revered assumptions of higher education, that Johnny (or Jonnie) is a "student." But where Farber relies on analogy, Kenner's development is inductive, making use of careful definitions and distinctions. Both writers conclude their argument by advocating change, but Farber demands an apocalyptic liberation of the mind, where Kenner suggests a practical alternative to "Johnnyism."

"The Student as Nigger"

Students are niggers. When you get that straight, our schools begin to make sense. It's more important, though, to understand why they're niggers. If we follow that question seriously enough, it will lead us past the zone of academic bullshit, where dedicated teachers pass their knowledge on to a new generation, and into the nitty-gritty of human needs and hangups. And from there we can go on to consider whether it might ever be possible for students to come up from slavery.

First let's see what's happening now. Let's look at the role students play in what we like to call education. At Cal State L.A., where I teach,* the students have separate and unequal dining facilities. If I

* Make that "taught."

take them into the faculty dining room, my colleagues get uncomfortable, as though there were a bad smell. If I eat in the student cafeteria, I become known as the educational equivalent of a niggerlover. In at least one building there are even rest rooms which students may not use. At Cal State, also, there is an unwritten law barring student-faculty lovemaking. Fortunately, this anti-miscegenation law, like its Southern counterpart, is not 100 percent effective.

Students at Cal State are politically disenfranchised. They are in an academic Lowndes County. Most of them can vote in national elections—their average age is about 26—but they have no voice in the decisions which affect their academic lives. The students are, it is true, allowed to have a toy government run for the most part by Uncle Toms and concerned principally with trivia. The faculty and administrators decide what courses will be offered; the students get to choose their own Homecoming Queen. Occasionally when student leaders get uppity and rebellious, they're either ignored, put off with trivial concessions, or maneuvered expertly out of position.

A student at Cal State is expected to know his place. He calls a faculty member "Sir" or "Doctor" or "Professor"—and he smiles and shuffles some as he stands outside the professor's office waiting for permission to enter. The faculty tell him what courses to take (in my department, English, even electives have to be approved by a faculty member); they tell him what to read, what to write, and, frequently, where to set the margins on his typewriter. They tell him what's true and what isn't. Some teachers insist that they encourage dissent but they're almost always jiving and every student knows it. Tell the man what he wants to hear or he'll fail your ass out of the course.

When a teacher says "jump," students jump. I know of one professor who refused to take up class time for exams and required students to show up for tests at 6:30 in the morning. And they did, by God! Another, at exam time, provides answer cards to be filled out—each one enclosed in a paper bag with a hole cut in the top to see through. Students stick their writing hands in the bags while taking the test. The teacher isn't a provo; I wish he were. He does it to prevent cheating. Another colleague once caught a student reading during one of his lectures and threw her book against the wall. Still another lectures his students into a stupor and then screams at them in a rage when they fall asleep.

Just last week during the first meeting of a class, one girl got up to leave after about ten minutes had gone by. The teacher rushed over, grabbed her by the arm, saying, "This class is NOT dismissed!" and led her back to her seat. On the same day another teacher began by informing his class that he does not like beards, mustaches, long hair on boys, or capri pants on girls, and will not tolerate any of that in his class. The class, incidentally, consisted mostly of high school teachers.

Even more discouraging than this master-slave approach to education is the fact that the students take it. They haven't gone through twelve years of public school for nothing. They've learned one thing and perhaps only one thing during those twelve years. They've forgotten their algebra. They've grown to fear and resent literature. They write like they've been lobotomized. But, Jesus, can they follow orders! Freshmen come up to me with an essay and ask if I want it folded, and whether their name should be in the upper right hand corner. And I want to cry and kiss them and caress their poor tortured heads.

Students don't ask that orders make sense. They give up expecting things to make sense long before they leave elementary school. Things are true because the teacher says they're true. At a very early age we all learn to accept "two truths," as did certain medieval churchmen. Outside of class, things are true to your tongue, your fingers, your stomach, your heart. Inside class things are true by reason of authority. And that's just fine because you don't care anyway. Miss Wiedemeyer tells you a noun is a person, place or thing. So let it be. You don't give a rat's ass; she doesn't give a rat's ass.

The important thing is to please her. Back in kindergarten, you found out that teachers only love children who stand in nice straight lines. And that's where it's been at ever since. Nothing changes except to get worse. School becomes more and more obviously a prison. Last year I spoke to a student assembly at Manual Arts High School and then couldn't get out of the goddamn school. I mean there was NO WAY OUT. Locked doors. High fences. One of the inmates was trying to make it over a fence when he saw me coming and froze in panic. For a moment I expected sirens, a rattle of bullets, and him clawing the fence.

Then there's the infamous "code of dress." In some high schools, if your skirt looks too short, you have to kneel before the principal in a brief allegory of fellatio. If the hem doesn't reach the floor, you go home to change while he, presumably, jacks off. Boys in high school can't be too sloppy and they can't even be too sharp. You'd think the school board would have been delighted to see all the black kids trooping to school in pointy shoes, suits, ties and stingy brims. Uh-uh. They're too visible.

What school amounts to, then, for white and black alike, is a 12-year course in how to be slaves. What else could explain what I see in a freshman class? They've got that slave mentality: obliging and ingratiating on the surface but hostile and resistant underneath.

As do black slaves, students vary in their awareness of what's going on. Some recognize their own put-on for what it is and even let their rebellion break through to the surface now and then. Others—including most of the "good students"—have been more deeply brainwashed. They swallow the bullshit with greedy mouths. They honest-to-God believe in grades, in busy work, in General Education requirements. They're pathetically eager to be pushed around. They're like those

old grey-headed house niggers you can still find in the South who don't
see what all the fuss is about because Mr. Charlie "treats us real good."

College entrance requirements tend to favor the Toms and screen out
the rebels. Not entirely, of course. Some students at Cal State L.A.
are expert con artists who know perfectly well what's happening. They
want the degree or the 2-S and spend their years on the old plantation
alternately laughing and cursing as they play the game. If their egos
are strong enough, they cheat a lot. And, of course, even the Toms are
angry down deep somewhere. But it comes out in passive rather than
active aggression. They're unexplainably thick-witted and subject to frequent spells of laziness. They misread simple questions. They spent their
nights mechanically outlining history chapters while meticulously
failing to comprehend a word of what's in front of them.

The saddest cases among both black slaves and student slaves are
the ones who have so thoroughly introjected their masters' values that
their anger is all turned inward. At Cal State these are the kids for
whom every low grade is torture, who stammer and shake when they
speak to a professor, who go through an emotional crisis every time
they're called upon during class. You can recognize them easily at finals
time. Their faces are festooned with fresh pimples; their bowels boil
audibly across the room. If there really is a Last Judgment, then the
parents and teachers who created these wrecks are going to burn in hell.

So students are niggers. It's time to find out why, and to do this we
have to take a long look at Mr. Charlie.

The teachers I know best are college professors. Outside the classroom
and taken as a group, their most striking characteristic is timidity.
They're short on balls. Just look at their working conditions. At a time
when even migrant workers have begun to fight and win, most college
professors are still afraid to make more than a token effort to improve
their pitiful economic status. In California state colleges, the faculties
are screwed regularly and vigorously by the Governor and Legislature
and yet they still won't offer any solid resistance. They lie flat on their
stomachs with their pants down, mumbling catch phrases like "professional dignity" and "meaningful dialogue."

Professors were no different when I was an undergraduate at UCLA
during the McCarthy era; it was like a cattle stampede as they rushed
to cop out. And in more recent years, I found that my being arrested in
demonstrations brought from my colleagues not so much approval or
condemnation as open-mouthed astonishment. "You could lose
your job!"

Now, of course, there's the Vietnamese war. It gets some opposition
from a few teachers. Some support it. But a vast number of professors
who know perfectly well what's happening, are copping out again. And
in the high schools, you can forget it. Stillness reigns.

I'm not sure why teachers are so chickenshit. It could be that academic training itself forces a split between thought and action. It might also be that the tenured security of a teaching job attracts timid persons and, furthermore, that teaching, like police work, pulls in persons who are unsure of themselves and need weapons and the other external trappings of authority.

At any rate teachers ARE short on balls. And, as Judy Eisenstein has eloquently pointed out, the classroom offers an artificial and protected environment in which they can exercise their will to power. Your neighbors may drive a better car; gas station attendants may intimidate you; your wife may dominate you; the State Legislature may shit on you; but in the classroom, by God, students do what you say— or else. The grade is a hell of a weapon. It may not rest on your hip, potent and rigid like a cop's gun, but in the long run it's more power- ful. At your personal whim—any time you choose—you can keep 35 students up for nights and have the pleasure of seeing them walk into the classroom pasty-faced and red-eyed carrying a sheaf of typewritten pages, with title page, MLA footnotes and margins set at 15 and 91.

The general timidity which causes teachers to make niggers of their students usually includes a more specific fear—fear of the students themselves. After all, students are different, just like black people. You stand exposed in front of them, knowing that their interests, their values and their language are different from yours. To make matters worse, you may suspect that you yourself are not the most engaging of persons. What then can protect you from their ridicule and scorn? Respect for authority. That's what. It's the policeman's gun again. The white bwana's pith helmet. So you flaunt that authority. You wither whisperers with a murderous glance. You crush objectors with erudition and heavy irony. And worst of all, you make your own attainments seem not accessible but awesomely remote. You conceal your massive ignorance—and parade a slender learning.

The teacher's fear is mixed with an understandable need to be admired and to feel superior—a need which also makes him cling to his "white supremacy." Ideally, a teacher should minimize the distance between himself and his students. He should encourage them not to need him—eventually or even immediately. But this is rarely the case. Teachers make themselves high priests of arcane mysteries. They become masters of mumbo-jumbo. Even a more or less conscientious teacher may be torn between the need to give and the need to hold back, between the desire to free his students and the desire to hold them in bondage to him. I can find no other explanation that accounts for the way my own subject, literature, is generally taught. Literature, which ought to be a source of joy, solace and enlightenment, often becomes in the classroom nothing more than a source of anxiety—at best an arena for expertise, a ledger book for the ego. Literature teachers, often afraid to join a real union, nonetheless may practice the worst kind of trade-unionism in the classroom; they do to literature what Beckmesser does to song in Wagner's "Meistersinger." The avowed purpose of English departments is to teach literature; too often their real function is to kill it.

Finally, there's the darkest reason of all for the master-slave approach to education. The less trained and the less socialized a person is, the more he constitutes a sexual threat and the more he will be subjugated by institutions, such as penitentiaries and schools. Many of us are aware by now of the sexual neurosis which makes white men so fearful of integrated schools and neighborhoods, and which make the castration of Negroes a deeply entrenched Southern folkway. We should recognize a similar pattern in education. There is a kind of castration that goes on in schools. It begins before school years with parents' first encroachments on their children's free unashamed sexuality and continues right up to the day when they hand you your doctoral diploma with a bleeding, shriveled pair of testicles stapled to the parchment. It's not that sexuality has no place in the classroom. You'll find it there but only in certain perverted and vitiated forms.

How does sex show up in school? First of all, there's the sadomasochistic relationship between teachers and students. That's plenty sexual, although the price of enjoying it is to be unaware of what's happening. In walks the teacher in his Ivy League equivalent of a motorcycle jacket. In walks the teacher—a kind of intellectual rough trade—and flogs his students with grades, tests, sarcasm and snotty superiority until their very brains are bleeding. In Swinburne's England, the whipped school boy frequently grew up to be a flagellant. With us the perversion is intellectual but it's no less perverse.

Sex also shows up in the classroom as academic subject matter— sanitized and abstracted, thoroughly divorced from feeling. You get "sex education" now in both high school and college classes: everyone determined not to be embarrassed, to be very up to date, very contempo. These are the classes for which sex, as Feiffer puts it, "can be a beautiful thing if properly administered." And then, of course there's still another depressing manifestation of sex in the classroom: the "off-color" teacher who keeps his class awake with sniggering sexual allusions, obscene titters and academic innuendo. The sexuality he purveys, it must be admitted, is at least better than none at all.

What's missing, from kindergarten to graduate school, is honest recognition of what's actually happening—turned-on awareness of hairy goodies underneath the pettipants, the chinos and the flannels. It's not that sex needs to be pushed in school; sex is push enough. But we should let it be, where it is and like it is. I don't insist that ladies in junior high school lovingly caress their students' cocks (someday maybe); however, it is reasonable to ask that the ladies don't, by example and stricture, teach their students to pretend that those cocks aren't there. As things stand now, students are psychically castrated or spayed—and for the very same reason that black men are castrated in Georgia: because they're a threat.

So you can add sexual repression to the list of causes, along with vanity, fear and will to power, that turn the teacher into Mr. Charlie. You might also want to keep in mind that he was a nigger once himself and has never really gotten over it. And there are more causes, some of which are better described in sociological than in psychological terms. Work them out, it's not hard. But in the meantime what we've got on our hands is a whole lot of niggers. And what makes this particularly grim is that the student has less chance than the black man of getting out of his bag. Because the student doesn't even know he's in it. That, more or less, is what's happening in higher education. And the results are staggering.

For one thing damn little education takes place in the schools. How could it? You can't educate slaves; you can only train them. Or, to use an even uglier and more timely word, you can only program them.

I like to folk dance. Like other novices, I've gone to the Intersection or to the Museum and laid out good money in order to learn how to dance. No grades, no prerequisites, no separate dining rooms; they just turn you on to dancing. That's education. Now look at what happens in college. A friend of mine, Milt, recently finished a folk dance class. For his final, he had to learn things like this: "The Irish are known for their wit and imagination, qualities reflected in their dances, which include the jig, the reel and the hornpipe." And then the teacher graded him, A, B, C, D, or F, while he danced in front of her. That's not education. That's not even training. That's an abomination on the face of the earth. It's especially ironic because Milt took that dance class trying to get out of the academic rut. He took crafts for the same reason. Great, right? Get your hands in some clay? Make something? Then the teacher announced a 20-page term paper would be required— with footnotes.

At my school we even grade people on how they read poetry. That's like grading people on how they fuck. But we do it. In fact, God help me, I do it. I'm the Commandant of English 323. Simon Legree on the poetry plantation. "Tote that iamb! Lift that spondee!" Even to discuss a good poem in that environment is potentially dangerous because the very classroom is contaminated. As hard as I may try to turn students on to poetry, I know that the desks, the tests, the IBM cards, their own attitudes toward school, and my own residue of UCLA method are turning them off.

Another result of student slavery is equally serious. Students don't get emancipated when they graduate. As a matter of fact, we don't let them graduate until they've demonstrated their willingness—over 16 years—to remain slaves. And for important jobs, like teaching, we make them go through more years just to make sure. What I'm getting at is that we're all more or less niggers and slaves, teachers and students alike. This is a fact you might want to start with in trying to understand wider social phenomena, say, politics, in our country and in other countries.

Educational oppression is trickier to fight than racial oppression. If you're a black rebel, they can't exile you; they either have to intimidate you or kill you. But in high school or college they can just bounce you out of the fold. And they do. Rebel students and renegade faculty members get smothered or shot down with devastating accuracy. Others get tired of fighting and voluntarily leave the system. This may be a mistake though. Dropping out of college for a rebel is a little like going North for a Negro. You can't really get away from it so you might as well stay and raise hell.

How do you raise hell? That's a whole other article. But just for a start, why not stay with the analogy? What have black people done? They have, first of all, faced the fact of their slavery. They've stopped kidding themselves about an eventual reward in that Great Watermelon Patch in the sky. They've organized; they've decided to get freedom now, and they've started taking it.

Students, like black people, have immense unused power. They could, theoretically, insist on participating in their own education. They could make academic freedom bilateral. They could teach their teachers to thrive on love and admiration, rather than fear and respect, and to lay down their weapons. Students could discover community. And they could learn to dance by dancing on the IBM cards. They could make coloring books out of the catalogs and they could put the grading system in a museum. They could raze one set of walls and let life come blowing into the classroom. They could raze another set of walls and let education flow out and flood the streets. They could turn the classroom into where it's at—a "field of action" as Peter Marin describes it. And believe it or not, they could study eagerly and learn prodigiously for the best of all possible reasons—their own reasons.

They could. Theoretically. They have the power. But only in a very few places, like Berkeley, have they even begun to think about using it. For students, as for black people, the hardest battle isn't with Mr. Charlie. It's with what Mr. Charlie has done to your mind.

1. The fundamental basis of analysis and argument in Farber's essay is analogical, but he also relies on an inductive method throughout his essay. How are these two methods related? How does Farber use them together to develop his proposition?

2. Farber interprets all his facts consistently, such as seeing separate dining rooms for students and faculty, as well as separate restrooms, as oppression. But could they be interpreted in other ways? How could his basic question—"What else could explain what I see in a freshman class?"—be answered differently?

3. What kind of voice do we hear, and what is the implied character of the "I"? Why does Farber use profanity and obscenity? How is the voice that Farber has chosen appropriate to his subject? How does it further his argument?

4. What are Farber's basic assumptions about teachers? One of Farber's presuppositions of analysis is that sex is at the heart of the relationships that comprise college culture. How is sex related to his proposition? What are his assumptions about the nature of sexuality, and how do they influence the structure of his argument?

5. When Farber turns to the implications of his proposition in the last four paragraphs, how does he demonstrate what is at stake? How does he look back to the development of his argument and ahead to the continuation of his analysis at the same time? In what ways is his last sentence more than a summary statement?

6. What does the word "Nigger" mean in this essay? How does Farber's use of this word increase the power of his argument?

"Don't Send Johnny to College"

Johnny goes by the official title of "student." Yet Johnny's is the face every professor would prefer to see anywhere but in his classroom, where it blocks with its dreary smile, or its stoical yawn, the educational process on which we are proud to spend annually billions of dollars. By his sheer inert numbers he is making the common pursuit of professors and students—real students—impossible.

No one, least of all his professor, wills Johnny an injustice. Even the dean of students, whose lot he renders abysmal, finds it impossible not to like him, though some miraculous multiplication of loafers and fish sends

Johnnies in an endless column trooping past the dean's receptionist, to stammer out their tale of dragging grades and just not digging the stuff.

Johnnies by the thousand, by the hundred thousand, clutter up every college in the land, where they long ago acquired a numerical majority. If you have a teenager in your home, thinking of college, the chances are you have Johnny. On behalf of my 400,000 colleagues in the academic profession, I'd be grateful if you'd keep him home.

Though Johnny is by definition multitudinous and anonymous, bits of Johnnyism stick in every teacher's mind. I remember the set neon smile that greeted me class after class for three whole weeks from a front-row seat just next to the door. The smile's owner and operator—let's call her Jonnie—never said a word, never took a note, never turned a page in her copy of *Gulliver's Travels*. Then, the day after I assigned a paper, the smile was gone, and so was she, apparently for good.

A month later, having heard that I would welcome some explanation, Jonnie turned up in my office, smiling. No, she couldn't do papers at all, not at all. Then what, pray, had brought her to a university, where, as everyone knows, one does papers? Well, she had enrolled on the advice of her psychiatrist. He had said the College Experience would be good therapy. Unwilling to monkey with therapy, I referred her, smile and all, to the dean. I've forgotten what he decided. There are so many Johnnies and Jonnies.

And there is no end to what their mentors and counselors, not to say psychiatrists, expect a university to do. Teach Johnny to behave like a gentleman. Prevent his simultaneous presence with Jonnie in parked cars after 10 P.M. Help him (her) get to know girls (boys). Improve his work habits. Open his mind (he has nothing but prejudices). Shut his mouth (he does nothing but talk). Tighten his morals. Loosen his imagination. Spread beneath his slack chin the incredible banquet of Western Civilization. And discharge him fit to earn a better living, make a better marriage and digest (Lord help him) *The New York Times*.

The parents and mentors who expect all this expect it not of the college but of the College Experience, which is turning, accordingly, into the experience of living in a whole cityful of Johnnies. (I've just been told by a Sunday supplement that within 35 years many colleges with enrollments of 100,000 to 200,000 will have become cities in their own right.)

Johnny (Jonnie) expects none of the wonders of the College Experience, except *in re* girls (boys). Johnny is amiably devoid of expectations. One might say that he goes where he's shoved. One might affirm with more tact that he lends himself amiably to the College Experience, having no better plans. That is what marks him as Johnny, not as a student. A student has a vocation for study. But there's really nothing that Johnny comes to campus burning to learn about.

"Real education," wrote Ezra Pound 30 years ago, "must ultimately be limited to men who INSIST on working; the rest is mere sheepherding."

The mind that insists on knowing is (alas) not to be identified by tests, which explains why, despite the well-publicized vigilance of admissions officers, the number of campus Johnnies keeps rising. A mind that insists on knowing has begun to focus its energies by the time it has been in the world 16 years. By 17 or 18—the age of a college freshman—it has learned the taste of knowledge and the sensation of reaching for more. It may spell erratically, if it is served (like Yeats) by a deficient visual memory. It may calculate imperfectly, if it is (like Einstein) more at home with concepts than with operations. There may be strange gaps in its information, since a young mind cannot be everywhere at once.

But what it does not know it will encounter with pleasure. And it *must* learn as a cat must eat. It may not yet know where its need for knowledge is meant to be satisfied. It may tack about, sails taut, without regard for curricular symmetry, changing majors perhaps more than once. But its tireless curiosity is unmistakable. In time, if all goes well, it will accept training, and the lifelong responsibilities of keeping itself trained.

But Johnny has no such appetite, no such momentum. When Johnny applies his brand-new ball-point to his first blue book, each sentence comes out smudged with his unmistakable pawprint. "Newspaper comics are good because they put a rosy glow on the grayish realities of the mind": There you have Johnny ingenuously expressing the state of *his* mind—a gray place which Pogo can occasionally animate, and a place of Good Things and Bad Things where Pogo is a Good Thing.

"The three main groups of people are the well-educated, semieducated and semiuneducated." There is all mankind characterized (a feat that taxed Aristotle), complete with a category for Johnny himself; he never forgets himself.

I am not inventing these examples. A colleague of mine gleaned a dozen like them in a single afternoon, from freshman themes at a university that accepts only the top one-eighth of the high-school crop. What they illustrate isn't primarily the "inability to express oneself," i.e., technical difficulties with the English language. What they illustrate is something deeper, probably irremediable; a happy willingness to emulate the motions of thought, since a teacher is standing there expecting such motions, along with a nearly total want of experience of what the process of thinking feels like.

"And this is why we should have no prejudice again Negroes and other lower races." That mind, we may say with some confidence, doesn't insist upon knowing. It doesn't know even its own most blatant contradictions. "To analyze this theory, it can be broken down into two parts: men and women." That's what men and women are, for the nonce—they are the parts of Johnny's theory. "The result is a ridiculous fiasco under which the roof falls in." It is indeed, and one does not know whether to marvel more at the oppressive weight of that fiasco, crashing through the roof like a half-ton bear, or at the innocent ease with which Johnny, supposing ideas to be weightless, pats them to and fro like bubbles.

But examples don't define a problem which by its very nature arises out of sheer multitudinousness. The amiable dumbbell has for decades been a part of campus folklore, like the absentminded professor. It is when you multiply him by a million that he grows ominous, swamping the campus as with creeping molasses. His uncle of 40 years ago, Joe College, had no more interest in learning that Johnny has, but none of Johnny's baleful power. With a certain talent for grotesque stylization, he conducted his entertaining ballet of raccoon coats, hip flasks, and whiffenpoofery, while the business of the academy, a considerably more modest business than today, went on.

What has created the Johnny problem isn't some freakish meta-morphosis of Joe College into numberless protozoa, but rather the nearly universal conviction that everybody ought to spend four years at college if it can possibly be managed.

Johnny's parents, needless to say, believe this. His state legislator, despite the fantastic costs, tries to believe it, since his constituents seem to. The prospective employer believes it: let Johnny check "none" where the personnel blank inquires after "college record," and Johnny will be lucky to be issued a pick and shovel, let alone a sample kit. Even the college, caught in competitions for funds (which tend to hinge on enrollments), has come to believe it believes it.

Meanwhile B.A.'s grow so common that employers who once demanded them now demand M.A.'s, and the Master's requirement in some fields (not just the academic) has been upgraded to the Ph.D. In the years since Robert M. Hutchins sardonically proposed that we achieve our desires with less trouble by granting every American citizen a B.A. at birth, we have moved closer and closer to a utopia in which everyone receives it at 21, in return for doing classroom time. One already hears talk of attendance being compulsory through age 20. In California, where problems tend to surface before New England need worry about them, the state population rose 50 percent in one decade, and the college population 82 percent. It grows easy to foresee the day when 50 percent of the population of California (and, after a suitable time lag, of Massachusetts, of New York, of Illinois and, yes of Montana) will be employed at teaching the other 50 percent, perhaps changing ends at the half.

Clearly something has got to bust, and no one doubts what: the idea of a university. As an institution for (in Thomas Jefferson's words) "the instruction of those who will come after us," it's already being trampled out of recognizable existence by hordes of Johnnies.

The real student, struggling against suffocation of the soul, draws back, or beefs about how "the class" is holding things up, or starts feeling superior (and energy expended in nourishing a feeling of superiority is wholly lost). At worst, from being eager he turns merely "sensitive," and allows his zeal to be leached away. He is deprived, and can rightfully resent being deprived, of the kind of company he deserves to expect at a place where, often at considerable sacrifice, he has elected to invest four years of his life.

The professors suffer too. For one thing, they are coming off the production line too rapidly (though the harried trustees, looking wildly around at teaching machines and television hookups say "Not rapidly enough!"). Since there's no way of growing scholars at a pace keyed to the amoebalike increase of Johnnies, substitutes have begun to be manufactured. As real students are swamped by Johnnies, real professors must coexist with a swarm of Johnny-professors.

And like the real students, the real professors grow obsessed with futility, and unless they succeed, as some do, in isolating themselves with advanced students, fall victim to the real occupational hazard of the profession: an inability to believe that anybody can be taught anything. I once heard of a man who was so startled by the discovery of a real student that, lest she slip over his horizon, he divorced his wife and married her. I don't believe that story, but it's indicative; the professor who told it to me found it believable.

There's no doubt that as a nation we settle for only the side effects and the fringe benefits of what we invest in universities: the products of physics labs and research stations, and the economic advantages, to which our economy has been attuned ever since the G. I. Bill, of keeping several million young people off the labor market as long as possible. We are getting even this, though, at the price of a colossal wastage of time and spirit—the time and spirit of the real students on whose behalf the system is allegedly being run. If by the year 2000, as President Clark Kerr of California expects, educational institutions will be the largest single force in the economy, and if attendance to the age of 20 is compulsory, as Dr. Dwayne Orton of I.B.M. expects, why then the economy will in the lifetime of most of us have begun devoting its principal energies to the maintenance of huge concentration camps for keeping Johnnies by the multimillion agreeably idle.

So do we kick out Johnny? Alas, things will never be that simple again. Our social and economic system has come to depend on Johnny, B.A., in ways that can probably never be unstitched. Moreover, the College Experience probably *is* the most important event in the lives of most of the people who undergo it, even of the hundreds of thousands who learn very little. It is their time of access to the intellectual traffic patterns that define the quality of American life. A Kansan and a Georgian who have both been to college—merely been there—will have more to say to one another than a Vermonter who has and a Vermonter who hasn't. The College Experience is our folk ritual for inducting our adolescents into the 20th century. As part of our established religion, it must be treated as immune from curtailment.

Very well, then: the College Experience for Johnny, in his Johnny-classrooms. But let us, in the name of sanity, allow the real students to have *their* version of the College Experience. That means either separate-but-equal facilities, or (better, I think), some college equivalent of the two-track high schools that already exist.

One way of arranging a two-track college with minimum disruption is to permit only the real students to pursue majors. The University of Toronto has been doing that for more than half a century. Two decades ago I was one of a group of 40 freshman English majors there. In the sophomore year there were 20 of us, in the junior year 10; there the ruthless cutting stopped. But the missing 30 were not slung out of school. All but a few hopeless cases were "permitted," as the official formula had it, "to transfer to the pass course," which meant that, if they wanted to stay on at college, they abandoned the major and enrolled in "pass arts."

Pass arts was a three-year humanities mixture, leading to the degree of B.A. And it wasn't a ghetto for dropouts; many students enrolled in it to start with. Its degree satisfied employers, parents and the Ontario College of Education. It satisfied Johnny just fine. It gave the university all the advantages of bigness, as the quality of the library testified. It wasn't conducive to snobbery or segregation; every honor student took a couple of pass courses a year, in subjects peripheral to his major.

It was, in short, a two-track system, with the tracks parallel, and with means for switching laggards onto the slow track.

Everyone, we agree, should have access to all the education he can absorb. Everyone who can absorb education deserves, I would add, a chance to absorb it, free from the distracting tramp of the million-footed Johnny. As colleges now operate, the idea that everybody should be sent to them is nonsense. The only hope is to start operating them differently, detached from the dogma that Johnny is by birthright a student. He needs, in fact, explicit treatment as a nonstudent. There's no inherent reason why the nation's universities shouldn't make special curricular arrangements for several million nonstudents, any more than there's an inherent reason why one of the nation's universities shouldn't be the world's largest purveyor of white mice. (One of them is.)

1. What is Kenner's definition of a "real student"? What is "Johnnyism" (par. 4)? What is Kenner's proposition? On the analogy of "The Student as Nigger," how would you fill in the blank: "Johnny as _____"?
2. Why does Kenner begin his essay (the first fifteen paragraphs) with examples? Does he also present conclusions here? What is the primary structure of the first part of his essay?
3. What are some of the specific ways in which Kenner develops his analysis in the second part of his essay (pars. 16–30)? Is Johnny the problem or the symptom?
4. What are Kenner's basic assumptions about the nature of education? About the future?
5. What is the function of the last five paragraphs?
6. Why does Kenner use predominantly short paragraphs?
7. What specific points or assumptions of Kenner's argument would Farber attack? Why?

"Sex and Secularization"/*Harvey Cox*

"Ethics and Unmarried Sex"/*Joseph Fletcher*

The following writers are not as much concerned with male and female roles as they are with human liberation. That is, each author desires the "humanization of sex." Cox argues for the freedom of sex from society's fraudulent images of "The Playboy" and "Miss America." Fletcher argues for its freedom from absolute codes of morality. Accordingly, Cox's chapter from *The Secular City*, a book celebrating the liberating rise of urban civilization and collapse of traditional religion, shares with Fletcher's essay a view of humans as primarily moral, as beings faced with choice. (They must decide how to handle their sexuality free from the dictates of God or culture.) Despite their common assumptions and aims, however, their argumentative strategies differ radically.

Although both authors begin with a clear statement of their proposition, Cox develops his argument through a detailed analysis of our culture and the function of "cultural-identity images," such as Miss America, while Fletcher relies on statistics and careful refutation. The larger structure of each essay is deductive, but images and symbols become evidence in Cox's strategy, whereas the facts and statistics of experience constitute evidence in Fletcher's. Cox immediately plunges us into a world of "demons," "tribal lore," and "shamans," which we are shocked to find is our own familiar world seen from a different perspective. He forces us to see in a different way, and once we have seen, his argument appears self-evident. In contrast, Fletcher immediately opposes himself to a world of absolute morality and attempts to lead us step by logical step to its inevitable refutation. We are convinced of his proposition by the staggering weight of accumulated evidence and the logic of its presentation, rather than by suddenly finding ourselves in an oppressive world. Compare these strategies as you read the following essays.

"Sex and Secularization"

No aspect of human life seethes with so many unexorcised demons as does sex. No human activity is so hexed by superstition, so haunted by residual tribal lore, and so harassed by socially induced fear. Within the breast of urban-secular man, a toe-to-toe struggle still rages between his savage and his bourgeois forebears. Like everything else, the images of sex which informed tribal and town society are expiring along with the eras in which they arose. The erosion of traditional values and the disappearance of accepted modes of behavior have left contemporary man free, but somewhat rudderless. Abhoring a vacuum, the mass media have rushed in to supply a new code and a new set of behavioral proto-types. They appeal to the unexorcised demons. Nowhere is the persistence of mythical and metalogical denizens more obvious than in sex, and the shamans of sales do their best to nourish them. Nowhere is the humanization of life more frustrated. Nowhere is a clear word of exorcism more needed.

How is the humanization of sex impeded? First it is thwarted by the parading of cultural-identity images for the sexually dispossessed, to make money. These images become the tyrant gods of the secular society, undercutting its liberation from religion and transforming it into a kind of neotribal culture. Second, the authentic secularization of sex is checkmated by an anxious clinging to the sexual standards of the town, an era so recent and yet so different from ours that simply to transplant its sexual ethos into our situation is to invite hypocrisy of the worst degree.

Let us look first at the spurious sexual models conjured up for our anxious society by the sorcerers of the mass media and the advertising guild. Like all pagan deities, these come in pairs—the god and his consort. For our purposes they are best symbolized by The Playboy and Miss America, the Adonis and Aphrodite of a leisure-consumer society which still seems unready to venture into full postreligious maturity and freedom. The Playboy and Miss America represent The Boy and The Girl. They incorporate a vision of life. They function as religious phenomena and should be exorcised and exposed.

THE RESIDUE OF TRIBALISM

Let us begin with Miss America. In the first century B.C., Lucretius wrote this description of the pageant of Cybele:

> Adorned with emblem and crown . . . she is carried in awe-inspiring state. Tight-stretched tambourines and hollow cymbals thunder all round to the stroke of open hands, hollow pipes stir with Phrygian strain. . . . She rides in procession through great cities and mutely enriches mortals with a blessing not expressed in words. They straw all her path with brass and silver, presenting her with bounteous alms, and scatter over her a snow-shower of roses.[1]

Now compare this with the annual twentieth-century Miss America pageant in Atlantic City, New Jersey. Spotlights probe the dimness like votive tapers, banks of flowers exude their varied aromas, the orchestra blends feminine strings and regal trumpets. There is a hushed moment of tortured suspense, a drumroll, then the climax—a young woman with carefully prescribed anatomical proportions and exemplary "personality" parades serenely with scepter and crown to her throne. At TV sets across the nation throats tighten and eyes moisten. "There she goes, Miss America—" sings the crooner. "There she goes, your ideal." A new queen in America's emerging cult of The Girl has been crowned.

Is it merely illusory or anarchronistic to discern in the multiplying pageants of the Miss America, Miss Universe, Miss College Queen type a residuum of the cults of the pre-Christian fertility goddesses? Perhaps, but students of the history of religions have become less prone in recent years to dismiss the possibility that the cultural behavior of modern man may be significantly illuminated by studying it in the perspective of the mythologies of bygone ages. After all, did not Freud initiate a revolution in social science by utilizing the venerable myth of Oedipus to help make sense out of the strange behavior of his Viennese contemporaries? Contemporary man carries with him, like his appendix and his fingernails, vestiges of his tribal and pagan past.

In light of this fertile combination of insights from modern social science and the history of religions, it is no longer possible to see in the Miss America pageant merely an overpublicized prank foisted on us by the advertising industry. It certainly is this, but it is also much more.

---

[1] This is quoted from Lucretius ii, 608f. in T. R. Glover, *The Conflict of Religions in the Early Roman Empire* (Boston: Beacon, 1960), p. 20. It was originally published in 1909 by Methuen & Co. Ltd.

It represents the mass cultic celebration, complete with a rich variety of ancient ritual embellishments, of the growing place of The Girl in the collective soul of America.

This young woman—though she is no doubt totally ignorant of the fact—symbolizes something beyond herself. She symbolizes The Girl, the primal image, the One behind the many. Just as the Virgin appears in many guises—as our Lady of Lourdes or of Fatima or of Guadalupe— but is always recognizably the Virgin, so with The Girl.

The Girl is also the omnipresent icon of consumer society. Selling beer, she is folksy and jolly. Selling gems, she is chic and distant. But behind her various theophanies she remains recognizably The Girl. In Miss America's glowingly healthy smile, her openly sexual but officially virginal figure, and in the name-brand gadgets around her, she personifies the stunted aspirations and ambivalent fears of her culture. "There she goes, your ideal."

Miss America stands in a long line of queens going back to Isis, Ceres, and Aphrodite. Everything from the elaborate sexual taboos surrounding her person to the symbolic gifts at her coronation hints at her ancient ancestry. But the real proof comes when we find that the function served by The Girl in our culture is just as much a "religious" one as that served by Cybele in hers. The functions are identical—to provide a secure personal "identity" for initiates and to sanctify a particular value structure.

Let us look first at the way in which The Girl confers a kind of identity on her initiates. Simone de Beauvoir says in *The Second Sex* that "no one is *born* a woman." [2] One is merely born a female, and "*becomes* a woman" according to the models and meanings provided by the civilization. During the classical Christian centuries, it might be argued, the Virgin Mary served in part as this model. With the Refor- mation and especially with the Puritans, the place of Mary within the symbol system of the Protestant countries was reduced or eliminated. There are those who claim that this excision constituted an excess of zeal that greatly impoverished Western culture, an impoverishment from which it has never recovered. Some would even claim that the alleged failure of American novelists to produce a single great heroine (we have no Phaedra, no Anna Karenina) stems from this self-imposed lack of a central feminine ideal.

Without entering into this fascinating discussion, we can certainly be sure that, even within modern American Roman Catholicism, the Virgin Mary provides an identity image for few American girls. Where then do they look for the "model" Simone de Beauvoir convincingly contends they need? For most, the prototype of femininity seen in their

[2] Simone de Beauvoir, *The Second Sex* (New York: Knopf, 1953; London: Cape), p. 41.

mothers, their friends, and in the multitudinous images to which they are exposed on the mass media is what we have called The Girl.

In his significant monograph *Identity and the Life Cycle,* Erik Erikson reminds us that the child's identity is not modeled simply on the parent but on the parent's "super-ego." [3] Thus in seeking to forge her own identity the young girl is led beyond her mother to her mother's ideal image, and it is here that what Freud called "the ideologies of the superego . . . the traditions of the race and the people" become formative. It is here also that The Girl functions, conferring identity on those for whom she is—perhaps never completely consciously—the tangible incarnation of womanhood.

To describe the mechanics of this complex psychological process by which the fledgling American girl participates in the life of The Girl and thus attains a woman's identity would require a thorough description of American adolescence. There is little doubt, however, that such an analysis would reveal certain striking parallels to the "savage" practices by which initiates in the mystery cults shared in the magical life of their god.

For those inured to the process, the tortuous nightly fetish by which the young American female pulls her hair into tight bunches secured by metal clips may bear little resemblance to the incisions made on their arms by certain African tribesmen to make them resemble their totem, the tiger. But to an anthropologist comparing two ways of attempting to resemble the holy one, the only difference might appear to be that with the Africans the torture is over after initiation, while with the American it has to be repeated every night, a luxury only a culture with abundant leisure can afford.

In turning now to an examination of the second function of The Girl—supporting and portraying a value system—a comparison with the role of the Virgin in the twelfth and thirteenth centuries may be helpful. Just as the Virgin exhibited and sustained the ideals of the age that fashioned Chartres Cathedral, as Henry Adams saw, so The Girl symbolizes the values and aspirations of a consumer society. (She is crowned not in the political capital, remember, but in Atlantic City or Miami Beach, centers associated with leisure and consumption.) And she is not entirely incapable of exploitation. If men sometimes sought to buy with gold the Virgin's blessings on their questionable causes, so The Girl now dispenses her charismatic favor on watches, refrigerators, and razor blades—for a price. Though The Girl has built no cathedrals, without her the colossal edifice of mass persuasion would crumble. Her sharply stylized face and figure beckon us from every magazine

[3] Erik Erikson, *Identity and the Life Cycle* (New York: International University Press, 1959).

and TV channel, luring us toward the beatific vision of a
consumer's paradise.

The Girl is *not* the Virgin. In fact she is a kind of anti-Madonna.
She reverses most of the values traditionally associated with the Virgin—
poverty, humility, sacrifice. In startling contrast, particularly, to the
biblical portrait of Mary in Luke 1:46–55, The Girl has nothing to
do with filling the hungry with "good things," hawking instead an
endless proliferation of trivia on TV spot commercials. The Girl exalts
the mighty, extols the rich, and brings nothing to the hungry but
added despair. So The Girl does buttress and bring into personal focus
a value system, such as it is. In both social and psychological terms,
The Girl, whether or not she is really a goddess, certainly acts
that way.

Perhaps the most ironic element in the rise of the cult of The Girl
is that Protestantism has almost completely failed to notice it, while
Roman Catholics have at least given some evidence of sensing its
significance. In some places, for instance, Catholics are forbidden to
participate in beauty pageants, a ruling not entirely inspired by prudery.
It is ironic that Protestants have traditionally been most opposed to lady
cults while Catholics have managed to assimilate more than one at
various points in history.

If we are correct in assuming that The Girl *functions* in many ways
as a goddess, then the cult of The Girl demands careful Protestant
theological criticism. Anything that functions, even in part, as a god
when it is in fact not God, is an idol. When the Reformers and their
Puritan offspring criticized the cult of Mary it was not because they
were anti-feminist. They opposed anything—man, woman, or beast (or
dogma or institution)—that usurped in the slightest the prerogatives that
belonged alone to God Almighty. As Max Weber has insisted, when the
prophets of Israel railed against fertility cults, they had nothing against
fertility. It is not against sexuality but against a cult that protest is
needed. Not, as it were, against the beauty but against the pageant.

Thus the Protestant objection to the present cult of The Girl must
be based on the realization that The Girl is an *idol*. She functions as the
source of value, the giver of personal identity. But the values she
mediates and the identity she confers are both spurious. Like every idol
she is ultimately a creation of our own hands and cannot save us.
The values she represents as ultimate satisfactions—mechanical comfort,
sexual success, unencumbered leisure—have no ultimacy. They lead
only to endless upward mobility, competitive consumption, and anxious
cynicism. The devilish social insecurities from which she promises to
deliver us are, alas, still there, even after we have purified our breaths,
our skins, and our armpits by applying her sacred oils. She is a
merciless goddess who draws us farther and farther into the net of

accelerated ordeals of obeisance. As the queen of commodities in an
expanding economy, the fulfillment she promises must always
remain just beyond the tips of our fingers.

Why has Protestantism kept its attention obsessively fastened on
the development of Mariolatry in Catholicism and not noticed the
sinister rise of this vampirelike cult of The Girl in our society? Unfortunately, it is due to the continuing incapacity of theological critics to
recognize the religious significance of cultural phenomena outside the
formal religious system itself. But the rise of this new cult reminds us
that the work of the reformer is never done. Man's mind is indeed—
as Luther said—a factory busy making idols. The Girl is a far more
pervasive and destructive influence than the Virgin, and it is to her and
her omnipresent altars that we should be directing our criticism.

Besides sanctifying a set of phony values, The Girl compounds her
noxiousness by maiming her victims in a Procrustean bed of uniformity.
This is the empty "identity" she panders. Take the Miss America
pageant, for example. Are these virtually indistinguishable specimens of
white, middleclass postadolescence really the best we can do? Do they
not mirror the ethos of a mass-production society, in which genuine
individualism somehow mars the clean, precision-tooled effect? Like
their sisters, the finely calibrated Rockettes, these meticulously measured
and pretested "beauties" lined up on the Boardwalk bear an ominous
similarity to the faceless retinues of goose-steppers and the interchange-
able mass exercisers of explicitly totalitarian societies. In short, *who*
says this is beauty?

The caricature becomes complete in the Miss Universe contest, when
Miss Rhodesia is a blonde, Miss South Africa is white, and Oriental
girls with a totally different tradition of feminine beauty are forced to
display their thighs and appear in spike heels and Catalina swim suits.
Miss Universe is as universal as an American adman's stereotype
of what beauty should be.

The truth is that The Girl can*not* bestow the identity she promises.
She forces her initiates to torture themselves with starvation diets and
beauty-parlor ordeals, but still cannot deliver the satisfactions she
holds out. She is young, but what happens when her followers, despite
added hours in the boudoir, can no longer appear young? She is happy
and smiling and loved. What happens when, despite all the potions and
incantations, her disciples still feel the human pangs of rejection and
loneliness? Or what about all the girls whose statistics, or "personality"
(or color) do not match the authoritative "ideal"?

After all, it is God—not The Girl—who is God. He is the center and
source of value. He liberates men and women from the bland uniformity of cultural deities so that they may feast on the luxurious
diversity of life He has provided. The identity He confers frees men

from all pseudo-identities to be themselves, to fulfill their human destinies regardless whether their faces or figures match some predetermined abstract "ideal." As His gift, sex is freed from both fertility cults and commercial exploitation to become the thoroughly human thing He intended. And since it is one of the last items we have left that is neither prepackaged nor standardized, let us not sacrifice it too hastily on the omnivorous altar of Cybele.

The Playboy, illustrated by the monthly magazine of that name, does for the boys what Miss America does for the girls. Despite accusations to the contrary, the immense popularity of this magazine is not solely attributable to pin-up girls. For sheer nudity its pictorial art cannot compete with such would-be competitors as *Dude* and *Escapade*. *Playboy* appeals to a highly mobile, increasingly affluent group of young readers, mostly between eighteen and thirty, who want much more from their drugstore reading than bosoms and thighs. They need a total image of what it means to be a man. And Mr. Hefner's *Playboy* has no hesitation in telling them.

Why should such a need arise? David Riesman has argued that the responsibility for character formation in our society has shifted from the family to the peer group and to the mass-media peer-group surrogates.[4] Things are changing so rapidly that one who is equipped by his family with inflexible, highly internalized values becomes unable to deal with the accelerated pace of change and with the varying contexts in which he is called upon to function. This is especially true in the area of consumer values toward which the "other-directed person" is increasingly oriented.

Within the confusing plethora of mass media signals and peer-group values, *Playboy* fills a special need. For the insecure young man with newly acquired free time and money who still feels uncertain about his consumer skills, *Playboy* supplies a comprehensive and authoritative guidebook to this forbidding new world to which he now has access. It tells him not only who to be; it tells him *how* to be it, and even provides consolation outlets for those who secretly feel that they have not quite made it.

In supplying for the other-directed consumer of leisure both the normative identity image and the means for achieving it, *Playboy* relies on a careful integration of copy and advertising material. The comic book that appeals to a younger generation with an analogous problem skillfully intersperses illustrations of incredibly muscled men and excessively mammalian women with advertisements for body-building

4 David Riesman, *The Lonely Crowd* (New Haven: Yale University Press, 1950; Harmondsworth, Middlesex: Penguin).

gimmicks and foam-rubber brassière supplements. Thus the thin-chested comic-book readers of both sexes are thoughtfully supplied with both the ends and the means for attaining a spurious brand of maturity. *Playboy* merely continues the comic-book tactic for the next age group. Since within every identity crisis, whether in teens or twenties, there is usually a sexual-identity problem, *Playboy* speaks to those who desperately want to know what it means to be a man, and more specifically a *male*, in today's world.

Both the image of man and the means for its attainment exhibit a remarkable consistency in *Playboy*. The skilled consumer is cool and unruffled. He savors sports cars, liquor, high fidelity, and book-club selections with a casual, unhurried aplomb. Though he must certainly *have* and *use* the latest consumption item, he must not permit himself to get too attached to it. The style will change and he must always be ready to adjust. His persistent anxiety that he may mix a drink incorrectly, enjoy a jazz group that is passé, or wear last year's necktie style is comforted by an authoritative tone in *Playboy* beside which papal encyclicals sound irresolute.

"Don't hesitate," he is told, "this assertive, self-assured weskit is what every man of taste wants for the fall season." Lingering doubts about his masculinity are extirpated by the firm assurance that "real men demand this ruggedly masculine smoke" (cigar ad). Though "the ladies will swoon for you, no matter what they promise, don't give them a puff. This cigar is for men only." A fur-lined canvas field jacket is described as "the most masculine thing since the cave man." What to be and how to be it are both made unambiguously clear.

Since being a male necessitates some kind of relationship to females, *Playboy* fearlessly confronts this problem too, and solves it by the consistent application of the same formula. Sex becomes one of the items of leisure activity that the knowledgeable consumer of leisure handles with his characteristic skill and detachment. The girl becomes a desirable—indeed an indispensable—"Playboy accessory."

In a question-answering column entitled "The Playboy Adviser," queries about smoking equipment (how to break in a meerschaum pipe), cocktail preparation (how to mix a Yellow Fever), and whether or not to wear suspenders with a vest alternate with questions about what to do with girls who complicate the cardinal principle of casualness either by suggesting marriage or by some other impulsive gesture toward a permanent relationship. The infallible answer from the oracle never varies: sex must be contained, at all costs, within the entertainment-recreation area. Don't let her get "serious."

After all, the most famous feature of the magazine is its monthly fold-out photo of a *play*mate. She is the symbol par excellence of recreational sex. When playtime is over, the playmate's function ceases, so she must be made to understand the rules of the game. As the crew-cut young man in a *Playboy* cartoon says to the rumpled and disarrayed girl he is passionately embracing, "Why speak of love at a time like this?"

The magazine's fiction purveys the same kind of severely departmentalized sex. Although the editors have recently dressed up the *Playboy* contents with contributions by Hemingway, Bemelmans, and even a Chekhov translation, the regular run of stories relies on a repetitious and predictable formula. A successful young man, either single or somewhat less than ideally married—a figure with whom readers have no difficulty identifying—encounters a gorgeous and seductive woman who makes no demands on him except sex. She is the prose duplication of the cool-eyed but hot-blooded playmate of the fold-out.

Drawing heavily on the fantasy life of all young Americans, the writers utilize for their stereotyped heroines the hero's schoolteacher, his secretary, an old girl friend, or the girl who brings her car into the garage where he works. The happy issue is always a casual but satisfying sexual experience with no entangling alliances whatever. Unlike the women he knows in real life, the *Playboy* reader's fictional girl friends know their place and ask for nothing more. They present no danger of permanent involvement. Like any good accessory, they are detachable and disposable.

Many of the advertisements reinforce the sex-accessory identification in another way—by attributing female characteristics to the items they sell. Thus a full-page ad for the MG assures us that this car is not only "the smoothest pleasure machine" on the road and that having one is a "love-affair," but most important, "you drive it—it doesn't drive you." The ad ends with the equivocal question "Is it a date?" [5]

Playboy insists that its message is one of liberation. Its gospel frees us from captivity to the puritanical "hatpin brigade." It solemnly crusades for "frankness" and publishes scores of letters congratulating it for its unblushing "candor." Yet the whole phenomenon of which *Playboy* is only a part vividly illustrates the awful fact of a new kind of tyranny.

Those liberated by technology and increased prosperity to new worlds of leisure now become the anxious slaves of dictatorial tastemakers. Obsequiously waiting for the latest signal on what is cool and what is awkward, they are paralyzed by the fear that they may hear pronounced on them that dread sentence occasionally intoned by "The Playboy Adviser": "You goofed!" Leisure is thus swallowed up in apprehensive competitiveness, its liberating potential transformed into a self-

---

[5] This whole fusing of sex and machine symbols in contemporary mass media was once brilliantly explored by Marshall McCluhan in *The Mechanical Bride,* now out of print.

destructive compulsion to consume only what is *à la mode*. *Playboy* mediates the Word of the most high into one section of the consumer world, but it is a word of bondage, not of freedom.

Nor will *Playboy's* synthetic doctrine of man stand the test of scrutiny. Psychoanalysts constantly remind us how deep-seated sexuality is in the human being. But if they didn't remind us, we would soon discover it ourselves anyway. Much as the human male might like to terminate his relationship with a woman as he would snap off the stereo, or store her for special purposes like a camel's-hair jacket, it really can't be done. And anyone with a modicum of experience with women knows it can't be done. Perhaps this is the reason *Playboy's* readership drops off so sharply after the age of thirty.

Playboy really feeds on the existence of a repressed fear of involvement with women, which for various reasons is still present in many otherwise adult Americans. So *Playboy's* version of sexuality grows increasingly irrelevant as authentic sexual maturity is achieved.

The male identity crisis to which *Playboy* speaks has as its roots a deep-set fear of sex, a fear that is uncomfortably combined with fascination. *Playboy* strives to resolve this antinomy by reducing the proportions of sexuality, its power and its passion, to a packageable consumption item. Thus in *Playboy's* iconography the nude woman symbolizes total sexual accessibility but demands nothing from the observer. "You drive it—it doesn't drive you." The terror of sex, which cannot be separated from its ecstasy, is dissolved. But this futile attempt to reduce the *mysterium tremendum* of the sexual fails to solve the problem of being a man. For sexuality is the basic form of all human relationship, and therein lies its terror and its power.

Karl Barth has called this basic relational form of man's life *Mitmensch*, co-humanity.[6] This means that becoming fully human, in this case a human male, requires not having the other totally exposed to me and my purposes—while I remain uncommitted—but exposing myself to the risk of encounter with the other by reciprocal self-exposure. The story of man's refusal so to be exposed goes back to the story of Eden and is expressed by man's desire to control the other rather than to *be with* the other. It is basically the fear to be one's self, a lack of the "courage to be."

Thus any theological critique of *Playboy* that focuses on its "lewdness" will misfire completely. *Playboy* and its less successful imitators are not "sex magazines" at all. They are basically antisexual. They dilute and dissipate authentic sexuality by reducing it to an accessory, by keeping it at a safe distance.

It is precisely because these magazines are antisexual that they deserve

[6] Karl Barth, *Church Dogmatics* (Edinburgh: T & T Clark, 1957), II/2.

the most searching kind of theological criticism. They foster a heretical doctrine of man, one at radical variance with the biblical view. For *Playboy's* man, others—especially women—are *for* him. They are his leisure accessories, his playthings. For the Bible, man only becomes fully man by being *for* the other.

Moralistic criticisms of *Playboy* fail because its antimoralism is one of the few places in which *Playboy* is right. But if Christians bear the name of One who was truly man because He was totally *for* the other, and if it is in Him that we know who God is and what human life is for, then we must see in *Playboy* the latest and slickest episode in man's continuing refusal to be fully human.

Freedom for mature sexuality comes to man only when he is freed from the despotic powers which crowd and cower him into fixed patterns of behavior. Both Miss America and The Playboy illustrate such powers. When they determine man's sexual life, they hold him in captivity. They prevent him from achieving maturity. They represent the constant danger of relapsing into tribal thralldom which always haunts the secular society, a threat from which the liberating, secularizing word of the Gospel repeatedly recalls it.

1. What is Cox's proposition? What does he mean by the word "humanization" (par. 2)? How does he support his proposition?
2. What are Cox's basic assumptions about the relationship of society and the media? About the individual and society? About sex and the media? About religion and sex? About contemporary humans and sex?
3. What is Cox's purpose in quoting Lucretious's description of the pageant of Cybele?
4. How does the question beginning paragraph six reveal Cox's awareness of his audience and aid the development of his analysis?
5. Trace the steps of Cox's argument concerning "The Girl," showing where and how it alternates between deductive and inductive strategies. What types of evidence does he use? What is his principal argumentative structure?
6. What is Cox's definition of an "idol" and why is it important to his argument? Is this concept a purely religious one?
7. How are Cox's arguments about "The Girl" and "The Boy" related? Are the questions leading to his analyses the same in both discussions?
8. What specific phrases and allusions are indicative of the "voice" that Cox has chosen? On the basis of these, characterize the implied speaker.

"Ethics and Unmarried Sex"

THE SITUATION

Back in 1960 Professor Leo Koch of the University of Illinois, a biologist, was fired for saying that it was ethically justifiable to approve of premarital intercourse. His offending statement was: "With modern contraceptives and medical advice readily available at the nearest drug store, or at least a family physician, there is no valid reason why sexual intercourse should not be condoned among those sufficiently mature to engage in it without social consequences and without violating their own codes of morality and ethics." [1] With due regard for his three qualifying factors—maturity, social concern, and integrity—we can say that Professor Koch's position is the one at which this position essay will arrive. We shall try, incidentally, to demonstrate that the fear of honest discussion revealed by Koch's dismissal is at least not universal. (Professor Koch shared the earlier opinion of Professor George Murdock of Yale that premarital intercourse would prepare young people for more successful marriages.[2] But this paper will not offer any analysis favoring or opposing the Murdock-Koch thesis about marriage preparation.)

The American Bar Association has lately urged the different states to review and revise their civil and criminal laws regulating sex acts. Few have done so—except for Illinois. Serious efforts are under way in California and New York in the face of strong opposition in the churches. A model code committee of the American Law Institute in 1956 reported out some important proposed changes in existing law, all in the direction of greater personal freedom sexually, and calling for a lowering of the age of consent to eliminate unjust convictions for statutory rape. Fornication is a criminal offense in thirty-six of our fifty states, the penalty running from $10.00 in Rhode Island to $500 plus two years in jail in Alaska. Fourteen states have no law against it, but in six of these States "cohabitation" (nonmarital intercourse consistently with the same person) is a criminal offense.

This is a typical anomaly of our sex laws. It makes the punishment for cohabitation heavier than for promiscuity, thus creating the absurd situation in which a measure of interpersonal commitment between such sexual partners is penalized and promiscuity or *casual* fornication is preferred! In Massachusetts, for example, the penalty for fornication is $30.00 or ninety days in jail, but for cohabitation it is $300 or as much as three years. While many states outlaw adultery, there are others that

[1] *Time*, April 18, 1960.
[2] *Time*, February 13, 1950.

allow extramarital sex—as in wife swapping clubs. California is an example.

A great deal of both clinical and taxonomic evidence has been gathered showing that sexual activity, or at least sexual exploration, occurs before marriage—unrecognized by the conventional wisdom. The Kinsey findings were that 67 per cent of college males are involved, 84 per cent of males who go as far as high school, and 98 per cent of those who only finish grade school. We can raise these figures for the intervening fifteen years or more, but very probably it is still true that there is a negative correlation between educational levels and nonmarital intercourse. With females the opposite is the case; the higher the school level the greater their frequency of fornication. College women rated 60 per cent in Kinsey's studies (1953), but the rate was discernibly higher for 1966.

In recent years there has been a considerable black market in oral contraceptives. They can be had from "a man on the corner" or from drug stores that just don't ask for a prescription. Five million pills were hijacked in Philadelphia two years ago. Incidentally, local investigators have learned that more pills are sold in the vicinity of colleges than elsewhere. Doctors give unmarried girls and women prescriptions for them even when they do not personally approve of their patients' use of them. They rarely refuse them to applicants, and practically never when the young woman is engaged to be married. A year's prescription costs from $5.00 to $25.00 as the fee. In some college health services the medical staff make this distinction, giving to the engaged and refusing the unengaged. Soon we will have injections and vaccines which immunize against ovulation for several months at a time, making things easier than ever. It is even likely that a morning-after pill is coming, an abortifacient.

This will be a blessing because of the increase of unintended pregnancies and venereal diseases, due to the new sexual freedom. The Surgeon General has said that 1,400 get a venereal disease every day in the year.[3] Syphilis increased by 200 percent from 1965 to 1966 among persons under twenty.[4] The rate of illegitimate pregnancies among teenagers doubled from 1940 to 1961, and it quadrupled among women in the ages of twenty to twenty-five. The highest incidence of pregnancy is among those least promiscuous, i.e., those who are least competent sexually. Yet the risks do not deter them anymore. Fifty percent of teen-age girls who marry are pregnant; 80 percent of those who marry teen-age boys. It is estimated that nearly 200,000 teen-agers are aborted every year.

[3] *Saturday Review,* December 12, 1964.
[4] *New York Times,* September 5, 1965.

Sociologists, psychologists, and psychiatrists give us many reasons for the spread of premarital sex. Popularity seeking, the need for a secure companion and dater, the prestige value of full sexual performance, the notion that it achieves personal self-identity, even—but rather rarely—the need for physical satisfaction, these are among the things most mentioned. It is probably still the case that the majority of young women and some young men ordinarily, except for an occasional lapse, stop short of coitus, practicing petting to the point of orgasm instead of actual intercourse. Yet from the moral standpoint it is doubtful that there is any real difference between a technical virgin and a person who goes "all the way." And as for the old double standard for masculine and feminine behavior, it is clearly on its way out in favor of a more honest and undiscriminatory sex ethic.

These changes in attitude are going on even among Christians. The Sycamore Community at Penn State made a survey anonymously of 150 men and women, mostly ministers or professors and their wives, and found that while 33 percent were opposed to premarital sex, 40 percent favored it selectively. Forty percent of their male respondents reported that they themselves engaged in it (a low percentage compared to the whole population), and 35 percent of the women so reported. Fifteen percent reported that they had or had had premarital coitus frequently or regularly. Of the married respondents 18 percent of the husbands and 15 percent of the wives reported extramarital sex acts, although one-third of them said they had petted short of coitus. Yet 40 percent felt it might be justifiable in certain situations.[5]

In order, however, to get a sharp focus on the ethical problem and a possible solution, let us agree to stay with *premarital* sex. And let us agree that this term covers both casual sexual congress and a more personalized experience with dating partners, "steadies," and a "shack up" friend.

THE PROBLEM

In terms of ethical analysis we have *two* problem areas. The first one is the problem of premarital sex for those whose moral standards are in the classical religious tradition, based on a faith commitment to a divine sanction—usually, in America, some persuasion or other of the Judaeo-Christian kind. The second area is the "secular" one, in which people's moral standards are broadly humanistic, based on a value commitment to human welfare and happiness. It is difficult, if not impossible, to say what proportion of our people falls in either area, but they exist certainly, and the "secular" area is growing all the time.

[5] *Sex Ethics: A Study by and for Adult Christians,* The Sycamore Community (State College, Pa.: 1965).

There is by no means a set or unchanging viewpoint in the religious camp. Some Christians are challenging the old morality of the marital monopoly of sex. The Sycamore report declares that "there are no distinctively Christian patterns of sexual behavior which can be characterized by the absence or presence of specific acts." Their report favors a more situational, less legalistic approach to sex ethics. "Let Christians," they say, "face squarely the fact that what the body of authoritative Christian thought passed off as God's revealed truth was in fact human error with a Pauline flavor. Let us remember this fact every time we hear a solemn assertion about this or that being God's will or *the* Christian ethic."

In contrast to situation ethics, or religious relativism, stands the legalistic ethics of universal absolutes (usually negatives and pro- hibitions), condemning every form of sexual expression except horizontal coitus eyeball-to-eyeball solely between the parties to a monogamous marriage contract. Thus one editorial writer in a semi-fundamentalist magazine said recently, and correctly enough, "The new moralists do not believe that the biblical moral laws are really given by God. Morals laws are not regarded as the products of revelation." [6] A growing company of church people are challenging fixed moral principles or rules about sex or anything else.

The idea in the past has been that the ideal fulfillment of our sex potential lies in a monogamous marriage. But there is no reason to regard this ideal as a legal absolute. For example, if the sex ratio were to be overthrown by disaster, polygamy could well become the ideal or standard. Jesus showed more concern about pride and hypocrisy than about sex. In the story of the "Woman Taken in Adultery" her accusers were guiltier than she. Among the Seven Deadly Sins lust is listed but not sex, and lust can exist in marriage as well as out. But even so, lust is not so grave a sin as pride. As Dorothy Sayers points out scornfully, "A man may be greedy and selfish; spiteful, cruel, jealous and unjust; violent and brutal; grasping, unscrupulous and a liar; stubborn and arrogant; stupid, morose and dead to every noble instinct" and yet, if he practices his sinfulness within the marriage bond he is not thought by some Christians to be immoral! [7]

The Bible clearly affirms sex as a high-order value, at the same time sanctioning marriage (although not always monogamy), but any claim that the Bible requires that sex be expressed solely within marriage is only an inference; there is nothing explicitly forbidding premarital acts. Only extramarital acts, i.e., adultery, is forbidden. Those Christians who are situational, refusing to absolutize any moral principle except "love

[6] *Christianity Today*, October 8, 1965.
[7] *The Other Six Deadly Sins*, (London: Hodder & Stoughton, 1961).

thy neighbor," cannot absolutize St. Paul's one-flesh (*henosis*) theory of marriage in I Corinthians 6.[8] Paul Ramsey of Princeton has tried to defend premarital intercourse by engaged couples on the ground that they become married thereby. But marriages are not made by the act itself; sexual congress does not create a marriage. Marriage is a mutual commitment, willed and purposed interpersonally. Besides, all such "ontological" or "naturalistic" reasoning fails completely to meet the moral question of nonmarital sex acts between *un*engaged couples, since it presumably condemns them all universally as unjustifiable, simply because they are nonmarital. It is still the old marital monopoly theory, only one step relaxed.[9]

The humanists in our "secular" society draw close to the nonlegalists, the nonabsolutists among Christians, when they choose concern for personal values as their ethical norm, for this is very close to the Biblical "love thy neighbor as thyself." Professor Lester Kirkendall, in a privately circulated position paper, "Searching for the Roots of Moral Judgments," puts the humanist position well:

> The essence of morality lies in the quality of interrelationships which can be established among people. Moral conduct is that kind of behavior which enables people in their relationships with each other to experience a greater sense of trust and appreciation for others; which increases the capacity of people to work together; which reduces social distance and continually furthers one's outreach to other persons and groups; which increases one's sense of self-respect and produces a greater measure of personal harmony.
>
> Immoral behavior is just the converse. Behavior which creates distrust destroys appreciation for others, decreases the capacity for cooperation, lessens concern for others, causes persons or groups to shut themselves off or be shut off from others, and decreases an individual's sense of self-respect is immoral behavior.
>
> This is, of course, nothing new. The concept has been implicit in religions for ages. The injunction "love thy neighbor as thyself" is a case in point.[10]

On this view sarcasm and graft are immoral but not sexual intercourse, unless it is malicious or callous or cruel. On this basis an act is not wrong because of the act itself but because of its *meaning*—its motive and message. Therefore, as Professor Kirkendall explains, the question "Should we ever spank a child?" can only be answered, "It depends upon the situation, on why it is done and how the child understands it."

In the same way, as a *Christian* humanist, Professor John Macmurray,

[8] I Cor. 6:16: "Do you not know that he who joins himself to a prostitute becomes one body with her? For as it is written, 'The two shall become one.'"
[9] See also *Consultation on Sex Ethics*, (Founex, Switzerland: World Council of Churches, July 6–10, 1964).
[10] See Kirkendall's *Premarital Intercourse and Interpersonal Relations*, (New York: Julian Press, 1961).

declares, "The integrity of persons is inviolable. You shall not use a person for your own ends or indeed for any ends, individual or social. To use another person is to violate his personality by making an object of him; and in violating the integrity of another, you violate your own." [11] Thus one of Kant's maxims, at least, has survived the ravages of time. And recalling Henry Miller's book titles, we might paraphrase Kant and Macmurray by saying, "The plexus of the sexus is the nexus."

Both religious and secular moralists in America's plural society need to remember that freedom *of* religion includes freedom *from* religion. There is no ethical basis for compelling noncreedalists to follow any creedal codes of behavior, Christian or non-Christian. A "sin" is an act against God's will, but if the agent does not believe in God he cannot commit sin; and even those who do believe in God disagree radically as to what God's will is. Speaking to the issue over birth control law, Cardinal Cushing of Boston says, "Catholics do not need the support of civil law to be faithful to their own religious convictions, and they do not need to impose their moral views on other members of society. . . ." What the Cardinal says about birth control applies just as much to premarital intercourse.

Harking back to the Group for the Advancement of Psychiatry report's support of sexual *laissez faire* on college campuses, we could offer an ethical proposition of our own: Nothing we do is truly moral unless we are free to do otherwise. We must be free to decide what to do before any of our actions even begins to be moral. No discipline but self-discipline has any moral significance. This applies to sex, politics, or anything else. A moral act is a free act, done because we want to do it.

Incidentally, but not insignificantly, let me remark that this freedom, which is so essential to moral acts, can mean freedom *from* premarital sex as well as freedom for it. Not everybody would choose to engage in it. Some will not because it would endanger a precious relationship, interpersonally; some because it would endanger the sense of personal integrity. Value sentiments or "morals" may be changing (they *are,* obviously), but we are still "living in the overlap" and a sensitive, imaginative person might both well and wisely decide against it. As Dr. Mary Calderone points out, very young men and women are not always motivated in the same way: "The girl plays at sex, for which she is not ready, because fundamentally what she wants is love; and the boy plays at love, for which he is not ready, because what he wants is sex." [12]

Many will oppose premarital sex for reasons of the social welfare, others for relationship reasons, and some for simply egoistic reasons.

[11] *Reason and Emotion,* (New York: Barnes & Noble, 1962), p. 39.
[12] *Redbook* Magazine (July, 1965).

We may rate these reasons differently in our ethical value systems, but the main point morally is to respect the freedom to choose. And short of coitus young couples can pet each other at all levels up to orgasm, just so they are honest enough to recognize that merely technical virgins are no better morally than those who go the whole way. In John Hersey's recent novel, the boy and girl go to bed finally but end up sleeping curled up at arm's length.[13] It is ethically possible, that is to say, to be undecided, conflicted, and immobilized. What counts is being honest, and in some cases decision can be mistaken. Let honesty reign then too. Bryan Green, the evangelist, once said that the engaged but unmarried should thank God for the "experience" and ask his forgiveness for a lack of discipline.[14]

THE SOLUTION

Just as there are two ethical orientations, theistic and humanistic, so there are two distinct questions to ask ourselves. One is: Should we prohibit and condemn premarital sex? The other is: Should we approve of it? To the first one I promptly reply in the negative. To the second I propose an equivocal answer, "Yes and no—depending on each particular situation." The most solid basis for any ethical approach is on the ground common to both the religiously oriented and the humanistically oriented—namely, the concern both feel for persons. They are alike *personalistically* oriented. For example, both Christians and non-Christians can accept the normative principle, "We ought to love people and use things: immorality only occurs when we love things and use people." They can agree also on a companion maxim: "We ought to love people, not rules or principles; what counts is not any hard and fast moral law but doing what we can for the good of others in every situation."

The first principle means that no sexual act is ethical if it hurts or exploits others. This is the difference between lust and love: lust treats a sexual partner as an object, love as a subject. Charity is more important than chastity, but there is no such thing as "free love." There must be some care and commitment in premarital sex acts or they are immoral. Hugh Hefner, the whipping boy of the stuffies, has readily acknowledged in *Playboy* that "personal" sex relations are to be preferred to impersonal.[15] Even though he denies that mutual commitment needs

[13] *Too Far to Walk*, (New York: Knopf, 1966).
[14] Quoted in R. F. Hettlinger, *Living with Sex: The Student's Dilemma*, (New York: Seabury, 1966), p. 139.
[15] December, 1964.

to go to the radical lengths of marriage, he sees at least the difference between casual sex and actually callous congress.

The second principle is one of situation ethics—making a moral decision hang on the particular case. How, here and now, can I act with the most concern for the happiness and welfare of those involved— myself and others? Legalistic moralism, with its absolutes and universals, always thou-shalt-nots, cuts out the middle ground between being a virgin and a sexual profligate.[16] This is an absurd failure to see that morality has to be acted out on a continuum of relativity, like life itself, from situation to situation.

The only independent variable is concern for people; love thy neighbor as thyself. Christians, whether legalistic or situational about their ethics, are agreed that the *ideal* sexually is the combination of marriage and sex. But the ideal gives no reason to demand that others should adopt that ideal or to try to impose it by law; nor is it even any reason to absolutize the ideal in practice for all Christians in all situations. Sex is not always wrong outside marriage, even for Christians; as St. Paul said, "I know . . . that nothing is unclean in itself." [17] Another way to put it is to say that character shapes sex conduct, sex does not shape character.

As I proposed some years ago in a paper in *Law and Contemporary Problems*, the Duke University law journal, there are only three proper limitations to guide both the civil law and morality on sexual acts.[18] No sexual act between persons competent to give mutual consent should be prohibited, except when it involves either the seduction of minors or an offense against the public order. These are the principles of the Wolfenden Report to the English Parliament, adopted by that body and endorsed by the Anglican and Roman Catholic archbishops. It is time we acknowledged the difference between "sins" (a private judgment) and "crimes" against the public conscience and social consensus.

Therefore, we can welcome the recent decision of the federal Department of Health, Education, and Welfare to provide birth control assistance to unmarried women who desire it. It is a policy which puts into effect the principles of the President's Health Message to Congress of March 1, 1966. If the motive is a truly moral one it will be concerned not only with relief budgets but with the welfare of the women and a concern to prevent unwanted babies. Why wait for even *one* illegitimate child to be born?

Dr. Ruth Adams, president of Wellesley College, has said that the

16 See Harvey Cox, *The Secular City*, (New York: Macmillan, 1965), p. 212.
17 Romans 14:14.
18 Joseph Fletcher, "Sex Offenses: An Ethical View," *Law and Contemporary Problems* (Spring, 1961), pp. 244–57.

college's role is to give information about birth control educationally but no medical assistance. Actually birth control for unmarried students, she thinks, is "the function of the student's private physician rather than the college." [19] This is the strategy being followed by most universities and colleges—to separate knowledge and assistance, relegating to off-campus doctors the responsibility of protecting the unmarried from unwanted pregnancies. As a strategy it obviously avoids a clash with those who bitterly oppose sexual freedom; it is therefore primarily a public relations posture. It bows the neck to people whose attitude is that if premarital sex can't be prevented then the next best thing is to prevent tragic consequences—a curiously sadistic kind of pseudo-morality.

But surely this policy of information but no personal help is an ethical evasion by the universities. If they accept a flat fee for watching over the students' health, is not contraceptive care included? If college health services are able to prescribe treatment which is better than students can get in a drugstore, they *ought* to provide it. They should give *all* the medical service needed except what is too elaborate or technical for their facilities. Nobody is suggesting that pills or IUD's or diaphragms should be sold in the campus bookstore, but they ought to be regarded as a medical resource *owed* to the student as needed and requested. This is the opinion of most physicians on college health services, and I would support it for ethical reasons—chiefly out of respect for personal freedom.

1. What is the function of the first section ("The Situation"), and how is it related to the other two sections of the essay? What is the purpose in this first section of discussing the prevalence of premarital sex and its relationship to the law? What kind of evidence does Fletcher muster here to prove his assertion about the prevalence of premarital sex?

2. How is Fletcher's main assumption in the first section related to his argument in the last two sections?

3. With regard to an ethical analysis, are there only "*two* problem areas"? Why does Fletcher make this distinction?

4. Fletcher advances the ethical proposition that "Nothing we do is truly moral unless we are free to do otherwise." How is this assumption the basis of his entire essay? How is it related to his controlling idea and argument?

5. What is Fletcher's presupposition about sexuality? Does he narrow it to coitus, or expand it to a larger aspect of human relationships? How does

[19] *New York Times*, March 22, 1966.

his definition of "sexuality" influence his argument? Is it true, where Fletcher agrees with Mary Calderone, that the girl plays at sex because she wants love, and the boy plays at love because he wants sex?

6. Why does Fletcher state in the *first* paragraph the "position" at which his essay will "arrive"?

"Psychology Constructs the Female"/*Naomi Weisstein*

"The Suicide of the Sexes"/*George Gilder*

While the following essays share a common concern, their audiences are divergent. Naomi Weisstein's study was written for a scholarly audience attending a professional convention. In contrast, George Gilder's discussion first appeared in a widely circulated slick magazine appealing to a relatively well-educated but more general group. These facts determine not only the authors' respective differences in documentation of sources, but in their points of view as well. Notice how the voices of the opening paragraphs indicate basic differences in the method and rigor of their succeeding arguments.

Both essays, however, arise from the same question regarding our sexuality: what is innate and what is conditioned by culture—are roles rooted in natural, biological "facts," or are they merely arbitrary cultural categories? Weisstein and Gilder oppose each other in their answers to this question, and the methods of their respective arguments also differ dramatically. Weisstein's strategy, in her carefully researched and documented paper, is to attack aggressively the assumptions of her antagonists, those psychologists who limit female possibilities. She asserts at the outset that Psychology "has nothing to say about what women are really like." She then structures her argument around this proposition, showing that psychologists present theory on the basis of faulty evidence. She is most rigorous about what constitutes evidence as opposed to assumption and, on this basis, challenges the authority of scientists and the validity of their methods.

Gilder also attacks the assumptions of his antagonists and begins with the proposition that sex, "the life force and cohesive impulse of a people," is at present "devalued and deformed." But where Weisstein depends on a strategy of refutation, Gilder's method is to outline a broad theory which he applies to disparate elements of our experience. He trusts the internal consistency of his argument to overwhelm his opponents. In short, Weisstein attacks by aiming a cannon at the foundations of her enemy's fortress, while Gilder attacks by laying siege to his antagonist, showing that further resistance is futile because he is surrounded.

"Psychology Constructs the Female"

It is an implicit assumption that the area of psychology that concerns itself with personality has the onerous but necessary task of describing the limits of human possibility. Thus, when we are about to consider the liberation of women, we naturally look to psychology to tell us what "true" liberation would mean: what would give women the freedom to fulfill their own intrinsic natures?

Psychologists have set about describing the true nature of women with a certainty and a sense of their own infallibility rarely found in the secular world. Bruno Bettelheim tells us that "we must start with the realization that, as much as women want to be good scientists or engineers, they want first and foremost to be womanly companions of men and to be mothers." [1] Erik Erikson, upon noting that young women often ask whether they can "have an identity before they know whom they will marry, and for whom they will make a home," explains somewhat elegiacally that "much of a young woman's identity is already defined in her kind of attractiveness and in the selectivity of her search for the man (or men) by whom she wishes to be sought. . . ." Mature womanly fulfillment, for Erikson, rests on the fact that a woman's ". . . somatic design harbors an 'inner space' destined to bear the offspring of chosen men, and with it, a biological, psychological, and ethical commitment to take care of human infancy." [2] Some psychiatrists even see the acceptance of woman's role by women as a solution to societal problems. "Woman is nurturance," writes Joseph Rheingold, a psychiatrist at Harvard Medical School, ". . . anatomy decrees the life of a woman . . . when women grow up without dread of their biological functions and without subversion by feminist doctrine, and therefore enter upon motherhood with a sense of fulfillment and altruistic sentiment, we shall attain the goal of a good life and a secure world in which to live it." [3]

These views from men who are assumed to be experts reflect, in a surprisingly transparent way, the cultural consensus. They not only assert that a woman is defined by her ability to attract men, but they see

[1] B. Bettelheim, "The Commitment Required of a Woman Entering a Scientific Profession in Present-day American Society," in *Woman and the Scientific Professions,* an MIT Symposium on American Women in Science and Engineering (Cambridge, Mass., 1965).

[2] E. Erikson, "Inner and Outer Space: Reflections on Womanhood," *Daedalus* 93 (1964): 582–606.

[3] J. Rheingold, *The Fear of Being a Woman* (New York: Grune & Stratton, 1964), p. 714.

no alternative definitions. They think that the definition of a woman in
terms of a man is the way it should be; and they back it up with psycho-
sexual incantation and biological ritual curses. A woman has an identity
if she is attractive enough to obtain a man, and thus, a home; for this
will allow her to set about her life's task of "joyful altruism and
nurturance." A woman's *true* nature is that of a happy servant.

Business certainly does not disagree. If views such as Bettelheim's and
Erikson's do indeed have something to do with real liberation for
women, then seldom in human history has so much money and effort
been spent on helping a group of people realize their true potential.
Clothing, cosmetics, and home furnishings are multimillion dollar
businesses. If you do not like investing in firms that make weaponry and
flaming gasoline, then there is a lot of cash in "inner space." Sheet
and pillowcase manufacturers are anxious to fill this inner space:

> Mother, for a while this morning, I thought I wasn't cut out for married life.
> Hank was late for work and forgot his apricot juice and walked out without
> kissing me, and when I was all alone I started crying. But then the postman
> came with the sheets and towels you sent, that look like big bandana handker-
> chiefs, and you know what I thought? That those big red and blue hand-
> kerchiefs are for girls like me to dry their tears on so they can get busy and do
> what a housewife has to do. Throw open the windows and start getting the
> house ready, and the dinner, maybe clean the silver and put new geraniums
> in the box. *Everything to be ready for him when he walks through that door.*[4]

Of course, it is not only the sheet and pillowcase manufacturers, the
cosmetics industry, and the home furnishings salesmen who profit from
and make use of the cultural definitions of men and women. The
example above is blatantly and overtly pitched to a particular kind of
sexist stereotype: the child nymph. But almost all aspects of the media
are normative, that is, they have to do with the ways in which beautiful
people, or just folks, or ordinary Americans, or extraordinary Americans
should live their lives. They define the possible, and the possibilities
are usually in terms of what is male and what is female.

It is an interesting but limited exercise to show that psychologists
and psychiatrists embrace these sexist norms of our culture, that they do
not see beyond the most superficial and stultifying conceptions of female
nature, and that their ideas of female nature serve industry and
commerce so well. Just because it is good for business does not mean it
is wrong. What I will show is that it is wrong; that there is not the
tiniest shred of evidence that these fantasies of servitude and childish
dependence have anything to do with women's true potential; that the
idea of the nature of human possibility which rests on the accidents of
individual development of genitalia, on what is possible today because

[4] Fieldcrest advertisement in the *New Yorker*, 1965. My italics.

of what happened yesterday, on the fundamentalist myth of sex-organ causality, has strangled and deflected psychology so that it is relatively useless in describing, explaining, or predicting humans and their behavior. It then goes without saying that present psychology is less than worthless in contributing to a vision that could truly liberate—men as well as women.

The central argument of my essay, then, is this. Psychology has nothing to say about what women are really like, what they need and what they want, essentially because psychology does not know. I want to stress that this failure is not limited to women; rather, the kind of psychology that has addressed itself to how people act and who they are has failed to understand in the first place why people act the way they do, and certainly failed to understand what might make them act differently.

These psychologists, whether engaged in academic personality research or in clinical psychology and psychiatry, make the central assumption that human behavior rests on an individual and inner dynamic, perhaps fixed in infancy, perhaps fixed by genitalia, perhaps simply arranged in a rather immovable cognitive network. But this assumption is rapidly losing ground as personality psychologists fail again and again to get consistency in the assumed personalities of their subjects.[5] Meanwhile, the evidence is accumulating that what a person does and who he believes himself to be will in general be a function of what people around him expect him to be, and what the overall situation in which he is acting implies that he is. Compared to the influence of the social context within which a person lives, his or her history and traits, as well as biological make-up, may simply be random variations, noise superimposed on the true signal that can predict behavior.

Some academic personality psychologists are at least looking at the counterevidence and questioning their theories; no such corrective is occurring in clinical psychology and psychiatry. Freudians and neo-Freudians, Adlerians and neo-Adlerians, classicists and swingers, clinicians and psychiatrists simply refuse to look at the evidence against their theory and practice. And they support their theory and their practice with stuff so transparently biased as to have absolutely no standing as empirical evidence.

To summarize: psychology has failed to understand what people are and how they act because (1) psychology has looked for inner traits when it should have been noting social context; and (2) theoreticians of

[5] J. Block, "Some Reasons for the Apparent Inconsistency of Personality," *Psychological Bulletin* 70 (1968): 210–212.

personality have generally been clinicians and psychiatrists, and they have never considered it necessary to offer evidence to support their theories.

THEORY WITHOUT EVIDENCE

Let us turn to the second cause of failure first: the acceptance by psychiatrists and clinical psychologists of theory without evidence. If we inspect the literature of personality, it is immediately obvious that the bulk of it is written by clinicians and psychiatrists whose major support for their theories is "years of intensive clinical experience." This is a tradition started by Freud. His "insights" occurred during the course of his work with his patients. Now there is nothing wrong with such an approach to theory *formulation;* a person is free to make up theories with any inspiration that works: divine revelation, intensive clinical practice, a random numbers table. However, he is not free to claim any validity for his theory until it has been tested and confirmed. But theories are treated in no such tentative way in ordinary clinical practice. Consider Freud. What he thought constituted evidence fell short of the most minimal conditions of scientific rigor. In *The Sexual Enlightenment of Children,* the classic document that is supposed to demonstrate empirically the existence of a castration complex and its connection to a phobia, Freud based his analysis on the reports of the father of the little boy, himself in therapy, and a devotee of Freudian theory.[6] I really do not have to comment further on the contamination in this kind of evidence. It is remarkable that only recently has Freud's classic theory on the sexuality of women—the notion of the double orgasm—been actually tested physiologically and found just plain wrong. Now those who claim that fifty years of psychoanalytic experience constitute evidence enough of the essential truths of Freud's theory should ponder the robust health of the double orgasm. Did women, until Masters and Johnson,[7] believe they were having two different kinds of orgasm? Did their psychiatrists cow them into reporting something that was not true? If so, were there other things they reported that were also not true? Did psychiatrists ever observe anything different from what their theories had led them to believe? If clinical experience means anything at all, surely we should have been done with the double-orgasm myth long before the Masters and Johnson studies.

[6] S. Freud, *The Sexual Enlightenment of Children* (New York: Collier Books, 1963).
[7] W. H. Masters and V. E. Johnson, *Human Sexual Response* (Boston: Little, Brown, 1966).

But certainly, you may object, "years of intensive clinical experience" are the only reliable measure in a discipline that rests for its findings on insights, sensitivity, and intuition. The problem with insight, sensitivity, and intuition is that they can confirm for all time the biases that one started out with. People used to be absolutely convinced of their ability to tell which of their number were engaging in witchcraft. All it required was some sensitivity to the workings of the devil.

Years of intensive clinical experience are not the same thing as empirical evidence. The first thing an experimenter learns in any kind of experiment that involves humans is the concept of the double blind. The term is taken from medical experiments, where one group is given a drug which is presumably supposed to change behavior in a certain way, and a control group is given a placebo. If the observers or the subjects know which group took which drug, the result invariably comes out on the positive side for the new drug. Only when it is not known which subject took which pill is validity remotely approximated. In addition, with judgments of human behavior, it is so difficult to precisely tie down just what behavior is going on, let alone what behavior should be expected, that one must test again and again the reliability of judgments. How many judges, blind, will agree in their observations? Can they repeat their own judgments at some later time? When in actual practice these judgment criteria are tested for clinical judgments, then we find that the judges cannot judge reliably, nor can they judge consistently; they do no better than chance in identifying which of a certain set of stories were written by men and which by women; which of a whole battery of clinical test results were the products of homosexuals and which were the products of heterosexuals,[8] and which of a battery of clinical test results and interviews (where questions are asked such as "Do you have delusions?") [9] were products of psychotics, neurotics, psychosomatics, or normals. Let me stress the implications of these findings. The ability of judges, chosen for their clinical expertise, to distinguish male heterosexuals from male homosexuals on the basis of three widely used clinical projective tests—the Rorschach, the TAT, and the MAP—was *no better than chance.* The reason this is such devastating news, of course, is that sexuality is supposed to be of fundamental importance in the deep dynamic of personality; if what is considered gross sexual deviance cannot be recognized, then what are psychologists talking about when they, for example, claim that at the basis of paranoid psychosis is "latent homosexual panic"? They cannot even identify what homosexual anything

[8] E. Hooker, "Male Homosexuality in the Rorschach," *Journal of Projective Techniques* 21 (1957): 18–31.
[9] K. B. Little and E. S. Schneidman, "Congruences among Interpretations of Psychological and Anamnestic Data," *Psychological Monographs* 73 (1959): 1–42.

is, let alone "latent homosexual panic." [10] More frightening, expert
clinicians cannot be consistent about what diagnostic category to assign
to a person, again on the basis of both tests and interviews; a number of
normals in the Little and Schneidman study were described as psychotic,
in such categories as schizophrenic with homosexual tendencies or
schizoid character with depressive trends. But most disheartening, when
the judges were asked to rejudge the test protocols some weeks later,
their diagnoses of the same subjects on the basis of the same protocols
differed markedly from their initial judgments. It is obvious that even
simple descriptive conventions in clinical psychology cannot be
consistently applied; that these descriptive conventions have any explana-
tory significance is therefore, of course, out of the question.

As a graduate student at Harvard some years ago, I was a member of
a seminar that was asked to identify which of two piles of a clinical
test, the TAT, had been written by males and which by females. Only
four students out of twenty identified the piles correctly; this was after
one and a half months of intensively studying the differences between
men and women. Since this result is below chance—that is, this result
would occur by chance about four out of a thousand times—we may
conclude that there *is* finally a consistency here; students are judging
knowledgeably within the context of psychological teaching about the
differences between men and women; the teachings themselves
are simply erroneous.

You may argue that the theory may be scientifically "unsound" but at
least it cures people. There is no evidence that it does. In 1952 Eysenck
reported the results of what is called an "outcome of therapy" study
of neurotics which showed that, of the patients who received psycho-
analysis, the improvement rate was 44 percent; of the patients who
received psychotherapy, the improvement rate was 64 percent; and of the
patients who received no treatment at all, the improvement rate was
72 percent.[11] These findings have never been refuted; subsequently later
studies have confirmed the negative results of the Eysenck study.[12] How

10 It should be noted that psychologists have been as quick to assert absolute truths about
the nature of homosexuality as they have about the nature of women. The arguments
presented in this essay apply equally to the nature of homosexuality; psychologists know
nothing about it; there is no more evidence for the "naturalness" of heterosexuality than
for the "naturalness" of homosexuality. Psychology has functioned as a pseudoscientific
buttress for our cultural sex-role notions, that is, as a buttress for patriarchal ideology
and patriarchal social organization. Women's liberation and gay liberation fight against
a common victimization.
11 H. J. Eysenck, "The Effects of Psychotherapy: An Evaluation," *Journal of Consulting
Psychology* 16 (1952): 319–324.
12 F. Barron and T. Leary, "Changes in Psychoneurotic Patients with and without Psychotherapy," *Journal of Consulting Psychology* 19 (1955): 239–245; A. E. Bregin,
"The Effects of Psychotherapy: Negative Results Revisited," *Journal of Consulting Psychology* 10 (1963): 244–250; R. D. Cartwright and J. L. Vogel, "A Comparison of

can clinicians and psychiatrists, then, in all good conscience, continue to practice? Largely by ignoring these results and being careful not to do outcome-of-therapy studies. The attitude is nicely summarized by J. B. Rotter: "Research studies in psychotherapy tend to be concerned more with psychotherapeutic procedure and less with outcome . . . to some extent, it reflects an interest in the psychotherapy situation as a kind of personality laboratory." [13] Some laboratory.

THE SOCIAL CONTEXT

Since clinical experience and tools can be shown to be worse than useless when tested for consistency, efficacy, agreement, and reliability, we can safely conclude that theories of a clinical nature advanced about women are also worse than useless. I want to turn now to the second major point in my essay: even when psychological theory is constructed so that it may be tested, and rigorous standards of evidence are used, it has become increasingly clear that in order to understand why people do what they do, and certainly in order to change what people do, psychologists must turn away from the theory of the causal nature of the inner dynamic and look to the social context within which individuals live.

Before examining the relevance of this approach for the question of women, let me first sketch the groundwork for this assertion. In the first place, it is clear that personality tests never yield consistent predictions; [14] a rigid authoritarian on one measure will be an unauthoritarian on the next. But the reason for this inconsistency is only now becoming clear; it seems overwhelmingly to have much more to do with the social situation in which the subject finds himself than with the subject himself.

In a series of brilliant experiments, R. Rosenthal and his coworkers have shown that if one group of experimenters has one hypothesis about what they expect to find, and another group of experimenters has the opposite hypothesis, both groups will obtain results in accord with their hypotheses.[15] The results obtained are not due to mishandling of data by

Changes in Psychoneurotic Patients during Matched Periods of Therapy and No-Therapy," *Journal of Consulting Psychology* 24 (1960): 121–127; E. Powers and H. Witmer, *An Experiment in the Prevention of Delinquency* (New York: Columbia University Press, 1951); C. B. Traux, "Effective Ingredients in Psychotherapy: An Approach to Unraveling the Patient-Therapist Interaction," *Journal of Counseling Psychology* 10 (1963): 256–263.
[13] J. B. Rotter, "Psychotherapy," *Annual Review of Psychology* 11 (1960): 381–414.
[14] Block, *op. cit.*
[15] R. Rosenthal and L. Jacobson, *Pygmalion in the Classroom: Teacher Expectation and Pupil's Intellectual Development* (New York: Holt, Rinehart & Winston, 1968); R. Rosenthal, *Experimenter Effects in Behavioral Research* (New York: Appleton-Century Crofts, 1966).

biased experimenters; rather, the bias of the experimenter somehow creates a changed environment in which subjects actually act differently. For instance, in one experiment subjects were to assign numbers to pictures of men's faces, with high numbers representing the subject's judgment that the man in the picture was a successful person, and low numbers representing the subject's judgment that the man in the picture was an unsuccessful person. One group of experimenters was told that the subjects tended to rate the faces high; another group of experimenters was told that the subjects tended to rate the faces low. Each group of experimenters was instructed to follow precisely the same procedure: they were required to read to subjects a set of instructions and to *say nothing else*. For the 375 subjects run, the results showed clearly that those subjects who performed the task with experimenters who expected high ratings gave high ratings, and those subjects who performed the task with experimenters who expected low ratings gave low ratings. How did this happen? The experimenters all used the same words, but something in their conduct made one group of subjects do one thing, and another group of subjects do another thing.

The concreteness of the changed conditions produced by expectation is a fact, a reality: even in two separate studies with animal subjects, those experimenters who were told that rats learning mazes had been especially bred for brightness obtained better learning from their rats than did experimenters believing their rats to have been bred for dullness.[16] In a very recent study Rosenthal and Jacobson extended their analysis to the natural classroom situation.[17] Here, they tested a group of students and reported to the teachers that some among the students tested "showed great promise." Actually, the students so named had been selected on a random basis. Some time later, the experimenters retested the group of students: those students whose teachers had been told that they were "promising" showed real and dramatic increments in their I.Q.'s as compared to the rest of the students. Something in the conduct of the teachers toward those who the teachers believed to be the "bright" students made those students brighter.

Thus, even in carefully controlled experiments and with no outward or conscious difference in behavior, the hypotheses we start with will influence the behavior of the subject enormously. These studies are extremely important when assessing the validity of psychological studies of women. Since it is beyond doubt that most of us start with notions

[16] R. Rosenthal and K. L. Fode, "The Effect of Experimenter Bias on the Performance of the Albino Rat," unpublished manuscript (Cambridge: Harvard University, 1960); R. Rosenthal and R. Lawson, "A Longitudinal Study of the Effects of Experimenter Bias on the Operant Learning of Laboratory Rats," unpublished manuscript (Cambridge: Harvard University, 1961).
[17] Rosenthal and Jacobson, *op. cit.*

about the nature of men and women, the validity of a number of observations of sex differences is questionable, even when these observations have been made under carefully controlled conditions. Second, and more important, the Rosenthal experiments point quite clearly to the influence of social expectation. In some extremely important ways, people are what you expect them to be, or at least they behave as you expect them to behave. Thus, if women, according to Bettelheim, want first and foremost to be good wives and mothers, it is extremely likely that this is what Bruno Bettelheim and the rest of society want them to be.

Another series of brilliant social psychological experiments point to the overwhelming effect of social context. These are the obedience experiments of Stanley Milgram in which subjects are asked to obey the orders of unknown experimenters, orders which carry with them the distinct possibility that the subject is killing somebody.[18] In Milgram's experiments a subject is told that he is administering a learning experiment and that he is to deal out shocks each time the other subject (in reality, a confederate of the experimenter) answers incorrectly. The equipment appears to provide graduated shocks ranging upward from 15 volts through 450 volts; for each of four consecutive voltages there are verbal descriptions such as "mild shock," "danger, severe shock," and, finally, for the 435 and 450 volt switches, a red XXX marked over the switches. Each time the stooge answers incorrectly the subject is supposed to increase the voltage. As the voltage increases, the stooge begins to cry in pain; he demands that the experiment stop; finally, he refuses to answer at all. When he stops responding, the experimenter instructs the subject to continue increasingly the voltage; for each shock administered the stooge shrieks in agony. Under these conditions about 62.5 percent of the subjects administered shocks that they believed to be possibly lethal.

No tested individual differences between subjects predicted how many would continue to obey and who would break off the experiment. When forty psychiatrists predicted how many of a group of 100 subjects would go on to give the lethal shock, their predictions were orders of magnitude below the actual percentages; most expected only one-tenth of one percent of the subjects to obey to the end.

But even though psychiatrists have no idea how people will behave in this situation, and even though individual differences do not predict which subjects will obey and which will not, it is easy to predict when subjects will be obedient and when they will be defiant. All the ex-

---

[18] S. Milgram, "Some Conditions of Obedience and Disobedience to Authority," *Human Relations* 18 (1965): 57–76; S. Milgram, "Liberating Effects of Group Pressure," *Journal of Personality and Social Psychology* 1 (1965): 127–134.

perimenter has to do is change the social situation. In a variant of Milgram's experiment, two stooges were present in addition to the "victim"; these worked along with the subject in administering electric shocks. When these two stooges refused to go on with the experiment, only 10 percent of the subjects continued to the maximum voltage. This is critical for personality theory. It says that behavior can only be predicted from the social situation, not from the individual history.

Finally, an ingenious experiment by S. Schachter and J. E. Singer showed that subjects injected with adrenalin, which produces a state of physiological arousal in all but minor respects identical to that which occurs when subjects are extremely afraid, became euphoric when they were in a room with a stooge who was acting euphoric, and became extremely angry when they were placed in a room with a stooge who was acting extremely angry.[19]

To summarize: if subjects under quite innocuous and noncoercive social conditions can be made to kill other subjects and under other types of social conditions will positively refuse to do so; if subjects can react to a state of physiological fear by becoming euphoric, because somebody else around is euphoric, or angry, because somebody else around is angry; if students become intelligent because teachers expect them to be intelligent, and rats run mazes better because experimenters are told the rats are bright, then it is obvious that a study of human behavior requires, first and foremost, a study of the social contexts within which people move, of the expectations about how they will behave, and of the authority that tells them who they are and what they are supposed to do.

BIOLOGICALLY BASED THEORIES

Two theories of the nature of women, which come not from psychiatric and clinical tradition, but from biology, can be disposed of now with little difficulty. The first biological theory of sex differences argues that since females and males differ in their sex hormones, and sex hormones enter the brain, there must be innate differences in nature.[20] But this argument only tells us that there are differences in physiological state. The problem is whether these differences are at all relevant to behavior. Recall that Schachter and Singer have shown that a particular physiological state can itself lead to a multiplicity of felt emotional

[19] S. Schachter and J. E. Singer, "Cognitive, Social, and Physiological Determinants of Emotional State," *Psychological Review* 69 (1962): 379–399.
[20] D. A. Hamburg and D. T. Lunde, "Sex Hormones in the Development of Sex Differences in Human Behavior," in E. Maccoby, ed., *The Development of Sex Differences* (Stanford: Stanford University Press, 1966), pp. 1–24.

states and outward behavior, depending on the social situation.[21] The second theory is a form of biological reductionism: sex-role behavior in some primate species is described, and it is concluded that this is the natural behavior for humans. Putting aside the not insignificant problem of observer bias (for instance, H. Harlow of the University of Wisconsin, after observing differences between male and female rhesus monkeys, quotes Lawrence Sterne to the effect that women are silly and trivial and concludes that "men and women have differed in the past and they will differ in the future"),[22] there are a number of problems with this approach.

The most general and serious problem is that there are no grounds to assume that anything primates do is necessary, natural, or desirable in humans, for the simple reason that humans are not nonhumans. For instance, it is found that male chimpanzees placed alone with infants will not "mother" them. Jumping from hard data to ideological speculation researchers conclude from this information that *human* females are necessary for the safe growth of human infants. Following this logic, it would be as reasonable to conclude that it is quite useless to teach human infants to speak since it has been tried with chimpanzees and it does not work.

One strategy that has been used is to extrapolate from primate behavior to "innate" human preference by noticing certain trends in primate behavior as one moves phylogenetically closer to humans. But there are great difficulties with this approach. When behaviors from lower primates are directly opposite to those of higher primates, or to those one expects of humans, they can be dismissed on evolutionary grounds—higher primates and/or humans grew out of that kid stuff. On the other hand, if the behavior of higher primates is counter to the behavior considered natural for humans, while the behavior of some lower primate is considered natural for humans, the higher primate behavior can be dismissed also on the grounds that it has diverged from an older, prototypical pattern. So either way, one can select those behaviors one wants to prove as innate for humans. In addition, one does not know whether the sex-role behavior exhibited is dependent on the phylogenic rank or on the environmental conditions (both physical and social) under which different species live.

Is there then any value at all in prime observations as they relate to human females and males? There is a value but it is limited: its function can be no more than to show some extant examples of diverse sex-role behavior. It must be stressed, however, that this is an extremely limited function. The extant behavior does not begin to suggest all the

[21] Schachter and Singer, *op. cit.*
[22] H. F. Harlow, "The Heterosexual Affectional System in Monkeys," *The American Psychologist* 17 (1962): 1–9.

possibilities, either for nonhuman primates or for humans. Bearing these caveats in mind, it is nonetheless interesting that if one inspects the limited set of existing nonhuman primate sex-role behaviors, one finds, in fact, a much larger range of sex-role behavior than is commonly believed to exist. Biology appears to limit very little; the fact that a female gives birth does not mean, even in nonhumans, that she necessarily cares for the infant (in marmosets, for instance, the male carries the infant at all times except when the infant is feeding).[23] Natural female and male behavior varies all the way from females who are much more aggressive and competitive than males (for example, Tamarins) [24] and male "mothers" (for example, Titi monkeys, night monkeys, and marmosets),[25] to submissive and passive females and male antagonists (for example, rhesus monkeys).[26]

But even for the limited function that primate arguments serve, the evidence has been misused. Invariably, only those primates have been cited that exhibit exactly the kind of behavior that the proponents of the biological basis of human female behavior wish were true for humans. Thus, baboons and rhesus monkeys are generally cited: males in these groups exhibit some of the most irritable and aggressive behavior found in primates, and if one wishes to argue that females are naturally passive and submissive, these groups provide vivid examples. There are abundant counterexamples, such as those mentioned above; in fact, in general a counterexample can be found for every sex-role behavior cited, including male "mothers." The presence of counterexamples has not stopped florid and overarching theories of the natural or biological basis of male privilege from proliferating. For instance, there have been a number of theories dealing with the innate incapacity of human males for monogamy. Here, as in most of this type of theorizing, baboons are a favorite example, probably because of their fantasy value: the family unit of the hamadryas baboon, for instance, consists of a highly constant pattern of one male and a number of females and their young. And again, the counterexamples, such as the invariably monogamous gibbon, are ignored.

An extreme example of this maiming and selective truncation of the evidence in the service of a plea for the maintenance of male privilege is a recent book, *Men in Groups*, by a man who calls himself Tiger.[27] The central claim of this book is that females are incapable of honorable

23 G. D. Mitchell, "Paternalistic Behavior in Primates," *Psychological Bulletin* 71 (1969): 399–417.
24 *Ibid.*
25 *Ibid.*
26 All these are lower-order primates, which makes their behavior with reference to humans unnatural, or more natural; take your choice.
27 M. Schwarz-Belkin, "Les Fleurs du Mal," in *Festschrift for Gordon Piltdown* (New York: Ponzi Press, 1914), claims that the name was originally *Mouse*, but this may be a reference to an earlier L. Tiger (putative).

collective action because they are incapable of "bonding" as in "male bonding." [28] What is male bonding? Its surface definition is simple: "a particular relationship between two or more males such that they react differently to members of their bonding units as compared to individuals outside of it." [29] If one deletes the word male, the definition, on its face, would seem to include all organisms that have any kind of social organization. But this is not what Tiger means. For instance, Tiger asserts that because females are incapable of bonding, they should be restricted from public life. Why is bonding an exclusively male behavior? Because, says Tiger, it is seen in male primates. All male primates? No, very few male primates. Tiger cites two examples where male bonding is seen: rhesus monkeys and baboons. Surprise, surprise. But not even all baboons: as mentioned above, the hamadryas social organization consists of one-male units; so does that of the Gelada baboon.[30] The great apes do not go in for male bonding much either. The male bond is hardly a serious contribution to scholarship; one reviewer for *Science* has observed that the book "shows basically more resemblance to a partisan political tract than to a work of objective social science," with male bonding being "some kind of behavioral phlogiston." [31]

In short, primate arguments have generally misused the evidence: primate studies themselves have, in any case, only the very limited function of describing some possible sex-role behavior; and at present, primate observations have been sufficiently limited so that even the range of possible sex-role behavior for nonhuman primates is not known. This range is not known since there is only minimal observation of what happens to behavior if the physical or social environment is changed. In one study different troops of Japanese macaques were observed.[32] Here, there appeared to be cultural differences: males in three out of the eighteen troops observed differed in their aggressiveness and infant-caring behavior. There could be no possibility of differential evolution here; the differences seemed largely transmitted by infant socialization. Thus, the very limited evidence points to some plasticity in the sex-role behavior of nonhuman primates; if we can devise experiments that massively change the social organization of primate groups, it is possible that we may observe great changes in behavior. At present, however, we must conclude that since nonhuman primates are too stupid to change their social conditions by themselves, the innateness and fixedness of

28 L. Tiger, *Men in Groups* (New York: Random House, 1969).
29 *Ibid.*, pp. 19–20.
30 Mitchell, *op. cit.*
31 M. H. Fried, "Mankind Excluding Woman," review of Tiger's *Men in Groups*, *Science* 165 (1969): 884.
32 J. Itani, "Paternal Care in the Wild Japanese Monkeys, *Macaca fuscata*," in C. H. Southwick, ed., *Primate Social Behavior* (Princeton, N.J.: Van Nostrand, 1963).

their behavior is simply not known. Thus, even if there were some way—which there is not—to settle on the behavior of a particular primate species as being the "natural" way for humans, we would not know whether or not this behavior was simply some function of the present social organization of that species. And finally, once again it must be stressed that even if nonhuman primate behavior turned out to be relatively fixed, this would say little about our behavior. More immediate and relevant evidence, that is, the evidence from social psychology, points to an enormous plasticity in human behavior, not only from one culture to the next, but from one experimental group to the next. One of the most salient features of human social organization is its variety; there are a number of cultures where there is at least a rough equality between men and women.[33] In summary, primate arguments can tell us very little about our innate sex-role behavior; if they tell us anything at all, they tell us that there is no one biologically natural female or male behavior and that sex-role behavior in nonhuman primates is much more varied than has previously been thought.

CONCLUSION

In brief, the uselessness of present psychology with regard to women is simply a special case of the general conclusion: one must understand social expectations about women if one is going to characterize the behavior of women.

How are women characterized in our culture and in psychology? They are inconsistent, emotionally unstable, lacking in a strong conscience or superego, weaker, nurturant rather than productive, intuitive rather than intelligent, and, if they are at all "normal," suited to the home and the family. In short, the list adds up to a typical minority-group stereotype of inferiority: [34] if women know their place, which is in the home, they are really quite lovable, happy, childlike, loving creatures. In a review of the intellectual differences between little boys and little girls, Eleanor Maccoby has shown that there are no intellectual differences until about high school, or, if there are, girls are slightly ahead of boys.[35] In high school girls begin to do worse on a few intellectual tasks, such as arithmetic reasoning, and beyond high school the achievement of women now measured in terms of productivity and accomplishment drops off even more rapidly. There are a number of other, nonintellectual tests which show sex differences; I chose the

33 M. Mead, *Male and Female: A Study of the Sexes in a Changing World* (New York: William Morrow, 1949).
34 H. M. Hacker, "Women as a Minority Group," *Social Forces* 30 (1951); 60–69.
35 Maccoby, *op. cit.*

intellectual differences since it is seen clearly that women start becoming inferior. It is useless to talk about women being different but equal; all of the tests I can think of have a "good" outcome and a "bad" outcome. Women usually end up at the "bad" outcome. In light of social expectations about women, what is surprising is not that women end up where society expects they will; what is surprising is that little girls do not get the message that they are supposed to be stupid until high school; and what is even more remarkable is that some women resist this message even after high school, college, and graduate school.

My essay began with remarks on the task of discovering the limits of human potential. Psychologists must realize that it is they who are limiting discovery of human potential. They refuse to accept evidence if they are clinical psychologists, or, if they are rigorous, they assume that people move in a context-free ether, with only their innate dispositions and their individual traits determining what they will do. Until psychologists begin respecting evidence and until they begin looking at the social contexts within which people move, psychology will have nothing of substance to offer in this task of discovery. I do not know what immutable differences exist between men and women apart from differences in their genitals; perhaps there are some other unchangeable differences; probably there are a number of irrelevant differences. But it is clear that until social expectations for men and women are equal, until we provide equal respect for both men and women, our answers to this question will simply reflect our prejudices.

1. What is the basic question at the heart of Weisstein's argument? Show specifically where she reveals this question.

2. Why does Weisstein wait until paragraphs five through seven to give her proposition? What is the purpose of the first four paragraphs?

3. Characterize the voice of the implied speaker in this essay. How are the formal references to sources and the tendency to phrases such as, "To summarize," consistent with this voice? How is the voice appropriate for the argument?

4. What is Weisstein's assumption about the formation of the human personality? How does this assumption influence her argument? Does she attempt to prove this assumption? Why is it "remarkable" to Weisstein, in the penultimate paragraph, that "some women resist this message from our culture, of their stupidity even after high school, college, and graduate school"? Given Weisstein's assumptions, can she explain this fact?

5. Show specific places (for example, par. 10) where Weisstein anticipates and refutes opposing arguments. What is her principal method of refutation?

6. Weisstein's argument is basically devoted to refuting major theories about the nature of women, but what does it say positively about women?

"The Suicide of the Sexes"

There's an extraordinary chorus in the land these days—all bouncing between water beds and typewriters and talk shows—making sexual liberation ring on the cash registers of revolution. They haven't much in common—these happy hookers, Dr. Feelgoods, answer men, evangelical lesbians, sensuous psychiatrists, pornographers, dolphins, swinging priests, polymorphous perverts, and playboy philosophers—but they are all at one in proclaiming the advent of a new age of freedom between the sexes.

Nothing is free, however, least of all sex, which is bound to our deepest sources of energy, identity, and emotion. Sex can be cheapened, of course, but then it becomes extremely costly to the society as a whole. For sex is the life force and cohesive impulse of a people, and their very character will be deeply affected by how sexuality is sublimated and expressed, denied or attained. When sex is devalued and deformed, as at present, the quality of our lives declines and the social fabric unravels.

Even our attitude toward the concepts "sex" and "sexuality" illustrates the problem. The words no longer evoke a broad pageant of relations and differences between men and women, embracing every aspect of their lives. Instead, "sex" and "sexuality" are assumed to refer chiefly to copulation, as if our sexual lives were restricted to the male limits, as if the experiences of motherhood were not paramount sexual events. In fact, sexual energy animates most of our activities and connects every individual to a family and a community, and through these to a past and future. Sexuality is best examined not as sexology, physiology, or psychology, but as a study encompassing all the deepest purposes of a society.

The differences between the sexes are perhaps the most important condition of our lives. With the people we know best, in the moments most crucial in our lives together, sexual differences become all-absorbing. Intercourse, marriage, conception of a child, childbearing, breast-feeding are all events when our emotions are most intense, our lives most thoroughly changed, and society perpetuated in our own image. And they are all transactions of sexual differences reaching in symbol or consequence into the future.

These differences are embodied in a number of roles. The central ones are mother-father, husband-wife. They form neat and apparently balanced pairs. But in the most elemental sexual terms, there is little balance at all. In most of the key sexual events of our lives, the male role is trivial, easily dispensable. Although the man is needed in intercourse, artificial insemination can make his participation rudimentary indeed. Otherwise the man is completely unnecessary. It is the woman who conceives, bears, and suckles the child. Males are the sexual outsiders and inferiors. A far smaller portion of their bodies is directly erogenous. A far smaller portion of their lives is devoted to specifically sexual activity. Their own distinctively sexual experience is limited to erection and ejaculation; their primary sexual drive leads only toward copulation. Beside the socially indispensable and psychologically crucial experiences of motherhood, men are irredeemably subordinate.

The nominally equivalent role of father is in fact a product of marriage and other cultural contrivances. There is no biological need for the father to be around when the baby is born and nurtured, and in many societies the father has no special responsibility to support the children he sires; in some, paternity isn't even acknowledged. Without long-term commitments to and from women—without the institution of marriage—men are exiles from the procreative chain of nature.

One of the best ways to enrage a young feminist today is to accuse her of having a maternal instinct. In a claim contrary to the evidence of all human history and anthropology—and to an increasing body of hormonal research*—most of these women assert that females have no more innate disposition to nurture children than do men. The usual refrain is, "I know lots of men with far more interest in babies than I have." But whether instinctual or not, the maternal role originates in the fact that only the woman is necessarily present at birth and has an easily identifiable connection to the child—a tie on which society can depend. This maternal feeling is the root of human sexuality. If it is not deeply cultivated among the women, it does not emerge among the men. The idea that the father is inherently equal to the mother within the family, or that he will necessarily be inclined to remain with it, is nonsense. The man must be made equal by the culture; he must be given a way to make himself equal.

A man's predicament begins in his earliest years. A male child is born, grows, and finds his being in relation to his own body and to the bodies of his parents, chiefly his mother. In trusting her he learns to trust himself, and trusting himself he learns to bear the slow dissolution

* The increasingly conclusive evidence that the two sex roles originate in profound biological differences is summarized and appraised in a brilliant new scholarly study by Steven Goldberg, *The Inevitability of Patriarchy* (Morrow).

of the primary tie. He moves away into a new world, into a sometimes frightening psychic space between his parents; and he must then attach his evolving identity to a man, his father. From almost the start, the boy's sexual identity is dependent on acts of exploration and initiative. Before he can return to a woman, he must assert his manhood in action. The Zulu warrior had to kill a man, the Irish peasant had to build a house, the American man must find a job. This is the classic myth and the mundane reality of masculinity, the low comedy and high tragedy of mankind.

Female histories are different. A girl's sexuality normally unfolds in an unbroken line, from a stage of utter dependency and identification with her mother through stages of gradual autonomy. Always, however, the focus of female identification is clear and stable. In a woman, moreover, sexual expression is not limited to a series of brief per-formances: her gender is affirmed and demonstrated monthly in menstruation, her breasts and womb further represent an extended sexual role. Even if a woman does not in fact bear a child, she is continually reminded that she can, that she is capable of performing the crucial act in the perpetuation of her family and the species. She alone can give sex an unquestionable meaning, an incarnate result.*

Regardless, then, of any other anxieties she may have in relation to her sexual role and how to perform it, she at least knows that she has a role. Her knowledge, indeed, is ontological: it is stamped in her very being—with the result that women rarely appreciate the significance of the absence of an extended sexual identity in men. Women take their sexuality for granted, when they are aware of it at all, and assume that were it not for some cultural peculiarity, some unfortunate wrinkle in the social fabric, men too might enjoy such deep-seated sexual authenticity.

Throughout the literature of feminism, in fact, there runs a puzzled complaint, "Why can't men *be* men, and just relax?" The reason is that, unlike femininity, relaxed masculinity is at bottom empty, a limp nullity. While the female body is full of internal potentiality, the male is internally barren (from the Old French *bar*, meaning man). Manhood at the most basic level can be validated and expressed only in action. For

* Doris Lessing, a writer frequently praised and published in *Ms.*, states the case with her usual vehemence. Speaking of feminist characters in her own work, she said in a recent interview, "We're very biological animals. We always tend to think that if one is in a violent state of emotional need, it is our unique emotional need or state, when in matter of fact it's probably just the emotions of a young woman whose body is demand-ing that she have children. . . . Anna and Molly [in *The Golden Notebook*] are women who are conditioned to be one way and are trying to be another. I know a lot of girls who don't want to get married or have children. And very vocal they are about it. Well, they're trying to cheat on their biology. . . . It will be interesting to see how they're thinking at thirty."

a man's body is full only of undefined energies. And all these energies need the guidance of culture. He is therefore deeply dependent on the structure of the society to define his role in it.

Of all society's institutions that work this civilizing effect, marriage is perhaps the most important. All the companionship, love, and inspiration that have come to be associated with marriage are secondary to its crucial social role. Marriage attaches men to families, the source of continuity, individuality, and order. As we should have long ago discovered from the frequent ineffectiveness of schools, prisons, mental hospitals, and psychiatric offices, the family is the only agency that can be depended upon to induce enduring changes in its members' character and commitment. It is, most importantly, the only uncoercive way to transform individuals, loose in social time and space, into voluntary participants in the social order.

Of course, families can exist without marriage. Almost always, they consist of women and children. The problem is this leaves the men awash in what one set of marriage counselors approvingly terms the "nowness of self." And the problem with *that* is the willingness with which men grasp their "nowness." Throughout history, societies have recognized the great price to be paid in securing family commitments from men. The alternative male pattern of brief sexual exploits and predatory economics accords very nicely indeed with the many millions of years of male evolution as a hunter. Women have had to use all their ingenuity, all their powers of sexual attraction and discrimination to induce men to create and support families. And the culture has had to invest marriage with all the ceremonial sanctity of religion and law. This did not happen as a way to promote intimacy and companionship. It evolved and survived in the course of sustaining civilized societies, where love, intimacy, and companionship might flourish.

MEN AND WORK

Every society has a sexual constitution that undergirds its economy, politics, and culture. Although its central concerns are marriages and families, nearly every contact among human beings contains a sexual charge. How all these charges are organized—the nature of the sexual constitution—will deeply influence the productivity and order of the community. It will determine whether social energies are short-circuited and dissipated, or whether they are accumulated and applied to useful pursuits. It will determine whether the society is a fabric of fully integrated citizens or whether it is an atomized flux, with disconnected individuals pursuing sex and sustenance on the most limited and antisocial scale.

At every job site, in every classroom, in every store, office, and factory, this system comes into play. To anyone else, a man at work is performing an economic task, subject to legal and political regulation. But to the man himself, this formal role probably seems incidental. To him the job is chiefly important because of the connections it affords with his co-workers and with the existing or prospective women and children in his life.

A job is thus a central part of the sexual constitution. It can affirm the masculine identity of its holder; it can make it possible for him to court women in a spirit of commitment; it can make it possible for him to be married and thereby integrated into a continuing community.

Crucial to the sexual constitution of employment is that, in one way or another, it assures that over the whole society, class by class, most men will make more money than most women. Above an absolute minimum that varies from country to country, pay and poverty are relative. And for most men, most importantly, that means relative to women. A man who does not make as much money as the significant women in his life—his girlfriend, wife, and closest co-workers—will often abandon his job and will pursue women in the plundering masculine spirit that the women's movement so woefully condemns.

The feminist contention that women do not generally receive equal pay for equal work, correct in statistical terms, may reflect a preference for male need and aggressiveness over female credentials. In any case, this tendency should be considered in light of the greater cost to the society of male unemployment. The unemployed male can contribute little to the society and will often disrupt it, while the unemployed woman may perform valuable work in creating and maintaining families. In effect, the system of discrimination, which the movement is perfectly right in finding nearly ubiquitous, tells women that if they enter the marketplace they will probably receive less pay than men, not because they could do the job less well but because they have an alter-native role of incomparable value to the society as a whole. The man, on the other hand, is paid more, not because of his special virtue, but because of the key importance of taming his naturally disruptive energies. The male job advantage, therefore, is based on the real costs of female careerism to raising children and socializing men. The society will have to pay these costs one way or another.

It is vital here to understand the sexual role of money. Particularly in relatively poor communities, a woman with more money than the men around her tends to demoralize them. Undermining their usefulness as providers, she weakens their connections with the community and pro-motes a reliance upon other, anti-social ways of confirming their masculinity: the priapic modes of hunting and fighting. A society of relatively wealthy and independent women will be a society of sexually and economically predatory males, or a society of narcotized drones who have abandoned sexuality entirely.

A male's money, on the other hand, is socially affirmative. If the man is unmarried, a much higher proportion of his money than a woman's will be spent on the opposite sex. His money gives him the wherewithal to undertake long-term sexual initiatives. It gives him an incentive to submit to female sexual patterns, for he knows he will retain the important role of provider. His sexual impulses can assume a civilizing, not a subversive, form.

The women's movement argues that most women work because they *need* the money. That is precisely the point, and these women must be permitted to earn it. (They will not be helped, incidentally, by the competition of increasing numbers of non-poor women for jobs.) Those who support children should receive child allowances. But men also need the money—and need an increment above the woman's pay— for unfortunately nonrational uses: for the "luxury" spending on women that is necessary if men are to establish and support families. The more men who are induced to serve as providers, the fewer women who will be left to support children alone.

Nothing is so important to the sexual constitution as the creation and maintenance of families. And since the role of the male as principal provider is a crucial prop for the family, the society must support it one way or the other. Today, however, the burdens of childbearing no longer prevent women from performing the provider role; and if day care becomes widely available, it will be possible for a matriarchal social pattern to emerge. Under such conditions, however, the men will inevitably bolt. And this development, an entirely feasible one, would probably require the simultaneous emergence of a police state to super- vise the undisciplined men and a child care state to manage the children. Thus will the costs of sexual job equality be passed on to the public in vastly increased taxes. The present sexual constitution is cheaper.

Of course, the male responsibility can be enforced in many other ways, coercively or through religious and social pressures. It is perfectly possible to maintain male providers without taking social costs into account in determining wages and salaries. In modern American society, however, the "social pressures" on women for marriage and family are giving way to pressures for career advancement, while the social pressures on men are thrusting them toward sexual hedonism. The society no longer recognizes, let alone communicates forcefully, the extraordinary social costs incurred when women neglect their role in male socialization. In fact, it has begun to actively promote the delights of easy sex, while indulging a pervasive cynicism toward married love.

At this point, therefore, any serious governmental campaign for equal pay for equal work would be destructive. It would endorse the false feminist assumption that a greatly expanded female commitment to careers would be economical—using "human resources" that are now "wasted." The fact is that the triumph of a careerist ideology among American women would impose ultimate costs to the society far greater than the net contribution of the additional women in the work force. Already, save for the exceptional minority, female careerism is imposing heavy psychological penalties on women themselves, since most of them will not be able to fulfill themselves in careers. The feminists would establish an ideal chiefly practicable for themselves. The rest of woman-kind would be told, preposterously, that they are inferior to men unless they make comparable salaries.

Perhaps the most quixotic of all feminist demands is that men at work treat women first as "human beings." Male psychology is in large part a reaction formation, shaped in relation to women. As women further invade realms conventionally regarded as masculine—and as masculine technology further transforms other male roles—men will increasingly define themselves as *not*-women, and their responses will be increasingly sexual. If all the usual job stresses are intensified by sexual competition, the men will retaliate through bureaucratic sabotage or overt vicious-ness on the job, or they will desperately try to escape—either to the street or to higher levels of the bureaucracy. Already subject to severe sexual strains from women, men will not easily endure professional ones.

THE EFFEMINATE STUD

In all these economic questions the feminists are right in virtually every superficial way. Men *do* get paid more than women; women *are* persistently discouraged from competing with men; the minority of women who are sufficiently motivated *can* perform almost every im-portant job in society as well as men; job assignments by sex *are* arbitrary and illogical; most women *do* work because they have to; the lack of public child care facilities *does* prevent women from achieving real financial equality or opportunity.

But at a deeper level feminist women are terribly wrong. For they fail to understand their own sexual power; and they fail to perceive the sexual constitution of our society, or if they see it, they underestimate its importance to civilization and to their own interests. In general, the whole range of the society, marriage, and careers—and thus social order —will be best served if most men have a position of economic superiority over the relevant women in the community, and if in most jobs the sexes tend to be segregated by either level or function.

These practices are seen as oppressive by some; but they make possible a society in which women can love and respect men and sustain durable families. They make possible a society in which men can love and respect women and treat them humanely.

What is happening in the United States today is a steady undermining of the key conditions of male socialization. From the hospital, where the baby is abruptly taken from its mother; to early childhood, when he may be consigned to public care; to the home, where the father is frequently absent or ineffectual; to the school, where the boy is managed by female teachers and is often excelled by girls; possibly to a college, where once again his training is scarcely differentiated by sex; to a job, which, particularly at vital entry levels, is often sexually indistinct and which may not even be better paid than comparable female employment—through all these stages of development the boy's innately amorphous and insecure sexuality may be further subverted and confused.

In the end his opportunity to qualify for a family—to validate in society his love and sex through becoming a husband and provider—may be jeopardized. The man discovers that manhood affords few wholly distinctive roles except in the military, which is less inviting than ever. The society prohibits, constricts, or feminizes his purely male activities. Most jobs reward obedience, regularity, and carefulness more than physical strength; and the amount of individual initiative and assertiveness that can be accommodated by the average enterprise is very small indeed. Thus the man will find few compensatory affirmations of masculinity to make possible his expected submission to female sexual and social rhythms; and without a confident manhood he feels a compulsive need to prove it sexually, which he will do in ways that feminists, like the respectable women they are, fear and despise.

The American woman, meanwhile, becomes increasingly self-sufficient. While men are almost completely dependent upon women for a civilized role in the society and for biological and sexual meaning, women are capable of living decent—though often discontented—lives without men. The culture no longer much disapproves of unmarried mothers. The state affords them welfare and, increasingly, day care and maternity leave. In any case, birth control and legalized abortion give women complete control of procreation; and sexual liberation—not to mention masturbation and lesbianism—opens sexual enjoyment to them with only the most tenuous commitment to males. In fact, women are more than ever willing to adopt as their own an impulsive male sexuality, and although men may consequently find sexual partners more readily than before the meaning of their sexuality is diminished and they can derive less assurance from it. How could it be otherwise when more and more men and women now confront each other, *Joy of Sex* manuals in hand, joined in a grim competition of orgasmic performance.

The barely discriminate ruttings of the liberated woman find a nice complement in the stud vanity of the swinging male.

The stud, like his chief activity, is without significance except in dramatizing the largely spurious glamour of primitive masculinity: the love-'em-and-leave-'em style of most of our male heroes in novels and films. But the ordinary man may also come to feel his sexual role devalued in a context of overt sexual liberation. And he too will turn away from the family. He watches televised football and other sports for hours on end and argues about them incessantly. He becomes easy prey to jingoism and the crudest appeals for law and order. And he is obsessed with women. He tries as much as possible to reduce them to their sexual parts, and to reduce their sexuality to his own limited terms: to meaningless but insistent copulation. Exiled from the world of women, he tries to destroy consciousness of its superiority by reducing it to his own level. He insists—against all his unconscious and ulterior knowledge—that women are as sexually contemptible as his society tells him he is.

He turns to pornography, with fantasies of sex and violence. His magazines—*Male* and *Crime* and *Saga* and *True Detective*, even respectably prurient publications like *Playboy* and its refined imitators—are preoccupied with barren copulation, or with war, perversion, and crime. He is an exile, an outlaw under the sexual constitution. Often he becomes a literal outlaw as well.

What he is *not* is a powerful oppressor, with hypertrophied masculinity. Such men lead impotent lives, and, as Rollo May asserts, violence is the product of impotence grown unbearable. Their problem is a society inadequately affirmative of masculinity: a society seduced by an obsessive rationalism and functionalism—a cult of efficiency, and a fetish of statistical equality—to eliminate many of the male affirmations which all human societies have created throughout history to compensate for male sexual insecurity and female sexual superiority. The women's movement seems determined to create more and more such exiled "chauvinist" males, all the while citing their pathetic offenses as a rationale for feminism.

Thus the society both provides for its own disruption and leaches itself of positive male energies. Engels said that marriage is the handmaiden of capitalism; one could say, however, that it is the handmaiden of any productive society. For male insecurity is also the "divine unease" that in socialized males, strong enough to submit to women, produces the driving force behind a society's achievements in industry, art, and science. It is wrong to suggest that either women's liberation or male irresponsibility is chiefly to blame for our current predicament. Both phenomena are reflections of larger trends in the society hostile to enduring love.

LOVE VS. SEX

The "love that dare not speak its name" used to be homosexual.
Today, it's the love between men and women, especially husbands and
wives. Feminists are not alone in their embarrassed confusion over this
subject, but as usual they are a highly visible symptom of the general
condition. They often avoid the problem by deferring a definition
to some post-revolutionary stage—to be achieved after the withering away
of masculinity—when people will at last recognize each other as
"human beings."

Until then they offer an alternative, appealing to many people who
are both disillusioned with their adolescent images of love and
excited by a sense of new possibilities of sexual freedom and variety.
For while love, in the form of euphoric monogamy, seems increasingly
elusive, sex as a way of communicating warmth and exchanging
pleasures seems increasingly available. It even appears that sex is best
when it is spontaneous: exempt from the psychological complications
of a deep love.

The movement women, with the strong support of the counselors
of sex technique, go on to argue that sexual relations will be most
gratifying if the conventional roles of the two sexes are not closely
observed. They advise that the old "missionary position" be frequently
abandoned (a male chauvinist relic, say the pamphleteers of *Out From
Under*). And they give the impression that ineffable pinnacles of
pleasure can be reached if couples are just willing, with the advice
of the new sex manuals, to overcome inhibitions and role-stereotypes—
leaving no erogenous zone unexplored, or orifice unfathomed. The
"tyranny of genital sex" is to be exuberantly overthrown, and oral and
anal access affirmed.

Pleasures, of course, can be given and received by a variety of people,
and since variety is refreshing there is seen to be little physical or
psychological reason for restricting sex to a single partner. And since
sexual orgasm, the supreme pleasure, is in fact considered crucial to
mental health, there seems little moral sanction either for depriving
those who have failed to find a long-term lover.

These attitudes are also convenient for homosexuals, who have long
since abandoned sexually determined roles and escaped from the genital
tyranny of the missionary position. The view that sex is best when
the partners perform in psychologically similar, if versatile, ways, in fact
leaves little grounds at all for objecting to inversion. It comes as no
surprise then that the proponents of gay liberation, as well as some
literary avatars of that movement such as Gore Vidal and Kate Millett,
should seem to be moving beyond a claim on our tolerance and

compassion to an advocacy of the wonderful benefits of a homosexual style of life.

It would be a great mistake, however, to identify this fashionable concept of sex chiefly with feminism and gay liberation. For, ironically enough, it is also the essential ideology of male chauvinism: the playboy philosophy. Although the chauvinists may secretly nurse visions of male dominance, they are delighted with the prospect of female liberation. Like that *Cosmopolitan* girl and the "human beings" of *Ms.*, the playboy philosophers want to "finally and unanswerably break the connection between sexual intercourse and reproduction." Like the feminist writers, the male chauvinists fantasize polymorphously aggressive women, free of inhibitions and fixations. And also like the feminists, the male chauvinists do not like to envisage their women dependent or—God forbid—pregnant.

In practice, this popular image of spontaneous and carefree "love between mature and equal human beings" is often workable. Mutual needs are fulfilled lovingly, as long as is mutually desired, and the couple parts amicably. Each partner is defined as autonomous: neither, in theory, can be deeply hurt by the departure of the other. In a mature relationship no one is believed to suffer the mawkish toils of dependency. The two partners are free. They are liberated at once *from* expectations of lifelong enchantment, rarely fulfilled, and *for* deep physical gratifications more easily attained. Thus, according to the theory, they will be happier and less vulnerable, dealing not with fantasies but with possibilities in the real world.

With respect to marriage, the feminists offer a similar blueprint. A recent best-selling book, *Open Marriage,* by two anthropologists, George and Nena O'Neill, is a representative vision. Much of the prospectus is remarkably silly. The O'Neills invite us to transcend "mere togetherness" and reach "the ultimate in cooperation . . . that creates, through expanding feedback and growth, a *synergic couple*" (their italics). If some of us are not yet ready for the "opening expanding energy system" of the "now" marriage, if "high points" and "peak experiences" and "super moments" inspire only vertigo, the authors will understand. They concede that there may be those who might prefer to "ignore the peaks [and] huddle in the narrow valleys" of "conditional and static trust, unequal status, limited love, and a closed, self-limiting energy system." But, if one really wants to have a fulfilling union, they are firm in declaring that only an "open marriage" will do.

Oddly, however, the terms of the O'Neill marriage contract turn out to be extremely strict. As in the image of sexual relations between "human beings," so the open marriage envisages two partners with completely flexible and reversible roles. The O'Neills categorically dismiss the notion of sex-assigned functions and responsibilities, for unless the woman earns money (preferably as much as the husband) and the man keeps house (also on equal terms) the O'Neills fear that the couple will have too little in common to "grow together." When one actually scrutinizes their notion, equality turns out to mean sameness. The man earns money; so must the woman. The man philanders; so must his wife. The man initiates sex; so must she. The woman decorates the house, cooks a meal, or makes a bed; the man must eventually reciprocate.

Children, of course, are rather awkward in this scheme and the O'Neills would have as little to do with them as possible. They positively celebrate the childless marriage and declare that "the importance of motherhood has been inflated out of all proportion." "Motherhood," they argue, "must be disentangled from the wife's role." It should be "optional" in an overpopulated world, rather than "glorified."

Actually, the danger of overpopulation has little to do with the O'Neills' advocacy of the optional status of children. What they really fear is the snare of domesticity. The home, they assert, "may have its pleasures, but none of them makes sufficient demands to bring about real growth." Domestic life programs the woman for "mediocrity and dulls her brain." Far better to get out into the world of business and the professions with all their "inspiring challenges" and "broadening vistas."

This view of the way to find both good sex and reasonably enduring love seems plausible to most sophisticated Americans. The feminists are no more daringly rebellious in their usual sexual imagery than is Hugh Hefner in his mock-heroic battle against the dread forces of American puritanism. Nonetheless, the feminists—as well as the playboy philosophers, the *Joy of Sex* technicians, and the gay liberationists—are grotesquely wrong about both love and sex.

These groups have at least this in common: an eagerness to divorce sex from procreation. This desire is hardly extraordinary. It is resisted only by the Catholic and Baptist churches and Norman Mailer, among major American institutions; and in the general alarm about over-population, it has gained the moral momentum of a crusade and the financial support of the major foundations. To a considerable extent, this effort is reasonable enough.

The members of the new sex coalition, however, go well beyond the search for a better contraceptive. They also want to eliminate the psycho-logical and symbolic connections between intercourse and childbirth. They may reluctantly acknowledge that in a sense procreation is the most important current role of intercourse—and certainly the key role in the history of mankind. They may even recognize that during the millions of years when the species evolved and our sexuality was formed, fertility determined survival. Nevertheless, they look forward to a time, not too far distant, when artificial means may be employed for human reproduction.

This ideology of non-procreative sex is not a trivial matter. We all know that in the age of contraception all sexual activity does not have to be intentionally procreative, if indeed it ever did. But it hardly follows that sexual pleasure is totally unrelated to the complex of drives and desires that converge to reproduce the species in a loving and secure environment. Nor does it follow that a complete break between procreative and erotic instincts will not ultimately undermine all forms of sexual pleasure. To state the question directly: does sex that is wholly detached from a procreative mode—that violates its genital focus and sense of futurity—does this kind of sex ultimately reduce sexual energy and undermine love? Does the separatist ideal of polymorphous pleasures so fail to correspond to the inner syntax of sexuality that it strains the bonds of human personality, becoming disintegrative, not integrative, of body and mind and spirit? To answer these questions, one must explore the ties between sexual pleasure, procreation, and love.

The beginning of a man's love in a civilized society lies in his desire, whether conscious or not, to have and keep his progeny. For this he must choose a particular woman. His love defines his choice. His need to choose evokes his love. His sexual drive lends energy to his love, and his love gives shape, meaning, and continuity to his sexuality. When he selects a specific woman, he in essence defines himself both to himself and to society. Afterwards, every sex act celebrates that definition and social engagement.

The sex act then becomes a human affirmation, involving a man's entire personality and committing it, either in fact or in symbol, to a long-term engagement in a meaningful future. In fact, one can say that the conscious or unconscious desire to have children with a specific partner is a workable definition of sexual love. It is not, in bold specific terms, the only definition. But across the range of sexual experience in a civilized society, this motive seems to run strongest in the phenomenon of love.

This concept of sexual love, originating in the desire for children and symbolized in genital intercourse, again emphasizes the differences between the sexes. A man's love is focused on the symbols and associations of a woman's procreative powers—embodied in her womb and her breasts and elaborated in her nurturant sentiments, her tender- ness, and her sense of futurity. The woman loves the man for his strength and protectiveness, for temperamental qualities that provide an ability to support and protect her while she bears their children—or while she surrenders to orgasm. She loves him for his ability to control her in sexual intercourse and for his submission to the extended demands of her sexuality.

Beyond these primal attractions, of course, both the man and woman will seek a companionable and compatible partner. Both, that is, will seek someone whom they can imagine enjoying over time and who respects the values they want to transmit to their children. Such a relationship, it should go without saying, will accommodate a wide range of sexual activity, from deliberate attempts to conceive children to casual sex play.

SENSUOUS MASSAGE

There is a mode of sex, however, that is not affirmative, that tends to tear apart the armature of sexuality and identity. That sort of sex occurs when the sex act does not express love, is not associated even unconsciously or symbolically with the aspiration to conceive children, and does not subordinate male instant gratification to female futurity. Then the sex act becomes a transient pleasure, an ephemeral kick, which, if pursued, leads to emotional fragmentation rather than to a sense of continuity with nature and society. If this kind of sex prevails, the male circuit of impulsive and predatory sexuality can become the dominant rhythm in the culture.

The women's movement, the male chauvinists, the gay liberationists, the sexologists, and the pornographers all tend to indulge and promote such a disintegration. All present alternatives to loving sexuality. The man and woman who are attempting to fulfill their sexual natures in an affirmative way are bombarded with contrary ideologies. The pornographer pervasively advertises the potential joys of promiscuity, of unknown but shapely bodies—continuously stimulates primal male impulses and subverts the effort to maintain monogamous ties. The sex manuals present utopian images of the bliss that comes with an abandonment of "inhibitions" and "stereotypes" that may be important to affirmative sexuality. The women's movement offers visions of a spurious sexual equality, in which women are to be considered as erotically impulsive as men, or more so. The gay liberationists romanticize a pattern in which ultimate sexual fulfillment is impossible and in which temporary gratification is paramount.

The danger in the sexual separatist program is that unsocialized men will become culturally dominant, while the civilized will have to resist the pressures of the society at large. A civilization dependent on families, on long-term commitments, will be confronted by a powerful mass culture propagating a sexuality of immediate gratifications. A society profoundly reliant on monogamy will face a culture advertising promiscuity. We find ourselves close to that situation today.

The effect on men is most immediate and far-reaching because their identities and secondary sexual behavior are more dependent on culture and therefore more vulnerable to shifts in social pressures. But ultimately the impact on women is just as tragic. Women face a cruel dilemma, exemplified in part by the current women's movement. Some have responded to the increasing abdication of men from civilized social and sexual patterns by trying to play both key roles, sustaining long-term commitments as well as familial responsibilities. The most talented and stable will succeed, thus perpetuating civilized behavior in the face of a hostile culture. Other women have chosen careers alone, while either forgoing sex or halfheartedly adopting the male pattern. Still others have enthusiastically embraced an essentially male chauvinist ethic of promiscuous "openness," narrowing their expectations of men and of the potentialities of their own bodies.

In the end, the sexuality of both men and women and the spirit of the community are reduced to the limited, barren, compulsive circuitry of uncivilized males. Confined in a shallow present, with little hope for the future or interest in the past, neither sex works or loves devotedly. While sex is given a steadily larger role, it loses contact with its procreative sources and becomes increasingly promiscuous and undifferentiated, homosexual and pornographic. It becomes what in fact our current liberationists—male and female—already imagine it to be, essentially a form of sensuous massage—a shapeless, dissolute, and destructive pursuit of ever more elusive pleasures by ever more drastic techniques. In the quest for a better orgasm or more intense titillation, a frustrated population goes on ever wilder goose chases in "little-known erogenous zones"—on ever more futile scavenger hunts for sexual erotica, picking up a whip here, an orgy there, but always returning to the sterile and shapeless lump of their own sexuality. Such are the aporias of carnal knowledge—the dead ends of "spontaneity."

Our sexual potentialities are to a great extent fixed. But what we do with them is determined by culture, which is shaped by us. The first and most important step in restoring a sense of order and purpose and community is to reestablish the social pressures and cultural biases in favor of durable monogamous love and marriage—the long-term feminine sexual patterns—that the women's movement and the playboy philosophers find so "oppressive." It is women who will most benefit in the beginning, for their discomfort in the toils of male sexuality is already inducing a revulsion toward sex altogether. But ultimately the whole

society gains. For as we cultivate more profound patterns of love and
sexuality, we will create a deeper sense of community, a more optimistic
embrace of the future, and a more productive society.

The differences between the sexes are the single most important
fact of human society. The drive to deny them—in the name of women's
liberation, marital openness, sexual equality, erotic consumption,
homosexual romanticism—must be one of the most quixotic crusades
in the history of the species. Yet in a way it is typical of crusades. For
it is a crusade against a particular incarnate humanity—men and women
and children—on behalf of a metaphysical "humanism." It seems
unlikely, however, that the particular men and women one meets in
the real world will ever voluntarily settle for long in an
open house of barren abstractions.

1. What voice do you hear speaking in the first paragraph?
2. What central value regarding society underlies Gilder's entire argument?
   How is this related to his proposition?
3. What is Gilder's fear—the main threat to the order and stability of society—
   throughout his argument? How does this fear shape his argument?
4. Gilder uses the word "costs" throughout his argument. Show specifically
   how he uses this and related words. Are "costs" legitimate evidence, or are
   they used as mere threats?
5. What are Gilder's basic presuppositions about the socialization and development of the male and female personalities?
6. What is the "sexual constitution"? How is the careful definition of this
   phrase crucial for Gilder's argument?
7. How is the paragraph beginning the second section ("The effeminate stud")
   a good argumentative strategy?
8. What is the relationship among the essay's four sections?
9. Show how the overall structure of Gilder's argument is deductive. What
   is the major premise regarding the differences between the sexes that he
   begins with?

SUGGESTIONS FOR WRITING

The first group of writing assignments asks you to present a personal opinion and to support it with evidence primarily from your experience. The second group also draws on your own experience (as must any good writing), but requires that you gather and evaluate evidence more formally, and from outside your personal experience.

I.

a. Have you ever deliberately broken a law? For example, a drug, traffic, or tax law. Why? What issues were involved? Would you recommend that others do the same? On what basis would you or would you not advocate their compliance? Analyze the consequences or lack of consequences of your action. Would you break this law again? If you haven't ever deliberately broken a law, are there any circumstances in which you think that this action would be permissible, or even morally obligatory?

b. Analyze a social institution or a social "happening" that has a ritual structure, one that follows a recurrent pattern (for instance, rock festival, marriage, spring vacation migration, funeral, college registration, club or class initiation, church service), and show why it is significant. What values does the "happening" embody? What kind of people are attracted, and why? What are the essential elements of the specific ritual?

c. Write a letter to someone who is offended by your life-style, a particular action you have taken, or a particular view you hold, to which you would consider yourself strongly committed. Define the conflict, defend your own position, anticipate opposing arguments, and suggest where they might be in error. This might be a letter to your parents defending a different sexual morality, or a different belief from theirs, for example, but keep in mind that your purpose is to convince, to effect a change of attitude in your audience, not merely to "tell them off."

d. After reading Jerry Farber's "The Student as Nigger," choose another analogy, one which you think fits your experience better, and write a similar analysis of the student experience, such as "The Student as Hero," "The Student as Imposter," "The Student as Guinea Pig," "The Student as IBM Card," or "The Student as Cockroach."

II.

a. Henry David Thoreau once said: "That government is best which governs least." Select some issue on which you think the government should *not* rule (for example, abortion, gun control, draft, censorship), and write an argument defending responsible free and personal choice in the matter. Or you can write an argument in which you disagree with Thoreau's statement, to show that the best government is that which intervenes in such things as food and drug purity, pollution, child labor, and mine safety.

b. You have been given ten minutes on public TV to justify and invite people to a demonstration for your favorite social or political cause. Explain the reasons for the demonstration and the procedure to be followed. Be careful to clarify the issue and outline the consequences of accepting or rejecting your proposal. Why is it important that the public support you? Why is it in their best interests to support you? If it isn't, why should they support you anyway?

c. You must write a position paper for a well-known national or local political figure on a sensitive issue (such as legalizing prostitution, changing the national anthem, barring a proposed nuclear reactor or oil pipeline). You are not primarily interested in the public that the politician must face; you are most concerned with convincing him to accept what you feel is the correct position in the matter.

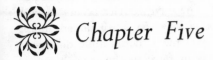 *Chapter Five*

Writing About a Symbolic World

INTRODUCTION

1. WHAT IS A "SYMBOLIC WORLD"?

So far, you've been writing about experiences that you have had or have observed in the world at large. Your emphasis has been on making the readers see a little more clearly how this world operates by showing them what it contains and how you think these contents should be viewed. This chapter asks you to look at more specialized or suggestive "worlds"—those of dreams, fantasies, short stories, and films. First we will attempt to define "world," then to discriminate everyday worlds from symbolic worlds. Finally we will try to show you how to analyze a symbolic world and how to incorporate this analysis into a coherent essay of your own.

We've all said of some odd character, "He lives in a world all his own," or "She's in another world." What do we mean? Something in this person's behavior, dress, even speech or facial expressions suggests to us that he or she is operating according to rules we either do not accept, or do not even perceive. What we are trying to express through such phrases is our awareness that there are people whose actions we cannot easily interpret. They do not fit into our "world," whether that world is the campus, the home, the church, or even the locker room.

"World," then, as we use it in this chapter, is a set of general expectations that completely encompass and set off an area so that only the "initiated" can understand what is going on within its boundaries. For example, in the world of football to "run with the ball" is a totally understandable and desirable activity; in basketball we know what the phrase means too, but we also realize that this action is something to be avoided. The same activity occurs in both worlds, but in one the fans cheer it, in the other they boo. Their understanding of the world of each sport makes them interpret the activities quite differently depending upon which set of expectations is in force in the game they are watching.

Clearly, we all participate in many worlds; campus, home, church, locker room only begin the list. Even language is a world in this sense. You participate in this world as soon as you admit that the following series of words is a sentence: *The dog is blue.* It has a noun that acts as a subject (*dog*); it has a verb that expresses a state of being as a predicate (*is*); it even has a predicate complement (*blue*) that tells you something about the subject. Finally, thanks to your sixth grade English teacher, you can see that this arrangement of words expresses a "complete thought." It does not matter that the thought is ridiculous, that it is out of keeping with what you know to be the normal coloring of dogs. Even if we cannot understand why the author should choose to mean something so absurd, we never fail to see that the sentence is English—it conforms to the grammar that patterns our language.

But, let's take a further example. Jesus once said "It is easier for a camel to go through the eye of a needle than for a rich man to enter the kingdom of God." We immediately understand the literal sense of the statement, as we do when we read, "The dog is blue." The world of both statements is clearly the English language. But the second statement includes enough information so that we know not only that we must interpret it according to the rules of English grammar, but also that to do *only* that will leave us without any real understanding of what the speaker means. We must enter another world in which these words have not only their literal meanings, but also a deeper significance. We must enter a *symbolic* world, for the speaker is far less concerned with camels and needle's eyes than he is with the relationship of material to spiritual values. The various details of everyday life—camels, needles, rich men—have been arranged into a statement which we interpret by discovering the unique relationship these parts have to each other and to the mythical "kingdom of God." Jesus is skeptical here of the spiritual sincerity of a man who spends his time pursuing material possessions. He cares very little about the impossibility his sentence proposes, except as it illustrates the point he is making.

Before we go any further, let's put together a definition of a symbolic world. Several things might be said. 1. A symbolic world is one that demands interpretation, one whose objects, events, characters and images beg to be seen in a "new" relationship. Just as you find people with no connection in your waking life in close association in your dreams, you may find strange, even disturbing associations of things in the symbolic world. For example, remember how strange mushrooms, caterpillars, and rabbits looked to Alice once she had entered her "wonderland"? 2. A symbolic world is *deliberately* created for the purpose of revealing something to its audience or recipient. This is apparent in art forms (short stories and films) but even in dreams the subconscious puts events together in a unique way that manifests something personal to the dreamer. 3. In spite of its differences from the everyday world, the symbolic world has a definite connection with our concrete existence, both in the material it uses (remember that in talking about heaven Jesus discusses camels, needles, and rich men) and in the meaning it suggests (Jesus brings up heaven in the first place to inspire a rich young man to give his riches to the poor on earth).

AN ACTIVITY

As a class, list as many symbolic worlds as you can think of. Write them on the board and list at least two specific examples beside each. Then discuss whether each symbolic world fulfills the three parts of our definition.

2. HOW DO YOU BEGIN TO ANALYZE A SYMBOLIC WORLD?

As we have said before, one inescapable quality of a symbolic world is that it *requires* analysis. If we are to understand this world, we must recognize its boundaries, observe and interpret its language, and surmise the creator's intentions. Only then can we feel confident in responding to its content.

We are reminded here of a student who was assigned to read Swift's "A Modest Proposal" without being told of its setting or message. Scanning its sentences quickly, he decided that the author was a raving madman. Swift's suggestion that the children of famine-starved Irish families be consumed as gourmet fare was clearly the cruelest thing that this student had ever read. But while his anger at such treatment of children is admirable, he is still a fool. For what he failed to notice was the ironic tone Swift used so skillfully— the deliberate double-meaning that transformed a literal travesty into a powerful plea for justice.

The student took the easy way out; he read with his eyes, but not with that essential combination of intellect and sensibility that makes one a responsive reader and effective writer. And that is really what this last chapter is all about. It is designed to help you become a responsive, articulate "analyst" not only of the world you experience every day, but of worlds that transform the everyday into highlighted, even fantastic, moments and situations (that is, the worlds of drama, literature, film, political satire and other "revelations").

Because of its complexity, a symbolic world requires analysis. It requires that you pay close attention to the minute particulars of its creation (language, focus, characterization, and so on). Likewise, it begs articulate response—clear interpretation and application of its meaning.

A woman in her eighth month of pregnancy once had a series of dreams in which she saw herself dying. Her terror of these dreams made her shun any waking memory of them; thus, they were repeated with increasing frequency. Finally, an insightful friend made her examine these nightmares. In the process the woman discovered that they conveyed a real but not a terrifying message. With the advent of motherhood, part of herself was indeed "passing away"—her freedom as well as her slender shape. With understanding came relief, and she set about preparing for the new self that was trying to emerge.

This story is not rare; you've all had dreams you had to "work through." We're now asking you to "work through" your responses to other symbolic worlds—ones set before you by writers with a variety of intentions. Such an exercise can help you in several ways. It will certainly increase your sensitivity to the work you choose to analyze. It will prepare you for written assignments in other classes that ask you to interpret and analyze symbolic worlds ranging from poems in literature courses, to biographies and personal memoires in history classes, to case studies in psychology classes. More important than either, however, it should make you a more responsive film-goer, novel-reader, and people-watcher.

A WRITING EXERCISE

As an exercise in "working through" a set of symbols, respond to the following questions. There are no right and wrong answers.

1. As you are walking through a forest, you come to a house that happens to be yours. What does it look like?
2. As you walk into the dining room you notice that there is a table. What does it look like? Is there anything on it?
3. Are there windows in the dining room? What do they look like? Do they have curtains?
4. As you go out the back door you see that beyond your property line there is an area on which nothing has been built. What does it look like?
5. You go for a walk and come to a body of water. What does it look like?
6. As you walk further, you find a cup. What does it look like? What do you do with it?
7. You also find a key. What does it look like? What do you do with it?
8. You start back to the house. As you approach the property line a creature approaches you. What does the creature look like? How do you react to it?

After you have recorded your answers to these questions, your teacher will suggest what area of your personality is being symbolized by each object and response. You will find that you haven't been writing mere descriptions of objects at all; you have been writing "symbolically" about yourself. To know this should make you see your answers in a completely new light.

Now let's turn to one of the basic problems involved in this kind of analysis. How do the readers of any given piece know whether they are reading "plain English" or being transported into a symbolic world? Titles don't always help. The words *Animal Farm* hardly indicate that an extended beast fable where pigs and cows parade as world politicians is being named. Length certainly doesn't help. A seventeen-syllable haiku can build a symbolic world as successfully as Herman Melville's expansive novel, *Moby Dick*. Content doesn't always help either. The matter of science fiction makes it recognizable as fantasy, but what about the matter of *The Adventures of Huckleberry Finn?* Boys did sail down the Mississippi on rafts in nineteenth century mid-America, but only one became the fictional representation of every person's desire to "light out for the territory."

We are forced to go back to the same elements of writing we have been discussing since Chapter One for clues. In fact, there are several ways in which a writer's *style* (the sum of all of his chosen techniques) can lure the reader down the "rabbit's hole" into the "wonderland" of the writer's choice.

VOICE

Tone of voice can be an important stylistic clue that you are entering a symbolic world. In "A Modest Proposal," Jonathan Swift tells us in modulated rational tones that the perfect solution to the hunger problem in Ireland is that citizens with money should purchase and consume the children of the poor. He elaborates his plan, showing its political expedience, giving recipes for the preparation of such a delicacy, and stressing the regard it will inspire among the poor of husband for pregnant wife and of parents for "valuable" offspring. His presentation is ghoulishly simple, and it is the simplicity itself that leads the readers "through the looking glass" of Swift's intentions into a world where all the ills that have been inflicted on the poor, by politician and landowner alike, are revealed to be as cruel as his proposed solution. The writer's motivation is anger; his voice is clear and rational; and the effect is *ironic*. Swift says one thing but means its opposite. He says his solution makes absolute sense and means that it is as coldly inhuman as present attitudes toward the poor. By using a clear logical voice to describe a horrible solution, Swift shocks the readers into facing the desperate ends of poverty and, hopefully, into planning for decent ways of feeding the poor.

But the voice of a piece does not have to create ironic effects in order to indicate that a world of evocative meanings is being created. In science fiction the most fantastic occurrences are spoken of as cold facts. Mr. X enters his time machine drinking a Pepsi Cola and steps out into the eighteenth century looking for a trash can to deposit his "empty." In such a work we are seduced into believing the world of fantasy because it is described with the paraphernalia and jargon of our present existence.

POINT OF VIEW

In Mark Twain's *Adventures of Huckleberry Finn*, voice is indistinguishable from point of view. Huck Finn tells his own story, embellishing it with country slang and sly wit. Such a device not only gives the tale more immediacy, it tells us instantly that the writer is creating an experience different from his own, as well as from the readers', and it draws the readers into a world where freedom from grammar becomes a corollary for freedom from other confines of the "snivilization" Huck Finn seeks to escape.

In Anton Chekhov's short story, "Gooseberries," point of view becomes even more complex and revealing. The author introduces us to two characters, Ivan Ivanovitch and Burkin, as they walk across an open field, get caught in the rain, and look for refuge in a neighbor's house. But the most "seductive" part of the story occurs when Ivan tells Burkin and the neighbor the story of his brother's life. At this point the narration takes on a life of its own. We forget about seeing events from the outside, and, instead, we become one with Ivan's listeners in the comfortable drawing room of the farmhouse. In short, we enter the world of Ivan and his brother.

FOCUS

Another stylistic device writers may use to prepare their readers for a symbolic venture is to focus on interior states of mind rather than on external events. Along with characters' physical attributes, we are handed their dreams, prejudices, fantasies, and fears. We are introduced to their interior worlds and thus prepare to tread the slippery, though significant, ground of the human psyche.

In Flannery O'Connor's short story "Revelation" the readers are forced to stay "inside" the pretensions and sufferings of a middle-aged woman during the course of a day in which her worthlessness is revealed to her. It is an odd and a painful focus, but one that pushes the readers into an understanding of the darker recesses of the human mind.

Likewise, in Ralph Ellison's "Battle Royal" the focus is on the emotional torture a group of black youths experience at the hands of sinister white businessmen out for an evening of "fun." Ellison achieves his focus by narrating the events of the evening from the point of view of one of the black participants. We learn, through what he tells us, what it feels like to be cruelly aroused by an unattainable woman, to be forced to punch your friends into bloody insensibility at the command of your worst enemy, and to be publicly humiliated for your intelligence. Again, it is a painful focus, one that forces us to face the tremendous complexity of human emotions and to face it from *inside* an experience that few of us will ever have.

PATTERNS OF IMAGERY

One of the ways we are made to face any experience is its sensuous appeal. An *image* is a phrase that holds an object or experience up to the readers' senses. A "red-tipped rose" appeals to the readers' sight, while a "tinkling bell" appeals to their hearing. A *pattern of imagery* occurs when a single sensory experience is repeated over and over in a single work, creating a special awareness in the readers—letting the readers know that that experience has a symbolic significance.

In Flannery O'Connor's short story, "Revelation," the image of pigs or hogs is used several times. Mrs. Turpin raises pigs; indeed, she sees the way she keeps her pigs as a sign of "class." When she is being assaulted by the strange girl, Mary Grace, she is called a "wart hog." And later in the day, when she finally comes to understand the full significance of this epithet, she is hosing down the pigs, trying to wash away their mud and stink. By tying all of these references together, O'Connor lets us know that there is a deep division in Mrs. Turpin. She feels, on the one hand, that she can make pigs respectable and clean; on the other hand, she must recognize the inevitable stench of her own self-righteousness. A vivid pattern of imagery can be an important clue that a symbolic world is being described.

CHARACTERIZATION

Symbolic worlds share many qualities with nonfiction in the development of character. You have only to reflect on your own efforts to write a character sketch to be aware that concrete observations, a consideration of motives, and an awareness of the characters' environment are all important in making them come alive on paper. But in some cases, readers become aware that they are approaching a symbolic world because of the allusive quality of the characters they meet. For example, they cannot get very far into Nathaniel Hawthorne's short story, "The Birthmark," before realizing that the characters are not complex embodiments of human emotions and desires, but are one-sided "types." Aylmer represents heartless idealism; Aminadab stands for the demonic side of human existence; and Georgiana symbolizes beauty and compassion. Hawthorne is writing a moral tale that requires a clear delineation of moral types, and it is his careful construction of these types that guides the readers to his meaning.

Thus, the authors' special use of writing elements that you have been working with all along makes you aware that you are entering a symbolic world—one that demands interpretation, is carefully contrived, and reflects back on the world you inhabit. An activity designed to help you further understand how these elements can be used to create a symbolic world follows.

A WRITING EXERCISE

Write on a piece of paper, "A large brown bear was walking down the street and met a kangeroo on her way to market." Record what the bear said to the kangeroo and what the kangeroo said to the bear.

Then write, "A thunderstorm suddenly came up." Again, record what the bear and the kangeroo said to one another.

Finally, write, "A bright green parrot, known to them both, flew over and was hit by lightning," and record the bear and the kangaroo's final exchange.

Now skip a line and finish the statement, "The moral of this story is . . ."

You have, obviously, constructed a beast fable—a simple symbolic world in which unusual events have happened, and in which you have made a concentrated effort to extract a universal meaning from the interrelation of concrete objects such as a thunderstorm, a country road, and a large brown bear. In the process you have manipulated point of view, focus, and voice in such a way that the readers are invited to see these objects in a new light.

By now you should have some idea of how a symbolic world "operates." But since this chapter is designed to help you *write* about symbolic worlds as well as comprehend them, Section 3 will discuss further structuring your responses to this type of world.

3. HOW DO YOU WRITE AN ANALYSIS OF A SYMBOLIC WORLD?

The process of analyzing a symbolic world is not substantially different from that of analyzing yourself or your culture. It requires that you form impressions of your subject matter (in this case, a short story), that you search out the concrete manifestations of these impressions, and that you allow impressions and details to modify one another. Through the interaction of general ideas and specific evidence you try to discover what the writer wants to reveal to you; and a clear statement of that discovery becomes the proposition for your written analysis.

For example, after reading Hawthorne's "Birthmark," you may feel that Georgiana has been treated most unfairly by her husband and his sinister helper. In order to test this feeling or impression you will have to go back to the kind of imagery that is used to describe these three main characters (is she described in admirable terms and they in more derogatory terms?), to the emotional focus of the story (do we see many things from Georgiana's perspective and, therefore, become sympathetic to her?), and to the outcome of the events (does she, in fact, suffer?). Through this examination of the particulars of the story, you may find that while Georgiana does suffer at the hand of her husband and Aminadab, she clearly *allows* this to happen. Such a realization will alter your initial impression and lead you on a search for clues as to *why* she is so passive. Eventually, this kind of movement between impressions and details should lead you to a thematic understanding of the story in general, and of the strangely appealing character, Georgiana, as well.

In the writing assignments that come at the end of this chapter we suggest that there are two kinds of written analyses. One demands an essay in which you *describe and interpret* the structure of a given symbolic world. The other calls for a prose "tale" or satire in which you *imitate* the structure of a given work. Both types of assignments require that you ask yourself several important questions after reading the work you will be analyzing.

1. Are there any images that are continually repeated in this story/satire? Are certain objects, actions, animals, emotions mentioned over and over? Why might this be?

2. Is the author's voice ironic, sarcastic, jocular, sneering, pretentious, and so on, in a noticeable way? Specifically, what language (words and phrases) reveals this attitude? What does this indicate about the author's approach to the subject and the approach he or she would like you to take?

3. In a more practical sense, what is the author's point of view? Where is the author standing in relation to you and to the actions of the work? Is the author talking to you directly? Or to someone else (maybe to himself)? Is he speaking as the author or as one of the participants in the action?

4. Where does the writer's (therefore, the reader's) attention seem to be focused in this story? Is it on emotional states of mind, on a particular prejudice, or on a single evocative event?

5. Does any event, image, or character in the work seem to have a universal significance? Does any detail or general theme become important because of its repetition in nearly everyone's experience?

The individual writing assignments will direct you in organizing and focusing your essay. But a general consideration of the basic method of presenting a literary analysis may be helpful. You will notice that this method is deductive and that it parallels the first three concerns of argument (proposition, evidence, implications).

First, you explain the story in terms of the aspect of the story that most interests you. This is your proposition. When you read Joyce Carol Oates' story, you will notice that she begins her analysis of "Revelation" by stating that the story has two extraordinary aspects: the revelation of bigotry and its self-destructive nature, and the protagonist's assumption that all physical life has a spiritual counterpart. All of her subsequent observations stem from these two central concerns.

Second, you explore how your theme or conclusion about what is important in the story is reinforced by the writers' methods. Here you discuss such items as point of view, focus, patterns of imagery, characterization, and voice, illustrating each observation with evidence from the stories. In her analysis, Joyce Carol Oates divides "Revelation" into two parts and examines the manifestations of prejudice and "spiritualism" in each.

Third, you evaluate the effectiveness of the writers' methods, and discuss the implications of accepting their meanings. You connect the revealed significance or main idea of the story with your world and see what powers of conviction this idea possesses. For example, Joyce Carol Oates concludes her essay on "Revelation" by illustrating that "it questions the very foundation of our assumptions of the ethical life" and that it does so with compelling force.

In all of this, however, remember that amusing the reader is always part of the story writer's craft. Don't dismiss possible meanings by shrugging your shoulders and saying, "Ah, he was only trying to tell a funny story." But at the same time, be ready to enjoy being taken out of your everyday world for a while and introduced to a world where different values and expectations operate. And, if you can, show in your essay how the writer has managed to make this excursion pleasant and to show you things you aren't likely to forget.

In summary, symbolic worlds are "places" that we visit in our dreams, in art, even in political satires. They are "places" where special values, ideas, and personalities prevail, but where the "furniture" (the objects, events, and character traits that inhabit them) is often recognizable. Symbolic worlds always have an author (even if it is the subconscious mind); they reveal important things to us about ourselves and the world we live in; and they beg us to interpret or analyze them. In many ways analysis of a symbolic world follows closely the procedure and outline for analyzing persons and cultural artifacts, and it is a useful exercise for seeing how language (the very medium of written analysis) can be submitted to close scrutiny and comment.

READINGS

"A Modest Proposal"/*Jonathan Swift*

The major tool of Swift's essay is a biting irony that forces us to accept the atrocities his "proposer" suggests as far more humane than anything anyone else has suggested to alleviate the suffering of the starving Irish poor. The speaker is sincere, well-prepared (notice how carefully he documents his proposal with statistics) and entirely rational. His argument is a model of clear organization. First he states the problem; then he presents his solution in elaborate detail; next he lists the advantages for all concerned that the acceptance of his proposal would yield. Following this elaboration, he anticipates possible objections and meets each one with counterarguments; finally he includes a personal disclaimer that he might gain any private benefit from the adoption of his proposal.

We are lured into the symbolic world of this essay by the matter-of-fact, disinterested voice of the careful, methodical planner. It is only when we are *inside* his world that we begin to see that the speaker is proposing a hideous moral idiocy. Yet the inescapable fact remains that the poor would be better off if such a plan were in effect. This ironic world repels us, forcing us back into the real world with our eyes opened once again to the cruelty of our neglect of starving human beings.

It is a melancholly Object to those, who walk through this great Town, or travel in the Country; when they see the *Streets,* the *Roads,* and *Cabbin-doors* crowded with *Beggars* of the Female Sex, followed by three, four, or six Children, *all in Rags,* and importuning every Passenger for an Alms. These *Mothers,* instead of being able to work for their honest Livelyhood, are forced to employ all their Time in stroling to beg Sustenance for their *helpless Infants;* who, as they grow up, either turn *Thieves* for want of Work; or leave their *dear Native Country, to fight for the Pretender in* Spain, or sell themselves to the *Barbadoes.*

I think it is agreed by all Parties, that this prodigious Number of Children in the Arms, or on the Backs, or at the *Heels* of their *Mothers,* and frequently of their *Fathers,* is *in the present deplorable State of the Kingdom,* a very great additional Grievance; and therefore, whoever could find out a fair, cheap, and easy Method of making these

Children sound and useful Members of the Commonwealth, would deserve so well of the Publick, as to have his Statue set up for a Preserver of the Nation.

But my Intention is very far from being confined to provide only for the Children of *professed Beggars:* It is of a much greater Extent, and shall take in the whole Number of Infants at a certain Age, who are born of Parents, in effect as little able to support them, as those who demand our Charity in the Streets.

As to my own Part, having turned my Thoughts for many Years, upon this important Subject, and maturely weighed the several *Schemes of other Projectors,* I have always found them grosly mistaken in their Computation. It is true a Child, *just dropt from its Dam,* may be supported by her Milk, for a Solar Year with little other Nourishment; at most not above the Value of two Shillings; which the Mother may certainly get, or the Value in *Scraps,* by her lawful Occupation of *Begging:* And, it is exactly at one Year old, that I propose to provide for them in such a Manner, as, instead of being a Charge upon their *Parents,* or the *Parish,* or *wanting Food and Raiment* for the rest of their Lives; they shall, on the contrary, contribute to the Feeding, and partly to the Cloathing, of many Thousands.

There is likewise another great Advantage in my *Scheme,* that it will prevent those *voluntary Abortions,* and that horrid Practice of *Women murdering their Bastard Children;* alas! too frequent among us; sacrificing the *poor innocent Babes,* I doubt, more to avoid the Expense than the Shame; which would move Tears and Pity in the most Savage and inhuman Breast.

The Number of Souls in *Ireland* being usually reckoned one Million and a half; of these I calculate there may be about Two hundred Thousand Couple whose Wives are Breeders; from which Number I subtract thirty thousand Couples, who are able to maintain their own Children; although I apprehend there cannot be so many, under *the present Distresses of the Kingdom;* but this being granted, there will remain an Hundred and Seventy Thousand Breeders. I again subtract Fifty Thousand, for those Women who miscarry, or whose Children die by Accident, or Disease, within the Year. There only remain an Hundred and Twenty Thousand Children of poor Parents, annually born: The Question therefore is, How this Number shall be reared, and provided for? Which, as I have already said, under the present Situation of Affairs, is utterly impossible, by all the Methods hitherto proposed: For we can *neither employ them in Handicraft or Agriculture;* we neither build Houses, (I mean in the Country) nor cultivate Land: They can very seldom pick up a Livelyhood *by Stealing* until they arrive at six Years old; except where they are of towardly Parts; although, I confess, they learn the Rudiments much earlier; during which Time, they can, however, be properly looked upon only as *Probationers*; as I have been informed by a principal Gentleman in the County of *Cavan*, who protested to me, that he never knew above one or two Instances under the Age of six, even in a Part of the Kingdom *so renowned for the quickest Proficiency in that Art*.

I am assured by our Merchants, that a Boy or a Girl before twelve Years old, is no saleable Commodity; and even when they come to this Age, they will not yield above Three Pounds, or Three Pounds and half a Crown at most, on the Exchange; which cannot turn to Account either to the Parents or the Kingdom; the Charge of Nutriment and Rags, having been at least four Times that Value.

I shall now therefore humbly propose my own Thoughts; which I hope will not be liable to the least Objection.

I have been assured by a very knowing *American* of my Acquaintance in *London*; that a young healthy Child, well nursed, is, at a Year old, a most delicious, nourishing, and wholesome Food; whether *Stewed, Roasted, Baked,* or *Boiled*; and, I make no doubt, that it will equally serve in a *Fricasie*, or *Ragoust*.

I do therefore humbly offer it to *publick Consideration*, that of the Hundred and Twenty Thousand Children, already computed, Twenty thousand may be reserved for Breed; whereof only one Fourth Part to be Males; which is more than we allow to *Sheep, black Cattle,* or *Swine*; and my Reason is, that these Children are seldom the Fruits of Marriage, *a Circumstance not much regarded by our Savages*; therefore, *one Male* will be sufficient to serve *four Females*. That the remaining Hundred thousand, may, at a Year old, be offered in Sale to the *Persons of Quality* and *Fortune*, through the Kingdom; always advising the Mother to let them suck plentifully in the last Month, so as to render them plump, and fat for a good Table. A Child will make two Dishes at an Entertainment for Friends; and when the Family dines alone, the fore or hind Quarter will make a reasonable Dish; and seasoned with a little Pepper or Salt, will be very good Boiled on the fourth Day, especially in *Winter*.

I have reckoned upon a Medium, that a Child just born will weigh Twelve Pounds; and in a solar Year, if tolerably nursed, encreaseth to twenty eight Pounds.

I grant this Food will be somewhat dear, and therefore very *proper for Landlords*; who, as they have already devoured most of the Parents, seem to have the best Title to the Children.

Infants Flesh will be in Season throughout the Year; but more plentiful in *March*, and a little before and after: For we are told by a grave * Author, an eminent *French* Physician, that *Fish being a*

---

* Rabelais.

prolifick Dyet, there are more Children born in *Roman Catholick Countries* about Nine Months after *Lent,* than at any other Season: Therefore reckoning a Year after *Lent,* the Markets will be more glutted than usual; because the Number of *Popish Infants,* is, at least, three to one in this Kingdom; and therefore it will have one other Collateral Advantage, by lessening the Number of *Papists* among us.

I have already computed the Charge of nursing a Beggar's Child (in which List I reckon all *Cottagers, Labourers,* and Four fifths of the *Farmers*) to be about two Shillings *per Annum,* Rags included; and I believe, no Gentleman would repine to give Ten Shillings for the *Carcase of a good fat Child;* which, as I have said, will make four Dishes of excellent nutritive Meat, when he hath only some particular Friend, or his own Family, to dine with him. Thus the Squire will learn to be a good Landlord, and grow popular among his Tenants; the Mother will have Eight Shillings net Profit, and be fit for Work until she produceth another Child.

Those who are more thrifty (*as I must confess the Times require*) may flay the Carcase; the Skin of which, artificially dressed, will make admirable *Gloves for Ladies,* and *Summer Boots for fine Gentlemen.*

As to our City of *Dublin;* Shambles may be appointed for this Purpose, in the most convenient Parts of it; and Butchers we may be assured will not be wanting; although I rather recommend buying the Children alive, and dressing them hot from the Knife, as we do *roasting Pigs.*

A very worthy Person, *a true Lover of his Country,* and whose Virtues I highly esteem, was lately pleased, in discoursing on this Matter, to offer a Refinement upon my Scheme. He said, that many Gentlemen of this Kingdom, having of late destroyed their Deer; he conceived, that the Want of Venison might be well supplied by the Bodies of young Lads and Maidens, not exceeding fourteen Years of Age, nor under twelve; so great a Number of both Sexes in every County being now ready to starve, for Want of Work and Service: And these to be disposed of by their Parents, if alive, or otherwise by their nearest Relations. But with due Deference to so excellent a Friend, and so deserving a Patriot, I cannot be altogether in his Sentiments. For as to the Males, my *American* Acquaintance assured me from frequent Experience, that their Flesh was generally tough and lean, like that of our School-boys, by continual Exercise, and their Taste disagreeable; and to fatten them would not answer the Charge. Then, as to the Females, it would, I think, with humble Submission, *be a Loss to the Publick,* because they soon would become Breeders themselves: And besides it is not improbable, that some scrupulous People might be apt to censure such a Practice (although indeed very unjustly) as a little bordering upon Cruelty, which, I confess, hath always been with me the strongest Objection against any Project, how well soever intended.

But in order to justify my Friend; he confessed, that this Expedient was put into his Head by the famous *Salmanaazor*, a Native of the Island *Formosa*, who came from thence to *London*, above twenty Years ago, and in Conversation told my Friend, that in his Country, when any young Person happened to be put to Death, the Executioner sold the Carcase to *Persons of Quality*, as a prime Dainty; and that, in his Time, the Body of a plump Girl of fifteen, who was crucified for an Attempt to poison the Emperor, was sold to his Imperial *Majesty's prime Minister of State*, and other great *Mandarins* of the Court, *in Joints from the Gibbet*, at Four hundred Crowns. Neither indeed can I deny, that if the same Use were made of several plump young girls in this Town, who, without one single Groat to their Fortunes, cannot stir Abroad without a Chair, and appear at the *Play-house*, and *Assemblies* in foreign Fineries, which they never will pay for; the Kingdom would not be the worse.

Some Persons of a desponding Spirit are in great Concern about that vast Number of poor People, who are Aged, Diseased, or Maimed; and I have been desired to employ my Thoughts what Course may be taken, to ease the Nation of so grievous an Incumbrance. But I am not in the least Pain upon that Matter; because it is very well known, that they are every Day *dying*, and *rotting*, by *Cold* and *Famine*, and *Filth*, and *Vermin*, as fast as can be reasonably expected. And as to the younger Labourers, they are now in almost as hopeful a Condition: They cannot get Work, and consequently pine away for Want of Nourishment, to a Degree, that if at any Time they are accidentally hired to common Labour, they have not Strength to perform it; and thus the Country, and themselves, are in a fair Way of being soon delivered from the Evils to come.

I have too long digressed; and therefore shall return to my Subject. I think the Advantages by the Proposal which I have made, are obvious, and many, as well as of the highest Importance.

For, *First*, as I have already observed, it would greatly lessen the *Number of Papists*, with whom we are yearly overrun; being the principal Breeders of the Nation, as well as our most dangerous Enemies; and who stay at home on Purpose, with a Design to *deliver the Kingdom to the Pretender*; hoping to take their Advantage by the Absence *of so many good Protestants*, who have chosen rather to leave their Country, than stay at home, and pay Tithes against their Conscience, to an idolatrous *Episcopal Curate*.

Secondly, The poorer Tenants will have something valuable of their own, which, by Law, may be made liable to Distress, and help to pay their Landlord's Rent; their Corn and Cattle being already seized, and *Money a Thing unknown*.

Thirdly, Whereas the Maintenance of an Hundred Thousand Children, from two Years old, and upwards, cannot be computed at less than ten Shillings a Piece *per Annum*, the Nation's Stock will be thereby encreased Fifty Thousand Pounds *per Annum;* besides the Profit of a new Dish, introduced to the Tables of all *Gentlemen of Fortune* in the Kingdom, who have any Refinement in Taste; and the Money will circulate among ourselves, the Goods being entirely of our own Growth and Manufacture.

Fourthly, The constant Breeders, besides the Gain of Eight Shillings *Sterling per Annum,* by the Sale of their Children, will be rid of the Charge of maintaining them after the first Year.

Fifthly, This Food would likewise bring great *Custom to Taverns,* where the Vintners will certainly be so prudent, as to procure the best Receipts for dressing it to Perfection; and consequently, have their Houses frequented by all the *fine Gentlemen,* who justly value themselves upon their Knowledge in good Eating; and a skilful Cook, who understands how to oblige his Guests, will contrive to make it as expensive as they please.

Sixthly, This would be a great Inducement to Marriage, which all wise Nations have either encouraged by Rewards, or enforced by Laws and Penalties. It would encrease the Care and Tenderness of Mothers towards their Children, when they were sure of a Settlement for Life, to the poor Babes, provided in some Sort by the Publick, to their annual Profit instead of Expence. We should soon see an honest Emulation among the married Women, *which of them could bring the fattest Child to the Market.* Men would become as *fond* of their Wives, during the Time of their Pregnancy, as they are now of their *Mares* in Foal, their *Cows* in Calf, or *Sows* when they are ready to farrow; nor offer to beat or kick them, (as it is too *frequent* a Practice) for fear of a Miscarriage.

Many other Advantages might be enumerated. For instance, the Addition of some Thousand Carcasses in our Exportation of barrelled Beef: The Propagation of *Swines Flesh,* and Improvement in the Art of making good *Bacon;* so much wanted among us by the great Destruction of *Pigs,* too frequent at our Tables, and are no way comparable in Taste, or Magnificence, to a well-grown fat yearling Child; which, roasted whole, will make a considerable Figure at a *Lord Mayor's Feast,* or any other publick Entertainment. But this, and many others, I omit; being studious of Brevity.

Supposing that one Thousand Families in this City, would be constant Customers for Infants Flesh; besides others who might have it at *merry Meetings,* particularly *Weddings* and *Christenings*; I compute that *Dublin* would take off, annually, about Twenty Thousand Carcasses; and the rest of the Kingdom (where probably they will be sold somewhat cheaper) the remaining Eighty Thousand.

I can think of no one Objection, that will possibly be raised against this Proposal; unless it should be urged, that the Number of People will be thereby much lessened in the Kingdom. This I freely own; and it was indeed one principal Design in offering it to the World. I desire the Reader will observe, that I calculate my Remedy *for this one individual Kingdom of* IRELAND, *and for no other that ever was, is, or I think ever can be upon Earth.* Therefore, let no man talk to me of other Expedients: *Of taxing our Absentees at five Shillings a Pound: Of using neither Cloaths, nor Houshold Furniture except what is of our own Growth and Manufacture: Of utterly rejecting the Materials and Instruments that promote foreign Luxury: Of curing the Expensiveness of Pride, Vanity, Idleness, and Gaming in our Women: Of introducing a Vein of Parsimony, Prudence and Temperance: Of learning to love our Country, wherein we differ even from* LAPLANDERS, *and the Inhabitants of* TOPINAMBOO: *Of quitting our Animosities, and Factions; nor act any longer like the* Jews, *who were murdering one another at the very Moment their City was taken: Of being a little cautious not to sell our Country and Consciences for nothing: Of teaching Landlords to have, at least, one Degree of Mercy towards their Tenants. Lastly, Of putting a Spirit of Honesty, Industry, and Skill into our Shop-keepers; who, if a Resolution could now be taken to buy only our native Goods, would immediately unite to cheat and exact upon us in the Price, the Measure, and the Goodness; nor could ever yet be brought to make one fair Proposal of just Dealing, though often and earnestly invited to it.*

Therefore I repeat, let no Man talk to me of these and the like Expedients; till he hath, at least, a Glimpse of Hope, that there will ever be some hearty and sincere Attempt to put *them in Practice.*

But, as to my self; having been wearied out for many Years with offering vain, idle, visionary Thoughts; and at length utterly despairing of Success, I fortunately fell upon this Proposal; which, as it is wholly new, so it hath something *solid* and *real,* of no Expence, and little Trouble, full in our own Power; and whereby we can incur no Danger in *disobliging* ENGLAND: For, this Kind of Commodity will not bear Exportation; the Flesh being of too tender a Consistence, to admit a long Continuance in Salt; *although, perhaps, I could name a Country, which would be glad to eat up our whole Nation without it.*

After all, I am not so violently bent upon my own Opinion, as to reject any Offer proposed by wise Men, which shall be found equally innocent, cheap, easy, and effectual. But before something of that Kind shall be advanced, in Contradiction to my Scheme, and offering a better; I desire the Author, or Authors, will be pleased maturely to consider two Points. *First,* As Things now stand, how they will be able to find Food and Raiment, for a Hundred Thousand useless Mouths and Backs? And *secondly,* There being a round Million of Creatures in human Figure, throughout this Kingdom; whose whole Subsistence, put into a common Stock, would leave them in Debt two Millions of Pounds *Sterling*; adding those, who are Beggars by Profession, to the Bulk of Farmers, Cottagers, and Labourers, with their Wives and Children, who are Beggars in Effect; I desire those Politicians, who dislike my Overture, and may perhaps be so bold to attempt an Answer, that they will first ask the Parents of these Mortals, Whether they would not, at this Day, think it a great Happiness to have been sold for Food at a Year old, in the Manner I prescribe; and thereby have avoided such a perpetual Scene of Misfortunes, as they have since gone through; by the *Oppression of Landlords*; the Impossibility of paying Rent, without Money or Trade; the Want of common Sustenance, with neither House nor Cloaths, to cover them from the Inclemencies of Weather; and the most inevitable Prospect of intailing the like, or greater Miseries upon their Breed for ever.

I profess, in the Sincerity of my Heart, that I have not the least personal Interest, in endeavouring to promote this necessary Work; having no other Motive than the *publick Good of my Country, by advancing our Trade, providing for Infants, relieving the Poor, and giving some Pleasure to the Rich.* I have no Children, by which I can propose to get a single Penny; the youngest being nine Years old, and my Wife past Child-bearing.

1. What is the effect of Swift's use of detail in this essay? How do statistics, recipes, and anecdotes support the symbolic world into which he wants to lead his readers?

2. What is the speaker's blind spot in this proposal? How does his choice of descriptive terms for the poor, whose plight he is supposedly committed to easing, reveal this blind spot?

3. What traits in the "proposer" are admirable? How does his style of writing show them to advantage? That is, how are we drawn into his scheme by his method of presentation? Be very specific in supporting your answer.

4. Throughout most of his essay Swift's own horror at the Irish situation is masked by the irony of his invented "proposer's" argument. Yet in a few places Swift allows irony to become sarcasm; his disgust at the conditions he describes breaks through the careful objective mask he has established. Where does this happen? Why does he suddenly shift the voice of his essay? What effect does this shift have?

5. How does the writer disarm possible objections to his proposition? Where specifically does he do this?

6. What is the purpose of the introduction (first seven paragraphs up to: "I shall now therefore humbly propose my own thoughts.")?

"The Birthmark"/*Nathaniel Hawthorne*

"The Birthmark" is one of Hawthorne's "moral tales." The focus of the story is on the moral questions it explores rather than the scenes, events, and characters we meet. Aylmer's great success as a "natural philosopher," his mysterious alchemistic experiments, even the growing repulsion he feels for his wife's minute blemish take on significance only as we gradually distinguish the two opposing moral themes which govern this symbolic world. Imperfection is a token of man's mortality—his humanity; but man's impatience with imperfection reveals his ability to aspire to the infinite—to have a god-like control over all things. It is the conflict between these two themes that gives significance to the world in which Aylmer works his mysterious experiments on his wife.

But as writers our ultimate concern is with Hawthorne's way of getting us to accept these moral ideas as the realities of his story—his strategy for leading us into Aylmer's strange world. How does he make us believe a world in which Aylmer's obsession and Georgiana's acquiescence seem not only congruent, but almost inevitable? One technique is to place his story in an alleged time and setting other than ours. At the outset of his tale, Hawthorne turns us to another "century" in which we are told that the "mysteries of nature," miracles, and the "spirit" are common preoccupations. Since we have no basis upon which to judge the truth of this assertion, we accept it. Consequently, though Aylmer is an "eminent" man of "fine countenance," we are prepared to accept his strange actions because we recollect that he has deep roots in this mysterious century, having given himself "too unreservedly to scientific studies." As you read the following story, then, observe other ways in which Hawthorne prepares you to accept unrealistic "realities" and his interpretation of them.

In the latter part of the last century there lived a man of science—an eminent proficient in every branch of natural philosophy—who not long before our story opens had made experience of a spiritual affinity more attractive than any chemical one. He had left his laboratory to the care of an assistant, cleared his fine countenance from the furnace-smoke, washed the stain of acids from his fingers, and persuaded a beautiful woman to become his wife. In those days, when the comparatively recent discovery of electricity, and other kindred mysteries of nature, seemed to open paths into the region of miracle, it was not unusual for the love of science to rival the love of woman in its depth and absorbing energy. The higher intellect, the imagination, the spirit, and even the heart, might all find their congenial aliment in pursuits which, as some of their ardent votaries believed, would ascend from one step of powerful

intelligence to another until the philosopher should lay his hand on the
secret of creative force, and perhaps make new worlds for himself. We
know not whether Aylmer possessed this degree of faith in man's
ultimate control over nature. He had devoted himself, however, too
unreservedly to scientific studies ever to be weaned from them by any
second passion. His love for his young wife might prove the stronger of
the two, but it could only be by intertwining itself with his love of
science and uniting the strength of the latter to its own.

Such a union accordingly took place, and was attended with truly
remarkable consequences and a deeply impressive moral. One day, very
soon after their marriage, Aylmer sat gazing at his wife with a trouble in
his countenance that grew stronger, until he spoke.

"Georgiana," said he, "has it never occurred to you that the mark upon
your cheek might be removed?"

"No, indeed," said she smiling; but, perceiving the seriousness of his
manner, she blushed deeply. "To tell you the truth, it has been so often
called a charm that I was simple enough to imagine it might be so."

"Ah! upon another face perhaps it might," replied her husband, "but
never on yours. No, dearest Georgiana; you came so nearly perfect from
the hand of Nature that this slightest possible defect—which we hesitate
whether to term a defect or a beauty—shocks me as being the visible
mark of earthly imperfection."

"Shocks you, my husband!" cried Georgiana, deeply hurt, at first
reddening with momentary anger, but then bursting into tears. "Then
why did you take me from my mother's side? You cannot love that
which shocks you."

To explain this conversation it must be mentioned that in the centre
of Georgiana's left cheek there was a singular mark deeply interwoven,
as it were, with the texture and substance of her face. In the usual state
of her complexion—a healthy though delicate bloom—the mark wore a
tint of deeper crimson which imperfectly defined its shape amid the
surrounding rosiness. When she blushed, it gradually became more
indistinct, and finally vanished amid the triumphant rush of blood that
bathed the whole cheek with its brilliant glow. But if any shifting
emotion caused her to turn pale, there was the mark again, a crimson
stain upon the snow, in what Aylmer sometimes deemed an almost
fearful distinctness. Its shape bore not a little similarity to the human
hand, though of the smallest pigmy size. Georgiana's lovers were wont
to say that some fairy at her birth-hour had laid her tiny hand upon the
infant's cheek, and left this impress there in token of the magic
endowments that were to give her such sway over all hearts. Many a
desperate swain would have risked his life for the privilege of pressing
his lips to the mysterious hand. It must not be concealed, however, that
the impression wrought by this fairy sign-manual varied exceedingly

according to the difference of temperament in the beholders. Some
fastidious persons—but they were exclusively of her own sex—affirmed
that the bloody hand, as they chose to call it, quite destroyed the effect
of Georgiana's beauty, and rendered her countenance even hideous.
But it would be as reasonable to say that one of those small blue stains
which sometimes occur in the purest statuary marble would convert the
Eve of Powers to a monster. Masculine observers, if the birthmark did
not heighten their admiration, contented themselves with wishing it
away that the world might possess one living specimen of ideal loveliness
without the semblance of a flaw.

  After his marriage—for he thought little or nothing of the matter
before—Aylmer discovered that this was the case with himself. Had she
been less beautiful—if Envy's self could have found aught else to sneer
at—he might have felt his affection heightened by the prettiness of this
mimic hand, now vaguely portrayed, now lost, now stealing forth again,
and glimmering to and fro with every pulse of emotion that throbbed
within her heart. But, seeing her otherwise so perfect, he found this one
defect grow more and more intolerable with every moment of their
united lives. It was the fatal flaw of humanity which Nature in one
shape or another stamps ineffaceably on all her productions, either to
imply that they are temporary and finite, or that their perfection must be
wrought by toil and pain. The crimson hand expressed the ineludible
grip in which mortality clutches the highest and purest of earthly mold,
degrading them into kindred with the lowest, and even with the very
brutes, like whom their visible frames return to dust. In this manner,
selecting it as the symbol of his wife's liability to sin, sorrow, decay and
death, Aylmer's sombre imagination was not long in rendering the
birthmark a frightful object, causing him more trouble and horror than
ever Georgiana's beauty, whether of soul or sense, had given him
delight.

  At all the seasons which should have been their happiest he
invariably, and without intending it—nay, in spite of a purpose to
the contrary—reverted to this one disastrous topic. Trifling as it at first
appeared, it so connected itself with innumerable trains of thought and
moods of feeling that it became the central point of all. With the
morning twilight Aylmer opened his eyes upon his wife's face and
recognized the symbol of imperfection; and when they sat together at
the evening hearth, his eyes wandered stealthily to her cheek, and
beheld, flickering with the blaze of the woodfire, the spectral hand that
wrote mortality where he would fain have worshipped. Georgiana soon
learned to shudder at his gaze. It needed but a glance, with the peculiar
expression that his face often wore, to change the roses of her cheek
into a deathlike paleness, amid which the crimson hand was brought
strongly out like a bass-relief of ruby on the whitest marble.

Late one night, when the lights were growing dim, so as hardly to betray the stain on the poor wife's cheek, she herself for the first time voluntarily took up the subject.

"Do you remember, my dear Aylmer," said she, with a feeble attempt at a smile—"have you any recollection of a dream last night about this odious hand?"

"None—none whatever," replied Aylmer, starting; but then he added in a dry, cold tone, affected for the sake of concealing the real depth of his emotion, "I might well dream of it, for before I fell asleep it had taken a pretty firm hold of my fancy."

"And you did dream of it," continued Georgiana, hastily; for she dreaded lest a gush of tears should interrupt what she had to say—"a terrible dream. I wonder that you can forget it. Is it possible to forget this one expression?—'It is in her heart now: we must have it out.' Reflect, my husband; for by all means I would have you recall that dream."

The mind is in a sad state when Sleep the all-involving cannot confine her spectres within the dim region of her sway, but suffers them to break forth, affrighting this actual life with secrets that perchance belong to a deeper one. Aylmer now remembered his dream. He had fancied himself with his servant Aminadab, attempting an operation for the removal of the birthmark. But the deeper went the knife, the deeper sank the hand, until at length its tiny grasp appeared to have caught hold of Georgiana's heart, whence, however, her husband was inexorably resolved to cut or wrench it away.

When the dream had shaped itself perfectly in his memory, Aylmer sat in his wife's presence with a guilty feeling. Truth often finds its way to the mind close-muffled in robes of sleep, and then speaks with uncompromising directness of matters in regard to which we practice an unconscious self-deception during our waking moments. Until now he had not been aware of the tyrannizing influence acquired by one idea over his mind, and of the lengths which he might find in his heart to go for the sake of giving himself peace.

"Aylmer," resumed Georgiana, solemnly, "I know not what may be the cost to both of us to rid me of this fatal birthmark. Perhaps its removal may cause cureless deformity. Or, it may be, the stain goes as deep as life itself. Again, do we know that there is a possibility, on any terms, of unclasping the firm grip of this little hand which was laid upon me before I came into the world?"

"Dearest Georgiana, I have spent much thought upon the subject," hastily interrupted Aylmer; "I am convinced of the perfect practicability of its removal."

"If there be the remotest possibility of it," continued Georgiana, "let the attempt be made, at whatever risk. Danger is nothing to me, for life, while this hateful mark makes me the object of your horror and disgust—life is a burden when I would fling down with joy. Either remove this dreadful hand or take my wretched life. You have deep science; all the world bears witness to it. You have achieved great wonders; cannot you remove this little, little mark which I cover with the tips of two small fingers? Is this beyond your power, for the sake of your own peace and to save your poor wife from madness?"

"Noblest, dearest, tenderest wife!" cried Aylmer, rapturously. "Doubt not my power. I have already given this matter the deepest thought— thought which might almost have enlightened me to create a being less perfect than yourself. Georgiana, you have led me deeper than ever into the heart of Science. I feel myself fully competent to render this dear cheek as faultless as its fellow, and then, most beloved, what will be my triumph when I shall have corrected what Nature left imperfect in her fairest work! Even Pygmalion, when his sculptured woman assumed life, felt not greater ecstasy than mine will be."

"It is resolved, then," said Georgiana, faintly smiling. "And, Aylmer, spare me not, though you should find the birthmark take refuge in my heart at last."

Her husband tenderly kissed her cheek—her right cheek, not that which bore the impress of the crimson hand.

The next day Aylmer apprised his wife of a plan that he had formed whereby he might have opportunity for the intense thought and constant watchfulness which the proposed operation would require, while Georgiana, likewise, would enjoy the perfect repose essential to its success. They were to seclude themselves in the extensive apartments occupied by Aylmer as a laboratory, and where during his toilsome youth he had made discoveries in the elemental powers of nature that had aroused the admiration of all the learned societies in Europe. Seated calmly in this laboratory, the pale philosopher had investigated the secrets of the highest cloud-region and of the profoundest minds; he had satisfied himself of the causes that kindled and kept alive the fires of the volcano, and had explained the mystery of fountains and how it is that they gush forth, some so bright and pure and others with such rich medicinal virtues, from the dark bosom of the earth. Here, too, at an earlier period, he had studied the wonders of the human frame, and attempted to fathom the very process by which Nature assimilates all her precious influences from earth and air and from the spiritual world to create and foster man, her masterpiece. The latter pursuit, however, Aylmer had long laid aside in unwilling recognition of the truth against which all seekers sooner or later stumble—that our great creative mother, while she amuses us with apparently working in the broadest sunshine, is yet severely careful to keep her own secrets, and in spite of her pretended openness shows us nothing but results. She permits us, indeed, to mar, but seldom to mend, and, like a jealous patentee, on no account to make. Now, however, Aylmer resumed these half-forgotten investigations—not, of course, with such hopes or wishes as first suggested them, but because they involved much physiological truth and lay in the path of his proposed scheme for the treatment of Georgiana.

As he led her over the threshold of the laboratory Georgiana was cold and tremulous. Aylmer looked cheerfully into her face with intent to reassure her, but was so startled with the intense glow of the birthmark upon the whiteness of her cheek that he could not restrain a strong convulsive shudder. His wife fainted.

"Aminadab! Aminadab!" shouted Aylmer, stamping violently on the floor.

Forthwith there issued from an inner apartment a man of low stature but bulky frame, with shaggy hair hanging about his visage, which was grimed with the vapors of the furnace. This personage had been Aylmer's underworker during his whole scientific career, and was admirably fitted for that office by his great mechanical readiness and the skill with which, while incapable of comprehending a single principle, he executed all the practical details of his master's experiments. With his vast strength, his shaggy hair, his smoky aspect, and the indescribable earthiness that incrusted him, he seemed to represent man's physical nature, while Aylmer's slender figure and pale, intellectual face were no less apt a type of the spiritual element.

"Throw open the door of the boudoir, Aminadab," said Aylmer, "and burn a pastille."

"Yes, master," answered Aminadab, looking intently at the lifeless form of Georgiana; and then he muttered to himself, "if she were my wife, I'd never part with that birthmark."

When Georgiana recovered consciousness, she found herself breathing an atmosphere of penetrating fragrance, the gentle potency of which had recalled her from her death-like faintness. The scene around her looked like enchantment. Aylmer had converted those smoky, dingy, sombre rooms where he had spent his brightest years in recondite pursuits into a series of beautiful apartments not unfit to be the secluded abode of a lovely woman. The walls were hung with gorgeous curtains which imparted the combination of grandeur and grace that no other species of adornment can achieve, and as they fell from the ceiling to the floor their rich and ponderous folds, concealing all angles and straight lines, appeared to shut in the scene from infinite space. For aught Georgiana knew, it might be a pavilion among the clouds. And Aylmer, excluding the sunshine, which would have interfered with his chemical processes, had supplied its place with perfumed lamps emitting flames of various hue, but all uniting in a soft, empurpled radiance. He now knelt by his wife's side, watching her earnestly, but without alarm, for

he was confident in his science, and felt that he could draw a magic
circle round her within which no evil might intrude.

"Where am I? Ah! I remember," said Georgiana, faintly; and she
placed her hand over her cheek to hide the terrible mark from
her husband's eyes.

"Fear not, dearest," exclaimed he. "Do not shrink from me. Believe
me, Georgiana, I even rejoice in this single imperfection, since it will be
such a rapture to remove it."

"Oh, spare me!" sadly replied his wife. "Pray, do not look at it again.
I never can forget that convulsive shudder."

In order to soothe Georgiana, and, as it were, to release her mind from
the burden of actual things, Aylmer now put in practice some of
the light and playful secrets which science had taught him among its
profounder lore. Airy figures, absolutely bodiless ideas and forms of
unsubstantial beauty, came and danced before her, imprinting their
momentary footsteps on beams of light. Though she had some indistinct
idea of the method of these optical phenomena, still the illusion was
almost perfect enough to warrant the belief that her husband possessed
sway over the spiritual world. Then, again, when she felt a wish to
look forth from her seclusion, immediately, as if her thoughts were
answered, the procession of external existence flitted across a screen. The
scenery and the figures of actual life were perfectly represented, but
with that bewitching yet indescribable difference which always makes a
picture, an image or a shadow, so much more attractive than the original.
When wearied of this, Aylmer bade her cast her eyes upon a vessel
containing a quantity of earth. She did so, with little interest at first,
but was soon startled to perceive the germ of a plant shooting upward
from the soil. Then came the slender stalk; the leaves gradually unfolded
themselves, and amid them was a perfect and lovely flower.

"It is magical," cried Georgiana; "I dare not touch it."

"Nay, pluck it," answered Aylmer—"pluck it and inhale its brief
perfume while you may. The flower will wither in a few moments, and
leave nothing save its brown seed-vessels; but thence may be perpetuated
a race as ephemeral as itself."

But Georgiana had no sooner touched the flower than the whole plant
suffered a blight, its leaves turning coal-black, as if by the agency of fire.

"There was too powerful a stimulus," said Aylmer, thoughtfully.

To make up for this abortive experiment, he proposed to take her
portrait by a scientific process of his own invention. It was to be effected
by rays of light striking upon a polished plate of metal. Georgiana
assented, but on looking at the result was affrighted to find the features
of the portrait blurred and indefinable, while the minute figure of a
hand appeared where the cheek should have been. Aylmer snatched
the metallic plate and threw it into a jar of corrosive acid.

Soon, however, he forgot these mortifying failures. In the intervals of study and chemical experiment he came to her flushed and exhausted, but seemed invigorated by her presence, and spoke in glowing language of the resources of his art. He gave a history of the long dynasty of the alchemists, who spent so many ages in quest of the universal solvent by which the golden principle might be elicited from all things vile and base. Aylmer appeared to believe that by the plainest scientific logic it was altogether within the limits of possibility to discover this long-sought medium; but, he added, a philosopher who should go deep enough to acquire the power would attain too lofty a wisdom to stoop to the exercise of it. Not less singular were his opinions in regard to the Elixir Vitae. He more than intimated that it was at his option to concoct a liquid that should prolong life for years—perhaps interminably—but that it would produce a discord in nature which all the world, and chiefly the quaffer of the immortal nostrum, would find cause to curse.

"Aylmer, are you in earnest?" asked Georgiana, looking at him with amazement and fear. "It is terrible to possess such power, or even to dream of possessing it."

"Oh, do not tremble, my love," said her husband; "I would not wrong either you or myself by working such inharmonious effects upon our lives. But I would have you consider how trifling in comparison, is the skill requisite to remove this little hand."

At the mention of the birthmark, Georgiana, as usual, shrank as if a red-hot iron had touched her cheek.

Again Aylmer applied himself to his labors. She could hear his voice in the distant furnace-room giving directions to Aminadab, whose harsh, uncouth, misshapen tones were audible in response, more like the grunt or growl of a brute than human speech. After hours of absence Aylmer reappeared, and proposed that she should now examine his cabinet of chemical products and natural treasures of the earth. Among the former he showed her a small vial in which, he remarked, was contained a gentle yet most powerful fragrance capable of impregnating all the breezes that blow across a kingdom. They were of inestimable value, the contents of that little vial; and as he said so he threw some of the perfume into the air and filled the room with piercing and invigorating delight.

"And what is this?" asked Georgiana, pointing to a small crystal globe containing a gold-colored liquid. "It is so beautiful to the eye that I could imagine it the Elixir of Life."

"In one sense it is," replied Aylmer—"or, rather, the Elixir of Immortality. It is the most precious poison that ever was concocted in this world. By its aid I could apportion the lifetime of any mortal at whom you might point your finger. The strength of the dose would determine whether he were to linger out years or drop dead in the midst of a breath. No king on his guarded throne could keep his life, if I, in my private station, should deem that the welfare of millions justified me in depriving him of it."

"Why do you keep such a terrific drug?" inquired Georgiana, in horror.

"Do not mistrust me, dearest," said her husband, smiling; "its virtuous potency is yet greater than its harmful one. But see! here is a powerful cosmetic. With a few drops of this in a vase of water freckles may be washed away as easily as the hands are cleansed. A stronger infusion would take the blood out of the cheek and leave the rosiest beauty a pale ghost."

"Is it with this lotion that you intend to bathe my cheek?" asked Georgiana, anxiously.

"Oh, no!" hastily replied her husband; "this is merely superficial. Your case demands a remedy that shall go deeper."

In his interviews with Georgiana, Aylmer generally made minute inquiries as to her sensations, and whether the confinement of the rooms and the temperature of the atmosphere agreed with her. These questions had such a particular drift that Georgiana began to conjecture that she was already subjected to certain physical influences, either breathed in with the fragrant air or taken with her food. She fancied, likewise— but it might be altogether fancy—that there was a stirring up of her system, a strange, indefinite sensation creeping through her veins and tingling, half painfully, half pleasurably, at her heart. Still whenever she dared to look into the mirror, there she beheld herself pale as a white rose and with the crimson birthmark stamped upon her cheek. Not even Aylmer now hated it so much as she.

To dispel the tedium of the hours which her husband found it necessary to devote to the processes of combination and analysis, Georgiana turned over the volumes of his scientific library. In many dark old tomes she met with chapters full of romance and poetry. They were the works of the philosophers of the Middle Ages, such as Albertus Magnus, Cornelius Agrippa, Paracelsus, and the famous friar who created the prophetic Brazen Head. All these antique naturalists stood in advance of their centuries, yet were imbued with some of their credulity, and therefore were believed, and perhaps imagined themselves, to have acquired from the investigation of nature a power above nature, and from physics a sway over the spiritual world. Hardly less curious and imaginative were the early volumes of the *Transactions* of the Royal Society, in which the members, knowing little of the limits of natural possibility, were continually recording wonders or proposing methods whereby wonders might be wrought.

But to Georgiana the most engrossing volume was a large folio from her husband's own hand in which he had recorded every experiment of his scientific career, with its original aim, the methods adopted for its development and its final success or failure, with the circumstances to which either event was attributable. The book, in truth, was both the history and emblem of his ardent, ambitious, imaginative, yet practical and laborious life. He handled physical details as if there were nothing beyond them, yet spiritualized them all, and redeemed himself from materialism by his strong and eager aspiration toward the infinite. In his grasp the veriest clod of earth assumed a soul. Georgiana, as she read, reverenced Aylmer, and loved him more profoundly than ever, but with less entire dependence on his judgment than heretofore. Much as he had accomplished, she could not but observe that his most splendid successes were almost invariably failures, if compared with the idea at which he aimed. His brightest diamonds were the merest pebbles, and felt to be so by himself, in comparison with the inestimable gems which lay hidden beyond his reach. The volume rich with achievements that had won renown for its author was yet as melancholy a record as ever mortal hand had penned. It was the sad confession and continued exemplification of the shortcomings of the composite man, the spirit burdened with clay and working in matter, and of the despair that assails the higher nature at finding itself so miserably thwarted by the earthly part. Perhaps every man of genius, in whatever sphere, might recognize the image of his own experience in Aylmer's journal.

So deeply did these reflections affect Georgiana that she laid her face upon the open volume and burst into tears. In this situation she was found by her husband.

"It is dangerous to read in a sorcerer's book," said he, with a smile, though his countenance was uneasy and displeased. "Georgiana, there are pages in that volume which I can scarcely glance over and keep my senses. Take heed lest it prove as detrimental to you."

"It has made me worship you more than ever," said she.

"Ah! wait for this one success," rejoined he, "then worship me if you will. I shall deem myself hardly unworthy of it. But come! I have sought you for the luxury of your voice; sing to me, dearest."

So she poured out the liquid music of her voice to quench the thirst of his spirit. He then took his leave with a boyish exuberance of gayety, assuring her that her seclusion would endure but a little longer, and that the result was already certain. Scarcely had he departed, when Georgiana felt irresistibly impelled to follow him. She had forgotten to inform Aylmer of a symptom which for two or three hours past had begun to excite her attention. It was a sensation in the fatal birthmark— not painful, but which induced a restlessness throughout her system. Hastening after her husband, she intruded for the first time into the laboratory.

The first thing that struck her eye was the furnace, that hot and feverish worker, with the intense glow of its fire, which by the quantities of soot clustered above it seemed to have been burning for ages. There was a distilling apparatus in full operation. Around the room were retorts, tubes, cylinders, crucibles and other apparatus of chemical research. An electrical machine stood ready for immediate use. The atmosphere felt oppressively close, and was tainted with gaseous odors which had been tormented forth by the processes of Science. The severe and homely simplicity of the apartment, with its naked walls and brick pavement, looked strange, accustomed as Georgiana had become to the fantastic elegance of her boudoir. But what chiefly—indeed, almost solely—drew her attention was the aspect of Aylmer himself.

He was pale as death, anxious and absorbed, and hung over the furnace as if it depended upon his utmost watchfulness whether the liquid which it was distilling should be the draught of immortal happiness or misery. How different from the sanguine and joyous mien that he had assumed for Georgiana's encouragement!

"Carefully now, Aminadab. Carefully, thou human machine! Carefully, thou man of clay!" muttered Aylmer, more to himself than his assistant. "Now, if there be a thought too much or too little, it is all over."

"Hoh! hoh!" mumbled Aminadab. "Look, master, look!"

Aylmer raised his eyes hastily, and at first reddened, then grew paler than ever, on beholding Georgiana. He rushed toward her and seized her arm with a grip that left the print of fingers upon it.

"Why do you come hither? Have you no trust in your husband?" cried he, impetuously. "Would you throw the blight of that fatal birth-mark over my labors? It is not well done. Go, prying woman, go!"

"Nay, Aylmer," said Georgiana, with a firmness of which she possessed no stinted endowment, "it is not you that have a right to complain. You mistrust your wife. You have concealed the anxiety with which you watch the development of this experiment. Think not so unworthily of me, my husband. Tell me all the risk we run, and fear not that I shall shrink, for my share in it is far less than your own!"

"No, no, Georgiana!" said Aylmer, impatiently; "it must not be."

"I submit," replied she, calmly. "And, Aylmer, I shall quaff whatever draught you bring me, but it will be on the same principle that would induce me to take a dose of poison if offered by your hand."

"My noble wife!" said Aylmer, deeply moved; "I knew not the height and depth of your nature until now. Nothing shall be concealed. Know, then, that this crimson hand, superficial as it seems, has clutched its grasp into your being with a strength of which I had no previous conception. I have already administered agents powerful enough to do aught except to change your entire physical system. Only one thing remains to be tried; if that fails us, we are ruined!"

"Why did you hesitate to tell me this?" asked she.

"Because, Georgiana," said Aylmer, in a low voice, "there is danger."

" 'Danger'! There is but one danger—that this horrible stigma shall be left upon my cheek," cried Georgiana. "Remove it, remove it, whatever be the cost, or we shall both go mad."

"Heaven knows your words are too true," said Aylmer, sadly. "And now, dearest, return to your boudoir. In a little while all will be tested."

He conducted her back, and took leave of her with a solemn tenderness which spoke far more than his words how much was now at stake.

After his departure Georgiana became wrapped in musings. She considered the character of Aylmer, and did it completer justice than at any previous moment. Her heart exulted while it trembled at his honorable love, so pure and lofty that it would accept nothing less than perfection, nor miserably make itself contented with an earthlier nature than he had dreamed of. She felt how much more precious was such a sentiment than that meaner kind which would have borne with the imperfection for her sake, and have been guilty of treason to holy love by degrading its perfect idea to the level of the actual. And with her whole spirit she prayed that for a single moment she might satisfy his highest and deepest conception. Longer than one moment, she well knew, it could not be, for his spirit was ever on the march, ever ascending, and each instant required something that was beyond the scope of the instant before.

The sound of her husband's footsteps aroused her. He bore a crystal goblet containing a liquor colorless as water, but bright enough to be the draught of immortality. Aylmer was pale, but it seemed rather the consequence of a highly-wrought state of mind and tension of spirit than of fear or doubt.

"The concoction of the draught has been perfect," said he in answer to Georgiana's look. "Unless all my science have deceived me, it cannot fail."

"Save on your account, my dearest Aylmer," observed his wife, "I might wish to put off this birthmark of mortality by relinquishing mortality itself, in preference to any other mode. Life is but a sad possession to those who have attained precisely the degree of moral advancement at which I stand. Were I weaker and blinder, it might be happiness; were I stronger, it might be endured hopefully; but, being what I find myself, methinks I am of all mortals the most fit to die."

"You are fit for heaven without tasting death," replied her husband. "But why do you speak of dying? The draught cannot fail. Behold its effect upon this plant."

On the window-seat there stood a geranium diseased with yellow blotches, which had overspread all its leaves, Aylmer poured a small quantity of the liquid upon the soil in which it grew. In a little time, when the roots of the plant had taken up the moisture, the unsightly blotches began to be extinguished in a living verdure.

"There needed no proof," said Georgiana quietly. "Give me the goblet; I joyfully stake all upon your word."

"Drink, then, thou lofty creature!" exclaimed Aylmer, with fervid admiration. "There is no taint of imperfection on thy spirit. Thy sensible frame, too, shall soon be all perfect."

She quaffed the liquid, and returned the goblet to his hand.

"It is grateful," said she, with a placid smile. "Methinks it is like water from a heavenly fountain, for it contains I know not what of unobtrusive fragrance and deliciousness. It allays a feverish thirst that had parched me for many days. Now, dearest, let me sleep. My earthly senses are closing over my spirit like the leaves around the heart of a rose at sunset."

She spoke the last words with a gentle reluctance, as if it required almost more energy than she could command to pronounce the faint and lingering syllables. Scarcely had they loitered through her lips ere she was lost in slumber. Aylmer sat by her side, watching her aspect with the emotions proper to a man the whole value of whose existence was involved in the process now to be tested. Mingled with this mood, however, was the philosophic investigation characteristic of the man of science. Not the minutest symptom escaped him. A heightened flush of the cheek, a slight irregularity of breadth, a quiver of the eyelid, a hardly perceptible tremor through the frame—such were the details which as the moments passed he wrote down in his folio volume. Intense thought had set its stamp upon every previous page of that volume, but the thoughts of years were all concentrated upon the last.

While thus employed he failed not to gaze often at the fatal hand, and not without a shudder. Yet once, by a strange and unaccountable impulse, he pressed it with his lips. His spirit recoiled, however, in the very act, and Georgiana, out of the midst of her deep sleep, moved uneasily and murmured, as if in remonstrance. Again Aylmer resumed his watch. Nor was it without avail. The crimson hand, which at first had been strongly visible upon the marble paleness of Georgiana's cheek, now grew more faintly outlined. She remained not less pale than ever, but the birthmark with every breath that came and went lost somewhat of its former distinctness. Its presence had been awful; its departure was more awful still. Watch the stain of the rainbow fading out of the sky, you will know how that mysterious symbol passed away.

"By Heaven, it is wellnigh gone!" said Aylmer to himself, in almost irrepressible ecstasy. "I can scarcely trace it now. Success! Success! And now it is like the faintest rose-color; the slightest flush of blood across her cheek would overcome it. But she is so pale!"

He drew aside the window-curtain and suffered the light of natural day to fall into the room and rest upon her cheek. At the same time he heard a gross, hoarse chuckle which he had long known as his servant Aminadab's expression of delight.

"Ah, clod! Ah, earthly mass!" cried Aylmer, laughing in a sort of frenzy. "You have served me well! Matter and spirit—earth and heaven—have both done their part in this. Laugh, thing of the senses! You have earned the right to laugh!"

These exclamations broke Georgiana's sleep. She slowly unclosed her eyes and gazed into the mirror which her husband had arranged for that purpose. A faint smile flitted over her lips when she recognized how barely perceptible was now that crimson hand which had once blazed forth with such disastrous brilliancy as to scare away all their happiness. But then her eyes sought Aylmer's face with a trouble and anxiety that he could by no means account for.

"My poor Aylmer!" murmured she.

"Poor? Nay—richest, happiest, most favored!" exclaimed he. "My peerless bride, it is successful. You are perfect!"

"My poor Aylmer!" she repeated with a more than human tenderness. "You have aimed loftily; you have done nobly. Do not repent that with so high and pure a feeling you have rejected the best the earth could offer. Aylmer, dearest Aylmer, I am dying."

Alas, it was too true! The fatal hand had grappled with the mystery of life, and was the bond by which an angelic spirit kept itself in union with a mortal frame. As the last crimson tint of the birthmark—that sole token of human imperfection—faded from her cheek, the parting breath of the now perfect woman passed into the atmosphere, and her soul, lingering a moment near her husband, took its heavenward flight. Then a hoarse, chuckling laugh was heard again. Thus ever does the gross fatality of earth exult in its invariable triumph over the immortal essence which in this dim sphere of half development demands the completeness of a higher state. Yet, had Aylmer reached a profounder wisdom, he need not thus have flung away the happiness which would have woven his mortal life of the selfsame texture with the celestial. The momentary circumstance was too strong for him: he failed to look beyond the shadowy scope of time, and, living once for all eternity, to find the perfect future in the present.

1. How does Hawthorne describe the characters, events, and scenes in his tale so that we do not expect a realistic account of scientific experimentation?

In addition to these passages, what sections present his central concerns outright? How are these two strategies of fantasy and realistic argument related?

2. Why does Aylmer need Aminadab? How does Hawthorne stress the symbolic significance of their association?

3. In real life Aylmer's obsession with Georgiana's birthmark would be in poor taste, to say the least. Why does Hawthorne indulge that obsession in the story? Why must Georgiana patiently bear her husband's peculiar behavior and finally submit to his experiment? That is, what does the mark come to symbolize? Trace the gradual growth of the symbol throughout the tale.

4. What is Hawthorne's position as narrator? Does he sympathize with Aylmer's obsession, or does he find it destructive? In either case, point out places in the tale where the narrator reveals himself.

5. What is the function of Aylmer's dream and Georgiana's persistence in bringing it to his consciousness?

6. How does the incident in which Georgiana examines her husband's books function in helping us to accept (to suspend our disbelief in) the world that Hawthorne creates?

"Battle Royal"/*Ralph Ellison*

What follows is the first chapter of Ellison's novel, *Invisible Man*, in which a young black man gradually discovers that he is socially, politically, and even physically a non-person—invisible. In the world of this chapter, irony is the rule. Nothing is as it appears. The Grandfather's dying words seem to contradict his whole life; the white leaders of the town are revealed as savage, drunken lechers; even the main character's graduation reward is transformed into a sick joke by the dream which ends the section.

This nightmare world is seen through the "I" Ellison has created to tell the story. We are limited to the narrator's point of view, and it's from his surreal vision, where reality, horror, and symbol merge, that Ellison's ironic world arises. For example, the narrator's simultaneous attraction to and revulsion from white women is vividly realized in his realistic description of the white whore with an American flag tattooed upon her belly. But she is also made unreal in her grotesque and manikin-like appearance. At this point she takes on a symbolic power, as she becomes the quintessential victim, full of "terror and disgust." By means of this technique, Ellison expresses the puzzlement and confusion through which the main character must struggle to find true values.

It goes a long way back, some twenty years. All my life I had been looking for something, and everywhere I turned someone tried to tell me what it was. I accepted their answers too, though they were often in contradiction and even self-contradictory. I was naïve. I was looking for myself and asking everyone except myself questions which I, and only I, could answer. It took me a long time and much painful boomeranging of my expectations to achieve a realization everyone else appears to have been born with: That I am nobody but myself. But first I had to discover that I am an invisible man!

And yet I am no freak of nature, nor of history. I was in the cards, other things having been equal (or unequal) eighty-five years ago. I am not ashamed of my grandparents for having been slaves. I am only ashamed of myself for having at one time been ashamed. About eighty-five years ago they were told that they were free, united with others of our country in everything pertaining to the common good, and, in everything social, separate like the fingers of the hand. And they believed it. They exulted in it. They stayed in their place, worked hard, and brought up my father to do the same. But my grandfather is the one. He was an odd old guy, my grandfather, and I am told I take after him. It was he who caused the trouble. On his deathbed he called my father to him and said, "Son, after I'm gone I want you to keep up the good fight. I never told you, but our life is a war and I have been a traitor all my born days, a spy in the enemy's country ever since I give up my gun back in the Reconstruction. Live with your head in the lion's mouth. I want you to overcome 'em with yeses, undermine 'em with grins, agree 'em to death and destruction, let 'em swoller you till they vomit or bust wide open." They thought the old man had gone out of his mind. He had been the meekest of men. The younger children were rushed from the room, the shades drawn and the flame of the lamp turned so low that it sputtered on the wick like the old man's breathing. "Learn it to the younguns," he whispered fiercely; then he died.

But my folks were more alarmed over his last words than over his dying. It was as though he had not died at all, his words caused so much anxiety. I was warned emphatically to forget what he had said and, indeed, this is the first time it has been mentioned outside the family circle. It had a tremendous effect upon me, however. I could never be sure of what he meant. Grandfather had been a quiet old man who never made any trouble, yet on his deathbed he had called himself a traitor and a spy, and he had spoken of his meekness as a dangerous activity. It became a constant puzzle which lay unanswered in the back of my mind. And whenever things went well for me I remembered my grandfather and felt guilty and uncomfortable. It was as though I was carrying out his advice in spite of myself. And to make it worse, everyone loved me for it. I was praised by the most lily-white men of the town. I was considered an example of desirable conduct—just as my grandfather had been. And what puzzled me was that the old man had defined it as *treachery*. When I was praised for my conduct I felt a guilt that in some way I was doing something that was really against the wishes of the white folks, that if they had understood they would have desired me to act just the opposite, that I should have been sulky and mean, and that that really would have been what they wanted, even though they were fooled and thought they wanted me to act as I did. It made me afraid that some day they would look upon me as a traitor and I would be lost. Still I was more afraid to act any other way because they didn't like that at all. The old man's words were like a curse. On my graduation day I delivered an oration in which I showed that humility was the secret, indeed, the very essence of progress. (Not that I believed this— how could I, remembering my grandfather?—I only believed that it worked.) It was a great success. Everyone praised me and I was invited to give the speech at a gathering of the town's leading white citizens. It was a triumph for our whole community.

It was in the main ballroom of the leading hotel. When I got there I discovered that it was on the occasion of a smoker, and I was told that since I was to be there anyway I might as well take part in the battle royal to be fought by some of my schoolmates as part of the entertainment. The battle royal came first.

All of the town's big shots were there in their tuxedoes, wolfing down the buffet foods, drinking beer and whiskey and smoking black cigars. It was a large room with a high ceiling. Chairs were arranged in neat rows around three sides of a portable boxing ring. The fourth side was clear, revealing a gleaming space of polished floor. I had some misgivings over the battle royal, by the way. Not from a distaste for fighting, but because I didn't care too much for the other fellows who were to take part. They were tough guys who seemed to have no grandfather's curse worrying their minds. No one could mistake their toughness. And besides, I suspected that fighting a battle royal might detract from the dignity of my speech. In those pre-invisible days I visualized myself as a potential Booker T. Washington. But the other fellows didn't care too much for me either, and there were nine of them. I felt superior to them in my way, and I didn't like the manner in which we were all crowded together into the servants' elevator. Nor did they like my being there. In fact, as the warmly lighted floors flashed past the elevator we had words over the fact that I, by taking part in the fight, had knocked one of their friends out of a night's work.

We were led out of the elevator through a rococo hall into an

anteroom and told to get into our fighting togs. Each of us was issued
a pair of boxing gloves and ushered out into the big mirrored hall, which
we entered looking cautiously about us and whispering, lest we might
accidentally be heard above the noise of the room. It was foggy with cigar
smoke. And already the whiskey was taking effect. I was shocked to see
some of the most important men of the town quite tipsy. They were
all there—bankers, lawyers, judges, doctors, fire chiefs, teachers,
merchants. Even one of the more fashionable pastors. Something we
could not see was going on up front. A clarinet was vibrating sensuously
and the men were standing up and moving eagerly forward. We were
a small tight group, clustered together, our bare upper bodies touching
and shining with anticipatory sweat; while up front the big shots were
becoming increasingly excited over something we still could not see.
Suddenly I heard the school superintendent, who had told me to come,
yell, "Bring up the shines, gentlemen! Bring up the little shines!"

We were rushed up to the front of the ballroom, where it smelled
even more strongly of tobacco and whiskey. Then we were pushed into
place. I almost wet my pants. A sea of faces, some hostile, some amused,
ringed around us, and in the center, facing us, stood a magnificent
blonde—stark naked. There was dead silence. I felt a blast of cold air
chill me. I tried to back away, but they were behind me and around me.
Some of the boys stood with lowered heads, trembling. I felt a wave of
irrational guilt and fear. My teeth chattered, my skin turned to goose
flesh, my knees knocked. Yet I was strongly attracted and looked in
spite of myself. Had the price of looking been blindness, I would have
looked. The hair was yellow like that of a circus kewpie doll, the
face heavily powdered and rouged, as though to form an abstract mask,
the eyes hollow and smeared a cool blue, the color of a baboon's butt.
I felt a desire to spit upon her as my eyes brushed slowly over her body.
Her breasts were firm and round as the domes of East Indian temples,
and I stood so close as to see the fine skin texture and beads of pearly
perspiration glistening like dew around the pink and erected buds of her
nipples. I wanted at one and the same time to run from the room, to
sink through the floor, or go to her and cover her from my eyes and the
eyes of the others with my body; to feel the soft thighs, to caress her
and destroy her, to love her and murder her, to hide from her, and yet to
stroke where below the small American flag tattooed upon her belly
her thighs formed a capital V. I had a notion that of all in the room she
saw only me with her impersonal eyes.

And then she began to dance, a slow sensuous movement; the smoke
of a hundred cigars clinging to her like the thinnest of veils. She seemed
like a fair bird-girl girdled in veils calling to me from the angry surface
of some gray and threatening sea. I was transported. Then I became
aware of the clarinet playing and the big shots yelling at us. Some
threatened us if we looked and others if we did not. On my right I saw

one boy faint. And now a man grabbed a silver pitcher from a table
and stepped close as he dashed ice water upon him and stood him up
and forced two of us to support him as his head hung and moans issued
from his thick bluish lips. Another boy began to plead to go home.
He was the largest of the group, wearing dark red fighting trunks much
too small to conceal the erection which projected from him as though
in answer to the insinuating low-registered moaning of the clarinet. He
tried to hide himself with his boxing gloves.

And all the while the blonde continued dancing, smiling faintly at the
big shots who watched her with fascination, and faintly smiling at our
fear. I noticed a certain merchant who followed her hungrily, his lips
loose and drooling. He was a large man who wore diamond studs in a
shirtfront which swelled with the ample paunch underneath, and each
time the blonde swayed her undulating hips he ran his hand through the
thin hair of his bald head and, with his arms upheld, his posture
clumsy like that of an intoxicated panda, wound his bellow in a slow
and obscene grind. This creature was completely hypnotized. The music
had quickened. As the dancer flung herself about with a detached
expression on her face, the men began reaching out to touch her. I could
see their beefy fingers sink into the soft flesh. Some of the other tried to
stop them and she began to move around the floor in graceful circles,
as they gave chase, slipping and sliding over the polished floor. It was
mad. Chairs went crashing, drinks were split, as they ran laughing and
howling after her. The caught her just as she reached a door, raised her
from the floor, and tossed her as college boys are tossed at a hazing,
and above her red, fixed-smiling lips I saw the terror and disgust in
her eyes, almost like my own terror and that which I saw in some of the
other boys. As I watched, they tossed her twice and her soft breasts
seemed to flatten against the air and her legs flung wildly as she spun.
Some of the more sober ones helped her to escape. And I started off
the floor, heading for the anteroom with the rest of the boys.

Some were still crying and in hysteria. But as we tried to leave we
were stopped and ordered to get into the ring. There was nothing to do
but what we were told. All ten of us climbed under the ropes and
allowed ourselves to be blindfolded with broad bands of white cloth.
One of the men seemed to feel a bit sympathetic and tried to cheer us up
as we stood with our backs against the ropes. Some of us tried to grin.
"See that boy over there?" one of the men said. "I want you to run across
at the bell and give it to him right in the belly. If you don't get him,
I'm going to get you. I don't like his looks." Each of us was told the
same. The blindfolds were put on. Yet even then I had been going over
my speech. In my mind each word was as bright as flame. I felt the
cloth pressed into place, and frowned so that it would be loosened
when I relaxed.

But now I felt a sudden fit of blind terror. I was unused to darkness.

It was as though I had suddenly found myself in a dark room filled with poisonous cottonmouths. I could hear the bleary voices yelling insistently for the battle royal to begin.

"Get going in there!"

"Let me at that big nigger!"

I strained to pick up the school superintendent's voice, as though to squeeze some security out of that slightly more familiar sound.

"Let me at those black sonsabitches!" someone yelled.

"No, Jackson, no!" another voice yelled. "Here, somebody, help me hold Jack."

"I want to get at that ginger-colored nigger. Tear him limb from limb," the first voice yelled.

I stood against the ropes trembling. For in those days I was what they called ginger-colored, and he sounded as though he might crunch me between his teeth like a crisp ginger cookie.

Quite a struggle was going on. Chairs were being kicked about and I could hear voices grunting as with a terrific effort. I wanted to see, to see more desperately than ever before. But the blindfold was tight as a thick skin-puckering scab and when I raised my gloved hands to push the layers of white aside a voice yelled, "Oh, no you don't, black bastard! Leave that alone!"

"Ring the bell before Jackson kills him a coon!" someone boomed in the sudden silence. And I heard the bell clang and the sound of the feet scuffling forward.

A glove smacked against my head. I pivoted, striking out stiffly as someone went past, and felt the jar ripple along the length of my arm to my shoulder. Then it seemed as though all nine of the boys had turned upon me at once. Blows pounded me from all sides while I struck out as best I could. So many blows landed upon me that I wondered if I were not the only blindfolded fighter in the ring, or if the man called Jackson hadn't succeeded in getting me after all.

Blindfolded, I could no longer control my motions. I had no dignity. I stumbled about like a baby or a drunken man. The smoke had become thicker and with each new blow it seemed to sear and further restrict my lungs. My saliva became like hot bitter glue. A glove connected with my head, filling my mouth with warm blood. It was everywhere. I could not tell if the moisture I felt upon my body was sweat or blood. A blow landed hard against the nape of my neck. I felt myself going over, my head hitting the floor. Streaks of blue light filled the black world behind the blindfold. I lay prone, pretending that I was knocked out, but felt myself seized by hands and yanked to my feet. "Get going, black boy! Mix it up!" My arms were like lead, my head smarting from blows. I managed to feel my way to the ropes and held on, trying to catch my breath. A glove landed in my mid-section and I went over again, feeling as though the smoke had become a knife jabbed into my guts. Pushed this way and that by the legs milling around me, I finally pulled erect and discovered that I could see the black, sweat-washed forms weaving in the smoky-blue atmosphere like drunken dancers weaving to the rapid drum-like thuds of blows.

Everyone fought hysterically. It was complete anarchy. Everybody fought everybody else. No group fought together for long. Two, three, four, fought one, then turned to fight each other, were themselves attacked. Blows landed below the belt and in the kidney, with the gloves open as well as closed, and with my eye partly opened now there was not so much terror. I moved carefully, avoiding blows, although not too many to attract attention, fighting from group to group. The boys groped about like blind, cautious crabs crouching to protect their mid-sections, their heads pulled in short against their shoulders, their arms stretched nervously before them, with their fists testing the smoke-filled air like the knobbed feelers of hypersensitive snails. In one corner I glimpsed a boy violently punching the air and heard him scream in pain as he smashed his hand against a ring post. For a second I saw him bent over holding his hand, then going down as a blow caught his unprotected head. I played one group against the other, slipping in and throwing a punch then stepping out of range while pushing the others into the melee to take the blows blindly aimed at me. The smoke was agonizing and there were no rounds, no bells at three minute intervals to relieve our exhaustion. The room spun round me, a swirl of lights, smoke, sweating bodies surrounded by tense white faces. I bled from both nose and mouth, the blood spattering upon my chest.

The men kept yelling, "Slug him, black boy! Knock his guts out!"

"Uppercut him! Kill him! Kill that big boy!"

Taking a fake fall, I saw a boy going down heavily beside me as though we were felled by a single blow, saw a sneaker-clad foot shoot into his groin as the two who had knocked him down stumbled upon him. I rolled out of range, feeling a twinge of nausea.

The harder we fought the more threatening the men became. And yet, I had begun to worry about my speech again. How would it go? Would they recognize my ability? What would they give me?

I was fighting automatically when suddenly I noticed that one after another of the boys was leaving the ring. I was surprised, filled with panic, as though I had been left alone with an unknown danger. Then I understood. The boys had arranged it among themselves. It was the custom for the two men left in the ring to slug it out for the winner's prize. I discovered this too late. When the bell sounded two men in tuxedoes leaped into the ring and removed the blindfold. I found myself facing Tatlock, the biggest of the gang. I felt sick at my stomach. Hardly had the bell stopped ringing in my ears than it clanged again and I saw him moving swiftly toward me. Thinking of nothing else to do I hit him smash on the nose. He kept coming, bringing the rank sharp violence of stale sweat. His face was a black blank of a face, only his eyes alive— with hate of me and aglow with a feverish terror from what had happened to us all. I became anxious. I wanted to deliver my speech and he came at me as though he meant to beat it out of me. I smashed him again and again, taking his blows as they came. Then on a sudden impulse I struck him lightly and as we clinched, I whispered, "Fake like I knocked you out, you can have the prize."

"I'll break your behind," he whispered hoarsely.

"For *them?*"

"For *me,* sonofabitch!"

They were yelling for us to break it up and Tatlock spun me half around with a blow, and as a joggled camera sweeps in a reeling scene, I saw the howling red faces crouching tense beneath the cloud of blue-gray smoke. For a moment the world wavered, unraveled, flowed, then my head cleared and Tatlock bounced before me. That fluttering shadow before my eyes was his jabbing left hand. Then falling forward, my head against his damp shoulder, I whispered,

"I'll make it five dollars more."

"Go to hell!"

But his muscles relaxed a trifle beneath my pressure and I breathed, "Seven?"

"Give it to your ma," he said, ripping me beneath the heart.

And while I still held him I butted him and moved away. I felt myself bombarded with punches. I fought back with hopeless desperation. I wanted to deliver my speech more than anything else in the world, because I felt that only these men could judge truly my ability, and now this stupid clown was ruining my chances. I began fighting carefully now, moving in to punch him and out again with my greater speed. A lucky blow to his chin and I had him going too—until I heard a loud voice yell, "I got my money on the big boy."

Hearing this, I almost dropped my guard. I was confused: Should I try to win against the voice out there? Would not this go against my speech, and was not this a moment for humility, for nonresistance? A blow to my head as I danced about sent my right eye popping like a jack-in-the-box and settled my dilemma. The room went red as I fell. It was a dream fall, my body languid and fastidious as to where to land, until the floor became impatient and smashed up to meet me. A moment later I came to. An hypnotic voice said FIVE emphatically. And I lay there, hazily watching a dark red spot of my own blood shaping itself into a butterfly, glistening and soaking into the soiled gray world of the canvas.

When the voice drawled TEN I was lifted up and dragged to a

chair. I sat dazed. My eye pained and swelled with each throb of my pounding heart and I wondered if now I would be allowed to speak. I was wringing wet, my mouth still bleeding. We were grouped along the wall now. The other boys ignored me as they congratulated Tatlock and speculated as to how much they would be paid. One boy whimpered over his smashed hand. Looking up front, I saw attendants in white jackets rolling the portable ring away and placing a small square rug in the vacant space surrounded by chairs. Perhaps, I thought, I will stand on the rug to deliver my speech.

Then the M.C. called to us, "Come on up here boys and get your money."

We ran forward to where the men laughed and talked in their chairs, waiting. Everyone seeemd friendly now.

"There it is on the rug," the man said. I said. I saw the rug covered with coins of all dimensions and a few crumpled bills. But what excited me, scattered here and there, were the gold pieces.

"Boys, it's all yours," the man said. "You get all you grab."

"That's right, Sambo," a blond man said, winking at me confidentially.

I trembled with excitement, forgetting my pain. I would get the gold and the bills, I thought. I would use both hands. I would throw my body against the boys nearest me to block them from the gold.

"Get down around the rug now," the man commanded, "and don't anyone touch it until I give the signal."

"This ought to be good," I heard.

As told, we got around the square rug on our knees. Slowly the man raised his freckled hand as we followed it upward with our eyes.

I heard, "These niggers look like they're about to pray!"

Then, "Ready," the man said. "Go!"

I lunged for a yellow coin lying on the blue design of the carpet, touching it and sending a surprised shriek to join those rising around me. I tried frantically to remove my hand but could not let go. A hot, violent force tore through my body, shaking me like a wet rat. The rug was electrified. The hair bristled up on my head as I shook myself free. My muscles jumped, my nerves jangled, writhed. But I saw that this was not stopping the other boys. Laughing in fear and embarrassment, some were holding back and scooping up the coins knocked off by the painful contortions of the others. The men roared above us as we struggled.

"Pick it up, goddamnit, pick it up!" someone called like a bass-voiced parrot. "Go on, get it!"

I crawled rapidly around the floor, picking up the coins, trying to avoid the coppers and to get greenbacks and the gold. Ignoring the shock by laughing, as I brushed the coins off quickly, I discovered that I could contain the electricity—a contradiction, but it works. Then the men began to push us onto the rug. Laughing embarrassedly, we struggled out of their hands and kept after the coins. We were all wet and slippery and hard to hold. Suddenly I saw a boy lifted into the air, glistening with sweat like a circus seal, and dropped, his wet back landing flush upon the charged rug, heard him yell and saw him literally dance upon his back, his elbows beating a frenzied tattoo upon the floor, his muscles twitching like the flesh of a horse stung by many flies. When he finally rolled off, his face was gray and no one stopped him when he ran from the floor amid booming laughter.

"Get the money," the M.C. called. "That's good hard American cash!"

And we snatched and grabbed, snatched and grabbed. I was careful not to come too close to the rug now, and when I felt the hot whiskey breath descend upon me like a cloud of foul air I reached out and grabbed the leg of a chair. It was occupied and I held on desperately.

"Leggo, nigger! Leggo!"

The huge face wavered down to mine as he tried to push me free. But my body was slippery and he was too drunk. It was Mr. Colcord, who owned a chain of movie houses and "entertainment palaces." Each time he grabbed me I slipped out of his hands. It became a real struggle. I feared the rug more than I did the drunk, so I held on, surprising myself for a moment by trying to topple *him* upon the rug. It was such an enormous idea that I found myself actually carrying it out. I tried not to be obvious, yet when I grabbed his leg, trying to tumble him out of the chair, he raised up roaring with laughter, and, looking at me with soberness dead in the eye, kicked me viciously in the chest. The chair leg flew out of my hand and I felt myself going and rolled. It was as though I had rolled through a bed of hot coals. It seemed a whole century would pass before I would roll free, a century in which I was seared through the deepest levels of my body to the fearful breath within me and the breath seared and heated to the point of explosion. It'll all be over in a flash, I thought as I rolled clear. It'll all be over in a flash.

But not yet, the men on the other side were waiting, red faces swollen as though from apoplexy as they bent forward in their chairs. Seeing their fingers coming toward me I rolled away as a fumbled football rolls off the receiver's fingertips, back into the coals. That time I luckily sent the rug sliding out of place and heard the coins ringing against the floor and the boys scuffling to pick them up and the M.C. calling, "All right, boys, that's all. Go get dressed and get your money."

I was limp as a dish rag. My back felt as though it had been beaten with wires.

When we had dressed the M.C. came in and gave us each five dollars, except Tatlock, who got ten for being last in the ring. Then he told us to leave. I was not to get a chance to deliver my speech, I thought. I was going out into the dim alley in despair when I was stopped and told to go back. I returned to the ballroom, where the men were pushing back their chairs and gathering in groups to talk.

The M.C. knocked on a table for quiet. "Gentlemen," he said, "we almost forgot an important part of the program. A most serious part, gentlemen. This boy was brought here to deliver a speech which he made at his graduation yesterday . . ."

"Bravo!"

"I'm told that he is the smartest boy we've got out there in Green-wood. I'm told that he knows more big words than a pocket-sized dictionary."

Much applause and laughter.

"So now, gentlemen, I want you to give him your attention."

There was still laughter as I faced them, my mouth dry, my eye throbbing. I began slowly, but evidently my throat was tense, because they began shouting, "Louder! Louder!"

"We of the younger generation extol the wisdom of that great leader and educator," I shouted, "who first spoke these flaming words of wisdom: 'A ship lost at sea for many days suddenly sighted a friendly vessel. From the mast of the unfortunate vessel was seen a signal: "Water, water; we die of thirst!" The answer from the friendly vessel came back: "Cast down your bucket where you are." The captain of the distressed vessel, at last heeding the injunction, cast down his bucket, and it came up full of fresh sparkling water from the mouth of the Amazon River.' And like him I say, and in his words, 'To those of my race who depend upon bettering their condition in a foreign land, or who underestimate the importance of cultivating friendly relations with the Southern white man, who is his next-door neighbor, I would say: "Cast down your bucket where you are"—cast it down in making friends in every manly way of the people of all races by whom we are surrounded . . .' "

I spoke automatically and with such fervor that I did not realize that the men were still talking and laughing until my dry mouth, filling up with blood from the cut, almost strangled me. I coughed, wanting to stop and go to one of the tall brass, sand-filled spittoons to relieve myself, but a few of the men, especially the superintendent, were listening and I was afraid. So I gulped it down, blood, saliva and all, and continued. (What powers of endurance I had during those days! What enthusiasm! What a belief in the rightness of things!) I spoke even louder in spite of the pain. But still they talked and still they laughed, as though deaf with cotton in dirty ears. So I spoke with greater emotional emphasis. I closed my ears and swallowed blood until I was nauseated. The speech seemed a hundred times as long as before, but I could not leave out a single word. All had to be said, each memorized nuance considered, rendered. Nor was that all. Whenever I uttered a word of three or more syllables a group of voices would yell for me to repeat it. I used the phrase "social responsibility" and they yelled:

"What's that word you say, boy?"

"Social responsibility," I said.

"What?"

"Social . . ."

"Louder."

". . . responsibility."

"More!"

"Respon-"

"Repeat!"

"-sibility."

The room filled with the uproar of laughter until, no doubt, distracted by having to gulp down my blood, I made a mistake and yelled a phrase I had often seen denounced in newspaper editorials, heard debated in private.

"Social . . ."

"What?" they yelled.

". . . equality-"

The laughter hung smokelike in the sudden stillness. I opened my eyes, puzzled. Sounds of displeasure filled the room. The M.C. rushed forward. They shouted hostile phrases at me. But I did not understand.

A small dry mustached man in the front row blared out, "Say that slowly, son!"

"What, sir?"

"What you just said!"

"Social responsibility, sir," I said.

"You weren't being smart, were you, boy?" he said, not unkindly.

"No, sir!"

"You sure that about 'equality' was a mistake?"

"Oh, yes, sir," I said. "I was swallowing blood."

"Well, you had better speak more slowly so we can understand. We mean to do right by you, but you've got to know your place at all times. All right, now, go on with your speech."

I was afraid. I wanted to leave but I wanted also to speak and I was afraid they'd snatch me down.

"Thank you, sir," I said, beginning where I had left off, and having them ignore me as before.

Yet when I finished there was a thunderous applause. I was surprised to see the superintendent come forth with a package wrapped in white tissue paper, and, gesturing for quiet, address the men.

"Gentlemen, you see that I did not overpraise this boy. He makes a good speech and some day he'll lead his people in the proper paths. And I don't have to tell you that this is important in these days and times. This is a good, smart boy, and so to encourage him in the right direction, in the name of the Board of Education I wish to present him a prize in the form of this . . ."

He paused, removing the tissue paper and revealing a gleaming calfskin brief case.

". . . in the form of this first-class article from Shad Whitmore's shop."

"Boy," he said, addressing me, "take this prize and keep it well. Consider it a badge of office. Prize it. Keep developing as you are and some day it will be filled with important papers that will help shape the destiny of your people."

I was so moved that I could hardly express my thanks. A rope of bloody saliva forming a shape like an undiscovered continent drolled upon the leather and I wiped it quickly away. I felt an importance that I had never dreamed.

"Open it and see what's inside," I was told.

My fingers a-tremble, I complied, smelling the fresh leather and finding an official-looking document inside. It was a scholarship to the state college for Negroes. My eyes filled with tears and I ran awkwardly off the floor.

I was overjoyed; I did not even mind when I discovered that the gold pieces I had scrambled for were brass pocket tokens advertising a certain make of automobile.

When I reached home everyone was excited. Next day the neighbors came to congratulate me. I even felt safe from grandfather, whose deathbed curse usually spoiled my triumphs. I stood beneath his photograph with my brief case in hand and smiled triumphantly into his stolid black peasant's face. It was a face that fascinated me. The eyes seemed to follow everywhere I went.

That night I dreamed I was at a circus with him and that he refused to laugh at the clowns no matter what they did. Then later he told me to open my brief case and read what was inside and I did, finding an official envelope stamped with the state seal; and inside the envelope I found another and another, endlessly, and I thought I would fall of weariness. "Them's years," he said. "Now open that one." And I did and in it I found an engraved document containing a short message in letters of gold. "Read it," my grandfather said. "Out loud!"

"To Whom It May Concern," I intoned. "Keep This Nigger-Boy Running."

I awoke with the old man's laughter ringing in my ears.

(It was a dream I was to remember and dream again for many years after. But at that time I had no insight into its meaning. First I had to attend college.)

1. Since the story is narrated in the first person it is hard for Ellison to state explicitly that his main character is painfully naive about his relations with southern whites. What techniques does the author use to convey this impression?
2. What effect does the scene with the dancing girl have? Is it a bit of added sensationalism, or is it thematically related to the picture that Ellison is attempting to sketch for us?
3. While Ellison's narrator is naive he is also thoughtful. Why does he choose to talk about this painful and humiliating incident? What is he trying to clarify for himself?
4. What does the "battle royal" reveal about relations between blacks and whites in this southern town? What does it reveal about the relations between blacks?
5. Would the narrative be essentially unchanged without the opening and closing incidents concerning the narrator's grandfather? What do the grandfather's enigmatic words come to symbolize in the story?
6. How does Ellison use precisely observed details and voices different from the narrator's (his grandfather's, the school superintendent's, and so on) to help create a world of anarchy and terror?

"Revelation"/*Flannery O'Connor*

The reader is asked to make a strange journey in this story from the detailed reality of a doctor's office to an apocalyptical vision of Judgment Day. But the real journey is made within the mind of Mrs. Turpin, an overweight, middle-aged, middle-class, southern white woman who is under the impression that she is "saved," "happy," and in love with everyone who is worth the loving. In fact, the reader finds out long before Mrs. Turpin does that she despises everyone who is not like herself and that dark recesses of self-doubt and self-hate lurk behind her "sweetness and light."

We are carried on this journey because Flannery O'Connor stays relentlessly close to her protagonist's opinions of things and because a pimple-faced college student confronts Mrs. Turpin early in the story with a blunt statement of her hypocrisy. The girl thus becomes the catalyst for the tortured woman's self-

"revelation." O'Connor skillfully reveals the world of Mrs. Turpin's self-righteousness by continually recording her mental asides. In this way we are quickly forced into a psychological confrontation with Mrs. Turpin which finds its physical equivalent in the explosive event at the center of the story. And it's through this disorienting shock that O'Connor introduces "revelation," a vision of truth, into the story. We accept this conclusion to our disturbing journey through a world of prejudice and delusion because in the narrator's voice and observations we have been carefully prepared for a Last Judgment. We have, in fact, been inside a world of impending doom from the beginning of the story.

The doctor's waiting room, which was very small, was almost full when the Turpins entered and Mrs. Turpin, who was very large, made it look even smaller by her presence. She stood looming at the head of the magazine table set in the center of it, a living demonstration that the room was inadequate and ridiculous. Her little bright black eyes took in all the patients as she sized up the seating situation. There was one vacant chair and a place on the sofa occupied by a blond child in a dirty blue romper who should have been told to move over and make room for the lady. He was five or six, but Mrs. Turpin saw at once that no one was going to tell him to move over. He was slumped down in the seat, his arms idle at his sides and his eyes idle in his head; his nose ran unchecked.

Mrs. Turpin put a firm hand on Claud's shoulder and said in a voice that included anyone who wanted to listen, "Claud, you sit in that chair there," and gave him a push down into the vacant one. Claud was florid and bald and sturdy, somewhat shorter than Mrs. Turpin, but he sat down as if he were accustomed to doing what she told him to.

Mrs. Turpin remained standing. The only man in the room besides Claud was a lean stringy old fellow with a rusty hand spread out on each knee, whose eyes were closed as if he were asleep or dead or pretending to be so as not to get up and offer her his seat. Her gaze settled agreeably on a well-dressed grey-haired lady whose eyes met hers and whose expression said: if that child belonged to me, he would have some manners and move over—there's plenty of room there for you and him too.

Claud looked up with a sigh and made as if to rise.

"Sit down," Mrs. Turpin said. "You know you're not supposed to stand on that leg. He has an ulcer on his leg," she explained.

Claud lifted his foot onto the magazine table and rolled his trouser leg up to reveal a purple swelling on a plump marble-white calf.

"My!" the pleasant lady said. "How did you do that?"

"A cow kicked him," Mrs. Turpin said.

"Goodness!" said the lady.

Claud rolled his trouser leg down.

"Maybe the little boy would move over," the lady suggested, but the child did not stir.

"Somebody will be leaving in a minute," Mrs. Turpin said. She could not understand why a doctor—with as much money as they made charging five dollars a day to just stick their head in the hospital door and look at you—couldn't afford a decent-sized waiting room. This one was hardly bigger than a garage. The table was cluttered with limp-looking magazines and at one end of it there was a big green glass ash tray full of cigaret butts and cotton wads with little blood spots on them. If she had had anything to do with the running of the place, that would have been emptied every so often. There were no chairs against the wall at the head of the room. It had a rectangular-shaped panel in it that permitted a view of the office where the nurse came and went and the secretary listened to the radio. A plastic fern in a gold pot sat in the opening and trailed its fronds down almost to the floor. The radio was softly playing gospel music.

Just then the inner door opened and a nurse with the highest stack of yellow hair Mrs. Turpin had ever seen put her face in the crack and called for the next patient. The woman sitting beside Claud grasped the two arms of her chair and hoisted herself up; she pulled her dress free from her legs and lumbered through the door where the nurse had disappeared.

Mrs. Turpin eased into the vacant chair, which held her tight as a corset. "I wish I could reduce," she said, and rolled her eyes and gave a comic sigh.

"Oh, *you* aren't fat," the stylish lady said.

"Ooooo I am too," Mrs. Turpin said. "Claud he eats all he wants to and never weighs over one hundred and seventy-five pounds, but me I just look at something good to eat and I gain some weight," and her stomach and shoulders shook with laughter. "You can eat all you want to, can't you, Claud?" she asked, turning to him.

Claud only grinned.

"Well, as long as you have such a good disposition," the stylish lady said, "I don't think it makes a bit of difference what size you are. You just can't beat a good disposition."

Next to her was a fat girl of eighteen or nineteen, scowling into a thick blue book which Mrs. Turpin saw was entitled *Human Development*. The girl raised her head and directed her scowl at Mrs. Turpin as if she did not like her looks. She appeared annoyed that anyone should speak while she tried to read. The poor girl's face was blue with acne and Mrs. Turpin thought how pitiful it was to have a face like that at that age. She gave the girl a friendly smile but the girl only scowled the harder. Mrs. Turpin herself was fat but she had always had good skin, and, though she was forty-seven years old, there was not a wrinkle in her face except around her eyes from laughing too much.

Next to the ugly girl was the child, still in exactly the same position, and next to him was a thin leathery old woman in a cotton print dress. She and Claud had three sacks of chicken feed in their pump house that was in the same print. She had seen from the first that the child belonged with the old woman. She could tell by the way they sat—kind of vacant and white-trashy, as if they would sit there until Doomsday if nobody called and told them to get up. And at right angles but next to the well-dressed pleasant lady was a lank-faced woman who was certainly the child's mother. She had on a yellow sweat shirt and wine-colored slacks, both gritty-looking, and the rims of her lips were stained with snuff. Her dirty yellow hair was tied behind with a little piece of red paper ribbon. Worse than niggers any day, Mrs. Turpin thought.

The gospel hymn playing was, "When I looked up and He looked down," and Mrs. Turpin, who knew it, supplied the last line mentally, "And wona these days I know I'll we-eara crown."

Without appearing to, Mrs. Turpin always noticed people's feet. The well-dressed lady had on red and grey suede shoes to match her dress. Mrs. Turpin had on her good black patent leather pumps. The ugly girl had on Girl Scout shoes and heavy socks. The old woman had on tennis shoes and the white-trashy mother had on what appeared to be bedroom slippers, black straw with gold braid threaded through them—exactly what you would have expected her to have on.

Sometimes at night when she couldn't go to sleep, Mrs. Turpin would occupy herself with the question of who she would have chosen to be if she couldn't have been herself. If Jesus had said to her before he made her, "There's only two places available for you. You can either be a nigger or white-trash," what would she have said? "Please, Jesus, please," she would have said, "just let me wait until there's another place available," and he would have said, "No, you have to go right now and I have only those two places so make up your mind." She would have wiggled and squirmed and begged and pleaded but it would have been no use and finally she would have said, "All right, make me a nigger then—but that don't mean a trashy one." And he would have made her a neat clean respectable Negro woman, herself but black.

Next to the child's mother was a red-headed youngish woman, reading one of the magazines and working a piece of chewing gum, hell for leather, as Claud would say. Mrs. Turpin could not see the woman's feet. She was not white-trash, just common. Sometimes Mrs. Turpin occupied herself at night naming the classes of people. On the bottom of the heap were most colored people, not the kind she would have been if she had been one, but most of them; then next to them—not above, just away from—were the white-trash; then above them were the home-owners, and above them the home-and-land owners, to which she and Claud belonged. Above she and Claud were people with a lot of money and much bigger houses and much more land. But here the complexity of it would begin to bear in on her, for some of the people with a lot of money were common and ought to be below she and Claud and some of the people who had good blood had lost their money and had to rent and then there were colored people who owned their homes and land as well. There was a colored dentist in town who had two red Lincolns and a swimming pool and a farm with registered white-face cattle on it. Usually by the time she had fallen asleep all the classes of people were moiling and roiling around in her head, and she would dream they were all crammed in together in a box car, being ridden off to be put in a gas oven.

"That's a beautiful clock," she said and nodded to her right. It was a big wall clock, the face encased in a brass sunburst.

"Yes, it's very pretty," the stylish lady said agreeably. "And right on the dot too," she added, glancing at her watch.

The ugly girl beside her cast an eye upward at the clock, smirked, then looked directly at Mrs. Turpin and smirked again. Then she returned her eyes to her book. She was obviously the lady's daughter because, although they didn't look anything alike as to disposition, they both had the same shape of face and the same blue eyes. On the lady they sparkled pleasantly but in the girl's seared face they appeared alternately to smolder and to blaze.

What if Jesus had said, "All right, you can be white-trash or a nigger or ugly"!

Mrs. Turpin felt an awful pity for the girl, though she thought it was one thing to be ugly and another to act ugly.

The woman with the snuff-stained lips turned around in her chair and looked up at the clock. Then she turned back and appeared to look a little to the side of Mrs. Turpin. There was a cast in one of her eyes. "You want to know wher you can get you one of themther clocks?" she asked in a loud voice.

"No, I already have a nice clock," Mrs. Turpin said. Once somebody like her got a leg in the conversation, she would be all over it.

"You can get you one with green stamps," the woman said. "That's most likely wher he got hisn. Save you up enough, you can get you most anythang. I got me some joo'ry."

Ought to have got you a wash rag and some soap, Mrs. Turpin thought.

"I get contour sheets with mine," the pleasant lady said.

The daughter slammed her book shut. She looked straight in front of her, directly through Mrs. Turpin and on through the yellow curtain and the plate glass window which made the wall behind her. The girl's eyes seemed lit all of a sudden with a peculiar light, an unnatural light like night road signs give. Mrs. Turpin turned her head to see if there was anything going on outside that she should see, but she could not see anything. Figures passing cast only a pale shadow through the curtain. There was no reason the girl should single her out for her ugly looks.

"Miss Finley," the nurse said, cracking the door. The gum-chewing woman got up and passed in front of her and Claud and went into the office. She had on red high-heeled shoes.

Directly across the table, the ugly girl's eyes were fixed on Mrs. Turpin as if she had some very special reason for disliking her.

"This is wonderful weather, isn't it?" the girl's mother said.

"It's good weather for cotton if you can get the niggers to pick it," Mrs. Turpin said, "but niggers don't want to pick cotton any more. You can't get the white folks to pick it and now you can't get the niggers— because they got to be right up there with the white folks."

"They gonna *try* anyways," the white-trash woman said, leaning forward.

"Do you have one of those cotton-picking machines?" the pleasant lady asked.

"No," Mrs. Turpin said, "they leave half the cotton in the field. We don't have much cotton anyway. If you want to make it farming now, you have to have a little of everything. We got a couple of acres of cotton and a few hogs and chickens and just enough white-face that Claud can look after them himself."

"One thang I don't want," the white-trash woman said, wiping her mouth with the back of her hand. "Hogs. Nasty stinking things, a-gruntin and a-rootin all over the place."

Mrs. Turpin gave her the merest edge of her attention. "Our hogs are not dirty and they don't stink," she said. "They're cleaner than some children I've seen. Their feet never touch the ground. We have a pig-parlor—that's where you raise them on concrete," she explained to the pleasant lady, "and Claud scoots them down with the hose every afternoon and washes off the floor." Cleaner by far than that child right there, she thought. Poor nasty little thing. He had not moved except to put the thumb of his dirty hand into his mouth.

The woman turned her face away from Mrs. Turpin. "I know I wouldn't scoot down no hog with no hose," she said the wall.

You wouldn't have no hog to scoot down, Mrs. Turpin said to herself.

"A-gruntin and a-rootin and a-groanin," the woman muttered.

"We got a little of everything," Mrs. Turpin said to the pleasant lady. "It's no use in having more than you can handle yourself with help like it is. We found enough niggers to pick our cotton this year but Claud he has to go after them and take them home again in the evening. They can't walk that half a mile. No they can't. I tell you," she said and laughed merrily, "I sure am tired of buttering up niggers, but you got to love em if you want em to work for you. When they come in the morning, I run out and I say, 'Hi yawl this morning?' and when Claud drives them off to the field I just wave to beat the band and they just wave back." And she waved her hand rapidly to illustrate.

"Like you read out of the same book," the lady said, showing she understood perfectly.

"Child, yes," Mrs. Turpin said. "And when they come in from the field, I run out with a bucket of icewater. That's the way it's going to be from now on," she said. "You may as well face it."

"One thang I know," the white-trash woman said. "Two thangs I ain't going to do: love no niggers or scoot down no hog with no hose." And she let out a bark of contempt.

The look that Mrs. Turpin and the pleasant lady exchanged indicated they both understood that you had to *have* certain things before you could *know* certain things. But every time Mrs. Turpin exchanged a look with the lady, she was aware that the ugly girl's peculiar eyes were still on her, and she had trouble bringing her attention back to the conversation.

"When you got something," she said, "you got to look after it." And when you ain't got a thing but breath and britches, she added to herself, you can afford to come to town every morning and just sit on the Court House coping and spit.

A grotesque revolving shadow passed across the curtain behind her and was thrown palely on the opposite wall. Then a bicycle clattered down against the outside of the building. The door opened and a colored boy glided in with a tray from the drug store. It had two large red and white paper cups on it with tops on them. He was a tall, very black boy in discolored white pants and a green nylon shirt. He was chewing gum slowly, as if to music. He set the tray down in the office opening next to the fern and stuck his head through to look for the secretary. She was not in there. He rested his arms on the ledge and waited, his narrow bottom stuck out, swaying slowly to the left and right. He raised a hand over his head and scratched the base of his skull.

"You see that button there, boy?" Mrs. Turpin said. "You can punch that and she'll come. She's probably in the back somewhere."

"Is thas right?" the boy said agreeably, as if he had never seen the button before. He leaned to the right and put his finger on it. "She sometime out," he said and twisted around to face his audience, his elbows behind him on the counter. The nurse appeared and he twisted back again. She handed him a dollar and he rooted in his pocket and made the change and counted it out to her. She gave him fifteen cents for a tip and he went out with the empty tray. The heavy door swung to slowly and closed at length with the sound of suction. For a moment no one spoke.

"They ought to send all them niggers back to Africa," the white-trash woman said. "That's wher they come from in the first place."

"Oh, I couldn't do without my good colored friends," the pleasant lady said.

"There's a heap of things worse than a nigger," Mrs. Turpin agreed. "It's all kinds of them just like it's all kinds of us."

"Yes, and it takes all kinds to make the world go round," the lady said in her musical voice.

As she said it, the raw-complexioned girl snapped her teeth together. Her lower lip turned downwards and inside out, revealing the pale pink inside of her mouth. After a second it rolled back up. It was the ugliest face Mrs. Turpin had ever seen anyone make and for a moment she was certain that the girl had made it at her. She was looking at her as if she had known and disliked her all her life—all of Mrs. Turpin's life, it seemed too, not just all the girl's life. Why, girl, I don't even know you, Mrs. Turpin said silently.

She forced her attention back to the discussion. "It wouldn't be practical to send them back to Africa," she said. "They wouldn't want to go. They got it too good here."

"Wouldn't be what they wanted—if I had anythang to do with it," the woman said.

"It wouldn't be a way in the world you could get all the niggers back over there," Mrs. Turpin said. "They'd be hiding out and lying down and turning sick on you and wailing and hollering and raring and pitching. It wouldn't be a way in the world to get them over there."

"They got over here," the trashy woman said. "Get back like they got over."

"It wasn't so many of them then," Mrs. Turpin explained.

The woman looked at Mrs. Turpin as if here was an idiot indeed but Mrs. Turpin was not bothered by the look, considering where it came from.

"Nooo," she said, "they're going to stay here where they can go to New York and marry white folks and improve their color. That's what they all want to do, every one of them, improve their color."

"You know what comes of that, don't you?" Claud asked.

"No, Claud, what?" Mrs. Turpin said.

Claud's eyes twinkled. "White-faced niggers," he said with never a smile.

Everybody in the office laughed except the white-trash and the ugly girl. The girl gripped the book in her lap with white fingers. The trashy woman looked around her from face to face as if she thought they were all idiots. The old woman in the feed sack dress continued to gaze expressionless across the floor at the high-top shoes of the man opposite her, the one who had been pretending to be asleep when the Turpins came in. He was laughing heartily, his hands still spread out on his knees. The child had fallen to the side and was lying now almost face down in the old woman's lap.

While they recovered from their laughter, the nasal chorus on the radio kept the room from silence.

> *"You go to blank blank*
> *And I'll go to mine*
> *But we'll all blank along*
> *To-geth-ther,*
> *And all along the blank*
> *We'll hep eachother out*
> *Smile-ling in any kind of*
> *Weath-ther!"*

Mrs. Turpin didn't catch every word but she caught enough to agree with the spirit of the song and it turned her thoughts sober. To help anybody out that needed it was her philosophy of life. She never spared herself when she found somebody in need, whether they were white or black, trash or decent. And of all she had to be thankful for, she was most thankful that this was so. If Jesus had said, "You can be high society and have all the money you want and be thin and svelte-like, but you can't be a good woman with it," she would have had to say, "Well don't make me that then. Make me a good woman and it don't matter what else, how fat or how ugly or how poor!" Her heart rose. He had not made her a nigger or white-trash or ugly! He had made her herself and given her a little of everything. Jesus, thank you! she said. Thank you thank you thank you! Whenever she counted her blessings she felt as buoyant as if she weighed one hundred and twenty-five pounds instead of one hundred and eighty.

"What's wrong with your little boy?" the pleasant lady asked the white-trashy woman.

"He has a ulcer," the woman said proudly. "He ain't give me a minute's peace since he was born. Him and her are just alike," she said, nodding at the old woman, who was running her leathery fingers through the child's pale hair. "Look like I can't get nothing down them two but Co' Cola and candy."

That's all you try to get down em, Mrs. Turpin said to herself. Too lazy to light the fire. There was nothing you could tell her about people like them that she didn't know already. And it was not just that they didn't have anything. Because if you gave them everything, in two weeks it would all be broken or filthy or they would have chopped it up for lightwood. She knew all this from her own experience. Help them you must, but help them you couldn't.

All at once the ugly girl turned her lips inside out again. Her eyes were fixed like two drills on Mrs. Turpin. This time there was no mistaking that there was something urgent behind them.

Girl, Mrs. Turpin exclaimed silently, I haven't done a thing to you! The girl might be confusing her with somebody else. There was no need to sit by and let herself be intimidated. "You must be in college," she said boldly, looking directly at the girl. "I see you reading a book there."

The girl continued to stare and pointedly did not answer.

Her mother blushed at this rudeness. "The lady asked you a question, Mary Grace," she said under her breath.

"I have ears," Mary Grace said.

The poor mother blushed again. "Mary Grace goes to Wellesley College," she explained. She twisted one of the buttons on her dress. "In Massachusetts," she added with a grimace. "And in the summer she just keeps right on studying. Just reads all the time, a real book worm. She's done real well at Wellesley; she's taking English and Math and History and Psychology and Social Studies," she rattled on, "and I think it's too much. I think she ought to get out and have fun."

The girl looked as if she would like to hurl them all through the plate glass window.

"Way up north," Mrs. Turpin murmured and thought, well, it hasn't done much for her manners.

"I'd almost rather to have him sick," the white-trash woman said, wrenching the attention back to herself. "He's so mean when he ain't. Look like some children just take natural to meanness. It's some gets bad when they get sick but he was the opposite. Took sick and turned good. He don't give me no trouble now. It's me waitin to see the doctor," she said.

If I was going to send anybody back to Africa, Mrs. Turpin thought, it would be your kind, woman. "Yes, indeed," she said aloud, but looking up at the ceiling, "it's a heap of things worse than a nigger." And dirtier than a hog, she added to herself.

"I think people with bad dispositions are more to be pitied than anyone on earth," the pleasant lady said in a voice that was decidedly thin.

"I thank the Lord he has blessed me with a good one," Mrs. Turpin said. "The day has never dawned that I couldn't find something to laugh at."

"Not since she married me anyways," Claud said with a comical straight face.

Everybody laughed except the girl and the white-trash.

Mrs. Turpin's stomach shook. "He's such a caution," she said, "that I can't help but laugh at him."

The girl made a loud ugly noise through her teeth.

Her mother's mouth grew thin and tight. "I think the worst thing in the world," she said, "is an ungrateful person. To have everything and not appreciate it. I know a girl," she said, "who has parents who would give her anything, a little brother who loves her dearly, who is getting a good education, who wears the best clothes, but who can never say a kind word to anyone, who never smiles, who just criticizes and complains all day long."

"Is she too old to paddle?" Claud asked.

The girl's face was almost purple.

"Yes," the lady said, "I'm afraid there's nothing to do but leave her to her folly. Some day she'll wake up and it'll be too late."

"It never hurt anyone to smile," Mrs. Turpin said. "It just makes you feel better all over."

"Of course," the lady said sadly, "but there are just some people you can't tell anything to. They can't take criticism."

"If it's one thing I am," Mrs. Turpin said with feeling, "It's grateful. When I think who all I could have been besides myself and what all I got, a little of everything, and a good disposition besides, I just feel like shouting, 'Thank you, Jesus, for making everything the way it is!' It could have been different!" For one thing, somebody else could have got Claud. At the thought of this, she was flooded with gratitude and a terrible pang of joy ran through her. "Oh thank you, Jesus, Jesus, thank you!" she cried aloud.

The book struck her directly over her left eye. It struck almost at the same instant that she realized the girl was about to hurl it. Before she could utter a sound, the raw face came crashing across the table toward her, howling. The girl's fingers sank like clamps into the soft flesh of her neck. She heard the mother cry out and Claud shout, "Whoa!" There was an instant when she was certain that she was about to be in an earthquake.

All at once her vision narrowed and she saw everything as if it were happening in a small room far away, or as if she were looking at it through the wrong end of a telescope. Claud's face crumpled and fell out of sight. The nurse ran in, then out, then in again. Then the gangling figure of the doctor rushed out of the inner door. Magazines flew this way and that as the table turned over. The girl fell with a thud and Mrs. Turpin's vision suddenly reversed itself and she saw everything large instead of small. The eyes of the white-trashy woman were staring hugely at the floor. There the girl, held down on one side by the nurse and on the other by her mother, was wrenching and turning in their grasp. The doctor was kneeling astride her, trying to hold her arm down. He managed after a second to sink a long needle into it.

Mrs. Turpin felt entirely hollow except for her heart which swung from side to side as if it were agitated in a great empty drum of flesh.

"Somebody that's not busy call for the ambulance," the doctor said in the off-hand voice young doctors adopt for terrible occasions.

Mrs. Turpin could not have moved a finger. The old man who had been sitting next to her skipped nimbly into the office and made the call, for the secretary still seemed to be gone.

"Claud!" Mrs. Turpin called.

He was not in his chair. She knew she must jump up and find him but she felt like some one trying to catch a train in a dream, when everything moves in slow motion and the faster you try to run the slower you go.

"Here I am," a suffocated voice, very unlike Claud's, said.

He was doubled up in the corner on the floor, pale as paper, holding his leg. She wanted to get up and go to him but she could not move. Instead, her gaze was drawn slowly downward to the churning face on the floor, which she could see over the doctor's shoulder.

The girl's eyes stopped rolling and focused on her. They seemed a much lighter blue than before, as if a door that had been tightly closed behind them was now open to admit light and air.

Mrs. Turpin's head cleared and her power of motion returned. She leaned forward until she was looking directly into the fierce brilliant eyes. There was no doubt in her mind that the girl did know her, knew her in some intense and personal way, beyond time and place and condition. "What you got to say to me?" she asked hoarsely and held her breath, waiting, as for a revelation.

The girl raised her head. Her gaze locked with Mrs. Turpin's. "Go back to hell where you came from, you old wart hog," she whispered. Her voice was low but clear. Her eyes burned for a moment as if she saw with pleasure that her message had struck its target.

Mrs. Turpin sank back in her chair.

After a moment the girl's eyes closed and she turned her head wearily to the side.

The doctor rose and handed the nurse the empty syringe. He leaned over and put both hands for a moment on the mother's shoulders, which were shaking. She was sitting on the floor, her lips pressed together, holding Mary Grace's hand in her lap. The girl's fingers were gripped like a baby's around her thumb. "Go on to the hospital," he said. "I'll call and make the arrangements."

"Now let's see that neck," he said in a jovial voice to Mrs. Turpin. He began to inspect her neck with his first two fingers. Two little moon-shaped lines like pink fish bones were indented over her windpipe.

There was the beginning of an angry red swelling above her eye. His fingers passed over this also.

"Lea' me be," she said thickly and shook him off. "See about Claud. She kicked him."

"I'll see about him in a minute," he said and felt her pulse. He was a thin grey-haired man, given to pleasantries. "Go home and have yourself a vacation the rest of the day," he said and patted her on the shoulder.

Quit your pattin me, Mrs. Turpin growled to herself.

"And put an ice pack over that eye," he said. Then he went and squatted down beside Claud and looked at his leg. After a moment he pulled him up and Claud limped after him into the office.

Until the ambulance came, the only sounds in the room were the tremulous moans of the girl's mother, who continued to sit on the floor. The white-trash woman did not take her eyes off the girl. Mrs. Turpin looked straight ahead at nothing. Presently the ambulance drew up, a long dark shadow, behind the curtain. The attendants came in and set the stretcher down beside the girl and lifted her expertly onto it and carried her out. The nurse helped the mother gather up her things. The shadow of the ambulance moved silently away and the nurse came back in the office.

"That ther girl is going to be a lunatic, ain't she?" the white-trash woman asked the nurse, but the nurse kept on to the back and never answered her.

"Yes, she's going to be a lunatic," the white-trash woman said to the rest of them.

"Po' critter," the old woman murmured. The child's face was still in her lap. His eyes looked idly out over her knees. He had not moved during the disturbance except to draw one leg up under him.

"I thank Gawd," the white-trash woman said fervently, "I ain't a lunatic."

Claud came limping out and the Turpins went home.

As their pick-up truck turned into their own dirt road and made the crest of the hill, Mrs. Turpin gripped the window ledge and looked out suspiciously. The land sloped gracefully down through a field dotted with lavender weeds and at the start of the rise their small yellow frame house, with its little flower beds spread out around it like a fancy apron, sat primly in its accustomed place between two giant hickory trees. She would not have been startled to see a burnt wound between two blackened chimneys.

Neither of them felt like eating so they put on their house clothes and lowered the shade in the bedroom and lay down, Claud with his leg on a pillow and herself with a damp washcloth over her eye. The instant she was flat on her back, the image of a razor-backed hog with warts on its face and horns coming out behind its ears snorted into her head. She moaned, a low quiet moan.

"I am not," she said tearfully, "a wart hog. From hell." But the denial had no force. The girl's eyes and her words, even the tone of her voice, low but clear, directed only to her, brooked no repudiation. She had been singled out for the message, though there was trash in the room to whom it might justly have been applied. The full force of this fact struck her only now. There was a woman there who was neglecting her own child but she had been overlooked. The message had been given to Ruby Turpin, a respectable, hard-working, church-going woman. The tears dried. Her eyes began to burn instead with wrath.

She rose on her elbow and the washcloth fell into her hand. Claud was lying on his back, snoring. She wanted to tell him what the girl had said. At the same time, she did not wish to put the image of herself as a wart hog from hell into his mind.

"Hey, Claud," she muttered and pushed his shoulder.

Claud opened one pale baby blue eye.

She looked into it warily. He did not think about anything. He just went his way.

"Wha, whasit?" he said and closed the eye again.

"Nothing," she said. "Does your leg pain you?"

"Hurts like hell," Claud said.

"It'll quit terreckly," she said and lay back down. In a moment Claud was snoring again. For the rest of the afternoon they lay there. Claud slept. She scowled at the ceiling. Occasionally she raised her fist and made a small stabbing motion over her chest as if she was defending her innocence to invisible guests who were like the comforters of Job, reasonable-seeming but wrong.

About five-thirty Claud stirred. "Got to go after those niggers," he sighed, not moving.

She was looking straight up as if there were unintelligible hand-writing on the ceiling. The protuberance over her eye had turned a greenish-blue. "Listen here," she said.

"What?"

"Kiss me."

Claud learned over and kissed her loudly on the mouth. He pinched her side and their hands interlocked. Her expression of ferocious concentration did not change. Claud got up, groaning and growling, and limped off. She continued to study the ceiling.

She did not get up until she heard the pick-up truck coming back with the Negroes. Then she rose and thrust her feet in her brown oxfords, which she did not bother to lace, and stumped out onto the back porch and got her red plastic bucket. She emptied a tray of ice cubes into it and filled it half full of water and went out into the back yard.

Every afternoon after Claud brought the hands in, one of the boys helped him put out hay and the rest waited in the back of the truck until he was ready to take them home. The truck was parked in the shade under one of the hickory trees.

"Hi yawl this evening?" Mrs. Turpin asked grimly, appearing with the bucket and the dipper. There were three women and a boy in the truck.

"Us doin nicely," the oldest woman said. "Hi you doin?" and her gaze stuck immediately on the dark lump on Mrs. Turpin's forehead. "You done fell down, ain't you?" she asked in a solicitous voice. The old woman was dark and almost toothless. She had on an old felt hat of Claud's set back on her head. The other two women were younger and lighter and they both had new bright green sun hats. One of them had hers on her head; the other had taken hers off and the boy was grinning beneath it.

Mrs. Turpin set the bucket down on the floor of the truck. "Yawl hep yourselves," she said. She looked around to make sure Claud had gone. "No. I didn't fall down," she said, folding her arms. "It was something worse than that."

"Ain't nothing bad happen to you!" the old woman said. She said it as if they all knew that Mrs. Turpin was protected in some special way by Divine Providence. "You just had you a little fall."

"We were in town at the doctor's office for where the cow kicked Mr. Turpin," Mrs. Turpin said in a flat tone that indicated they could leave off their foolishness. "And there was this girl there. A big fat girl with her face all broke out. I could look at that girl and tell she was peculiar but I couldn't tell how. And me and her mama were just talking and going along and all of a sudden WHAM! She throws this big book she was reading at me and . . ."

"Naw!" the old woman cried out.

"And then she jumps over the table and commences to choke me."

"Naw!" they all exclaimed, "naw!"

"Hi come she do that?" the old woman asked. "What ail her?"

Mrs. Turpin only glared in front of her.

"Somethin ail her," the old woman said.

"They carried her off in an ambulance," Mrs. Turpin continued, "but before she went she was rolling on the floor and they were trying to hold her down to give her a shot and she said something to me." She paused. "You know what she said to me?"

"What she say?" they asked.

"She said," Mrs. Turpin began, and stopped, her face very dark and heavy. The sun was getting whiter and whiter, blanching the sky overhead so that the leaves of the hickory tree were black in the face of it. She could not bring forth the words. "Something real ugly," she muttered.

"She sho shouldn't said nothin ugly to you," the old woman said. "You so sweet. You the sweetest lady I know."

"She pretty too," the one with the hat on said.

"And stout," the other one said. "I never knowed no sweeter white lady."

"That's the truth befo' Jesus," the old woman said. "Amen! You des as sweet and pretty as you can be."

Mrs. Turpin knew just exactly how much Negro flattery was worth and it added to her rage. "She said," she began again and finished this time with a fierce rush of breath, "that I was an old wart hog from hell."

There was an astounded silence.

"Where she at?" the youngest woman cried in a piercing voice. "Lemme see her. I'll kill her!"

"I'll kill her with you!" the other one cried.

"She b'long in the sylum," the old woman said emphatically. "You the sweetest white lady I know."

"She pretty too," the other two said. "Stout as she can be and sweet. Jesus satisfied with her!"

"Deed he is," the old woman declared.

Idiots! Mrs. Turpin growled to herself. You could never say anything intelligent to a nigger. You could talk at them but not with them. "Yawl ain't drunk your water," she said shortly. "Leave the bucket in the truck when you're finished with it. I got more to do than just stand around and pass the time of day," and she moved off and into the house.

She stood for a moment in the middle of the kitchen. The dark protuberance over her eye looked like a miniature tornado cloud which might any moment sweep across the horizon of her brow. Her lower lip protruded dangerously. She squared her massive shoulders. Then she marched into the front of the house and out the side door and started down the road to the pig parlor. She had the look of a woman going single-handed, weaponless, into battle.

The sun was a deep yellow now like a harvest moon and was riding westward very fast over the far tree line as if it meant to reach the hogs before she did. The road was rutted and she kicked several good-sized stones out of her path as she strode along. The pig parlor was on a little knoll at the end of a lane that ran off from the side of the barn. It was a square of concrete as large as a small room, with a board fence about four feet high round it. The concrete floor sloped slightly so that the hog wash could drain off into a trench where it was carried to the field for fertilizer. Claud was standing on the outside, on the edge of the concrete, hanging onto the top board, hosing down the floor inside. The hose was connected to the faucet of a water trough nearby.

Mrs. Turpin climbed up beside him and glowered down at the hogs inside. There were seven long-snouted bristly shoats in it—tan with liver-colored spots—and an old sow a few weeks off from farrowing. She was lying on her side grunting. The shoats were running about shaking themselves like idiot children, their little slit pig eyes searching the floor for anything left. She had read that pigs were the most intelligent animal. She doubted it. They were supposed to be smarter than dogs. There had even been a pig astronaut. He had performed his assignment perfectly but died of a heart attack afterwards because they left him in his electric suit, sitting upright throughout his examination when naturally a hog should be on all fours.

A-gruntin and a-rootin and a-groanin.

"Gimme that hose," she said, yanking it away from Claud. "Go on and carry them niggers home and then get off that leg."

"You look like you might have swallowed a mad dog," Claud observed, but he got down and limped off. He paid no attention to her humors.

Until he was out of earshot, Mrs. Turpin stood on the side of the pen, holding the hose and pointing the stream of water at the hind quarters of any shoat that looked as if it might try to lie down. When he had had time to get over the hill, she turned her head slightly and her wrathful eyes scanned the path. He was nowhere in sight. She turned back again and seemed to gather herself up. Her shoulders rose and she drew in her breath.

"What do you send me a message like that for?" she said in a low fierce voice, barely above a whisper but with the force of a shout in its concentrated fury. "How am I a hog and me both? How am I saved and from hell too?" Her free fist was knotted and with the other she gripped the hose, blindly pointing the stream of water in and out of the eye of the old sow whose outraged squeal she did not hear.

The pig parlor commanded a view of the back pasture where their twenty beef cows were gathered around the haybales Claud and the boy had put out. The freshly cut pasture sloped down to the highway. Across it was their cotton field and beyond that a dark green dusty wood which they owned as well. The sun was behind the wood, very red, looking over the paling of trees like a farmer inspecting his own hogs.

"Why me?" she rumbled. "It's no trash around here, black or white, that I haven't given to. And break my back to the bone every day working. And do for the church."

She appeared to be the right size woman to command the arena before her. "How am I a hog?" she demanded. "Exactly how am I like them?" and she jabbed the stream of water at the shoats. "There was plenty of trash there. It didn't have to be me.

"If you like trash better, go get yourself some trash then," she railed. "You could have made me trash. Or a nigger. If trash is what you wanted why didn't you make me trash?" She shook her fist with the hose in it and a watery snake appeared momentarily in the air. "I could quit working and take it easy and be filthy," she growled. "Lounge about the sidewalks all day drinking root beer. Dip snuff and spit in every puddle and have it all over my face. I could be nasty.

"Or you could have made me a nigger. It's too late for me to be a nigger," she said with deep sarcasm, "but I could act like one. Lay down in the middle of the road and stop traffic. Roll on the ground."

In the deepening light everything was taking on a mysterious hue. The pasture was growing a peculiar glassy green and the steak of highway had turned lavender. She braced herself for a final assault and this time her voice rolled out over the pasture. "Go on," she yelled, "call me a hog! Call me a hog again. From hell. Call me a wart hog from hell. Put that bottom rail on top. There'll still be a top and bottom!"

A garbled echo returned to her.

A final surge of fury shook her and she roared, "Who do you think you are?"

The color of everything, field and crimson sky, burned for a moment with a transparent intensity. The question carried over the pasture and across the highway and the cotton field and returned to her clearly like an answer from beyond the wood.

She opened her mouth but no sound came out of it.

A tiny truck, Claud's, appeared on the highway, heading rapidly out of sight. Its gears scraped thinly. It looked like a childs toy. At any moment a bigger truck might smash into it and scatter Claud's and the niggers' brains all over the road.

Mrs. Turpin stood there, her gaze fixed on the highway, all her muscles rigid, until in five or six minutes the truck reappeared, returning. She waited until it had had time to turn into their own road. Then like a monumental statue coming to life, she bent her head slowly and gazed, as if through the very heart of mystery, down into the pig parlor at the hogs. They had settled all in one corner around the old sow who was grunting softly. A red glow suffused them. They appeared to pant with a secret life.

Until the sun slipped finally behind the tree line, Mrs. Turpin remained there with her gaze bent to them as if she were absorbing some abysmal life-giving knowledge. At last she lifted her head. There was only a purple streak in the sky, cutting through a field of crimson and leading, like an extension of the highway, into the descending dusk. She raised her hands from the side of the pen in a gesture hieratic and profound. A visionary light settled in her eyes. She saw the streak as a vast swinging bridge extending upward from the earth through a field of living fire. Upon it a vast horde of souls were rumbling toward heaven. There were whole companies of white-trash, clean for the first time in their lives, and bands of black niggers in white robes, and battalions of freaks and lunatics shouting and clapping and leaping like frogs. And bringing up the end of the procession was a tribe of people whom she recognized at once as those who, like herself and Claud, had always had a little of everything and the God-given wit to use it right. She leaned forward to observe them closer. They were marching behind the others with great dignity, accountable as they had always been for good order and common sense and respectable behavior. They alone were on key. Yet she could see by their shocked and altered faces that even their virtues were being burned away. She lowered her hands and gripped the rail of the hog pen, her eyes small but fixed unblinkingly on what lay ahead. In a moment the vision faded but she remained where she was, immobile.

At length she got down and turned off the faucet and made her slow way on the darkening path to the house. In the woods around her the invisible cricket choruses had struck up, but what she heard were voices of the souls climbing upward into the starry field and shouting hallelujah.

1. What do we learn of Mrs. Turpin's biases and concealed spitefulness in the doctor's office scene? We are never told directly of her "blind spots"; how are we made to perceive them?

2. Look closely at events that immediately precede the book throwing scene. Who caused the action and how? What is the stylistic and psychological effect of having, "The book struck her directly over her left eye" follow immediately after Mrs. Turpin's exclamation, "O thank you, Jesus, Jesus, thank you!"?

3. Look carefully at Mrs. Turpin's immediate reactions to the blow. Why does she look for a further "revelation" from this girl? What has this strange girl come to symbolize to her?

4. Why does Mrs. Turpin tell her tale to the "niggers"? Is it in keeping with the values of her world for her to tell them, or is this an indication of a changing world? Do you get any other hints that the blacks symbolize changing times in this story?

5. All through the story we hear of Mrs. Turpin's fantasies. For the most part, they perpetuate her illusions of supremacy. What do you make of the final vision? Is it fantasy or reality?

6. How has O'Connor prepared us throughout the story for accepting the Judgment Day at its conclusion as a natural consequence of the world she has drawn us into? Note specifically in the story all the allusions to an apocalypse. For example, what do we hear in the background throughout the scene in the doctor's office?

"The Visionary Art of Flannery O'Connor"/*Joyce Carol Oates*

In this critical essay, Joyce Carol Oates not only presents us with a thoughtful definition of a symbolic world ("It is a world of meanings, naturalistic details crowded one upon another until they converge into a higher significance; an antinaturalistic technique, perhaps, but one that is firmly based in the observed world."), she also makes Flannery O'Connor's short story "Revelation" come alive as such a "world of meanings." These meanings, centering on the constricting nature of bigotry and self-righteousness, are explored through an analysis of Mrs. Turpin's smugness. They are then applied to the lives of the readers through the suggestion that we all possess a smugness that deserves censure. Thus, while Oates maintains the necessary detachment of a "critic," illustrating her points convincingly with details from the story, she also allows the story to question *her* values—to "strike her on the forehead" and hopefully change her way of thinking.

The organization of the analysis is relatively simple. Oates discusses at some length her belief that bigotry and judgment are O'Connor's major concerns. Then she divides the story into two parts and illustrates the evidence for small-mindedness and spiritual censure in each. Finally, she declares that Mrs. Turpin is, in fact, all of us and that her revelation must also be ours.

As you read, notice how throughout the essay Oates brings words and phrases from "revelation" into her own sentences, never letting us forget that her focus is on O'Connor's use of language.

The triumph of "Revelation" is its apparently natural unfolding of a series of quite extraordinary events, so that the impossibly smug, self-righteous Mrs. Turpin not only experiences a visual revelation but is prepared for it, demands it, and is equal to it in spite of her own bigotry. Another extraordinary aspect of the story is the protagonist's assumption —an almost automatic assumption—that the vicious words spoken to her by a deranged girl in a doctor's waiting room ("Go back to hell where you came from, you old wart hog") are in fact the words of Christ, intended for her alone. Not only is the spiritual world a literal, palpable fact, but the physical world—of other people, of objects and events— becomes transparent, only a means by which the "higher" judgment is delivered. It is a world of meanings, naturalistic details crowded one upon another until they converge into a higher significance; an anti-naturalistic technique, perhaps, but one that is firmly based in the observed world. O'Connor is always writing about original sin and the ways we may be delivered from it, and therefore she does not—cannot—

believe in the random innocence of naturalism, which states that all men are innocent and are victims of inner or outer accidents. The naturalistic novel, which attempts to render the "real" world in terms of its external events, must hypothesize an interior randomness that is a primal innocence, antithetical to the Judaeo-Christian culture. O'Connor uses many of the sharply observed surfaces of the world, but her medieval sense of *correspondentia*, or the ancient "sympathy of all things," forces her to severely restrict her subject matter, compressing it to one or two physical settings and a few hours' duration. Since revelation can occur at any time and sums up, at the same time that it eradicates, all of a person's previous life, there is nothing claustrophobic about the doctor's waiting room, "which was very small," but which becomes a microcosm of an entire godless society.

"Revelation" falls into two sections. The first takes place in the doctor's waiting room; the second takes place in a pig barn. Since so many who live now are diseased, it is significant that O'Connor chooses a doctor's waiting room for the first half of Mrs. Turpin's revelation, and it is significant that Gospel hymns are being played over the radio, almost out of earshot, incorporated into the mechanical vacant listlessness of the situation: "When I looked up and He looked down . . . And wona these days I know I'll we-eara crown." Mrs. Turpin glances over the room, notices white-trashy people who are "worse than niggers any day," and begins a conversation with a well-dressed lady who is accompanying her daughter: the girl, on the verge of a breakdown, is reading a book called *Human Development*, and it is this book that will strike Mrs. Turpin in the forehead. Good Christian as she imagines herself, Mrs. Turpin cannot conceive of human beings except in terms of class, and is obsessed by a need to continually categorize others and speculate upon her position in regard to them. The effort is so exhausting that she often ends up dreaming "they were all crammed in together in a box car, being ridden off to be put in a gas oven." O'Connor's chilling indictment of Mrs. Turpin's kind of Christianity grows out of her conviction that the displacement of Christ will of necessity result in murder, but that the "murder" is a slow steady drifting rather than a conscious act of will.

The ugly girl, blue-faced with acne, explodes with rage at the inane bigotry expressed by Mrs. Turpin and throws the textbook at her. She loses all control and attacks Mrs. Turpin; held down, subdued, her face "churning," she seems to Mrs. Turpin to know her "in some intense and personal way, beyond time and place and condition." And the girl's eyes lighten, as if a door that had been tightly closed was now open "to admit light and air." Mrs. Turpin steels herself, as if awaiting a revelation: and indeed the revelation comes. Mary Grace, used here by O'Connor as the instrument through which Christ speaks, bears some resemblance to other misfits in O'Connor's stories—not the rather stylish, shabby-glamorous men, but the pathetic overeducated, physically unattractive girls like Joy-Hulga of "Good Country People." That O'Connor identifies with these girls is obvious; it is *she,* through Mary Grace, who throws that textbook on human development at all of us, striking us in the foreheads, hopefully to bring about a change in our lives.

Mrs. Turpin is shocked, but strangely courageous. It is rare in O'Connor that an obtuse, unsympathetic character ascends to a higher level of self-awareness; indeed, she shows more courage than O'Connor's intellectual young men. She has been called a wart hog from hell and her vision comes to her in the pig barn, where she stands above the hogs that appear to "pant with a secret life." It is these hogs, the secret panting mystery of life itself, that finally allow Mrs. Turpin to realize her vision. She seems to absorb from them some "abysmal life-giving knowledge," and at sunset she stares into the sky, where she sees

> . . . a vast swinging bridge extending upward from the earth through a field of living fire. Upon it a vast horde of souls were rumbling toward heaven. There were whole companies of white-trash, clean for the first time in their lives, and bands of black niggers in white robes, and battalions of freaks and lunatics shouting and clapping and leaping like frogs. And bringing up the end of the procession was a tribe of people whom she recognized at once as those who, like herself and Claud, had always had a little of everything. . . . They were marching behind the others with great dignity, accountable as they always had been for good order and common sense and respectable behavior. They alone were on key. Yet she could see by the shocked and altered faces that even their virtues were being burned away. . . .

This is the most powerful of O'Connor's revelations, because it questions the very foundations of our assumptions of the ethical life. It is not simply our "virtues" that will be burned away, but our rational faculties as well, and perhaps even the illusion of our separate, isolated egos. There is no way in which the ego can confront Mrs. Turpin's vision except as she does—"her eyes small but fixed unblinkingly on what lay ahead."

1. How do you think Oates feels about Mrs. Turpin? Does she despise, like, respect, or fear her? What details in the analysis make you confident of your opinion? Why do you think Oates feels this way?
2. What does the last sentence of the essay mean: "There is no way in which the ego can confront Mrs. Turpin's vision except as she does—'her eyes small but fixed unblinkingly on what lay ahead.' "? Has Oates ended her analysis

by giving you a definite statement or by dropping a question in your lap? Why has she done this?

3. How are the three parts of Oates' analysis (proposition, evidence, evaluation) related. How does she move from one to the other?

4. Why do you suppose Oates quotes such a large portion of Mrs. Turpin's "vision" in her essay? Would a paraphrase have suited her purposes as well?

5. Cite passages where Oates has made the language of "Revelation" her own language (such as when she speaks of the reader as being struck in the forehead by the story, just as Mrs. Turpin was struck in the forehead by Mary Grace's book, or where she incorporates short quotes from the story into her own sentences). What does this illustrate about the way Oates has read the story? How is it an effective device in bringing us into contact with the story?

6. How would you evaluate Oates' *voice* in this story? Is she speaking to you as a scholar, a friend, a teacher, a judge? What phrases convince you of this?

"Gooseberries"/*Anton Chekhov*

"Gooseberries" is what is commonly called a "frame story." Within a carefully chosen setting, one character tells a tale to two others, attempting to elicit a response from them that is both alike and different from the response Chekhov wishes to elicit from us. That is, we experience in his story a world within a world, each a commentary on the other.

Having taken refuge from a sudden storm in a country farmhouse, Ivan Ivanovitch tells his host and another friend about his brother who left the Exchequer to become a complacent country landowner. Adopting the less attractive characteristics of the aristocracy, he thought himself both happy and divorced from suffering in the world. His condition is symbolized for Ivan Ivanovitch in the fact that he has made a sweet fetish of gooseberries, which are, to Ivan's taste, a sour fruit.

Ivan tells this story to exorcise his own complacency and that of his audience; the narration is both confession and exhortation. But the two listeners, bored by the confession and irritated by the exhortation, retire into the clean linen of their feather beds. The narrator concludes by commenting that they "did not go into the question whether what Ivan Ivanovitch had just said was right and true." And this is the question Chekhov also intends for us. Both the teller (Ivan) and the subject of his tale (his brother Nikolay) are naive, and we find it difficult to accept either man's position as "right and true." But this is exactly the point. By constructing two worlds that challenge each other, Chekhov forces us to consider the rightness and truth of the story *he* is telling about *both* Ivan and his brother. Refusing to allow us an easy out, he makes us uncomfortable. Note the contrasts between the two worlds of this story (the frame and Ivan's tale) and generalize about their purposes.

The whole sky had been overcast with rain-clouds from early morning; it was a still day, not hot, but heavy, as it is in grey dull weather when the clouds have been hanging over the country for a long while, when one expects rain and it does not come. Ivan Ivanovitch, the veterinary surgeon, and Burkin, the high-school teacher, were already tired from walking, and the fields seemed to them endless. Far ahead of them they could just see the windmills of the village of Mironositskoe; on the right stretched a row of hillocks which disappeared in the distance behind the village, and they both knew that this was the bank of the river, that there were meadows, green willows, homesteads there, and that if one stood on one of the hillocks one could see from it the same vast plain, telegraph-wires, and a train which in the distance looked like a crawling caterpillar, and that in clear weather one could even see the town. Now, in still weather, when all nature seemed mild and dreamy, Ivan Ivanovitch and Burkin were filled with love of that countryside, and both thought how great, how beautiful a land it was.

"Last time we were in Prokofy's barn," said Burkin, "you were about to tell me a story."

"Yes; I meant to tell you about my brother."

Ivan Ivanovitch heaved a deep sigh and lighted a pipe to begin to tell his story, but just at that moment the rain began. And five minutes later heavy rain came down, covering the sky, and it was hard to tell when it would be over. Ivan Ivanovitch and Burkin stopped in hesitation; the dogs, already drenched, stood with their tails between their legs gazing at them feelingly.

"We must take shelter somewhere," said Burkin. "Let us go to Alehin's; it's close by."

"Come along."

They turned aside and walked through mown fields, sometimes going straight forward, sometimes turning to the right, till they came out on the road. Soon they saw poplars, a garden, then the red roofs of barns; there was a gleam of the river, and the view opened on to a broad expanse of water with a windmill and a white bath-house: this was Sofino, where Alehin lived.

The watermill was at work, drowning the sound of the rain; the dam was shaking. Here wet horses with drooping heads were standing near their carts, and men were walking about covered with sacks. It was

damp, muddy, and desolate; the water looked cold and malignant. Ivan
Ivanovitch and Burkin were already conscious of a feeling of wetness,
messiness, and discomfort all over; their feet were heavy with mud, and
when, crossing the dam, they went up to the barns, they were silent,
as though they were angry with one another.

In one of the barns there was the sound of a winnowing machine,
the door was open, and clouds of dust were coming from it. In the
doorway was standing Alehin himself, a man of forty, tall and stout,
with long hair, more like a professor or an artist than a landowner. He
had on a white shirt that badly needed washing, a rope for a belt, drawers
instead of trousers, and his boots, too, were plastered up with mud and
straw. His eyes and nose were black with dust. He recognized Ivan
Ivanovitch and Burkin, and was apparently much delighted to see them.

"Go into the house, gentlemen," he said, smiling; "I'll come directly,
this minute."

It was a big two-storeyed house. Alehin lived in the lower storey,
with arched ceilings and little windows, where the bailiffs had once
lived; here everything was plain, and there was a smell of rye bread,
cheap vodka, and harness. He went upstairs into the best rooms only on
rare occasions, when visitors came. Ivan Ivanovitch and Burkin were met
in the house by a maid-servant, a young woman so beautiful that they
both stood still and looked at one another.

"You can't imagine how delighted I am to see you, my friends,"
said Alehin, going into the hall with them. "It is a surprise! Pelagea,"
he said, addressing the girl, "give our visitors something to change into.
And, by the way, I will change too. Only I must first go and wash,
for I almost think I have not washed since spring. Wouldn't you like to
come into the bath-house? and meanwhile they will get things ready
here."

Beautiful Pelagea, looking so refined and soft, brought them towels
and soap, and Alehin went to the bath-house with his guests.

"It's a long time since I had a wash," he said, undressing. "I have got
a nice bath-house, as you see—my father built it—but I somehow never
have time to wash."

He sat down on the steps and soaped his long hair and his neck, and
the water round him turned brown.

"Yes, I must say," said Ivan Ivanovitch meaningly, looking at his
head.

"It's a long time since I washed . . ." said Alehin with embarrassment, giving himself a second soaping, and the water near him turned
dark blue, like ink.

Ivan Ivanovitch went outside, plunged into the water with a loud
splash, and swam in the rain, flinging his arms out wide. He stirred the
water into waves which set the white lilies bobbing up and down; he

swam to the very middle of the millpond and dived, and came up a
minute later in another place, and swam on, and kept on diving, trying
to touch the bottom.

"Oh, my goodness!" he repeated continually, enjoying himself
thoroughly. "Oh, my goodness!" He swam to the mill, talked to the
peasants there, then returned and lay on his back in the middle of the
ready to go, but he still went on swimming and diving. "Oh, my good-
pond, turning his face to the rain. Burkin and Alehin were dressed and
ness! . . ." he said. "Oh, Lord, have mercy on me! . . ."

"That's enough!" Burkin shouted to him.

They went back to the house. And only when the lamp was lighted
in the big drawing-room upstairs, and Burkin and Ivan Ivanovitch,
attired in silk dressing-gowns and warm slippers, were sitting in
arm-chairs; and Alehin, washed and combed, in a new coat, was
walking about the drawing-room, evidently enjoying the feeling of
warmth, cleanliness, dry clothes, and light shoes; and when lovely
Pelagea, stepping noiselessly on the carpet and smiling softly, handed
tea and jam on a tray—only then Ivan Ivanovitch began on his story,
and it seemed as though not only Burkin and Alehin were listening, but
also the ladies, young and old, and the officers who looked down upon
them sternly and calmly from their gold frames.

"There are two of us brothers," he began—"I, Ivan Ivanovitch, and
my brother, Nikolay Ivanovitch, two years younger. I went in for a
learned profession and became a veterinary surgeon, while Nikolay sat
in a government office from the time he was nineteen. Our father,
Tchimsha-Himalaisky, was a kantonist, but he rose to be an officer and
left us a little estate and the rank of nobility. After his death the little
estate went in debts and legal expenses; but, anyway, we had spent our
childhood running wild in the country. Like peasant children, we
passed our days and nights in the fields and the woods, looked after
horses, stripped the bark off the trees, fished, and so on. . . . And, you
know, whoever has once in his life caught perch or has seen the
migrating of the thrushes in autumn, watched how they float in flocks
over the village on bright, cool days, he will never be a real townsman,
and will have a yearning for freedom to the day of his death. My brother
was miserable in the government office. Years passed by, and he went
on sitting in the same place, went on writing the same papers and
thinking of one and the same thing—how to get into the country. And
this yearning by degrees passed into a definite desire, into a dream of
buying himself a little farm somewhere on the banks of a river or a lake.

"He was a gentle, good-natured fellow, and I was fond of him, but I
never sympathized with this desire to shut himself up for the rest of his
life in a little farm of his own. It's the correct thing to say that a man
needs no more than six feet of earth. But six feet is what a corpse needs,

not a man. And they say, too, now, that if our intellectual classes are attracted to the land and yearn for a farm, it's a good thing. But these farms are just the same as six feet of earth. To retreat from town, from the struggle, from the bustle of life, to retreat and bury oneself in one's farm—it's not life, it's egoism, laziness, it's monasticism of a sort, but monasticism without good works. A man does not need six feet of earth or a farm, but the whole globe, all nature, where he can have room to display all the qualities and peculiarities of his free spirit.

"My brother Nikolay, sitting in his government office, dreamed of how he would eat his own cabbages, which would fill the whole yard with such a savoury smell, take his meals on the green grass, sleep in the sun, sit for whole hours on the seat by the gate gazing at the fields and the forest. Gardening books and the agricultural hints in calendars were his delight, his favourite spiritual sustenance; he enjoyed reading newspapers, too, but the only things he read in them were the advertisements of so many acres of arable land and a grass meadow with farm-houses and buildings, a river, a garden, a mill and millponds, for sale. And his imagination pictured the garden-paths, flowers and fruit, starling cotes, the carp in the pond, and all that sort of thing, you know. These imaginary pictures were of different kinds according to the advertisements which he came across, but for some reason in every one of them he had always to have gooseberries. He could not imagine a homestead, he could not picture an idyllic nook, without gooseberries.

" 'Country life has its conveniences,' he would sometimes say. 'You sit on the verandah and you drink tea, while your ducks swim on the pond, there is a delicious smell everywhere, and . . . and the gooseberries are growing.'

"He used to draw a map of his property, and in every map there were the same things—(a) house for the family, (b) servants' quarters, (c) kitchen-garden, (d) gooseberry-bushes. He lived parsimoniously, was frugal in food and drink, his clothes were beyond description; he looked like a beggar, but kept on saving and putting money in the bank. He grew fearfully avaricious. I did not like to look at him, and I used to give him something and send him presents for Christmas and Easter, but he used to save that too. Once a man is absorbed by an idea there is no doing anything with him.

"Years passed: he was transferred to another province. He was over forty, and he was still reading the advertisements in the papers and saving up. Then I heard he was married. Still with the same object of buying a farm and having gooseberries, he married an elderly and ugly widow without a trace of feeling for her, simply because she had filthy lucre. He went on living frugally after marrying her, and kept her short of food, while he put her money in the bank in his name.

"Her first husband had been a postmaster, and with him she was

accustomed to pies and home-made wines, while with her second
husband she did not get enough black bread; she began to pine away
with this sort of life, and three years later she gave up her soul to God.
And I need hardly say that my brother never for one moment imagined
that he was responsible for her death. Money, like vodka, makes a man
queer. In our town there was a merchant who, before he died, ordered a
plateful of honey and ate up all his money and lottery tickets with the
honey, so that no one might get the benefit of it. While I was inspecting
cattle at a railway-station, a cattle-dealer fell under an engine and had
his leg cut off. We carried him into the waitingroom, the blood was
flowing—it was a horrible thing—and he kept asking them to look for
his leg and was very much worried about it; there were twenty roubles
in the boot on the leg that had been cut off, and he was afraid they
would be lost."

"That's a story from a different opera," said Burkin.

"After his wife's death," Ivan Ivanovitch went on, after thinking for
half a minute, "my brother began looking out for an estate for himself.
Of course, you may look about for five years and yet end by making a
mistake, and buying something quite different from what you have
dreamed of. My brother Nikolay bought through an agent a mortgaged
estate of three hundred and thirty acres, with a house for the family,
with servants' quarters, with a park, but with no orchard, no gooseberry-
bushes, and no duck-pond; there was a river, but the water in it was the
colour of coffee, because on one side of the estate there was a brickyard
and on the other a factory for burning bones. But Nikolay Ivanovitch
did not grieve much; he ordered twenty gooseberry-bushes, planted them,
and began living as a country gentleman.

"Last year I went to pay him a visit. I thought I would go and see
what it was like. In his letters my brother called his estate 'Tchum-
baroklov Waste, alias Himalaiskoe.' I reached 'alias Himalaiskoe' in the
afternoon. It was hot. Everywhere there were ditches, fences, hedges,
fir-trees planted in rows, and there was no knowing how to get to the
yard, where to put one's horse. I went up to the house, and was met
by a fat red dog that looked like a pig. It wanted to bark, but it was too
lazy. The cook, a fat, barefooted woman, came out of the kitchen, and
she, too, looked like a pig, and said that her master was resting after
dinner. I went in to see my brother. He was sitting up in bed with a
quilt over his legs; he had grown older, fatter, wrinkled; his cheeks, his
nose, and his mouth all stuck out—he looked as though he might begin
grunting into the quilt at any moment.

"We embraced each other, and shed tears of joy and of sadness at the
thought that we had once been young and now were both grey-headed
and near the grave. He dressed, and led me out to show me the estate.

" 'Well, how are you getting on here?' I asked.

" 'Oh, all right, thank God; I am getting on very well.'

"He was no more a poor timid clerk, but a real landowner, a gentleman. He was already accustomed to it, had grown used to it, and liked it. He ate a great deal, went to the bath-house, was growing stout, was already at law with the village commune and both factories, and was very much offended when the peasants did not call him 'Your Honour.' And he concerned himself with the salvation of his soul in a substantial, gentlemanly manner, and performed deeds of charity, not simply, but with an air of consequence. And what deeds of charity! He treated the peasants for every sort of disease with soda and castor oil, and on his name-day had a thanksgiving service in the middle of the village, and then treated the peasants to a gallon of vodka—he thought that was the thing to do. Oh, those horrible gallons of vodka! One day the fat landowner hauls the peasants up before the district captain for trespass, and next day, in honour of a holiday, treats them to a gallon of vodka, and they drink and shout 'Hurrah!' and when they are drunk bow down to his feet. A change of life for the better, and being well-fed and idle develop in a Russian the most insolent self-conceit. Nikolay Ivanovitch, who at one time in the government office was afraid to have any views of his own, now could say nothing that was not gospel truth, and uttered such truths in the tone of a prime minister. 'Education is essential, but for the peasants it is premature.' 'Corporal punishment is harmful as a rule, but in some cases it is necessary and there is nothing to take its place.'

" 'I know the peasants and understand how to treat them,' he would say. 'The peasants like me. I need only to hold up my little finger and the peasants will do anything I like.'

"And all this, observe, was uttered with a wise, benevolent smile. He repeated twenty times over 'We noblemen,' 'I as a noble'; obviously he did not remember that our grandfather was a peasant, and our father a soldier. Even our surname Tchimsha-Himalaisky, in reality so incongruous, seemed to him now melodious, distinguished, and very agreeable.

"But the point just now is not he, but myself. I want to tell you about the change that took place in me during the brief hours I spent at his country place. In the evening, when we were drinking tea, the cook put on the table a plateful of gooseberries. They were not bought, but his own gooseberries, gathered for the first time since the bushes were planted. Nikolay Ivanovitch laughed and looked for a minute in silence at the gooseberries, with tears in his eyes; he could not speak for excitement. Then he put one gooseberry in his mouth, looked at me with the triumph of a child who has at last received his favourite toy, and said:

" 'How delicious!'

"And he ate them greedily, continually repeating, 'Ah, how delicious! Do taste them!'

"They were sour and unripe, but, as Pushkin says:

" 'Dearer to us the falsehood that exalts
   Than hosts of baser truths.'

"I saw a happy man whose cherished dream was so obviously fulfilled, who had attained his object in life, who had gained what he wanted, who was satisfied with his fate and himself. There is always, for some reason, an element of sadness mingled with my thoughts of human happiness, and, on this occasion, at the sight of a happy man I was overcome by an oppressive feeling that was close upon despair. It was particularly oppressive at night. A bed was made up for me in the room next to my brother's bedroom, and I could hear that he was awake, and that he kept getting up and going to the plate of gooseberries and taking one. I reflected how many satisfied, happy people there really are! What a suffocating force it is! You look at life: the insolence and idleness of the strong, the ignorance and brutishness of the weak, incredible poverty all about us, overcrowding, degeneration, drunkenness, hypocrisy, lying. . . . Yet all is calm and stillness in the houses and in the streets; of the fifty thousand living in a town, there is not one who would cry out, who would give vent to his indignation aloud. We see the people going to market for provisions, eating by day, sleeping by night, talking their silly nonsense, getting married, growing old, serenely escorting their dead to the cemetery; but we do not see and we do not hear those who suffer, and what is terrible in life goes on somewhere behind the scenes. . . . Everything is quiet and peaceful, and nothing protests but mute statistics: so many people gone out of their minds, so many gallons of vodka drunk, so many children dead from malnutrition. . . . And this order of things is evidently necessary; evidently the happy man only feels at ease because the unhappy bear their burdens in silence, and without that silence happiness would be impossible. It's a case of general hypnotism. There ought to be behind the door of every happy, contented man some one standing with a hammer continually reminding him with a tap that there are unhappy people; that however happy he may be, life will show him her laws sooner or later, trouble will come for him—disease, poverty, losses, and no one will see or hear, just as now he neither sees nor hears others. But there is no man with a hammer; the happy man lives at his ease, and trivial daily cares faintly agitate him like the wind in the aspen-tree—and all goes well.

"That night I realized that I, too, was happy and contented," Ivan Ivanovitch went on, getting up. "I, too, at dinner and at the hunt liked to lay down the law on life and religion, and the way to manage the peasantry. I, too, used to say that science was light, that culture was essential, but for the simple people reading and writing was enough for the time. Freedom is a blessing, I used to say; we can no more do without it than without air, but we must wait a little. Yes, I used to talk like that, and now I ask, 'For what reason are we to wait?' " asked Ivan Ivanovitch, looking angrily at Burkin. "Why wait, I ask you? What grounds have we for waiting? I shall be told, it can't be done all at once; every idea takes shape in life gradually, in its due time. But who is it says that? Where is the proof that it's right? You will fall back upon the natural order of things, the uniformity of phenomena; but is there order and uniformity in the fact that I, a living, thinking man, stand over a chasm and wait for it to close of itself, or to fill up with mud at the very time when perhaps I might leap over it or build a bridge across it? And again, wait for the sake of what? Wait till there's no strength to live? And meanwhile one must live, and one wants to live!

"I went away from my brother's early in the morning, and ever since then it has been unbearable for me to be in town. I am oppressed by its peace and quiet; I am afraid to look at the windows, for there is no spectacle more painful to me now than the sight of a happy family sitting round the table drinking tea. I am old and am not fit for the struggle; I am not even capable of hatred; I can only grieve inwardly, feel irritated and vexed; but at night my head is hot from the rush of ideas, and I cannot sleep. . . . Ah, if I were young!"

Ivan Ivanovitch walked backwards and forwards in excitement, and repeated: "If I were young!"

He suddenly went up to Alehin and began pressing first one of his hands and then the other.

"Pavel Konstantinovitch," he said in an imploring voice, "don't be calm and contented, don't let yourself be put to sleep! While you are young, strong, confident, be not weary in well-doing! There is no happiness, and there ought not to be; but if there is a meaning and an object in life, that meaning and object is not our happiness, but something greater and more rational. Do good!"

And all this Ivan Ivanovitch said with a pitiful, imploring smile, as though he were asking him a personal favour.

Then all three sat in arm-chairs at different ends of the drawing-room and were silent. Ivan Ivanovitch's story had not satisfied either Burkin or Alehin. When the generals and ladies gazed down from their gilt frames, looking in the dusk as though they were alive, it was dreary to listen to the story of the poor clerk who ate gooseberries. They felt inclined, for some reason, to talk about elegant people, about women. And their sitting in the drawing-room where everything—the chandeliers in their covers, the arm-chairs, and the carpet under their feet—reminded them that those very people who were now looking down from their frames had once moved about, sat, drunk tea in this room, and the fact that lovely Pelagea was moving noiselessly about was better than any story.

Alehin was fearfully sleepy; he had got up early, before three o'clock

in the morning, to look after his work, and now his eyes were closing;
but he was afraid his visitors might tell some interesting story after he
had gone, and he lingered on. He did not go into the question whether
what Ivan Ivanovitch had just said was right and true. His visitors did
not talk of groats, nor of hay, nor of tar, but of something that had no
direct bearing on his life, and he was glad and wanted them to go on.

"It's bed-time, though," said Burkin, getting up. "Allow me to wish
you good-night."

Alehin said good-night and went downstairs to his own domain, while
the visitors remained upstairs. They were both taken for the night to a
big room where there stood two old wooden beds decorated with
carvings, and in the corner was an ivory crucifix. The big cool beds,
which had been made by the lovely Pelagea, smelt agreeably of clean
linen.

Ivan Ivanovitch undressed in silence and got into bed.

"Lord forgive us sinners!" he said, and put his head under the quilt.

His pipe lying on the table smelt strongly of stale tobacco, and
Burkin could not sleep for a long while, and kept wondering where the
oppressive smell came from.

The rain was pattering on the window-panes all night.

1. Chekhov carefully sets the scene for Ivan Ivanovitch's narrative account of
   his brother. What is significant about such details as Alehin's plain fare, Ivan
   Ivanovitch's "delicious" swim, "pretty" Pelagea's silent sweetness? Is there
   something ironic about Ivan Ivanovitch's response to all of this?
2. The frame story begins drenched in wetness and washing and ends with rain.
   What is the function of this imagery? What is the relation of the world of
   the frame story to that of the internal story?
3. Why is Nikolay Ivanovitch obsessed with gooseberry bushes? Does he love the
   taste or the idea of their fruit? Do you see any correlation between this object
   and the smell of Ivan's pipe that figures in the beginning and the ending?
4. How does Chekhov keep you aware that the internal story is just that—a
   narrative whose "telling" is as interesting as its content? (Look at events that
   precede, interrupt, and follow the internal story.)
5. Why does Ivan Ivanovitch find the pig image so appropriate to a description
   of his brother's farm? Do you see any correlation between Nikolay's piggish
   complacency and Mrs. Turpin's moral hypocrisy in "Revelation"?
6. How do you account for Alehin's and Burkin's response to Ivan Ivanovitch's
   story? Did they understand it? Did Ivan?

SUGGESTIONS FOR WRITING

1. Using the pattern of Swift's essay, write your own "modest proposal" for some current social problem. Be sure to cover three areas—a description of the problem, a careful explanation of the proposed solution, and a masked presentation of your actual solution. Notice that Swift's argument gains momentum from its detailed presentation. This involves pseudostatistics and arguments to support the mock proposal as well as actual facts that depict the problem in its full urgency. Notice also that except for one or two emphatic statements, Swift's essay maintains a cool ironic tone. Follow Swift as faithfully as possible in these two points.

2. After reading Hawthorne's "Birthmark" write a moral tale of your own. Remember that your events and characters must make literal sense as well as dramatize some moral conflict. Like Hawthorne, you must find ways of directing your readers to the moral conflict.

3. Analyze the use of violence in Ralph Ellison's "Battle Royal." Explain how violence is connected with the author's main idea or theme. Then consider his development of violence in the story. How does a description of the setting prepare the readers for the violence that follows? How do "games" perpetuate and structure the violence? How does the point of view of the story (first person narrative) allow the readers to feel its full impact? Finally, assess what the main character gains from his experience with violence. What does he learn about himself and his options in the world? Has violence ever taught you a similar lesson?

4. Why does "Battle Royal" begin and end with the grandfather's "philosophy"? First explain what you think his philosophy means. Explore the grandfather's "voice" when he describes it (is he sarcastic, coolly logical, or angry?) and the events that have determined his perspective on black-white relations. Then see how the grandfather's philosophy connects with the major action of the story. Does what happens in the narrative amplify or contradict what he says? Use details from the story to support your conclusion. Last, assess the narrator's final understanding of his grandfather's words. Does he share his grandfather's opinions after his ordeal? Do you?

5. Both "Revelation" and "Gooseberries" present a "class" problem. Mrs. Turpin constantly evaluates herself and others in terms of an intricate hierarchy of social standings, while Ivan's brother, Nikolay, tries to become a "country gentleman" by buying a farm and planting gooseberry bushes. But in spite of all their pretensions, each suffers from rural middle-class complacency. State what you think each character illustrates through his or her preoccupation with social class. Indicate how their preoccupations make them complacent. Then explore ways in which these two characters "operate." What are their attitudes toward themselves and toward others (particularly "in-

feriors")? Notice any likenesses in the imagery with which they are described and any gestures that they share. Finally, evaluate what happens to these two characters, and try to relate their preoccupations to your own attitudes toward social class.

6. In "Revelation" the author's focus is clearly on Mrs. Turpin's states of mind. Nevertheless, there are several important secondary characters in the story (Claud, Mary Grace, the "white trashy woman," and so on). State what you think is the author's point in surrounding Mrs. Turpin with these minor characters. Then explore the individual relationship that each minor character has with Mrs. Turpin. How does each character help to define Mrs. Turpin's "world"? What aspect of her personality does each one evoke? Finally, evaluate the effectiveness of this "arrangement" of personalities. Does it work well to "draw out" Mrs. Turpin's ingrained prejudices. Is this, in fact, the way prejudices are revealed in your world?

7. What is all the fuss about gooseberries in Chekhov's short story, "Gooseberries"? What is the central significance Chekhov gives to gooseberries in the story? Once you have stated this general meaning, examine individual uses of gooseberries. Why are they so important to Nikolay? What is important about their taste? What connection do gooseberries have with Ivan's pipe (end of the story)? Why do they become the title? Finally, evaluate the effectiveness of this central symbol. Does it adequately convey Chekhov's main theme or idea? Can you think of an object that you have made a "fetish" (sacred object) out of as Nikolay has done with gooseberry bushes? Does your fetish say something important about your values?

GLOSSARY

Abstract and *Concrete*   The concrete is the detail of experience accessible to the senses; the abstract is the general observation that arises from these details.

Analogy   A device by which writers clarify their subject by comparing it to a similar, and usually more familiar, object, idea, or experience.

Analysis   The process of taking some object, experience, or idea apart in order to discover and understand its structure.

Anecdote   A brief narrative of a self-contained event.

Argument   A form of analysis in which the logical presentation of evidence leads the readers to take seriously the writer's proposition.

Concrete   see *Abstract*

Deduction and *Induction*   Induction is the process of developing an argument by moving from evidence to conclusion. Deduction is the reverse process in which the writer first states the conclusions and then moves to supportive evidence.

Describe   The process of revealing the uniqueness of an object, person, or event through the use of sensory details.

Evidence   The support that writers give to their proposition or theme. Evidence can be personal experience, observations of others, or facts and ideas gleaned from others.

Focus   The way in which writers narrow their subjects to a particular idea or object and concentrate on concrete details that manifest this restricted subject.

Image   A device by which writers present a sensory experience directly.

Induction   see *Deduction*

Intention   What writers want to *do* to their audience: to educate, to entertain, to persuade, and so forth.

Irony   A device by which writers suggest one meaning by seeming to state its opposite.

Minute Particulars   The individual, concrete details that make up any total experience; the individual sense impressions as distinguished from the general impression the experience makes.

Narrate   The process of recounting a sequence of events.

Perception   What observers "take in" about their experiences in the world. Any perception is a complex of sense impressions, the observers' moods and biases, and any other factors that make them "see" in a particular way at a particular time.

Point of View   The position writers take with regard to their subject. That position can be a physical one (above, below, to the left), an emotional one (disgust, elation, curiosity), or a cultural one (vocational, ethical, regional).

Proposition   The controlling idea of a piece of writing. In its most explicit form (argument) it is called the proposition or *thesis;* in its most implicit form (fiction) it is called the *theme.*

Selection   The process by which writers sort through the possible details and ideas that relate to a given subject and select those that best emphasize their chosen *focus, point of view,* and *proposition* or *theme.*

Structure   The organizational pattern of a piece of writing which determines the relationship between its various elements, such as evidence, attitudes, and conclusions.

Style   The total verbal pattern of a piece of writing defined by writers' intentions, their relationship to their audience, and the relationships among all of the integral parts of the piece.

Symbol   A device by which writers present a familiar image to the readers that is what it says it is, but that also reveals a different, usually more suggestive or universal, meaning that is in keeping with the theme of the work.

Theme   see *Proposition*

Thesis   see *Proposition*

Unity   The quality of all good writing which makes the readers sense an essential relationship between all the parts and the whole essay, a singleness of purpose and effect.

Voice   The way writers choose to "sound" to their audience. It involves the writers' attitudes toward their audience and their attitude toward their subject. (You may hear this concept spoken of as *tone* in other contexts.)